ZEN AND THE HEART OF PSYCHOTHERAPY

ZEN AND THE HEART OF PSYCHOTHERAPY

By

Robert Rosenbaum, Ph.D.

USA	Publishing Office:	BRUNNER/MAZEL *A member of the Taylor & Francis Group* 325 Chestnut Street Philadelphia, PA 19106 Tel: (215) 625-8900 Fax: (215) 625-2940
	Distribution Center:	BRUNNER/MAZEL *A member of the Taylor & Francis Group* 47 Runway Road, Suite G Levittown, PA 19057 Tel: (215) 269-0400 Fax: (215) 269-0363
UK		BRUNNER/MAZEL *A member of the Taylor & Francis Group* 1 Gunpowder Square London EC4A 3DE Tel: +44 171 583 0490 Fax: +44 171 583 0581

Zen and the Heart of Psychotherapy

2 3 4 5 6 7 8 9 0

Printed by Edwards Brothers, Ann Arbor, MI, 1998.

A CIP catalog record for this book is available from the British Library.
    The paper in this publication meets the requirements of the ANSI Standard Z39.48-1984 (Permanence of Paper).

Library of Congress Cataloging-in-Publication Data
            Available by request from publisher.

Selections from "Among School Children" reprinted with permission of Scribner, a Division of Simon & Schuster from THE COLLECTED WORKS OF W.B. YEATS, Volume I: THE POEMS, revised and edited by Richard J. Finneran. Copyright © 1928 by Macmillan Publishing Company; copyright renewed by Georgia Yeats. "Herman Mellville" excerpt from W.H. AUDEN: COLLECTED POEMS by W.H. Auden. Reprinted by permission of Random House, Inc. "The Joy of Fishes" by Thomas Merton, from THE WAY OF CHUANG TZU. Copyright © 1965 by the Abbey of Gethsemani. Reprinted by permission of New Directions Publishing Corp. "Actualizing the Fundamental Point," "The Point of Zazen, After Zen Master Hongzhi," "Rules for Zazen," and "Snow" from MOON IN A DEWDROP: WRITINGS OF ZEN MASTER DOGEN, edited by Kazuaki Tanahashi. Copyright © 1985 by the San Francisco Zen Center. Reprinted by permission of North Point Press, a division of Farrar, Straus & Giroux, Inc. I GOT PLENTY O'NUTTIN', words and music by George Gershwin, DuBose and Dorothy Heyward and Ira Gershwin. © 1935 (Renewed 1962) George Gershwin Music, Ira Gershwin Music and DuBose and Dorothy Heyward Memorial Fund. All Rights Administered by WB Music Corp. All Rights Reserved. Used by Permission WARNER BROS. PUBLICATIONS U.S. INC., Miami, FL 33014.

ISBN 0-87630-891-4 (case)
ISBN 1-58391-040-9 (paper)

For my mother
—her heart warmed Vimalakirti's house
"When Goldie smiled, the sun came out."

Contents

Preface and Meal Chant

When I began this book I was having troubles reconciling my family life, my psychotherapeutic work, and my Zen practice.

Each morning I would wake up, go to the Berkeley Zen Center, and meditate for an hour in the calm, still quiet. Then I would get into my car, drive down to the clinic in the large health maintenance organization in which I worked as a psychotherapist, and see client after client. Most of my clients had chaotic life circumstances or serious medical problems; they initially saw me only at the urging of the medical staff across the street and often came to therapy resentful at not being helped by their doctor, or fearful of going crazy, desperate to find some relief from their pain and suffering. At the end of the day I would drive back home and reunite with my wife, back from her work, and our two young daughters. There we would try to handle the practical tasks of keeping the family going, wrestling with the pushes and pulls each of us experienced as we tried to juggle our individual needs with the life we spent together. Most nights, by the time it came to go to sleep, I was utterly exhausted.

My wife and daughters were not attracted to Buddhism and would sometimes get upset when I took time from our family to go off to the Zen center. It was difficult to find a way to apply meditation practice to family arguments: Sitting down, ringing a bell, and stopping to take a few deep breaths before talking things out felt rather artificial and certainly didn't go over well with my teenage daughter. Practice in the Zendo involved discovering how little I knew, learning to temper my self-importance and bow humbly to my fellow practitioners and teachers, attempting to let go of judgments and accept each thing as it is. This often did not mesh well with practice in the medical center, where hospital consults required quick judgments and confident assertiveness, and psychotherapy clients often looked for the security of professional certitude and expert advice on how to change. As my Zen practice led me to respect my clients more and more, how could I exercise my desire to bow to my clients without making them uncomfortable? Meanwhile in the Zendo, as meditation started to arouse old psychological issues, how could I reconcile the urge to weep with the silence of the meditation hall?

While I've been working on this book over the past several years my parents have died, my sister has gone through a serious illness, my children have grown. One of my daughters suffered her adolescence quite painfully; we felt heartbroken when she had to leave our household for a while. At the same time, the circumstances of my work as a psychotherapist were also changing. With the advent of managed care, the context in which I practice psychotherapy has altered from a profession centered on client needs to a business oriented to the vagaries of profit and loss. In my clinic we have always practiced brief therapy, but in the past this was governed largely by our need to serve our community and meet the large demand with a small staff. Now our clinic has a larger staff but practices brief therapy with one eye on economic indicators; measurements of productivity and cost compete with, and sometimes threaten to overshadow, the experience of working intimately in the service of a human being in pain.

In the midst of these events I decided to receive lay ordination as a Buddhist practitioner and commit myself to following the Buddhist precepts. At Berkeley Zen Center we mark this stage in our practice by sewing a *rakusu*, a rectangular cloth with straps that we wear during meditation as a symbol of donning Buddha's robe. Our teacher writes our new Buddhist name and a poem on the back of the rakusu. We assemble the rakusu by sewing together eight pieces of cloth to make a new garment, meanwhile saying a short phrase, a kind of prayer, with each stitch.

Sewing the rakusu from different pieces of fabric, it became difficult to evade the question: How do I make my life a whole cloth?

I didn't find it satisfying to simply add some Buddhist practices, such as mindfulness meditation, to my arsenal of therapeutic techniques—even though I found adding these techniques useful. Nor did it feel quite right to simply add psychological inquiry or some variety of psychotherapy to the experiences that arose in meditation—although again, this was a valuable supplement. With my family uninterested in taking on Buddhist practice, it wasn't possible to have us meditate or go to the Zendo together; adding a moment of silence before a meal at home or a family picnic at the Zendo didn't quite satisfy the urge for integration.

How could I do psychotherapy practice, family practice, and Zen practice without adding to or taking anything away from each one?

To help me puzzle out this issue, I decided to take each of the Buddhist texts we chanted at the Berkeley Zen Center in the mornings and write a chapter on its implications for the practice of psychotherapy and its relationship to the rest of my life. As I worked on this, I developed a deep love and appreciation for these texts. I wanted to share these texts with fellow psychotherapists and other people who didn't necessarily practice Zen or Buddhism but who might find in these texts some hints on how to live their lives and practice their professions. This book is the result.

This book is about how to practice with our lives, and how to come to life in our practice. Each chapter of the book examines some aspect of sewing together the practice of Zen with the realization of psychotherapy, and its implications for daily life. The first two chapters present Zen Master Dogen's practical instructions and guidelines for practice. In the third chapter, the Metta Sutta raises some basic issues of how to promote happiness for ourselves and others. The texts of the last four chapters are somewhat less straightforward; they bring up questions about intimacy, personal identity, what we can rely on, and how we find our way during our difficulties. Although there is a logical progression to the chapters, each chapter can be read on its own if the reader is interested in how a particular text might inform his or her psychotherapy or life circumstances.

This book, like the Zen writings which form its basis, raises more questions than it answers. As you read it you may discover that it does not teach anything new in the way of techniques or necessarily suggest that you do something different than what you are already doing. The book is not about how to reconcile Buddhism and psychotherapy in theory, it is not about how as therapists we can employ Buddhist methods for psychotherapeutic ends, nor even about learning Buddhist techniques for our own self-improvement. Although I provide many clinical examples[1] and personal anecdotes, the goal of this book is not to provide a manual for therapists or a set of prescriptions for self-help: It doesn't say *what* we should be doing to be good therapists, Zen students, parents, or lovers (because I don't know the answers to these questions), but rather the book is about working on *how* we can do what we are already doing so that we do it more wholeheartedly, bringing our self fresh to each moment.

This is not easy, because many of the moments of our lives are painful. We have only a little control over what life brings to us; often we can't get what we want and we can't avoid what we don't want. This is the beginning of both psychotherapy and spiritual practice, because it leads us to the question of how we deal with what is in front of us.

Faced with difficulties in our lives, we often try to find out what we "should" be doing in order to get to some better, more ideal state. We look for something to cling to, some thing to believe in. As we grow from children into mature adults, we want to make something of ourselves, but often feel we lack something. In our insecurity we think we must learn some special knowledge, attain some special accomplishments, create some stable, secure identity to be our selves. We feel there is something we must *do* in order to realize our lives. Gradually, as we deal with one event after another, we realize that our lives have been works in progress from the moment we were conceived, and that we are always being our self.

Most Zen students feel that they meditate to become enlightened. So we start to practice, and every morning we wake up early, get dressed, and go down to the Zendo to sit on our cushions. Gradually, the truth begins to dawn on us: We wake up *before* we meditate. We open our eyes before we become enlightened. We go down to the Zendo not to run after and find a way to possess enlightenment, but rather as a way to express our true nature, to realize our true selves.

Most people assume that clients come to psychotherapists in order to heal and become more whole. In every psychotherapy session, however, as we talk to another human being, we are listened to and start to listen. Gradually, we begin to hear the music we are making of our lives, and the truth begins to dawn on therapist and client alike: The impulse that brings us to therapy is the source of the healing. What is communicated is not so important as the communicating itself: We go to therapy not to become some ideal person but to become who we are; in becoming who we are we realize our true selves.

As we go through all this, we begin to have faith in ourselves. Having faith in ourselves doesn't mean thinking that I can personally handle anything that comes to me: Rather, having faith in ourselves involves a process of falling apart and discovering that somehow we come back together again. We learn that having faith in ourselves requires that we have faith in life. Having faith in life doesn't mean we'll get what we want or avoid pain: Having faith in life involves having faith in something larger than ourselves, although it includes our selves.

In Zen, we sometimes call this spacious largeness "Big Mind," that mind that is not confined to individual brains but that manifests as the universal, intimate interconnectedness of all things. If we have faith in this mind, therapists and clients can trust the therapy; Zen practitioners can trust in the practice, lovers can trust in compassion and kindness. We can trust that one thing follows and is related to another in what Buddhists call the "Wheel of the Law." We begin to sense that even in our difficulties, life and death, health and sickness are cousins, members of some larger family of which we are also part.

Getting married, having a child, doing meditation, seeing a client in psychotherapy—all require an act of faith. Reading a book requires an act of faith: Who knows what you will find? But having faith is not a question of clinging to a particular set of beliefs, a particular set of Buddhist practices or psychotherapeutic techniques. Having faith involves the opposite: It requires that we let go of what we are clinging to.

As we hold on to less and less, we are more and more open to what this moment of meditation, psychotherapy, or family life requires of us. How can we respond to whatever our client says, our child requests, or our lover invites? How can we face our inner demons and the oppressive tyrants of the world without returning greed for greed and hate for hate? This very questioning is our faith, our mode of renewing ourselves, our Way of reminding ourselves to appreciate our lives. If we hold to our beliefs, we oppose our beliefs to others. If we do not cling to any particular thing, we can have pure faith and perfect freedom.

Life is full of dilemmas and snarls in which we may easily lose sight of this. When we are stuck in our personal despair, it helps to remind ourselves of this larger picture. Practice is about how, in the midst of the difficulties of our lives, we keep faith in mind.

This book is about how, in the midst of a psychotherapeutic practice that exposes us hourly to the pains and difficulties of being human, we can keep faith in mind. In Japanese, the character for "mind" is the same as the character for "heart." Keeping faith in mind is ultimately a matter of learning to live whole-heartedly. My hope is that this book may serve to increase your appreciation of life by facilitating the rediscovery of the sincere heart of your own practice.

ACKNOWLEDGMENTS

We all have many ways of reminding ourselves to appreciate our lives. Some of us say a grace before our meal, a little expression of thanks for whatever is offered to us. At Berkeley Zen Center, before we eat our meals we say a chant[2] that I'd like to offer as a grace before the main body of this book:

> Innumerable labors brought us this food.
> May we know how it comes to us.
> Receiving this offering,
> let us consider whether our virtue and practice deserve it.
> Desiring the natural order of mind,
> let us be free from greed, hate and delusion.
> We eat to support life and to practice the way of Buddha.
>
> This food is for the three treasures:
> For our teachers, family, and all people
> And for all beings in the three worlds.
> The first portion is for the precepts:
> The second is for the practice of samadhi:
> The third is to save all beings.
> Thus we eat this food and awaken with everyone.

Innumerable labors went into this book. It could not exist without the life of the tree that went into its pages and the sweat of the printer that went into its ink. It could not exist without the myriad human beings whose spiritual seeking gave rise to the Zen masters who wrote the words to which I am responding. It could not exist without the patience and love of my wife, Judi Davis, and our children, Anna and Bekka. It could not exist without the encouragement of my sister Elana Rosenbaum and my brother-in-law David Levitin. It could not exist without my loving parents, now deceased, and all their parents and family before them. It could not exist without my friends who have offered support and suggestions; I would especially like to thank John Dyckman, who worked as coauthor with me on some similar projects. This book could not exist without all the teachers I have had; I am particularly grateful to Ellen Dennis, who taught me about generosity; to Taitetsu Unno, who introduced me to Zen by sponsoring a sesshin with Joshu Sasaki Roshi; and to my Dharma teacher, Sojun Mel Weitsman.

This book could not exist without the practice of all the people who make the Berkeley Zen Center possible, and the inspiring example of our teacher, Sojun Roshi. I would like to thank all the Sangha members who took the time to review the manuscript and offered their encouragement and advice. This book could not exist without all the clients who were willing to share their lives with me, and all my coworkers who keep our clinic running.

This book could not exist without the three treasures of Buddha, Dharma, and Sangha and all my teachers, all my family, all people and all beings past, present and future. This book came to me through all of them: I am quite sure neither my virtue nor practice deserve it, for it is not possible to personally deserve the abundance of love, compassion, acceptance, and joy that I have been fortunate to experience: I can only accept it with respect and gratitude and express my deep appreciation.

Any wisdom in this book is not mine but comes from the whole succession of ancestors, teachers, family, all people and all beings. The errors in this book are mine. Alhough I have tried as much as I can to keep the book free from a desire for personal gain, to not show off or to put down people with whom I disagree, to avoid misleading through obfuscation and ignorance, all of these creep in. Please don't let me confuse you.

This book could not exist without you, the reader. I thank you for picking it up and being open to partake of it, but I must confess at the start: You already have whatever wisdom this book has to offer. Any wisdom in this book is a wisdom we all have, we all share and partake of. I offer this book in the hope that it may be of some help in letting you become more familiar with what, in your heart of hearts, you already know. I offer this book in the hope that it will encourage us to act well toward others so that, immersing ourselves in our true nature, we help others. I offer this book in appreciation for this opportunity to wake up in company with you, together with all beings.

Credo

Poets mapping pathways of the heart
Confess the lines by which they draw their charts
Catch the cartographers.
The fact is, the most apt articulation
Can never capture quite in art
The wonder of a plain, mundane sensation.

Sisters hoping to communicate
breathe in breathe out a poem we must translate
Linked by relationship.
We need a form, a raft, a joyful beacon
Compassion's singing incarnate
Love's language finding paths to meet and seek in.

In silence surprise speech; in speech find silence.
Accept the open gates of subtle guidance
Kind winds' largesse: to navigate non-violence.

Dogen's Rules for Zazen[1]

1

Practicing Zen is zazen. For zazen a quiet place is suitable. Lay out a thick mat. Do not let in drafts or smoke, rain or dew. Protect and maintain the place where you settle your body. There are examples from the past of sitting on a diamond seat and sitting on a flat stone covered with a thick layer of grass.

Day or night the place of sitting should not be dark; it should be kept warm in winter and cool in summer.

2

Set aside all involvements and let the myriad things rest. Zazen is not thinking of good, not thinking of bad. It is not conscious endeavor. It is not introspection.

Do not desire to become a buddha; let sitting or lying down drop away. Be moderate in eating and drinking. Be mindful of the passing of time, and engage yourself in zazen as though saving your head from fire. On Mt. Huangmei the Fifth Ancestor practiced zazen to the exclusion of all other activities.

3

When sitting zazen, wear the kashaya and use a round cushion. The cushion should not be placed all the way under the legs, but only under the buttocks. In this way the crossed legs rest on the mat and the backbone is supported with the round cushion. This is the method used by all buddha ancestors for zazen.

Sit either in the half-lotus position or in the full-lotus position. For the full-lotus put the right foot on the left thigh and the left foot on the right thigh. The toes should lie along the thighs, not extending beyond. For the half-lotus position, simply put the left foot on the right thigh.

4

Loosen your robes and arrange them in an orderly way. Place the right hand on the left foot and the left hand on the right hand, lightly touching the ends of the thumbs together. With the hands in this position, place them next to the body so that the joined thumb-tips are at the navel.

Straighten your body and sit erect. Do not lean to the left or right; do not bend forward or backward. Your ears should be in line with your shoulders, and your nose in line with your navel.

Rest your tongue against the roof of your mouth, and breathe through your nose. Lips and teeth should be closed. Eyes should be open, neither too wide, nor too narrow. Having adjusted body and mind in this manner, take a breath and exhale fully.

Sit solidly in samadhi and think not-thinking. How do you think not-thinking? Nonthinking. This is the art of zazen.

Zazen is not learning to do concentration. It is the dharma gate of great ease and joy. It is undefiled practice-enlightenment.

Chapter 1

Full Engagement: Dogen's Rules for Zazen

INTRODUCTION

Zazen is sitting quietly doing nothing. Sitting on a cushion, spine straight, legs crossed, eyes half-open, facing a wall: What could this possibly teach us about doing psychotherapy?

The short answer is that zazen teaches nothing at all beyond being itself. Sitting quietly, doing nothing is just sitting: There's nothing more. It's just sitting being itself, me being myself. There is no use to it at all: One Zen master said that when he died, he wanted people to say: "He wasted his whole life in zazen."[2]

A forty-three-year-old man came to me in a deep depression. After many years of struggling with pain from back injuries, the discomfort had finally become unendurable. His physician had told him that he would no longer be able to perform his usual work, placed him on total disability, and referred him for vocational rehabilitation. He had previously taken pride in his ability to work hard at physical labor. Now, his back problems were severe enough his physician had told him he shouldn't do any housework or even pick up his eleven-month-old son. While he was waiting for his rehabilitation program to begin, he was staying around the house doing nothing.

He couldn't stand doing nothing. He ruminated about financial problems, despite the fact that his wife was successfully supporting the family. He became insecure in his relationship, worrying (despite his spouse's supportive reassurances) that his wife would leave him because he wasn't contributing enough to the family. Feeling guilty about doing nothing, he wouldn't leave the house to do things he used to enjoy and which he still could do, such as take a walk or go fishing.

He acknowledged that other people with disabilities still had a right to live and be happy even if they couldn't be conventionally productive or useful; however, he couldn't apply this to himself. The therapy focused on his beliefs about what he "ought" to be able to do to justify his existence and give meaning to his life.

"Doc," he frequently said, "being like this doesn't fit my image of what it means to be a man. It's not *me*. I just don't feel like myself. How can I be myself if I can't lift anything?"

How can I be myself when I can't do the things that maintain my image of myself? How can I be truly myself? This is the root problem behind all our individual lives, the thrust that brings clients and therapists to the practice of psychotherapy and students to the Zendo. The issue is reflected in every client's questioning; it comes up in condensed form in the following Zen anecdote:[3]

A monk named Hui Chao asked Fa Yen, "Hui Chao asks the Teacher, what is Buddha?"
Fa Yen said, "You are Hui Chao."

The Zen student strives to realize Buddhahood; the psychotherapy client tries to realize psychological health. Fa Yen reminds us that the answer to our quest is not something outside ourselves, but a matter of realizing who we are, of understanding our own true being.

How can I be truly myself? Is there something special I have to do? That can't be right: I must admit I am myself all the time, no matter what I'm doing. We get into difficulties, in part, because we mistake our ideas about who we think we ought to be with what we are actually experiencing. Often under the pressure of life events, what I'm going through will not match the image of who I want to be or who I think I am. If I try to hold on to my image of what I "really ought" to be, I may be in for a struggle.

On the other hand, if I make no special effort to improve or actualize myself, that doesn't feel right either. Then I'm just passively waiting while my time on earth elapses in a slothful slow dying. Surely I must express myself in my activity. But I cannot solve the problem of being myself just through thinking about who I am. I cannot "be myself" without engaging in activity, without *being* myself. Thinking about being myself is not the same (although it is a part of) being myself; thinking about doing something is not the same as doing it. Thought is not the same as experience. I cannot be a therapist without doing psychotherapy, no matter how many books I may read on the subject. Therapists cannot fully understand clients by *thinking* about them; no matter how much of their history we may read from chart notes, our theories about our clients will be different from the clients themselves. We must personally engage with our clients in an active relationship if we wish to teach and be taught.

We cannot understand ourselves without understanding others. There is no way we can understand anything fully—not even a stone, let alone a person—by observing it "from the outside." But how can I get "inside" another person? For that matter, how can I get "inside" myself without twisting myself into knots?

Zazen is undivided activity in which there is neither "outside" nor "inside." Zazen is manifesting my true self intertwined with all being. Just as we cannot understand clients without interacting with them, trying to understand zazen by reading a book is fruitless unless we actually do zazen. It's possible to become intrigued or curious, but it is not possible to understand sitting zazen without sitting zazen.

To do zazen, we only need to lay aside all our preconceived notions, all our thoughts/feelings/sensations/desires, open up to each moment as we breathe in, and let go of each moment as we breathe out. Then sitting quietly, doing nothing, far beyond teaching and learning, thinking, or not-thinking, we find ourselves face-to-face with our most intimate selves. We discover all the thoughts, judgments, and feelings that rise up from all our old habits. We discover how our personality tries to assert itself in the barest circumstances; we learn how we are always separating ourselves from ourselves and the world around us. We discover that ultimately there is no thing that makes me more or less special than you or any other thing in the entire universe, no thing that stands between our selves and our fundamental true nature.

Learning how we separate ourselves from ourselves, we learn to be more perceptive of how our clients separate themselves from themselves. Learning how we separate ourselves from others, we learn compassion for how our clients erect walls between themselves and the people and circumstances of their lives. Practicing zazen we practice just being alive and just dying; these are the basic activities of being human, the rest is superstructure. Discovering that ultimately there is nothing between our selves and our experience, we discover the blossom that unfolds when client and therapist touch each other in the immediacy of each moment.

WHY MEDITATE?

Most mornings I get up early out of bed, shake off my sleep, and then go wake up by sitting down and meditating for an hour. A friend of mine, a psychotherapist in the clinic where I work who is even more "type A" than I am, can't understand spending an hour a day sitting quietly doing nothing. He asks me, "Why do you do this?"

My friend will not understand, I think, if I explain that it is just my foolishness at work. He thinks I should get something out of doing this: There must at least be some physical health benefit or psychological insight to come out of it. But zazen doesn't work quite this way.

I still cling to the idea, a bit, that I will get something out of doing zazen—if nothing else, I have hoped I will get freedom from the idea that I will get something out of it. Over the years, I have learned how attached I am to getting something out of what I do: Being aware of my hopes for personal gain eases their pressure a bit and makes me less a prisoner of my desires.

Still, the issue of what motivates my sitting zazen remains. Recently I read a helpful book by David Brazier,[4] in which he suggests that Buddhism is about "a willingness to lay down one's life for the Truth all the time." I read this and was very impressed. This seemed like a good motivation I could appropriate to myself: I could tell my friend that I sit down on my cushion every morning to seek for Truth!

I think this is tempting but dangerous. Brazier says, "Everyone is willing to lay down their life for something. When we find out what we are willing to lay down our life for, then we know what our religion is." So I asked myself, "What is my religion and my Truth? For what am I willing to lay down my life?" I came up with various images: Like many people, I immediately thought of laying down my life while rescuing my children from a burning building.

I think I'd do that. Maybe I'd have some selfish hesitation for a moment, maybe I wouldn't. But just because I would rescue my children from a burning building, does this make them my truth and my religion? There is something disturbing about the idea of making any one object—even the love I bear for my children—the repository of the meaning of my life. To do so can burden them and entrap me. If I am doing zazen and searching for some particular truth, I may be ensnared by a circumscribed vision of enlightenment. If I am doing psychotherapy with a client with some preconceived idea of what a truly ideal outcome should look like, both the client and I may get ensnared by a limited vision of what "psychological health" should be, however much that image may not fit that client.

If I fashion truth into some particular image and place it in some graspable thing, there is a danger that I will turn it into an idol to be worshipped. The problem with worshipping idols—whether they be a god, a person, or a political idea—is that we tend to get attached to them and make them into our personal possessions. If someone threatens them we can become fearful and angry. If I am attached to a particular Truth I may be willing to lay down my life for it, but this impulse to sacrifice all to some religious Truth rather easily seems to turn into a willingness to wage a holy war to force others to lay *their* lives down for the Truth.

So I get nervous when I see Truth with a capital "T." I get nervous when anyone says they know what Truth is: This seems to lead to the Crusades. I get nervous when someone tells me they know what kind of therapy works for what kind of diagnosis. I feel more comfortable not having a preformed therapy that is the answer for every patient who comes in with a diagnosable complaint, and I prefer being unsure but curious about what therapy will emerge from the mysterious process of meeting a particular client at a particular time. I feel more comfortable not knowing what Truth is. I feel more comfortable not knowing why I sit down and meditate every day.

When I first began meditating I thought I would meditate and learn the Truth, and that knowing the Truth I would become powerful and wise. Gradually, meditating taught me how much I did not know. I was willing to accept that humbling experience as the ticket of admission to learn the Real Truth. Then, gradually, meditating taught me not just how much I did not know, but how much I *could not* and never would know. This was painful but curiously liberating, this not-knowing. For a while I thought if I could just become innocent enough, pure enough, silent and still and not-knowing enough, Truth would reveal itself to me.

Sometimes gradually, sometimes with occasional flashes of insight, it became clear that I had been making a fundamental mistake: I had been thinking Truth was somehow separate from me, separate from my search for it. I thought perhaps it existed outside of me, somewhere in the universe, or perhaps it was hidden deep inside of me: Either way, I had thought Truth was an unchanging thing which I could reach out and grasp. Meditating, it becomes clearer and clearer that Truth is not graspable; Truth is, like meditation, always changing even as it stays the same; Truth is not something to be reached, but something to practice.

It's important to devote oneself not to Truth but to practicing being truthful. So I think I sit down on my cushion to meditate every day for practice in entering the burning building, no matter what it may hold. Feeling the flames that threaten to engulf me, I get some practice for how to stay calm and not be afraid to enter the bonfires of suffering that clients bring to my office.

I sit down on the cushion for the practice it affords in laying my life down. When I lay my life down to just sit, I learn something about how to acknowledge all my selfish desires and something about how to set them aside; I learn something about how to bring myself to practice some activity that carries me along so that I forget about myself. Sitting on the cushion, carried by the currents of truth into just sitting, I learn something about how to let go of my favorite ideas when I meet a client in the burning building of psychotherapy.

FLAVORS OF ZAZEN AND PSYCHOTHERAPY

Sitting zazen has something of the flavor of psychoanalysis. Some schools of Zen sit facing a wall; some sit facing outward into space. Whichever way you sit, the empty space that confronts you is more silent than the most quiet psychotherapy session, more mercilessly neutral than the strictest Freudian analyst. Inevitably, one comes up against the walls we build within ourselves. The structure of zazen, where we sit still no matter what feelings or thoughts come up, creates a safe "holding environment" in whose security repressions may loosen. Feelings, thoughts, sensations emerge, and with no one there to blame or bounce off of, our projections twist back upon themselves until our innermost desires and fears are left nakedly visible. Sitting quietly, doing nothing, we do everything we can to escape from ourselves, only to find that there is no escape.

I remember the first times I sat down to do zazen. I was a college student in the days of psychedelics, free love, and the antiwar movement. One of my professors knew a Zen priest recently arrived from Japan; we went to his living room and he showed us how to sit zazen. Proud of my experience doing yoga, secretly wishing to impress a girl in the class I had a crush on, I sat with my legs crossed in the lotus position: Instructed to take long deep breaths and count each exhalation, I expected this would lead to some special mystic state in which I'd have a blissful time.

Time certainly did show up as a member of this party, but bliss wasn't so apparent. After five or ten minutes of not moving physically, something seemed terribly wrong and each second seemed an eternity. My body trembled all over, desperately wanting to move. Pain shot through my legs. My mind raced with thoughts. My desires clashed, caught between wanting to move and wanting to conquer my pain and succeed at sitting still. I had not suspected that I lived not just with the Vietnam war many miles away but also with a war within myself.

I tend to try hard to master myself. It has been difficult to learn to trust the experience of the moment and just settle in. So I trembled through many years of zazen.

There is an old joke in psychoanalytic circles that goes, "The problem with self-analysis is that the countertransference is terrible." In zazen, transference and countertransference rise up together, meet each other, fight, and eventually make friends and reconcile. As emotions, fantasies, and critical judgments rise and fall, we ride these waves to discover that countertransference and transference are mere solipsistic phantoms, a series of relationships that emerge among various parts of our selves, each of which wants to claim primacy. Gradually it dawns on us: No single part of our selves stands alone. Sinking into silence, some larger container emerges. Going to the root and deeper than the roots of countertransference and transference we find that the object of our relationship is the very universe that upholds us. Discovering what Zen calls our original face before we were born, we realize that what seemed to be vast cold stretches of vacant black space is the ocean that holds the stars: We find that the universe is compassionately smiling, and that gentle smile is us.

Sitting zazen has something of the flavor of cognitive therapy. In the absence of external distractions, thoughts fill the vacuum in the mind. Fantasies and "old tapes" play in a continuous loop: We drift back to images of the past and jump forward to pictures of the future. Strong feelings seemingly come out of nowhere, triggered by a thought, a memory, a body sensation. Sometimes during zazen the mind slides into pleasant daydreams, sometimes into vivid nightmares. Sometimes we get locked in battles with ourselves and sweat breaks out all over the body. Sometimes there is a pleasurable peace and balance.

Whatever the experience, it soon becomes clear that there is no external stimulus acting in the present moment and that we are creating our own suffering. The nasty boss is not there in the meditation hall; our anger is being stoked by the "shoulds" and "how dare yous" in our mind. The angry mother is not there in the meditation hall; our memories, our fears, and our tight muscles are arising from our mind. The lover who has deserted us is not there in the meditation hall; our sadness and yearning come from desires we are holding in our mind. The teacher whose approval we want is not there in the meditation hall; our trying so hard is directed toward images in our mind.

As we begin to realize the grip these thoughts and emotions and desires have on us, the real teacher—mindful awareness—begins to emerge. This real teacher is instructing us constantly, but we don't often take time to pay attention. Each impulse, fantasy, and fear is an opportunity for a lesson if we don't get stuck in our habitual responding. In order to get out of the habitual responding, we learn to note whatever our experience might be without either holding on to it or pushing it away.

This is not so easy. Perhaps some old, maybe previously repressed, memory of being sexually abused comes up. It takes some practice to learn how not to be caught by the feelings of fear, loathing, and aversion that arise and not just hurriedly push the feelings and the images away. Once we stop avoiding, it takes some practice to learn how to not be caught by horrid fascination or a desire for emotional catharsis, which tempts us to pursue the feelings and the mental pictures. Eventually, if some feeling or fantasy of being wise, enlightened, and at peace comes to visit, it can be hard to not try to hold on to this heavenly place.

Zazen is about learning how to balance between aversion and attachment without getting caught by or standing separated from the experience. Zazen is about letting experiences roll by like white clouds in a vast sky, watching and being both sky and clouds together.

Because sitting in zazen provides a period of no movement, no acting on the thoughts/feelings/sensations/desires, there is no outlet for actions that might reinforce the old patterns: The only outlet is to increase awareness. As awareness widens, the automatic repetitiveness of the mind's formations lessens. Becoming aware of the feelings as just feelings, becoming aware of the thoughts as just thoughts, becoming aware of the physical sensations as just sensations, becoming aware of the desires as just desires, a space opens up, a wider container embraces experience, and freedom becomes more than just a word.

Sitting zazen has something of the flavor of family-systems psychotherapy. Body and mind greet each other, and all their sons, daughters, parents, aunts, uncles, and cousins clamor out their conflicting desires. Mom is jealous of Aunt Ethel getting all the attention; like siblings, one thought ("My boss has really been pushing me lately") begrudges the attention lavished on any other thought ("She's getting a lot of pressure from her supervisor"). Your big brother, the feeling of despair, tries to convince you it really knows what's going on in the world; your little sister (bubbles of silly giggles) runs by as one sibling emotion after another clamors for attention. Each thought and feeling tries to hold on, carry the mind away, and be ruler of the roost, but one thought follows another, one feeling follows another. Each can lay claim only to being a small part of the whole family, of the total picture.

Dad sits down to read the paper after a hard day's work; sitting on the cushion, visual perceptions fill the mind. Just at that point the telephone rings with a phone call from Grandma and one's sense of hearing is on the phone (must the person on the next cushion breathe so *noisily?*). While meditating, the impulse to get up and move (Uncle Larry always did have wanderlust) meets the impulse to sit there calmly forever, even after the bell rings to end the session (Aunt Jane had agoraphobia and didn't leave the house for years). When pain visits, the Will says: Body, don't move! (is that Uncle George's authoritarian voice?) while Mind says: You can't tell my Body what to do! (Don't pick on my little sister, you bully!). Mind thinks Body belongs to it, Body asserts its autonomy and tells Mind who is boss, like a husband and wife sparring.

Like a huge extended family gathered around the Thanksgiving table carrying on multiple conversations at once, within the mind each thought and perception arises and clamors to assert its identity; within the body, tens of thousands of muscles talk to each other so that as the chin tilts downward the hips swivel slightly to meet the different distribution of weight. Your wife goes away on a business trip, and shortly afterwards your mother-in-law slips and breaks her leg: Sitting zazen, a muscle in the buttocks releases, giving rise to a tingle—and a wave of emotion—in some seemingly unrelated muscle on the side of the face.

Sitting quietly, we become aware of each thought, each feeling, each sensation in each cell of our body. How can we ever balance them to achieve harmony? How can any family ever reconcile the conflicting needs and desires of all its members?

Zazen is undivided activity; its very undividedness reveals the myriad ways in which I engage in conflicts with myself. A family is inextricably bound by blood; tied together, we seek ways to assert our individual existence. If my sister presses me to do one thing when I want to do another, sometimes it's easy to forget we both come from the same parents; we may even resent the fact that we come from the same parents and are bound to each other. The same holds true for the larger family of humankind: If the driver in front of me on the freeway is slow or has cut me off, it's easy to forget that we are sharing the same road.

Sitting on the cushion, to the extent that I feel that the pain in my knees has an independent existence from my desire to realize Zen, some part of me resists the pain and becomes locked in a battle. If I feel my mind must master my body or vice versa, then the marriage of body and mind becomes a struggle of "who's on top" more bitter than any lovers' quarrel.

Eventually zazen brings the realization that we are all in this together, and that the only way to harmonize the different streams in zazen is to accept them all, each one for what it is. Shunryu Suzuki, the founder of San Francisco and Berkeley Zen centers, used to teach meditation by instructing us if a thought, a feeling, a sensation, an impulse arises while doing zazen, to hold that thought, feeling, or memory as tenderly in our hands as if it were a vulnerable child.

In zazen we are always giving birth to the family that is our self, experiencing each aspect rising and dying away. We discover that body and mind are as interdependent as breathing in and breathing out, parent and child, lover and loved. I can only experience the sensations of the body through the mind. I can only actualize the mind's formations through the body. If the mind is smiling, the pain in the knees softens a bit; if the body is straight and balanced, the mind aligns and quiets itself. Physical form, thoughts, feelings, impulses, and consciousness can exist only in relation to each other. In zazen I learn through pain and comfort that I don't *have* a knee: For that moment, I *am* my knee. Body and mind can't be separate from each other but must inter-be.

This realization of interdependence, of interbeing, is central to Buddhism and to any ecological or systemic approach to psychotherapy. Therapists cannot exist without clients, and psychotherapy clients can only be defined in relation to psychotherapists. I can't be a parent without having a child; I can't be a child without having parents. However, it sometimes is hard to acknowledge our interdependence, because this goes against our egotistical pride. When I was a teenager, I wanted to think I existed without any relationship to my parents and that I was sufficient to myself. When I became a parent, it was easy to see how my children needed a parent for *their* identities, but it took me several years to realize how they are an inextricable part of who I am. I had to go beyond saying "I have two daughters" to acknowledging that "I am a father." If I say that I have two daughters, I can treat them as appendages, as if I have some permanent inner intrinsic identity that I retain whether or not I have children; to say I am a father is to acknowledge that something about me, about who I am, alters forever when I hold my daughter in my arms, she hugs me, and our lives intertwine eternally.

The family functions best if each member is allowed to truly be him- or herself; each member is able to be truly himself or herself when receiving the support of the whole family. Because lives intertwine, family members are always communicating with each other, providing feedback that forms the basis for each to respond to the other. Similarly, there is a constant feedback activity in zazen and psychotherapy, where each response constitutes its own next stimulus. In zazen knees, spine, thoughts, breath in, breath out, feelings, all have a wordless dialogue with each other to constantly make adjustments to find a balance this moment. If I think *this,* the body feels *that,* which leads me to think something else. In therapy the client pauses, the therapist wakes up and raises an eyebrow, the client takes a deep breath and decides to say a little more (or less) than he or she planned. Responding to responses, constantly making adjustments: This is how client and therapist dance together, linked as surely as body and mind.

Widening the field, creating a larger container, we discover that every one of us is part of a family that lets each member be the center of the Family, but that no member is more the center than any other member. In zazen the more time we spend sitting alone, the more we discover that we are linked to everyone who is living, has ever lived, or will live. There is a paradox to this feedback process more profound than any reverse psychology.[5] The paradox is one of joining: When *I* realize that *we* are all in this together, "me" and "you," "it" and "I" touch each other as parts of one whole, fingers of one hand. Then none of my thoughts are alien, none of my sensations "not-me," and compassion links us together. Zazen cultivates this compassion; psychotherapy sows the seeds from this healing fruit.

PSYCHOTHERAPY AS ZAZEN: PRACTICAL RULES

Practicing Zen is zazen...

Practicing psychotherapy is not something that we can read in a treatment manual and then apply to a patient like pasting a decal onto a model. Practicing psychotherapy in all its actual messiness is psychotherapy itself. When we practice psychotherapy, we practice it not just in what we say but in everything we do: how we greet our clients; how we walk with them from the waiting room; how we sit with them in the office; how we perceive them with our five senses; how we feel with them, think with them, enter awareness with them. The activity of practicing psychotherapy is the fruit of psychotherapy; the forms of psychotherapy are psychotherapy itself. Body and mind are not separate: target, arrow, and archer converge. Client and therapist, therapist and client, problem and solution, solution and problem: These arise together.

Set aside all involvements and let the myriad things rest.

Walking from the office to the waiting room to see a client, we can practice leaving behind all traces of any previous sessions with anybody else, meanwhile dropping all residues of our own personal concerns. A good way of doing this is to pause for a second and take a deep breath when stepping out of the office, gently bringing the mind to focus on the immediate experience of the moment. Relaxing body and mind can be consciously cultivated by staying aware of your movement step by step, noticing your breathing and allowing it to find its rhythm with your walking. Letting the mind attend to what is immediately in front of it frees it from remembering the last client or anticipating the next.

Meeting the client in the waiting room is a precious opportunity. We may never see this person again; a whole life—in fact, a series of generations of lives—is awaiting us there. In our rendezvous with each client, we have an opportunity to learn and to share what is best in us. I try to greet each client as if for that moment they are the only other person in the world, mentally bowing to them in respect and joy for this opportunity. Whether shaking hands or merely making eye contact, if we take a half a second to come to a complete stop and pause for just a moment that is slightly more than socially conventional, we can create a space that allows us to more truly meet the client.

Walking back to the office with the client, being aware of the pace allows us to match our pace with the client's and begin the process of empathic attunement. Walking this way while finding your own rhythm, your own center of balance step by step alongside the client is a kind of intervention, an experiment in leading by following. By slowing down slightly, taking it one step at a time and enjoying the stroll, you are both modeling for the client and offering an invitation to act as host to the client. How the client responds to the invitation is instructive: If we find a mutual rhythm, we can enjoy it together. If we are out of step, compassion can provide hints on how to respond to our guest.

When we reach the office, I let the client precede me into the room; before I enter the room, out of sight of the client (so as not to burden her or him), I bow to the client. One can do this mentally, but I prefer to anchor myself in the physical movement of an actual bow. In this bow, I attempt to let go of everything that preceded this session, to drop everything I ever thought I knew, and to open myself to learn whatever is to be learned in the oncoming meeting. Bowing offers a way to express respect and gratitude to everything in the client bringing them to seek health and connectedness; the bow also acknowledges the suffering and pain that bring our clients to us and reminds us to meet the suffering and pain with kindness, equanimity, and compassion. Bowing, we are offering ourselves fully to the meeting of self and other, and to finding joy in the meeting.

When you enter the office and close the door behind you, you are opening another gate in front of you. It is pleasant to take a moment at this point to survey the field facing you as you open this gate. When I go walking in the hills near my house, at the top of one rise is a fence with a simple gate to prevent cattle from grazing too far; after going through the gate, I have to loop some wire back over the fence post to secure the gate firmly. Once done with that, I can turn around and enjoy the vista of green fields and rolling hills. Entering the office, closing the door, and turning to the client is like this.

Zazen is not thinking of good, not thinking of bad.

Dogen offers good advice for the psychotherapist: Leave judgments outside the office. Let go of worrying about "good" or "bad"; as we let go of trying to be a perfect therapist and begin accepting ourselves as we are each moment, we can accept our clients as they are each moment and thus help them to accept themselves. Awareness of the flow of our breathing is a good practice for this. Accepting each breath as it is, shallow or deep, fast or slow, breathing in we open up; breathing out, we let go, and life moves in the midst of a vast stillness.

*Be mindful of the passing of time, and engage yourself in zazen
as though saving your head from fire.*

Knowing that we may never see this client again helps us to be mindful of the burning immediacy of this session. The urgency is *now.* However, even in the midst of the fires of the client's (and our own) suffering, we seek the calm center. Panic will not put out the flames but fan them. Breathing naturally, deeply, freely from the diaphragm helps anchor us in the certainty of the alternation of expiration with inspiration; this being so, each part of each breath can rest in itself, without anticipating what comes next. Each portion of each breath is complete this moment and serves as a reminder that we work with our clients in being-time, not in clock-time.

Working one moment at a time, each moment is fresh and offers a universe of possibilities. The past is gone, the future not here yet, the present cannot be grasped.[6] Each of us, together with our clients, is constantly disappearing and reappearing in each moment.

Straighten your body and sit erect.

It might sound strange, but of all the different alterations in therapeutic theory and technique I've experimented with over the past 20 years, altering the way I physically sit with a client has had perhaps the most profound effect on my practice. The therapist's chair is a crucial tool for the practice of psychotherapy; sitting with good posture throughout a session helps you give a client the quality of your full attention. Clients respond to this effort. Sitting straight and balanced also lets you become more easily aware of cues in your body that can alert you to how you are responding to the client, and it allows you to relax without slumping or caving in to the sleepiness of a soft chair.

Facing clients with the spine erect while letting the center of gravity drop lower helps give a sense of stability that can help us meet whatever comes up without losing our balance. If we are not leaning to left or right, forward or backward—if we are not attached to any particular stance or viewpoint—we are less likely to lose our way as we encounter the emotional pushes and pulls with which the client is wrestling. At the same time, it is important to not be rigid; if we are able to lean to the left or to the right, we can meet our clients wherever they are. The important thing here is always to be gravitating towards the center. Awareness of breath and posture allows us to notice if, in response to the interpersonal and affective pressures of the encounter with the client, we are beginning to get off-center and starting to react with constriction or fear; restoring breath and posture helps us recover our equilibrium. Being thrown off balance and recovering *is* the therapeutic work. Practice develops the container for this work.

Eyes should be open, neither too wide, nor too narrow.

If we open our eyes wide and look out at the world, we will see clients as objects separate from ourselves. There diagnosis is easy, communion is difficult. If we narrow our eyes and look only within ourselves, each word from the client will just show us our own reactions. There communion is easy, but finding a detached perspective to helping our client can be difficult.

We must see the world as the client sees it, but although we enter our clients' houses for a visit, we must not settle down to live there and let the doors shut on us and them. Although we try to experience things as our clients do, our reading of our clients' lives must always be from our own perspective; thus sometimes we widen the field of vision to provide a new perspective for our client, other times we narrow our eyes to find a therapeutic focus in our response. Because our response is our own, it offers the client's experience back to him or her in a new form. An orchestra playing in an empty hall sounds different than if an audience is present; the listeners absorb the sound and thus contribute to and alter that to which they are resonating. The same thing occurs when listening in psychotherapy. Seeing the client through the ears, hearing the client through the eyes, tasting their lives and offering ours, we can let the client freely come and go and let ourselves freely go and come in this meeting.

> *Sit solidly in samadhi and think not-thinking. How do you think not-thinking? Nonthinking.*

How do we sit and think not-thinking? This is the question zazen poses us: How can we fit knowing and doing together and live our lives in undivided activity? Zen practice does not involve suppressing thoughts and feelings, nor does it involve getting caught up in them, but instead finding a middle way. A classic Zen text, the *Book of Serenity*, quotes one of the scriptures with slightly more detailed instructions on this matter:

> At all times don't produce delusive thoughts.
> Also don't try to annihilate deluded states of mind.
> In realms of false conceptions don't add knowledge.
> And don't find reality in no knowledge.[7]

If we're balanced at the impossible midpoint of all these pulls, there is no room for the possibility of adding or subtracting our personal concerns: There is room only for genuinely being ourselves. This is the place we always are at, if we can only accept it and engage fully in whatever we are doing, with whatever is right in front of us. When we are fully engaged, we're in a place beyond thinking and nonthinking.

When we are fully engaged in the activity of psychotherapy, we think not-thinking. We do this by making any necessary judgments about a client from the standpoint of nonjudgmental, complete acceptance of the client. Such acceptance is beyond thinking or nonthinking: It is simply two human beings being alive with and to each other. Then if a client cries or laughs, we have an immediate response: It is only afterwards (even if only half a second later) that we respond to our response. So long as we are paying attention to the client, we will respond to him or her and the therapy will go forward. But it is not always easy to maintain our attention. It is easy to daydream during either zazen or psychotherapy: To keep our immediate responses to our clients fresh and clean, we must stay alert and awake while remaining simultaneously relaxed and open.

To do this, we must bring all our resources to bear on our work. We put forth effort to help our client as we would help ourselves, even before we help ourselves. This requires we bring everything we have ever learned to the treatment: analytic thought and experiential passion, fantasy and memory, acceptance and desire. The problem is that the different parts of ourselves often fight each other to achieve primacy, and in the process we get distracted: The trick is to bring these together. Then we can take guidance from a little poem written by Aitken-Roshi:

> When the children fight in the car
> I vow with all beings
> to show how the car doesn't move
> unless all of its parts are engaged.[8]

Our task in psychotherapy is to engage all the parts. We must bring our whole body and mind to work with a client and unify our effort. Once we have done this, though, we need to get on with the task of driving the car. Once we have consciously gathered all we can of ourselves, we need to drop everything and respond to the traffic that's immediately in front of us. In Zen, this is called dropping body and mind. In psychotherapy, we learn as much as we can in order to forget everything we know, drop all our agendas, opinions, and pre-formed theories, and then just do psychotherapy by responding whole-heartedly to the client facing us.

> *Zazen is not learning to do concentration. It is the dharma*
> *gate of great ease and joy. It is undefiled practice-enlightenment.*

There is a good deal of mystique about both Zen and psychotherapy. Clients often think therapists have special knowledge and abilities and are surprised to learn that therapists get depressed and anxious, have fights with their spouses and problems with their children. Zen students often think Zen masters have special accomplishments and arcane powers of mystical concentration.

Zazen is not about gaining some special ability but about enjoying the ordinary moments of our lives. Psychotherapy is not about becoming an ideal person, but about becoming a real person. In both, we have to let go of achieving anything in particular and learn to enjoy practicing with whatever we encounter. Often this involves forgetting about the expertise we have acquired and simply immersing ourselves in the task at hand.

Climbing the ladder from the pool to the high board, a diver brings her years of practice, her hours of adjusting the tuck of her chin and the angle of her arms, her memory of reviewing the tapes of her somersaults and her splashes, to each rung of the ladder. When she jumps off the board, body and mind unite and for a moment she forgets everything as she gives herself over to water, gravity, space.

Yet few, if any, dives are a perfect "10." The feet can always be pointed more, the entry into the water can always have a little less splash, the tuck of the somersault can always be a little tighter. The diver looks at the scores she has received for a dive, compares these to her own body's sense of the dive, consults with the coach outside and the coach inside—and climbs the ladder to do it again.

Perhaps the diver has been motivated to succeed by a desire for fame and wealth, perhaps by her ego's stubbornness in wanting mastery over a difficult task. It will be hard to sustain this motivation over many hours and many years of cold waters and dank locker rooms, of frustrating slips and painful failures. The diver's ego will rebel against the discipline required; as long as the dive is something outside of herself to be conquered, it will be a struggle. Her self-consciousness and her desires will get in the way of a smooth entry into the water.

Still every dive, awkward or smooth, describes a complete arc into the deep pool. This is true even if the diver is self-conscious or absent-minded. As she practices over and over, the diver will tend to devote herself more to the diving itself than to what she hopes to get out of it; her growing love of diving sustains her more than a desire to see her picture on a box of Wheaties. Each time the diver steps onto the board, she forgets herself a little further as she lets herself go into the dive more fully. Eventually the diver holds nothing back of herself and, becoming a vehicle of the dive, enters into the ease and joy of diving.

Zazen and working with clients are like this: great effort and concentration make way for the ease and joy of forgetting ourselves in our activity. In psychotherapy, this means meeting another human being in the fullness of their happiness and suffering.

Therapists are often anxious, feeling compelled to accomplish something but fearing we are not up to the task. Self-centered concerns about our performance can get in the way of meeting our clients heart to heart. To allay our anxiety, we often try to develop special abilities and techniques to help our clients. Learning and practicing technique is useful. But as we come to know more we stand in danger of becoming attached to our expertise and risk seeing clients only through the particular lens of what we know. Then therapy can begin to seem boring, a mechanical exercise that becomes a job, not a journey.

In contrast, doing therapy time and again can help us deepen a continual sense of wonder if we approach therapy not as a test of our mastery, but as an opportunity to renew our practice of helping others. Like the diver who practices again and again but finds each dive is different, each session is a fresh opportunity, and we find not only that there are numerous clients who simply do not fit into diagnostic or treatment categories, but that every client is unique in each session. As we become more comfortable with not having all the answers, each session evolves into an exploration of how to test the waters with the particular client in front of us.

We all have our share of belly flops and of wonderful moments. However, more than any particular success or failure, it is simply doing the activity over and over—meeting a client while letting go of our expectations and self-centered preoccupations—that allows the process of psychotherapy to slowly teach us to trust it. Session after session we dive into psychotherapy, in search of ourselves and each other. Each moment of each session is a complete plunge off the board. We make many mistakes in psychotherapy, but practicing therapy and accepting, learning from, and rejoicing in its imperfections becomes the therapy itself. Gradually we just do the therapy without worrying about it and find happiness in the practice.

In these days of managed care in which each session needs to be justified and rationalized, it may be hard for us to do psychotherapy without pretending that we know what we are doing or advertising ourselves as accomplishing some goal. But just as doing zazen ultimately is not about attaining some special abilities of concentration, being a psychotherapist is ultimately not about leading clients to some preconceived, socially sanctioned outcome.

Zazen and psychotherapy are both practices of constant discovery, learning again and again how to engage with others without getting stuck in any preconceived direction of where we should be headed. When we can wake up and cultivate a fresh, open mind each moment with a client, we open a gate to freedom for ourselves and our clients. If we and our clients hold nothing back and immerse ourselves in our meeting, we become like a windbell—all the events of our lives call forth our sound. When there's some turbulence, we ring; when there is a lull, our weight and shape bring us back to a balanced resting place. Still or moving, zazen and therapy ring out: Whether giving forth dark bass notes or clear bright trebles, in sorrow and happiness they sound the tones of great ease and joy.

Awakening the Thought of Enlightenment

My daughter asked a riddle:
Why did the boy look in the mirror with his eyes closed?
She answered:
To see himself asleep.
Then laughing, turned the page.

Dogen's Guidelines for Practicing the Way[1]
(excerpts)

1

The necessity of arousing way-seeking mind

Way-seeking mind... is the mind which sees the impermanence of all phenomena in this world, including the mind itself.

2

Once you hear the true teaching, you should practice it without fail

One phrase offered by a loyal minister can have the power to alter the course of the nation.

3

You should enter the buddha way through practice

You must understand that we practice within delusions and attain realization before you recognize it.... Practicing brings about realization; realization finds itself through practice.

4

Do not practice Buddha's teaching with gaining-mind

Proceed with the mind which neither clings to nor rejects anything.... Practice without thinking of gaining something in return. Buddhas have sympathy for all living beings and help them through compassion, [but] everything they do is neither for themselves nor others. A practitioner should not practice buddha-dharma for his own sake, to gain fame and profit, to attain good results, or to pursue miraculous powers. Practice the buddha-dharma only for the sake of buddha-dharma. This is the way.

5

You should find a true teacher to practice Zen and learn the way

A true teacher has to be free from egocentric views and not fettered by emotional feelings; his practice corresponds to his understanding.

6

Things which should be kept in mind in practicing Zen

Brilliance is not primary, knowledge is not primary; intellect, conscious endeavor, memory, imagination and introspection are not primary. Without resorting to any of these, harmonize body-and-mind and enter the buddha way.

7

Those who long to leave the world and practice buddha-dharma must study Zen

The dharma turns you, and you turn the dharma. When you turn the dharma, you are leading and the dharma is following. When dharma turns you, the dharma is leading and you are following. These two aspects are always present.

8

The activities of Zen monks

Please try releasing your hold. Open your hands. Just let everything go, and see: What is body and mind. What are daily activities?... Ultimately, what are mountains and rivers, the great earth, human beings, animals, and houses? Take a careful look at these things again and again: it is clear the dichotomy of movement and stillness does not arise at all. However, at this time, nothing is fixed.

9

You should practice everywhere toward the way

The Buddha-Way is right under your feet. Immersed in the way, clarify it right on the spot. Soaked through by enlightenment, you completely become yourself.

To be immersed in the way means to forget any traces of enlightenment... let body and mind drop off; throw away delusion and enlightenment.

10

Immediately hitting the mark

To realize buddha directly through nothing other than your body and mind is to accept the Way and hit the mark immediately. Not trying to change your body or mind, just following the realization of the true teacher completely, is called being here or settling down.

To follow buddha completely means you do not have your old views. Since you just settle down right here, you do not seek a new nest in which to settle.

Chapter 2

Building the Sanctuary: Dogen's Guidelines for Practicing the Way

Practicing the Buddha Way, each time we sit down on our cushion our zazen is different. We have to alter our responses to meet the unique shape of each breath, each thought, each feeling and sensation. At the same time, every meditation session shares an underlying unity with every other time we meditated and taps into the same source that supports anyone who is meditating, has meditated, or will meditate. How we reconcile this sameness and difference sitting on the cushion clarifies and teaches how to live our life each moment.

Practicing psychotherapy, each meeting with each client is unique. We have to alter our responses to meet the particular person at his or her particular place. At the same time, not only do clients with similar problems share similar patterns of experience, but they also share a basic humanity that connects us all and makes psychotherapy possible. How we reconcile this sameness and difference in the consulting room clarifies and teaches how we live our lives outside the therapeutic frame.

Each of us has to discover our own way to practice what we do. Dogen's guidelines for practice help point the way.

The necessity of arousing Way-Seeking Mind

Way-Seeking mind... is the mind which sees the impermanence
of all phenomena in this world, including the mind itself.

Practicing Buddhism, we become aware of impermanence and its two corre-
lates: suffering and release from suffering. Practicing psychotherapy, if we want
to be helpful to our clients we need an intimate acquaintance with the taste of
suffering. The First Noble Truth of Buddhism is that life is filled with suffering.
We must come to terms with this. Usually, when we first begin to practice, we are
looking for a way out of suffering. Gradually, our practice affords us a way *in*.

We need to give up the idea that suffering is an aberration, which, when
avoided, brings happiness. We need to do this not because, as therapists, we must
immerse ourselves in miserable experiences, wear a hair shirt, and drink bitter
tea. Rather, we need to do this because we cannot fully understand our own
and our clients' pain without coming to terms with the inevitability of impermanence. The simple fact is, everything in life passes away. Change and loss are
inevitable. This does not mean that we must teach ourselves and our clients to
become resigned to feeling unhappy: Rather, it means that *all* our experiences—
including the unpleasant ones—must be encompassed within the therapeutic
setting.

That Buddhism treats life as inextricable from suffering doesn't mean that life
is doomed to be miserable. To say "life is suffering" sounds gloomy, but really this
is neither pessimistic, optimistic, or idealistic. This is simply describing life the
way it is. It is not that suffering is good or bad, any more than life is good or
bad. Buddhism asks us to stop standing apart from life, judging it from a small
personal perspective of whether we like it or not. Buddhism asks us to step into
life and be fully open to it the way it is, without walling ourselves off.

Gautama Buddha grew up in a luxurious palace in which he was not only
screened from all personal misery but protected even from witnessing the misery
of others.[2] Eventually, as a young man, this protective screen wore thin; while
away from the palace, he encountered an old person, a sick person, and a corpse.
Each time he asked his advisors, "What is this?" He discovered that suffering
existed, and that it was ultimately unavoidable. Once he became aware of the
inevitability of suffering, however, he did not run back to hide in his palace; he
left his shelter and began his quest.

When Buddha left the palace, it is not that he learned that old age, sickness,
and death exist and are inherently awful. Old age, after all, can be a time of rest
and repose; death can be a merciful release; illness can lead to an appreciation of
health and sometimes even provides increased strength as we acquire immunity
against future infection. Instead, when he left his palace, Buddha learned the fundamental truth of impermanence. He discovered that old age puts an end to youth;
that sickness puts an end to health; that death puts an end to life.

All things end. All experience inherently is always impermanent and ungraspable. We can take a photograph of an experience, or videotape it, or inscribe it
in memory, but it won't be the same as the actual experience. This is both our
doom and our blessing because, of course, horrible, terrifying, and grief-stricken
experiences are just as transient and ungraspable as joyous ones.

No thing lasts forever.[3] We know this, but we tend to live in the illusion that the way things are now is the way that they always have been and always will be. When we are young, we may know intellectually that we will grow up, but in our innermost being we feel as if we will never suffer age and death. As we get older, we know we were younger but it becomes difficult to get in touch with what it felt like. I was sure, when I was twenty years old and had driven my parents to Mt. Rainier National Park, that my parents could walk faster and further if they really wanted to: I simply could not relate to what a body felt like when it was slowed by age. Now, twenty-five years later, I ask myself whether, when I was her age, I really could have been as impassioned as my teenaged daughter is now. At this time it takes an active effort of not only memory but also imagination to make a bridge between my experience and hers. My life now feels like my life forever, but life doesn't stand still.

Life is not a thing that has the quality of being transient: Life *is* transience flowing. In each moment, no matter how short, experience rises and passes away. Each moment of experience stretches out to be complete and vanishes into another moment. As you breathe, reading this passage, you can only exist moment-by-moment, constantly dying and being reborn.

Sweltering in the summer heat, it feels inescapable; we forget how, at the end of February when we complained about the numbness in our toes, it seemed that the icy winter would last forever. Immersed in the rebirth of spring, it feels for a while as if all of life is a blossom. Each season of our life is complete in and of itself, not a waystation to someplace else; each season does not "go" anywhere and is eternal in the moment. However, at the same time, each season and each moment is evanescent and constantly flowing. We can sometimes see this combination of movement and abiding more clearly through the eyes of a child; consider this poem my ten-year-old daughter wrote:

> When the Fall leaves, where has it gone?
> Into the sun?
> Racing the river?
> Forever gone only
> to return again.
> Watching Winter, Spring, Summer go flying past
> Just then Fall catches up
> Creeping up on Summer once more
> Chasing it away for another season
> Until it comes back
> to play tag with Spring.

Nonetheless, despite the passage of the seasons, despite the evidence of the ongoing changes in our bodies, often our clients feel that life is standing still. Immersed in misery, they may complain that they *always* feel bad, or that they have the same problem time and time again. The client comes seeking change but fears he or she will be mired in the current misery forever. The therapist needs a deep knowledge of impermanence to provide the client, not so much in words as in certainty of manner, the reassurance that all things, even this suffering, inevitably change.

Depression provides the classic example of this side of impermanence. Depression, of course, often is a response to loss; it usually involves looking back to the past. A wife has left a husband; a husband has died. A client's daughter has come down with multiple sclerosis. A novelist finds she cannot write as she used to. A man who was a pilot retires and cannot find any reason to live because he no longer can fly. A client comes in with nightmares about the auto accident he was in, in which he lost a leg.

It may seem odd to suggest that a therapeutic attitude based on the inevitability of impermanence could be helpful for clients experiencing depression following a loss. Yet, anybody experiencing depression knows that one of its hallmarks is the feeling that the current sadness and despair are eternal. Former joys are hard to recall and feel unreal if they can be recalled, and the current misery is experienced as if it will blanket life forever more. This illusion of constancy in depression holds a seductive comfort: At least it is predictable. Perhaps by imposing a sense of static permanence, depression provides an illusion of control and stability (however miserable) to fend off the anxiety of the flux and fragility of life.

Therapists sometimes unwittingly reinforce the sense of depression as a large, immovable object when we choose global "depression" as the target of treatment rather than dealing with the specific, concrete life experiences a client is having. If we categorize an unhappy person who is not sleeping or eating as depressed, we may stop looking for useful interventions beyond the medicine bottle. We are more likely to find interventions to deal with sleep problems, lack of pleasurable activities, and ruminative thoughts if we stay with specific client experiences: What does he do right before he goes to bed? Where does he sit when he has his ruminative thoughts? What pleasurable things will he be engaged in when he's feeling better, and how can he start doing them now?

If we examine our lives carefully, we discover that we are *always* feeling differently, that we live our lives moment-by-moment. The client who sits in my office saying he is "always" depressed got dressed that morning. At the moment he was tying his shoes he was neither depressed nor happy: He was simply tying his shoes.

If we label suffering unhappiness as "depression," it can be difficult to deal with because we approach it as a personal trait or a persistent condition. Specific incidents of unhappiness, in contrast, can be dealt with as part of the vicissitudes of life, difficulties that come and go partially dependent on our actions, partially dependent on the vicissitudes of random fortune. This can lead us to be more aware of the fluctuations in our thoughts and feelings moment-by-moment, and this impermanence gives us room to make changes even in the face of loss.

Paradoxically, we can recover from loss by giving up hope of ever being able to regain the idealized past and grasp it in an unattainable idealized future.[4] Once clients accept that they cannot regain the past, they can take realistic steps to discover and respond flexibly to wherever their present path currently places them. Emerging from depression requires accepting the inevitability of loss, opening up to the surprising changes each moment can offer, and letting the transience of life heighten our appreciation rather than sink us into despair.

Knowing the truth of impermanence helps free us and our clients from feeling stuck in their symptoms. But our clients often come to us with a paradoxical attitude towards impermanence. On the one hand, the client fears he will be permanently mired in his problem; on the other hand, when entertaining the possibility that he need not stay permanently stuck, he fears the impermanence of change. Clients may wish to get back to some previous state, but often have some (accurate) sense that once the past is gone and something has changed, they can never recover their exact former ways of being. Something new is in store, and the fact that my life is subject to uncertainty and that my very sense of who I am is not permanently stable can cause apprehension.

Anxiety is the classic example of this side of impermanence. Anxiety is often a response to feeling out of control or not knowing what the future will hold. Anxiety usually involves anticipation. An executive may become anxious that he cannot protect his staff from downsizing; a worker comes in to treatment fearing possible layoffs will make her unable to provide for her family. An earthquake shakes the World Series, a firestorm rips through the Oakland Hills, and we are all shaken loose from our false sense of security. Clients come in fearing that their futures will not go according to plan: A dissertation needs to be written, and the student doesn't know (and fears) how she will perform. A medical test, a surgery is scheduled; the worried client doesn't know how it will turn out.

Here the therapist needs a knowledge of impermanence to provide the client a sense that in the midst of change, if we can stay open to whatever comes and not cling to our old ideas, beneath the waves of change lies an ocean of deeper, calmer currents. It may seem odd to suggest that a therapeutic attitude based on accepting, rather than controlling, the uncertainty that attends impermanence could be helpful for clients experiencing fear of the unknown. Yet anxiety worsens the more we try to control the uncontrollable. A patient with panic attacks learns that sometimes breathing exercises work to nip them in the bud, sometimes they don't; if in doing the breathing exercise the client is worrying about whether or not the exercise will work ("what if this is a heart attack... what if I can't control this and I faint and get embarrassed?"), she is more likely to become tense and less likely to intercept the panic attack. If the client simply attends to the breathing and remains aware of the muscle sensations as just muscle sensations, the racing heart as just a racing heart, being grounded in the immediacy of bodily experience helps reduce the future-oriented interpretations of experience that stimulate fear.[5] The paradox of anxiety is that one controls it by letting go, being aware of and accepting the limits of one's own control without feeling swept away entirely.

Once a client accepts that he or she cannot control the future, then it becomes possible to take realistic steps in the present and respond flexibly to wherever the path leads. We don't know what's around the bend, but we can keep our eyes open not with apprehension but with curiosity. We don't know whether the next breath will be shallow or deep, but we do know that if we hold on to the breath, both the inhalation and exhalation will feel constricted. So we go along with each breath and make adjustments as we go along, comfortable with impermanence. We trip over our own feet less if we avoid plotting out some ideal highway in our minds but rather meet the terrain as it is.

There is another aspect to impermanence that commonly brings clients to psychotherapy. Sometimes it is neither the impermanence of past or future, but the uncertainties of a metamorphosis in the present that initiates a visit.

A woman came to therapy when, after seeing the grandfather who raped her when she was five years old, she began having nightmares again. Therapists often see this kind of situation, in which clients reexperience a trauma again and again: This seems at first glance to be the opposite of impermanence, because the past can feel eternal when it haunts the present. If we examine the situation more closely, however, we can see currents of change even in traumas that seem permanent and inescapable.

This client's encounter with her grandfather arose because her grandmother had just died, and my client felt her mother (the grandmother's daughter) needed her during the mourning period. She decided to accompany her mother, even though she knew it would involve seeing the grandfather she had avoided for twenty years, due to his being unrepentant about the molestation. She did meet her grandfather, who neither apologized nor denied the sexual abuse: In a drunken rage he reviled her and blamed her for being seductive and causing the sexual abuse. The client was upset about the encounter and needed to process it, but this is not so important as the fact that something had already changed within her, *before* she saw her grandfather.

In deciding to see her grandfather, some shift had occurred. Therapy was able to help the client appreciate the compassion that brought her to her mother's side at a time of need, and the strength she had shown in her ability to confront the man who had abused her (she had dealt with her grandfather's verbal abuse assertively without lapsing into rage or depression).

The fear and self-doubt that had held her in their grip for most of her adult life and prevented her from confronting the perpetrator of the abuse had loosened. These reactions to her rape had been an important "part of her" and intrinsic to what she thought of as her personality, but the fears, pain, and suffering of the past were themselves impermanent. She had thought of the trauma as something essential to herself: When in its impermanence the trauma began to loosen its hold, in effect she was coming to therapy to deal with this unexpected change in herself and where it might lead from here.

In this case something that had seemed stable throughout most of adult life shifted. The shift is not just in the sense of victimization, or in helplessness; the shift occurs when I stop thinking that just because such-and-such happened to me, I am fated to be a certain kind of person. I can recognize that everything in life is impermanent, including *me*. This can bring gut-wrenching terror, or profound peace.

From the time I was seven years old, I was afraid of death. There were many roots to this. I saw the emotional anguish involved in the painful, conflicted deaths of my maternal grandparents who came to live with us when I was three years old. They were profoundly demented and depressed; my grandmother would put her head in the oven and turn on the gas, when she wasn't flying into irrational rages. I saw my mother's difficulties in dealing with the living deaths of her parents, her guilt and rage when, feeling it wasn't safe to keep them in the house any longer, she sent them to a nursing home where they died shortly after.

Further stimulating my fear of death, in grade school we would have "duck and cover" drills to prepare for the nuclear attack that would incinerate us all. Lying in bed awake at night, whenever I confronted the idea that my consciousness, this awareness that I called "me" could somehow vanish or disappear, not just for an evening of sleep but forever, I would feel waves of panic at the shear unknown nothingness of it all.

Growing up in a major American city at the height of the Cold War, I had enough fear of death via a nuclear Armageddon that when it was time to go away to college I was happy to go to a school in a more rural setting, thinking this would at least help protect me from immediate incineration in an atomic fireball. Sometime in the first week or two, I mentioned this to a friend who replied, incredulously, "Don't you know we're just a few miles away from a major Air Force base? We'd be prime targets!" Adding to this, the international political situation at the time was quite unstable. A day or so after, I was walking through some farmland when I heard air raid sirens go off. A minute or so later, a throbbing roar from the sky started coming closer, so loud and so deep the ground trembled. Some huge jet, a warplane no doubt, was approaching inexorably. I was all alone in an empty field. The sirens, the sound, the recent revelation of the Air Force base target, and my own fears combined, and suddenly I was absolutely certain: Nuclear war was immediately at hand, and in a few minutes at most, the Bomb would go off.

I was terrified. I looked around for shelter, but there was none; I was standing in a flat empty field, cleared of trees. There was no escape.

At that moment, something curious happened. Knowing there was nothing I could do, fear drained away. I had previously always feared death, but never really accepted that I would die; in fact, my fear was based on the frantic hope that somehow, through some trick, this consciousness that was "me" would manage to escape and survive forever. Now, suddenly, I knew I would die, that no struggle would, ultimately, prevent it.

Many years later, during my father's terminal illness from cancer, he maintained a cheerful optimism. His doctors had told him that he had only a few months to live, but he survived almost two years from his diagnosis. Each morning he would wake up, rub the sleep from his eyes, look around, and a big smile would appear on his face. "I'm *here!*" he would proclaim. He spent his days contentedly, sitting in the sun, listening to music, chatting with neighbors, reading to his granddaughter. When my daughter told us she was scared of coming home from school one day to find him dead, he reassured her: "I'm not scared of my dying... why should you be?"

Then one day, just a few days before his death, a visible change occurred. His lungs were failing, and the hospice workers had brought in an oxygen tank for us to use. He started having trouble breathing, and my sister and I hooked up the oxygen for the first time. My father became irritable: The mask wasn't right, the flow wasn't right, the tank must be defective. No matter how many adjustments we made, it didn't do much good. Suddenly my father stopped being irritable, and a look of surprise crossed his face. "It's not working," he said quietly, in a tone of disbelief. It was obvious he had thought the oxygen would give him a new lease on life. Despite his distended stomach, despite his inability to walk on his own, despite his pain, despite all his reassurances about not being afraid of death, you could see: Up to this moment, he had never really believed he would die.

Now death was at hand. At first he was quiet; then he struggled painfully for the next few days. Toward the end, when he was semiconscious, each breath was an effort, staving off death. My sister and I sat next to him, sometimes meditating together, sometimes just sitting.

At the very end, as happens to so many people, he stopped fighting and experienced a release. His breath became calm, his face relaxed. My father continued to breathe quietly for a little while longer, then stopped. Peace returned. My sister and I stayed with him for a while, realizing we were together in a different way. It was my birthday.

My sister felt initially sorry for me (and I initially felt sorry for myself); my sister mentioned to our hospice worker that my father had died on my birthday. The hospice worker looked at me and gave me a gift by saying:

"How wonderful!"

The hospice worker offers a reminder: Birth and death are constantly touching each other. Years before, in the midst of the roaring approach of the plane that I thought held the fires of a hydrogen bomb, a calm stillness prevailed. I looked around at the field, and the sky was a very beautiful blue. The brown grasses of autumn were a preparation for winter; the maple leaf on the ground spoke, in its colors, not only of one tree's life but of roots eating soil, leaves drinking rain, buds singing light, returning all this to the source from which it had been borrowed and would emerge again. Acceptance took the place of despair: The fusion bomb that went off was the discovery of the connectedness of my life with my death, of the inevitable intertwining of my existence and passing away with the existence and passing away of all things. Face to face with impermanence beyond the possibility of my being able to escape or control it, fear finally gave way to wonder.

A friendship with impermanence helps us appreciate each moment for what it is. As I write this, my sister has just come home from the hospital where she spent five weeks in a bone-marrow transplant procedure for her cancer. The treatment nearly killed her; she developed complications and couldn't breathe, let alone walk or eat. When she finally was able to return home, she was very weak, with the metallic taste of anticancer medicines in her mouth and high doses of steroids leaving her muscles buckling under her so that she would fall unexpectedly.

The main words she used at this time were: "This is so wonderful." She would comment on how wonderful it was to be able to sit up on the sofa in the sun, and look out the window; how wonderful it was to be able to be dressed in clothes again, how wonderful it was to breathe fresh air on her patio.

In Buddhism, there is the story of a man in a jungle who finds himself pursued by a tiger.[6] He runs away as fast as he can, until he finds himself on the edge of a cliff with a steep, fatal drop. Fortunately, there is a small shrub sprouting out a little way down the cliff face. He climbs down to the shrub to escape the tiger and holds on for dear life. The tiger comes to the cliff edge and swipes at him just as the roots of the shrub begin to pull away from the cliff face. Turning his face, the man sees one red strawberry on the shrub, so ripe it is about ready to fall off. The man plucks it and puts it in his mouth. As the sweet juice of the strawberry touches his palate and the taste pervades his consciousness fully, in that moment he forgets the tiger, forgets the fall, forgets himself, and lives his life fully.

I often tell this story in the stress-reduction class I teach. But once a client responded, "Yeah, well I wouldn't waste time tasting no strawberry. I'd be looking for a way out of there." I asked him, "But what if there's no way out?" The client replied, "Well at least I'd go down fighting."

The question for all of us facing impermanence, whether in a psychotherapy session or a meditation hall, is: How do we want to taste that strawberry that is ripe on the vine for just a short time? If we go down fighting trying to grasp what cannot be grasped, like the client above, we may not taste life fully. If we go down fighting taking joy in the fight itself, that's tasting the strawberry in a different way, isn't it?

We fight hard against the fact of impermanence, running from the tiger, fleeing our deaths by seeking some semblance of stability. The rules we have about how to do therapy—whether they are rules derived from therapy manuals or rules imposed by health insurance committees—are attempts to encapsulate and control the wonderful wild chaos of our professional work. The neuroses with which we bind ourselves are "rules" we impose on ourselves in an attempt to achieve some control, some predictability over the constant novelty of the swirling currents of our lives and deaths.[7]

Zen practice reminds us, however, that there is an alternative to fighting against impermanence: We can instead embrace it fully. A Zen teacher has said, when handling a teacup, "Knowing this glass is fragile, and will break if I drop it, I can fully appreciate and enjoy the beauty of the glass as I hold it carefully."[8] Once we see life as impermanent, a continually fluctuating ebb and flow, we discover it's not a question of life changing frequently: Rather, life is *always* changing. We can enjoy the fact that no two breaths are alike, let alone any two psychotherapy sessions.

Our clients come to us to find a way of adjusting to the fact that they, and the circumstances of their lives, are always changing. If life were unchanging there would be neither a need for psychotherapy nor, if there were a need, would psychotherapy be possible. It is the constancy of change that both motivates psychotherapy and enables it to take place. As therapists, we must find ways of adjusting to the fact that we, together with our clients, are continually changing. We cannot do this if we insist that a certain kind of therapy should always be applied to a particular presenting problem, because this "permanent" solution is not fully responsive to the changing experience of individual clients. If as a therapist I can enjoy the impermanence of my own existence and the mutability of any expertise I have, when I see a client I can acknowledge that I am different from when I saw her last. Then I will be more open to seeing that she too is different from when I saw her last.

Although many of us might agree abstractly that life is always changing, it is a little harder to acknowledge that I, together with everyone I encounter, am not only immersed in this always-changing river but am an always-changing river myself. We see this in brief solution-oriented psychotherapy, in which we are taught to ask clients at the start of each session, "What's different since the last time we met? What's changed?" In my experience, the majority of clients respond to this with: "Not much." The textbooks[9] suggest meeting the client's protestation of no change with careful inquiry about specific details in an effort to discover exceptions to the problem and help clients become aware of how patterns that seem invariable to them are filled with natural fluctuations that they can influence. Still, many clients minimize or discount any changes that are discovered, treating them as differences that *don't* make a difference in their lives. To the extent that they feel the therapist has an agenda and is attached to the idea that things are improving, clients seem to hold on to the idea that they aren't getting better.

When a client is asked, "What's changed?" he or she usually thinks that the therapist is asking about the symptom and whether it has improved; the client often has some particular idea about how the symptom "ought" to change in order to signify improvement and, if experience hasn't matched this idea, will reply, "Not much."

A client came to see me distraught after her husband of 30 years had left her, leaving behind a taped message telling her everything he disliked about her. Her husband hadn't been clear, though, about whether he wanted a permanent divorce. The client had problems adjusting to an empty house and was crying and having difficulties sleeping and problems concentrating.

When I asked her at the next session what had changed, she replied, "Nothing." By this the client meant, "My husband hasn't come back to me and I'm still upset."

In fact, though, quite a bit had changed. The client's daughter had called and informed me that three days ago the client had wandered in a daze to a highway overpass, climbed over and prepared to jump off; a passing motorist stopped her car and talked the client out of it. In response, the client's family and friends had rallied around; worried about leaving her alone, a constant stream of people had kept her company for the previous three days. The client was no longer in an empty house and, supported by these people, she had phone conversations with her husband in which she stopped crying: She told him he needed to stop playing games and tell her by next Wednesday whether he wanted a divorce or whether he wanted to look into getting back together and working on the relationship.

Both the client's symptoms, and the circumstances of her life, had changed markedly. She was fixated, however, on a particular vision of what would constitute "change:" Her husband would apologize and come back to her. The task of therapy involved the need to broaden this vision; if the client could see her life in a wider way, one that included more than just her marital relationship, there would be an important shift in her experience of both herself and others whether her husband returned to her or not.

As therapists, we are constantly faced with the task of meeting a client at his or her view of the world while simultaneously challenging that view. When a client says "no change," either disagreeing with the client or agreeing with the client can lead to a therapeutic impasse. We have to make a response that doesn't entangle us in either position, neither saying too much nor too little. We're in the position of the monks Shou-shan confronted:[10]

> The priest Shou-shan held up his short bamboo staff before his assembly and said, "You monks, if you call this a staff, you're entangled. If you don't call this a staff, you ignore the fact. Tell me, what do you call it?"
>
> Robert Aitken-Roshi comments: "The problem is that if you don't say it, you won't express yourself. If you do say it, you will say too much."

When we engage a client not with our professional identity but with our whole person, we can respond naturally by joining the client in the ebb and flow of the therapy rather than trying to stand outside it as a privileged expert. So when a client says to me, "No change," I usually just say, "Really?!" Another good response is "Oh?!"

The essence is not in the words but in the expression, the tone of voice, raised eyebrow, and gentle smile that express "?!" This punctuation—accepting the client and simultaneously expressing a genial, challenging disbelief rooted in one's knowledge of the ubiquitousness of change—is the active intervention. After "?!" we can have an interesting conversation about what's going in the client's life. But "?!" can only be expressed if the therapist, grounded in impermanence, is not attached to any particular vision of what "should" happen in the therapy and is willing to matter-of-factly greet whatever is actually going on.

Therapy seems to flow more freely when I can remain confident that life is changing for the client, when I can be curious about the client's felt experience in the midst of the ups and downs of life but have no special predilection for the change going in any particular direction. If I adopt an attitude that I, and the client, can learn and appreciate something from each incident that transpires in my life and my client's, then no matter what has happened or failed to happen, every event becomes an instructive part of the psychotherapy. Then each session offers an opportunity to explore a new direction.

> *Once you hear the true teaching, you should practice it without fail*

> *One phrase offered by a loyal minister can have the power to alter the course of the nation.*

Significant shifts in a life can occur any moment. Most people have experienced some moments in their lives when everything seemed to stop, when some sudden realization—some insight, some strong feeling—pierced them through and through, the world spun slightly, and, when things settled down, some important personal shift occurred. Often these moments come when we least expect them. Sometimes in Zen this can be a *kensho*, a brief experience of enlightenment. In psychotherapy, we sometimes refer to this as the "aha!" experience.

Much of the time, however, we tend to forget such experiences can occur. We make plans—life plans, treatment plans—and try to proceed according to plan. Plans can be useful, but if we are too attached to sticking to the plan, we may close off to the possibility of spontaneous, sudden change.

Some years ago, my friend Moshe Talmon[11] noticed a curious fact; somewhere between a third and a half of all clients in our clinic only came in for a single psychotherapy session. This was true for all therapists, regardless of what kind of theoretical orientation they practiced. Moshe was intrigued, and then did something courageous: He decided to call up the clients he had seen who had not come back after the first therapy session and ask them what had happened. He was somewhat trepidatious about this, worried he would hear all about his failures as a therapist. Instead, to his surprise, he discovered a majority of his clients hadn't come back for a simple reason: They were feeling better.

Moshe reviewed the literature and discovered a number of studies indicating that clients could improve even after a single therapy session. Moshe then asked me if I'd like to participate in a research project on the subject. I agreed, although I was skeptical about the whole idea of clients changing in a single session.

> Shortly after beginning the project, I went on vacation and took a backpack trip by myself in the mountains. I hadn't quite settled into "vacation mode" yet, and as I hiked along I found myself musing about the futility of single-session therapies. Inspired by the stability of the huge mountains that loomed on either side of the valley I was traversing, I thought: "Perhaps some change can occur in a single session, but surely it can't be *significant* change. Lasting change requires gradual processes like those that mold mountains: What's required is time, slow erosion, wind and rain sculpting the face of the stone over and over again."
>
> At that point, the trail turned around a bend, and I came face to face with a huge avalanche chute. Half of a mountain, seemingly, had slid down into the valley the previous winter, changing both mountain and valley forever, all in the course of fewer than 30 seconds.
>
> I decided to take the notion of change occurring in single sessions of therapy more seriously.[12]

Since that time I have seen many clients whose lives have altered during a single session of psychotherapy. I have also seen more clients who required numerous sessions and varying lengths of time. Unfortunately the issue of single-session therapy has become embroiled in the economic battles being waged by competing factions in the field of health care, but the basic idea behind it is rather simple: However skilled the dancer, all dance occurs one step at a time. Our lives take place moment by moment. All therapies are single-session therapies, in that all therapies must take place one meeting at a time.

Zen practice encourages us to pay full attention and bring our whole being to each moment of our life without regard to whether it is repetitious or novel, exciting or dull. Sometimes Zen practice may appear boring: Sitting on the cushion following breath after breath, washing the windows time and again, we may make the mistake of thinking this is all preparation for some special breakthrough of enlightenment. In therapy sometimes a session may appear mundane, uninteresting, or stale; we may think a session is merely a prelude or preparation for significant events that we anticipate will follow later. If we approach our lives and our therapy this way, we are waiting for a Godot who may never arrive. If we wait for our life, we will miss it. Therapy, like life, is always right in front of us, actualizing itself one moment at a time; we have no existence in the past or the future. We are always, each instant, creating in this moment what we have been and are becoming.

I find it refreshing to approach each session of therapy—including the first one—as if it might be the last. Who knows what life will bring my client and myself after this session? A thousand different things could happen so we might never see each other again. Approaching therapy one session at a time helps me stay open to the possibility that my client might, this very session, make whatever change is necessary to open a new pathway of the heart. If as therapists we cannot accept that change can occur in a lightning flash, we may miss an opportunity where a client suddenly gasps and, slightly dizzy, sees the world spin and settle in a way different from what they've ever experienced before. Here, as Dogen says, "one phrase offered by a loyal minister can have the power to alter the course of the nation."

On the other hand, if we put our faith in the brilliance of the "aha!" experience, we may not respect the hard work that goes into producing the ripeness, and the hard work that follows to incorporate new perspectives into ongoing life. The fact is, the process of change is always both sudden *and* gradual. Our human experience is marked by quantum shifts in being as well as by development over time. All our lives begin with a discrete event: birth. In birth, something truly new becomes tangible and fully present in its own, unimaginably unique way. Each of us has a birth day that is special to us and to those who care about us. It is also true, however, that although we are born at a particular time—a Saturday at 2:03 in the afternoon— before we were born there was a long gestation period. This gestation period includes not just our own intrauterine development, not just the fertilization of egg by sperm, but the lives of our parents up until that quickening, and the gestation period of our parents in their wombs, and their parents and all the ancestors before them. Furthermore, although we may have appeared in this world on a Saturday at 2:03 in the afternoon, now that we are born we have our whole life to live, together with the lives that we touch and the lives that will come after us.

We are born again each moment, we die again each moment, and our lives go on forever, stretching back to the origins of the universe and forward through all the ripples that spread from this pebble's hitting the water. This is where psychotherapy sessions take place.

At one point, Zen Buddhism experienced a conflict between those who advocated techniques aimed at producing sudden versus gradual enlightenment. Each is simply one side of the same process.

A case of sudden change after gradual practice: A woman had suffered from migraines for 10 years. She had come to a behavioral medicine class I cotaught and participated assiduously. She practiced daily relaxation exercises, improved her assertive behavior, did Tai Chi, all to no avail: The migraines continued. She asked to see me individually for hypnosis.

We did a rather standard hypnotic treatment. After trance induction, a suggestion is made that the client can take a journey and, on the journey, discover a special house. This house turns out to be the house that houses the client: the house of the body. The client enters the house, wanders around until she comes to a room with a closed door; this room is the "nerve center, the control room" of the house. When she goes into the room, she can discover the controls that affect pain perception, blood flow, and anything else that affects headaches.

Within the control room, this client discovered a computer keyboard that "programmed" her headaches. Responding to the suggestion that she could make whatever adjustments she needed, she went to the keyboard and considered hitting the "delete" key. But something about this didn't feel right to her. So she hit the "shift" key instead, and felt the program change.

Follow-up a year later revealed that since the single session of hypnosis, she had not experienced any more migraines. She nevertheless continued her Tai Chi, relaxation exercises, and assertiveness because they all helped her feel good.

A case of gradual practice after sudden change:[13] Another woman came to me for hypnosis for migraines. She had a long history of migraines; five years ago she had seen a hypnotherapist and had been free of migraines for a month. Unfortunately, the migraines then recurred. She went back to the hypnotherapist, but it didn't work again. She went to other hypnotherapists but continued to have migraines. She then went to various neurologists and internists, hoping to find a medicine that would alleviate her migraines once and for all. None of the medicines she tried worked well for her. She continued to take medicines and went to a variety of alternative practitioners, hoping to find a "magic bullet," but without success. She also came to our headache class, but although she attended weekly, she never practiced any of the exercises in between class sessions.

When she came in to me she was irritable and nervous, with tight facial muscles and general body tension. She was in an unsatisfactory marital relationship and had difficulties with her children. She worked long hours and then came home and did housework to try to keep the house perfect.

She requested hypnosis. I told her I'd be glad to do hypnosis, but because she'd had so many disappointments, I wanted to maximize our chances of success. Consequently, I preferred to do the hypnosis after she began a regular schedule of daily relaxation exercises. She agreed. The next session, however, it turned out she had only been able to listen to the relaxation tape once; her job and family duties interfered on other occasions. We met over a period of time, helping her carve out time for herself, helping her learn to be more assertive with her family, examining and reducing her perfectionism.

A session came in which she mentioned she had a good rhythm to her life. She was going out with friends, developing hobbies more, involved in a yoga class and doing the yoga exercises daily. She was having more fun than she'd had in years. I mentioned to her that it seemed she had set up a firm foundation: If she wanted, we could do the hypnosis now to help her reduce her migraines.

She looked a little started. "Hypnosis? I guess we can," she said, "but I have to tell you, I haven't had a migraine for a long time."

Zen Buddhism is full of tales of sudden enlightenment, and many in the West first approach it seeking a quick, easy path. This ignores the necessary interplay between long training and sudden realization:

Hsiang-yen had studied many years and learned a great deal from Pai-chang, but when Pai-chang died his training was incomplete, so he went to study with Kuei-shan. Hsiang-yen was rather proud of his knowledge, but when Kuei-shan asked him, "Show me your own being before your parents were born," Hsiang-yen couldn't reply. He went back to his room, reviewed all his notes from Pai-chang's lectures, but couldn't find anything. He went back to Kuei-shan and said, "I have failed. Please teach me." Kuei-shan, though, wouldn't take the bait. Kuei-shan told him, "I really have nothing to teach you. And if I tried to express something, later you would revile me. Besides, whatever understanding I have is my own and will never be yours."

Hsiang-yen got discouraged. He felt he never would attain enlightenment, and decided to become a "rice-gruel" monk. He asked permission, and received it, to leave the monastery and just go work as a humble caretaker of a nearby neglected tomb. So he built a small hut near the tomb and spent his days cleaning the grounds, sweeping.

One day while sweeping up fallen leaves, his bamboo broom caught a stone and it sailed through the air and hit a stalk of bamboo with a little sound. *Tock!* With that *tock!* he was awakened. Hurrying to his hut, he bathed and then offered incense and bowed in the direction of Kuei-shan's temple, crying out aloud, "Your kindness is greater than that of my parents. If you had explained it to me, I would never have known this joy."[14]

Aitken-Roshi comments: To get that moment of enlightenment, Hsiang-yen had to give up any thought of mastery, and just keep on sweeping for a long time. When he did this, Hsiang-yen felt like a failure, but in fact he was practicing without fail.

Practicing the true teaching without fail does not mean, "Don't make mistakes. Don't fail." Such a perfectionistic attitude would be sure to paralyze Zen students, therapists, and clients by setting up some ideal standard; if we are always measuring ourselves against some idea of what we "ought" to be doing then we separate ourselves from the doing itself.

The nature of impermanence means that all things are "failing" all the time; all things fall short of attaining a frozen, absolute "ideal" state. We live our lives in a messy reality; a Zen student may aspire to sit zazen like the smooth, calm alabaster statue of the Buddha on the altar, but in actual sitting will quickly discover the body's flesh, blood, sweat, and hair, the mind's "impure" thoughts, feelings, sensations, and impulses. A clinician may study the master therapists, the gems of psychoanalytic interpretations, hypnotic metaphors, family reframings, and cognitive insight, only to discover that when he or she tries to imitate these with a client the words come out agrammatical and studded with awkward malapropisms, "unhs," and "ahems."

> When I was doing my internship, I became enamored of the work of a prominent family therapist. I watched a videotape of one of his sessions, and it seemed brilliant. The videotape would stop at various points in the session and point out how every action of the therapist—the way he took off his coat, the way he leaned forward or back, the phrasing of his words—achieved a specific therapeutic end. I tried self-consciously to work similarly but was awkward and self-critically miserable.
>
> I happened to remark to a friend of mine (not a psychotherapist) how much I admired this therapist, and my friend said "Really? Oh, he's my uncle." I was awed and envious. I told my friend about the videotape's testimony to her uncle's superlative skill.
>
> My friend replied genially, "Oh, I'm sure my uncle will be glad you liked it. He put a lot of work into it. I remember when Uncle was preparing that videotape. He reviewed hundreds of videotapes he'd made until he found a session he felt satisfied with... then he spent several months editing it carefully so it would be a good teaching tool. I remember he had to throw out lots of the session."

> A friend of mine was in her first year at the Tassajara Zen monastery. Sitting intensively, she came up against all her ideas of what she saw as imperfections in herself. She felt hopelessly inadequate. She went for a walk alone in the woods, sobbing, tears streaming down her cheeks. This made her feel even worse: Surely the fact that she was crying meant that she had not achieved the inner poise and calm equilibrium that "should" be the hallmark of the Zen student. To make matters worse, a revered Zen master happened to pass her in the woods, saw her tears, and walked by her with what she thought was a stern expression, without speaking to her. She felt mortified and ashamed.
>
> Later that day she happened to be sitting across from the Zen master while everyone was eating a formal meal in the meditation hall. These meals have a very strict protocol; everyone sits in the zazen position while food is consumed in complete silence. There is a specific form for how to bow to the food server, which bowl to pick up when, where to place the chopsticks, and so forth. Any unusual action sticks out like a sore thumb, and beginning students usually are fearful of making a mistake. In particular, they tend to fear dropping something; if you drop something the noise resounds through the hall and all eyes seem to snap to you. You cannot go pick it up. Instead, a server marches down the hall, stoops and retrieves the dropped object, bows to you as you bow back, then marches back down the hall. If you are self-conscious, it can be excruciating.
>
> While my friend was sitting and eating, she found the Zen master across from her staring at her across his bowl of rice, even as he ate with his chopsticks. She

felt even more self-conscious. The Zen master waited until he got her eye then, still staring at her, took his chopsticks and threw them down on the floor. Clack! All eyes turned and people almost gasped; the Master had made a mistake! He had dropped his chopsticks! The master waited composedly while a server retrieved them, bowed to the server, and resumed eating calmly.

After the meal, the Zen master came up to my friend. In a fierce voice, he asked her, "Is there any shame to a Zen master dropping his chopsticks in the meditation hall?"

"No, teacher," said my friend.

The Zen master looked at her keenly.

"So! Then is there any shame to a Zen student crying in the woods?"

"No, teacher," said my friend.

Real life is not the edited perfected movie we run through our minds; real life is bigger than that. Each moment encompasses more than we can possibly capture in an image of success or failure.

If we can let go of success or failure, we can plunge in to each moment. Practice simply means bringing our whole self to each moment, doing the best we can. "Practicing without fail" simply means practicing all the time, trying to be alert and awake each moment. "Practicing without fail" means acknowledging we are always and will always be failing and falling short of the ideal; therefore we are free to plunge in and find the best word we can, the best posture we can, the best action we can, each moment—then let go of it and go on to the next. This way, we have infinite opportunities for practice. This way, we can recognize that each moment is, in its own way, perfect. Each action our client takes is a complete expression of the client at that moment; each action we take in therapy is a complete expression of the therapy at that moment.

Things which should be kept in mind in practicing Zen

> *Brilliance is not primary, knowledge is not primary; intellect, conscious endeavor, memory, imagination and introspection are not primary. Without resorting to any of these, harmonize body-and-mind and enter the buddha way.*

Athletes and artists usually discover that when they try to produce brilliant work, they get something stiff and unsatisfactory. In contrast, if questioned after what observers would call a brilliant performance, the athlete or artist usually doesn't talk about how brilliant they were, but rather how natural it all seemed: They were "in the groove" or their effort "just flowed." Therapists do the same thing, especially novice therapists. In general, the harder they try to force a "good session," the more it slips out of reach.

When my colleagues and I studied single-session therapies we videotaped our sessions, and at the onset each of us worried, "Am I competent? What if it turns out my colleagues can help clients in a single session, and I can't?" So we tried to force each session to become a brilliant single-session therapy.

The more we tried to be brilliant and make the therapy "special," the more the process of therapy bogged down and became less effective. When we relaxed and simply dealt with each moment of each session the best we could, the therapy unfolded in an easy flow.

When we examined the outcomes of our therapies, we learned something very interesting. We each had several sessions we thought had gone particularly well and thought would have good outcomes. In fact, it turned out many of these "great" sessions had only fair-to-middling outcomes. In contrast, many of the interviews that had seemed rather bland and run-of-the-mill turned out to have the best outcomes.

Brilliance can get in the way: We squint in the bright sun but in ordinary sunlight can see quite a long way and get on with our work. True ordinariness is special, for it embraces life as it is. When we can work with the ordinary, we are freed from fears of success or failure. Visions of success and yearnings to be special can paralyze us and our clients.

Tom was a forty-year-old man who suffered from chronic depression and lamented that throughout his life he had never realized his potential. He was a very intelligent, even brilliant, man who saw only his failures and never his successes. He had recently obtained his Ph.D. and had just started working in a prestigious setting in a demanding field. The immediate problem was that he needed to produce some projects but dreaded that his work would be no good, that he would be ridiculed and exposed as a fraud. He felt paralyzed. He would stare at the pages of a professional book whose material he needed to learn but be unable to read it; he would stare at his computer screen but be unable to write. He felt a failure.

He maintained he'd always been a failure. He pointed out he had had a ten-year period in which he was severely alcoholic. When I asked him how, if he were a total failure, he had managed to stop drinking and obtain a Ph.D., he said that had been mere "grunt work." He had to force himself to do it, step by step: Surely this was an indication that he was untalented and stupid.

As we explored this further, it turned out he had an idea that truly talented people were able to accomplish what they did effortlessly and immediately. He recalled that as a boy he had played saxophone rather well and had a dream of becoming a professional jazz musician. Then one day he heard a recording of Charlie Parker, riffing at giddy heights of improvisational ecstasy. Tom said hearing this, he felt crushed: It was clear to him that Parker was so talented that his music just poured forth from him as a natural phenomenon. Tom was sure Parker had never had to practice, that he "had it" from the beginning. He knew that if he were ever to be as good as Parker, he'd have to practice for years: The fact that he needed to practice clearly indicated that he wasn't talented, therefore it didn't make sense to even try. So he quit, and felt like a failure.

Tom still maintained the same attitude now. When he sat down to read a professional book, he would read a paragraph or two and not understand it immediately. This indicated to him that he wasn't a competent professional. He would skim ahead to other chapters and, finding he could not understand them (because they built on earlier chapters), felt that this confirmed he was stupid. He would become anxious and depressed, be unable to concentrate, and give up.

I remembered how when I first went to college I took a philosophy course and was dismayed to discover that, when I sat down to read ten pages of Husserl, it took me several hours. I was sure this meant that I was not intelligent enough to appreciate abstract thinking... until I heard another student complaining of the same thing. Tom, however, had isolated himself and never discovered that everyone had to walk before they could run. However, sharing my own experience with him and suggesting that his need to learn things in small chunks was normal didn't provide Tom much relief.

I asked Tom to stand up to do an experiment. We both stood side by side and faced the office door, some eight or nine feet away. "That door is the gate," I said to him. "Let's go through it." He looked puzzled, but started to walk toward the door.

"No," I said, restraining him. "Let's do it your way." He asked me what I meant. "According to you, if we're going to really be good at this, we have to get to the door without taking any intermediary steps." He laughed with some discomfort and made as if to sit down.

"No, you can't sit down," I said. "To do that, you'd have to walk from here to the chair. You'd have to take some steps. And after all, you can't take even a single step one foot forward. If you think about it, you'll find your conscious mind doesn't know how to walk. Close your eyes, and see what happens if you try to walk by having your mind order specific muscles what to do."

At this point we were both standing still, Tom with his eyes closed, looking rather sad, and I said, "When you were young, you had to *learn* to walk. You had to practice how to walk not just for months, but for years and years.

"When you analyze walking from here to your chair, your mind knows it's impossible. You know that to do that, you'd first have to go halfway from here to there. To get halfway from here to there, you have to go half that distance first... and half that distance before that... and so forth. You can never get there from here."

He paused, momentarily confused, tense, and paralyzed. Then he shrugged it off. "Oh, that old paradox," he said, a little put out. "That's just words."

"But how can I get from here to there?" I asked him.

Somewhat defiantly, he walked over, sat down, and crossed his arms. "You just do it," he said.

"Yes." I replied.

The solution from here was obvious. He accepted an assignment to reserve an hour, go out to a coffee shop (where he did most of his reading), and read *no more than* the first three pages of his book during that hour. When he returned the following session, he had completed a good deal of the required reading.

"If I just take it page by page, and don't go on to the next page until I understand the first, I can manage it. I'm still slower than I like, but that's OK," he said. We then applied the same principle to his writing. He found he could write e-mail messages without a problem. So he started writing his project with e-mails; then gradually expanded into paragraphs, pages, and soon—in less time than he had anticipated—his project was completed. On follow-up several years later, Tom was doing well professionally.

Zen teaches us to take things one page at a time, to deal with the page in front of us. The danger both in therapy and in spiritual practice is that we may search for some special, magical experience that obscures the fact that we are already awake and enlightened. Zen constantly tries to bring us back to the magic of the mundane:

> A monk said to Chao-chou:[15] "I have just entered this monastery. Please teach me."
> Chao-chou said, "Have you eaten your rice gruel?"
> The monk said, "Yes, I have."
> Chao-chou said, "Wash your bowl." The monk understood.

How can we, as therapists, keep from complicating things beyond this? In our textbooks of psychotherapy we read about complex case formulations and therapeutic interventions; we become intrigued with discovering projective identifications and the timing of transference interpretations, double binds and asking experience of experience questions, of tracing schemas and devising ways to interrupt irrational thoughts. Once we're in the psychotherapy office, however, psychotherapy consists of two people sitting down together, listening and talking to each other. It all becomes very simple, but not easy. How can we stay on track and not get lost in our theories and anxieties?

In the Zendo, life is boiled down to its essentials and there is not much to attend to besides sitting on the cushion, eating the meal, and cleaning up afterwards. At the end of a meditation retreat, students often talk about how they can adopt a calm, balanced attitude in the rarefied atmosphere of the Zendo but complain it is difficult to maintain this in the everyday world in which we are all bombarded by myriad conflicting demands and concerns. The answer Buddhism poses to this challenge is to stop seeking some special ideal state, and to practice finding ourselves wherever we are, each moment.

> *You should enter the buddha way through practice*
>
> *You must understand that we practice within delusions and attain realization before you recognize it.... Practice brings about realization; realization find itself through practice.*

We wake up *before* we go sit down on our cushion in the Zendo; the client coming to therapy has initiated their healing *before* the first therapy session, when he'd already made the decision to change, and phoned to make an appointment. Practice and realization, insight and action, express each other.

The solutions to clients' problems are not different from the relationship with the problem they enact in the psychotherapy. This does not mean they must "work through" the problems to *get to* resolutions: The working through *is* the resolution.

> Nancy, a thirty-five-year-old single woman, was taking care of her elderly mother who had Alzheimer's disease. Nancy came to me because she was having problems deciding whether to have her mother institutionalized. The decision had awakened all the ambivalent feelings she had about her mother, as well as Nancy's conflicts about to

what extent she felt comfortable doing things for herself rather than for other people. Nancy wanted to go back to school and finish her professional degree, resume dating, and generally "get a life" for herself but felt guilty about doing this: Nancy felt she ought to sacrifice her own desires in order to care for her mother, whom she loved sincerely.

Nancy was an intelligent, insightful woman who was stuck, constantly oscillating between the two evenly balanced poles of her decision. We spent several sessions exploring her feelings and thoughts, but whenever we tried to plunge more deeply into one side of the matter, she would shift to the other side. We tried exploring psychodynamic aspects, without much success. We tried cognitive-behavioral techniques and various "homework assignments," also without much success.

Finally I said to her, "We don't seem to be getting anywhere. I think we're going around in circles." Nancy agreed.

I said, "I can give you a technique which will help clarify for you which decision to make. This technique will require up to, but not more than, an entire day's effort, and will result in a final decision you can stick to. But I don't think you're quite ready to do so yet. If I tell you how to go about making the decision, I'd like you to promise me that you won't do this until you're good and ready. Furthermore, once I tell you the technique, if you agree it sounds useful, I think it makes sense that we postpone further meetings until after you've done the technique, because otherwise we'll just keep going round and round in circles here."

Nancy agreed to all these conditions.

"Very well. You know the Nordstrom's store in downtown San Francisco? When you're ready to make a firm decision, go to that store. Get there when it first opens, and prepare to spend the whole day there, if necessary. You'll find they have a very unique escalator: It curves around and around in circles, going up and down five stories or so. Your job is to go to the store and go down to the basement. Fix in your mind the idea that you're going 'round and 'round about this issue with taking care of your mother and your desires to strike off on your own. Then start at the basement and get on the escalator going up. Go 'round and 'round the escalator until you get to the top; then go 'round and 'round the escalator until you get to the bottom.

"You may experience a lot of thoughts and feelings. Don't get off the escalator, no matter how bored, frustrated, anxious, or depressed you may become, until this is settled. At a certain point, going 'round and 'round, your decision will become clear to you. Then you can get off and leave that spiral behind you and get on, wholeheartedly, with what you know you need to do.

"I would appreciate it if you could please come back and tell me what happens."

Nancy looked rather startled but agreed. I didn't see her for several months. When she came back, her decision had been made.

"I just wanted to tell you that I feel much better. It worked... but it didn't work like I thought it would. I thought I'd go there and something special would happen. But instead, what happened was that in trying to decide when to go do this, I found myself thinking about my situation with my mother and seeing it from all different angles. I dreamed about it, I talked to friends about it, because I knew that at some point I'd have to get on and off that escalator. And you know what happened?

"On the day I went to the store and was about to get on the escalator, I realized that *I'd already made my decision.* I rode the escalator for a little while just to be sure, but I already felt at peace about it."

Nancy's practice called forth her realization, even before she was aware of her decisions. Nancy could only practice, though, by immersing herself in her doubts. This is the way our life works. We need to accept the fact that we make decisions in the midst of indecision, that enlightened Zen practice takes place in the midst of delusion.

Integrative and insightful psychotherapy takes place in the midst of self-division and its inevitable correlate, self-deceit. Clients come to us aware of their suffering but often unable to have a clear view of their contribution to it; they are mired in their habitual ways of thinking, in the repetitive patterns of their inter-actions with others, in their impulses and defenses. Yet in the midst of all this suffering, there is something else going on; the client has some awareness that he or she needs to turn a corner. In the midst of self-delusion, the blossoming of self-realization arises as we practice with our neuroses and our character warps. Our hurts offer us the field for our healings.

> At the end of one long meditation retreat, we had an opportunity for a question-and-answer session with our teacher. We sat in the meditation hall and one at a time stood up, walked to the center of the hall, and asked the teacher a question, and he would reply.
>
> This had been a difficult retreat for me. I had come in to the Zendo expecting to have a week of calm peace; instead, throughout the meditation I found myself buffeted by strong feelings. I decided to ask the teacher about it.
>
> I stood up, walked to the center, bowed, and said,
>
> "Teacher, I've been sitting on my meditation cushion for the past week. For no reason I can tell, all my peace of mind has deserted me. I sit here in pain, not just physical pain, but emotional pain. Waves of anger rush through me, to be replaced by sadness. I don't find any particular thoughts or ideas, but I sit on the cushion in anguish, tears streaming down my cheeks. I can't figure it out. What is this?"
>
> The teacher replied with one word:
>
> "Nirvana."

MINDFULNESS[16]

How do we recognize and dwell in nirvana in the midst of our own and our clients' suffering? How can we recognize the treasure-house of life when we are wracked with sadness and anger; when it seems every word we say to a client backfires; when our boss criticizes us, our wife disappoints us, and our child doesn't listen? When our body gets sick, when we do something we swore we'd never do again, how can we approach all of this in a way that leads not to despair but to healing? How do we arouse practice in the midst of delusion, and experience this practice as enlightenment?

Both psychotherapy and Buddhism suggest that a good place to start is by stepping back a bit from our lives and increasing our awareness. Once we become aware of the traps that we build for ourselves, we can start to see options for acting and feeling differently. Increasing awareness can widen our field of view and increase our freedom of movement, but increasing awareness can also become a problem if it becomes a morbid kind of self-consciousness.

Sometimes when Zen students become aware of their selfish desires and attachments, they feel that they are bad students. Sometimes when psychotherapy clients become aware of the role they play in their suffering, they feel guilty or self-blaming in a way that plays into their neuroses. As clients become more aware of their suffering, they often can feel that there is something "wrong" with them and label themselves. They say things like, "I am an adult child of an alcoholic. I'm codependent. I have to learn how to take care of myself more." This kind of awareness can create more restriction rather than more freedom if, after recognizing how they were trapped by an old idea of how they "ought" to be (i.e., self-sacrificing), it simply substitutes another idea of how they "ought" to be (i.e., self-indulgent). This is just another trap. I have seen clients who label themselves "codependents" feel guilty when they generously help someone out, feeling they are not being "true to themselves."

The images we form of who we should be create a very narrow vision of truth. This kind of awareness, which stands back and treats self and others as labeled objects, offers objectivity but not engagement or compassion. It can lead to rumination and fear, to obsessive worrying about whether our efforts in therapy or zazen will bear fruit, and to restricted ideas about what the fruit of practice "should" look like.

If an apple tree were self-conscious in this way it might worry, before it bore fruit, that it did not know what apples looked like and feared it could not make good apples. If the tree tried to make an apple purely through thinking and extrapolating from its isolated individual existence and past experience, the tree might wind up creating an apple that looked something like a branch, a leaf, or a root, because these would be the only things of which the apple tree was aware so far. It takes faith for the apple tree to allow itself to blossom. It takes faith for clients or Zen students to know that they would not be seeking peace or wholeness if they were not already, in some fundamental way, peaceful and whole.

Mindfulness is the Buddhist term for a kind of awareness that bypasses the "shoulds" and "shouldn'ts" of experience and returns to the experience itself. Mindfulness includes knowledge *and* faith, stepping back from experience to increase perspective while simultaneously immersing itself deeper into the experience. Mindfulness involves paying attention to what we are doing with a certain set of attitudes that affect *how* we pay attention so that it connects us to, rather than separates us from, our lives. In a nutshell, *mindfulness is simply being open to life as it is, paying attention to our life in all its fullness from the standpoint of life itself, without excluding anything or adding anything to it.* As we practice mindfulness with our clients, we teach ourselves and our clients how to be as fully alive as we can be, and our practice becomes our realization even before we recognize it—our practice "calls forth" our life.

Table 2.1 Attitudes For Mindfulness

Nonjudging	Patience
Awareness without categorizing or criticizing	Don't rush
Simply pay attention	Give yourself room
Watch whatever comes up	Be open to the present moment
Don't impose ideas of what experience "should" be	

Acceptance	Letting go
See things as they are in the present	Nonattachment
Don't deny, resist, avoid	Don't hold on to the pleasant or reject the unpleasant
Acceptance is not resignation, defeat, or passivity	Let things be as they are
	Recognize without pursuing

Openness: beginner's mind	Trust
No preconceptions	Be yourself
Start again with each moment	Honor your feelings
Each time is the first time	
Avoid getting stuck in ruts	

Nonstraining	Steady practice
Not trying, but doing	Take responsibility for yourself
Not forcing a particular goal or purpose	Self-discipline to persevere
	Commitment to practice regularly

Table 2.1 lists some of the attitudes it is helpful to cultivate in order to strengthen our ability to be mindful: nonjudging, acceptance, letting go, openness, patience, nonstraining, trust, and steady practice.

What gets in the way of being mindful of our experience is that we are constantly coloring it. We do this in two ways: by adding something "extra" to our experience, and by "tuning out" or suppressing parts of our experience.

When we tune out our experience, we don't pay full attention to what we are doing and what is happening to us. This is normal but constricting. If we are driving along the road thinking about the work waiting for us at our job, we probably will not notice or fully appreciate the purple of the ice plants in bloom along the margins of the freeway. If while meeting with a client we are thinking about how many other clients we have to see today to satisfy our employer, we may not notice that the client opposite us is feeling ignored.

The last time I had something to eat, was I fully aware of its texture and fragrance? Did I savor its taste and notice its color? Did I hear the sounds it made as I chewed it while being aware of the muscles in my jaw and throat that enabled me to take it in? Did I notice how my breathing changed as I was eating? Was I distracted at all, thinking of what I would be doing next, or what had happened earlier in the day?

The last time I met with a client, was I fully aware of the smoothness of his skin, or the calluses on the palms of his hands? Did I savor his efforts to live his life the best he could, despite the obstacles he encountered? Did I taste his despair and glory in the colors of his life? Did I hear not just his words, but the sound of his swallowing back tears and the tension in his voice even as he smiled and laughed? Was I aware of the tension in my thighs and ankles as he told me of his work dodging molten steel in the foundry? Did I notice how my breathing responded to his? Was I distracted, or was I fully sharing my life with his, his with mine?

We all are always missing a lot. Becoming more aware immeasurably enriches our clinical work and our personal lives. The paradox is that even as we are missing a good deal of what is going on right under our nose, we are also cluttering up our minds by adding extra layers to the experiences that we do attend to.

The most common way we add something extra is by imposing judgments and opinions about our experience on top of the experience itself. Our minds are constantly speeding along, chattering, comparing, judging good and bad, right and wrong, remembering, fantasizing, anticipating, commenting on our experience. We spend much of our time thinking about what has happened in the past and wondering or wishing for a different future, forming opinions about what is happening now and comparing it with some wished-for mental ideal. This happens so fast and so constantly that we're hardly aware of it. If we're stuck in traffic on the way to work, we may think to ourselves, "They really shouldn't do road work at this time in the morning... those idiots, where are my tax dollars going?... there's too much traffic these days... I'm going to be late." Our judgments may very well be justified, but that's not the point; in the process of constantly commenting on life, we often miss out on life the way it actually is. Our judgments sometimes get in the way of taking a deep breath, relaxing behind the wheel, and looking around to notice the blue of the sky overhead.

In clinical practice, we often encounter heavy traffic that seems to get in the way of a smooth ride. Especially if we are feeling pressured by having a limited number of sessions due to insurance constraints, we may begin judging either the client or ourselves. We may start telling ourselves we're not up to the job of being brief therapists, offering a running commentary: "That was a stupid intervention I just made... I don't know what to do now, but time's running out, I have to do something... maybe I need more training in brief therapy." We may start labeling the client with diagnoses of personality disorders and resistance: "This person's not psychologically minded... that client's family is really underorganized... this person's childhood was so deprived, he can't possibly get better in brief treatment." Whether we are judging the client or ourselves, our chattering mind takes us away from the engaged listening and responding in the present that forms the heart of simply doing the therapy and letting it work or not.

It doesn't work to *suppress* our chattering mind: It just comes back, stronger than before. There is nothing wrong with opinions, wishes, memories, or other thoughts about an experience; it's just that these can take up a lot of our attention and shove our current experience into the background where we can't appreciate it fully. If we cultivate mindfulness and become more aware of the full breadth of our experience—including how our mind is chattering—we simply redirect our attention to take in more of the immediate encounter. We get back to life itself, rather than the judgments we are making about life.

The act of judging can be subtle. Judging is not only a matter of criticizing; judging arises whenever we make a comparison. When we compare our experience to something else from our memories or anticipations it can take away from the immediate experience itself. We wind up reacting to our expectations about the experience, rather than to the experience itself. If we buy an apple pie thinking, "This looks as good as the ones my mother used to make," then when we taste the pie we'll be tasting our memories and our wishes right along with the pie. If we see a client and relate him or her to another case we've seen or read about, we may start interacting with a prototypical "case" rather than with the real person in front of us at this moment.

We need to make judgments in our clinical practice in order to choose our actions and decide on the best interventions of which we are capable. However, if we are *always* making judgments, we run the risk of not taking the time to just step back, see things as they are, and be guided by whatever comes up. Psychotherapy often works best when we make a conscious effort to suspend judgments for a period of time. Our judgments inherently edit our experience. When we widen our field of awareness, looking at whatever is happening without classifying it or criticizing it, just putting our bare attention on it without adding any opinions or old mental habits about what the experience "should" be, we have an opportunity to embrace all the experience that is *actually* occurring, rather than picking and choosing based on our *ideas* about what is or should be happening.

Judging takes us out of the real world of life as it is and into the conceptual world of "good" and "bad." When we start judging that things are not as they "should" be we stand a good chance of starting to feel annoyed, anxious, or upset. When we start judging that things are going well, we stand a good chance of starting to feel excited, wanting to hold on to what's happening or get more of what feels good. Contrary to the teachings of capitalism, however, more is not necessarily better.

If we grab overly eagerly at good things we're like the fish who, pursuing the worm, bites down on the hook: We get caught by our desires. Consumerist culture is full of such baited hooks, of promises that obtaining more material things will bring happiness. Pursuing happiness through accumulating possessions often serves only to ensnare us in debt, envy, and greed.

Psychotherapy also has its share of advertisements, books, and workshops that promise if we just accumulate more expertise our work with clients will become easy and successful. However, amassing a large collection of psychological knowledge may not make as much difference as a single new awareness that gets translated into action. In psychotherapy more is not necessarily better: If a feeling of intimacy arises in a therapy session but we try to push too much for more affect, the feeling in the room can become forced and the client's walls will go back up. Three new insights gained over many sessions will not necessarily be more helpful than a single deeply moving session that provides a pivot on which a client can swivel to see the world in a new way.

"More" and "less," "good" and "bad" are judgments. Judgments engender desires, hopes, and fears that can lead to rejection and avoidance, avidity and agitation. During psychotherapy or zazen, whether we fear that something negative will happen or yearn for something special to occur we can wind up straining if we pursue or flee from the mirages of our ideas. Mindfulness encourages us, instead, to relax into the current moment, whatever it may consist of. Working with what is "here" rather than worrying about where we are going, we are less likely to strain overmuch. Avoiding straining in mindfulness doesn't mean not working hard; it simply means that instead of "trying" to do something, we relax, forget our old ideas, and do the best we can. Mindfulness involves 100% of our effort and attention—not 90%, but not 110% either.[17] We need not dawdle, but we also need not hurry.

Mindfulness involves being patient and gentle with ourselves. We need to model this for our clients, who usually are quite harsh on themselves. So as therapists we need to accept our limitations and not strive excessively hard to do too much too soon. The most common mistake I notice beginners making when they start to do brief psychotherapy is to feel rushed, pressured to accomplish a lot in a short time. When we become mindful of each moment, however, we have many, many opportunities in each session to develop a meaningful encounter with a client, so there's no need to rush or push ourselves. Whatever is happening here in this session, now, is where the action is. Each moment of each session, whether boring or exciting, rough or smooth, makes its own contribution.

Mindfulness helps us learn from each experience by fostering a sense of openness and acceptance. Acceptance doesn't mean not doing anything. Accepting things as they are doesn't mean giving in to them, resigning ourselves to our lot and feeling hopelessly fatalistic. Rather, acceptance involves the strength to deal with the truth. The first step in dealing with anything is seeing it clearly. Mindfulness involves seeing and accepting things as they are without either rejecting or grasping at what we see. Our lives can be shocking, or strange, or intense; mindfulness requires that we don't close our eyes to what's happening.

If we accept things as they are without avoiding or clinging to them, they can't trap us; we let them be whatever they are and recognize them without getting caught by them. So mindfulness is about freedom, about maintaining an open mind in which all our experiences, thoughts, and feelings have room to come and go. When we suspend judgment and cultivate acceptance, we model for our clients an attitude in which they need not get caught in the opinions and desires they usually hold on to. In psychotherapy we implicitly ask our clients to make an experiment in mindfulness; we encourage them to intentionally let go of their old habits and ideas and, without being attached to anything in particular, to let themselves roam freely without getting stuck on any one thing.

Letting go can be difficult, because we all have lots of habits and automatic ways of doing things; we all have cherished ideas we cling to that lead us to act less than ideally in the immediate situation. The flip side of this, fortunately, is that we have lots of opportunities to free ourselves from our old habits. Each time we notice ourselves or our clients getting stuck in our fears and wishes, likes and dislikes, if we gently let go and attend to the immediate experience of that moment of fear or defensiveness, rather than to our editorializing thoughts or reactive feelings about the experience, we'll be able to make some new discoveries. When a feeling or thought comes up we notice it, accept it, let it pass, and come back to what's happening *right now.*

Mindfulness simply means being aware of *what is happening right now at this moment.* It is easier to accept our experience as it is if we can realize that it is not a frozen fate but a moving stream. Mindfulness brings home the truth of impermanence so that we experience life as always flowing. As we become more mindful, we become more rooted in the present, rather than weighed down by the past or yearning or fearing for the future. Accepting things as they are right now, we begin to discover that "now" is always moving, so that even our difficulties are vehicles of change.

When we do this, our feelings and our thoughts often quiet down a bit as we appreciate whatever the moment is bringing to us. So mindfulness is about appreciating our lives, about emptying ourselves of the ghosts of expectations so we can experience the fullness of life as it is. As we become more able to do this, we gradually strengthen our sense of inner calm, composure, and self-possession. As we learn to accept life without rejecting anything or holding on too tight, we also learn to accept ourselves as a whole, rather than building our identity on the "good parts" and fearing that the "bad parts" will shame us. If we stop rejecting ourselves and let go of pushing ourselves into images and molds that don't fit, we begin to discover our unique abilities and qualities. We learn to trust ourselves more and more, honoring our feelings without being ruled by them. In my experience, as I do this, it "rubs off" on my clients; our meeting becomes a continuous series of opportunities for us to practice mindfulness together.

One of my clients has written eloquently about her therapeutic journey in a way that exemplifies the openings that can come when we experience our lives mindfully. The specifics of her problems and the details of her therapy are not important here. Suffice it to say that growing up in a fatalistic, critical family environment made it hard for her, as an adult, to trust herself or accept her imperfections. This led her to feel alienated from her own inner experience. During the therapy she worked hard to cultivate a nonjudgmental increased awareness, but she tended to judge how well she was succeeding in being nonjudging! She found it difficult to fully accept herself and felt skeptical that increasing acceptance would be sufficient to help her feel better. Nevertheless she persisted, even in the face of considerable pain and suffering. Eventually she reached a turning point. She described her experience in a letter to me:

> [My dialogue with myself] has been, these last few weeks, by turns painful, chaotic, and now finally, somewhat calm... I have not trusted the process too much, as you know, but nevertheless I have been swept up into it...
>
> Freedom, self-definition was something I so wanted, and yet remained so relentlessly elusive. There was always some-one—my father, my lovers—to whom I owed compliance, or something—my pain—which demanded attention. So while I had these dreams of liberation, I have lived a kind of double existence. I have felt fragmented, distracted, ill-at-ease, both in my mind and my body...
>
> After our meeting on Thursday, I finally accepted what was happening, that I'd played the same, old theme again, only with you this time. But it was different because you encouraged me to witness and try to understand it: to catch, out of the corner of my eye, my shadow in motion...
>
> ...Fatalism has been an easy out. I realized that feeling messed up was a kind of reflex, a way of evading the difficulty of working through a problem. Essentially you said (if I may para-phrase) "hey, why are you so special? You're a mess, but we're all a mess, because life's a mess. And you're re-creating even more of a mess because you're adding another layer of tragedy with your fatalism and depression... It was helpful to see it as a habit that can be tossed aside... a thing the mind does, it doesn't define your being.
>
> So I've emerged from the travail of the last couple weeks somewhat dazed. I say dazed because I feel different, and yet not different in the way I'd imagined when I first began this process. I remember wanting so badly that, like a butterfly, I might shed my ugly old skin, my leaden, terrestrial existence, and lift off airborne, beautiful and new.
>
> Of course, this is not a fitting story for human creatures; it is the story I have been trapped in, rather than liberated by... And yet I do feel different. I am still the same old me, but I feel a certain peace and stillness, like the calm after a storm. A certain solidity of being. The anxiety, the sense of fragmentation and distraction is lessened... There's an expression in French, "etre bien dans la peau"—"to feel good in one's skin"—a feeling of being at ease, which is what I am close to feeling. Of course I still have worries, but they seem more external, in a way, less rooted in my being...
>
> It is interesting, the way fragmentation has evolved into complexity. Suddenly, the flow of emotions which had weighted me down, torn me in different directions, now flows free, opens up new possibilities. Emotions which in former times held me hostage now move through me with greater ease. I'd felt an infi-nite, encompassing sadness stretching steadily, relentlessly from past through the present out into an endless future. Now, al-though I'm inside of that sadness, I don't feel that I will drown

in it... I have also been generating a lot of ideas about my future. Normally I would feel overwhelmed by so many options,
but now I am learning to sit still and look at them.

The other night I had a dream... there was a fire, an internal fire which I hope has burned itself out. Something has been
cleared out...

BEGINNER'S MIND

Mindfulness is about clearing out our selves. When we let go and accept things as
they are, moving and changing, we open up to fresh ideas and experiences. Then
each moment can be a new adventure. In order to cultivate this aspect of mindfulness, we can approach everything as if it were the first time we are encountering
it, without any preconceptions. Children take an object and, not knowing what
it's "supposed to" be, use it in some creative way that looks like a lot of fun.
Mindfulness helps us recover this fruitful innocence.

There is a Zen saying: "In the beginner's mind, there are many possibilities,
but in the expert's there are few." [18] It is easy to become proud of what we know
and to wish to demonstrate the mastery we have obtained. If we become too attached to this, however, we can run into the problem of the monk in the following
story: [19]

Jiufeng worked as an attendant of Shishuang. When Shishuang passed away, the community wanted to invite the first-ranked monk in the hall to succeed to the abbacy.
Jiufeng did not agree; he said, "Wait until I have questioned him—if he understands
our late teacher's meaning, I'll serve him like our late teacher."

Then Jiufeng asked the chief monk, "The late teacher said, 'Cease, desist; spend
ten thousand years in one thought; be cold ashes, dead trees; be a censer in an ancient
shrine, be a strip of pure white silk.' Now tell me, what does this illustrate?"

The chief monk said, "It illustrates the teaching of Uniform Oneness."

Jiufeng said, "Then you still don't understand our late teacher's meaning."

The chief monk said, "Oh no? You don't agree with me? Set up some incense!"

The chief monk then lit the incense and said, "If I don't understand our late
teacher's meaning, then I won't be able to pass away while this incense is burning."

So saying, the chief monk sat down in meditation and (through the power of his
meditation), passed away. He died.

Jiufeng then patted him on the back and said, "As far as dying seated or standing is concerned, you're not lacking. But as for our late teacher's meaning, you still
haven't dreamed of seeing it."

As psychotherapists, we can become as fond of our expert psychological
knowledge as the chief monk was of his expert knowledge of Uniform Oneness.
However, if we become too sure that a particular answer goes with a particular
question, we can get into trouble. We can kill ourselves working too hard to fit
things into predetermined molds. If we hold on too tight to what we know, we
have less space available for learning. In both psychotherapy and Zen practice

we are always on a pilgrimage, but it is important to not be overly positive about where we are heading or how to get there, as Dizang[20] reminds us:

> Dizang asked Fayan, "Where are you going?"
>> Fayan said, "Around on pilgrimage."
>> Dizang said, "What is the purpose of pilgrimage?"
>> Fayan said, "I don't know."
>> Dizang said, "Not knowing is nearest."

If I know in advance the endpoint of my pilgrimage, all along the path I may feel far from my goal. If I let myself just pay attention to the process of traveling, arriving at my destination ceases to be the be-all and end-all. Not knowing where I'm going, my journey is joyful because every step brings me to an interesting spot.

These days when we have to justify our work to the insurance companies who are paying the bills, it is not easy to stand up for the importance of not knowing. Our professional societies have tended to fight back against having judgments imposed on us by outside authorities by asserting the importance of our professional knowledge. But what motivates scientific inquiry is not what we know, but what we *don't* know.

Even should we avoid the certainties imposed by outside authorities, if we assume we have personal expert knowledge to offer a client, we may see the client only through the lens of our particular expertise. If we become skilled in a particular psychotherapeutic intervention or school of therapy, we sometimes tend to view the intervention as the Answer to everything. Then we are likely to become less flexible and may try to force the client to fit our method rather than meet her or him where he or she needs to be met:

> About 15 years ago, when I was a novice therapist, a man came to see me because he had problems urinating in public restrooms. My client had no problem with urinary retention when he was alone. However, when he entered a public restroom he would become extremely self-conscious and anxious; this in turn would lead to muscle tightness that would make it more difficult to urinate, resulting in a vicious circle. He was sure other people noticed his inability to urinate and felt he was less than a man because of the problem. Because he was a salesman who worked far from home and only had crowded public restrooms available to him during his workday, he wound up holding his bladder for painfully long periods of time.
>
> My client told me that he had no traumatic childhood memories, but that he had read enough about psychotherapy so he guessed the treatment would involve talking about his childhood. I was originally trained psychodynamically, but around this time I had become impressed by the research literature that seemed to suggest that cognitive and behavioral interventions were more efficacious. In fact, I had just successfully treated another patient with a similar problem using these techniques. So I reassured the patient there was no need to go into his early memories; we could deal with this through relaxation training and systematic and in-vivo desensitization.

It didn't work. Despite learning progressive muscle relaxation, going through a desensitization hierarchy, and having successful experiences in the public restrooms in the medical center, he continued to have the problem in his daily life. He kept insisting throughout the desensitization treatment that he really thought it wouldn't work, and that he needed to talk about his childhood; I kept assuring him we just had to do this step-by-step and the problem would improve.

In retrospect, I realize I was holding on to my preferred method as much as he was holding on to his urine. I worry about cases like this sometimes when I see how the field is moving toward establishing a list of "approved" treatments for specific problems.

Later I would see other clients with a presenting problem of urinary retention. Some required desensitization; some required interpersonal psychotherapy; some improved with hypnosis; and some just needed to talk. Most of the clients I've seen with this problem feel intense shame; they fear losing control and wetting themselves, or feel embarrassed at not being able to urinate on demand, or feel defective in some other way. Cultivating a mindful attitude of acceptance and nonjudging, in which there is no success and no failure, seems more crucial to helping the client than any particular technique.

But each case is unique. One of my female clients got over her problem with urinary retention when she started carrying a small squeeze bottle filled with water in her purse; she would go into a stall, squeeze the bottle to produce a stream of fluid into the toilet and then, knowing anyone else in the bathroom would hear the sound and assume she was urinating "normally," she could relax and go about her business. Although the idea of the squeeze bottle surfaced within the first few sessions of the therapy, the client did not make use of it until we dealt with her feelings of being crippled by a childhood disease that had left her with a mildly abnormal gait. After dealing with that, she was able to use the mechanical device; within a few weeks she no longer needed to use the bottle. She had postponed getting married, fearing her problem would keep her from going away on a honeymoon. She soon married and is now raising a family.

If for each person I see I want to find an appropriate intervention that fits not the problem, but the client, I find that for each case I first need to let go of all my "knowledge" and listen with a "beginner's mind" that has no attachment to doing things one way rather than another. This is true not just for our personal experience but also for our relationships. I've always remembered something my teacher suggested when I was first learning family therapy: to try, when we wake up each morning and see our partner on the pillow beside us, to look at them as if we were seeing them for the first time. This is difficult but rewarding. When I work with couples who come to me complaining of "poor communication," I suggest the best thing they can do to improve their communication is to forget they know anything about each other, to acknowledge they can never know each other completely, and to approach the other person as a fascinating, unfathomable mystery.

When the certainty of rules crowds out the excitement of exploration, stale prescriptions can get in the way of fresh discoveries and the beginner's enthusiasm for therapy can turn into the expert's burnout. Mindfulness helps us approach our experience with fresh, open curiosity, with the wonder that we experience when we encounter anything for the first time. When we are mindful in this way, we and our clients can make a fresh start each moment and enjoy our lives as they unfold continuously before us.

Do not practice Buddha's teaching with gaining-mind

Proceed with the mind which neither clings to nor rejects anything.... Practice without thinking of gaining something in return. Buddhas have sympathy for all living beings and help them through compassion, [but] everything they do is neither for themselves nor others. A practitioner should not practice buddha-dharma for his own sake, to gain fame and profit, to attain good results, or to pursue miraculous powers. Practice the buddha-dharma only for the sake of the buddha-dharma. This is the way.

We are used to the notion that spiritual practice should not be practiced for the sake of personal gain. It might seem strange to suggest that psychotherapy also should not be practiced for the sake of personal gain. The whole idea of psychotherapy seems to be that the client should gain something: namely, a cure for what ails him or her. Didn't the days of doing psychotherapy just for some vague ideal of personal exploration go out with brief therapy and the managed-care revolution? Meanwhile, as therapists, while our primary concern may be to help our clients, we want to earn a good living and maybe even obtain some recognition for our work.

We know it's helpful in therapy for the therapist to accept clients with unconditional positive regard and not push them to be any particular way: Increasingly, however, we are required to move therapy toward specified goals in specified periods of time. We know that meditation rests on the open acceptance of all our experience we call mindfulness, yet we often strive to achieve some specific peaceful feeling or gain some sort of spiritual attainment. We know in our journeys in life we enjoy ourselves more when we have fewer expectations, yet we keep trying to mold life to fit into what we want it to be, so that we "get something" from it.

It's good to have some goals in life. However, if we become too focused on gaining some particular outcome, we may suffer from tunnel vision. If we get attached to our goal, it can become the only thing we'll see. If we are beachcombing and only let ourselves look for driftwood, excluding everything else from our attention, we may overlook the beautiful shell right beneath our feet. When we practice psychotherapy, we need a focus to guide us, but we also need to avoid becoming overly restricted by concern for whether we are achieving the goal.

We are encouraged more and more to evaluate whether we are reaching our goals and whether the therapy is "working." We have to prove to clients and insurance companies that the therapy is worth it, that they are getting their money's worth. The problem with this is that as soon as we ask, "Am I getting something from this? Is this worth it?" we set up obstacles to ourselves: Such evaluations add expectations and judgmental doubting that distracts us from the experience itself.

> When I was an undergraduate in college, I took a course in yoga from one of my professors.[21] This genial man made no claims to being an adept at yoga—he was an ex-Marine, a wrestling coach, and an administrator—but he had learned a little yoga from a friend and offered a beginning course.
>
> Some time after completing his course, I learned that there would be a visiting Indian preacher who would offer a yoga course. I was interested in attending but wasn't sure whether I should spend some of my meager funds on the fee. I didn't know his qualifications; he wasn't a certified "guru" but simply a Methodist preacher; I worried I'd be spending my money without much benefit. I asked my professor about this and never forgot his advice.
>
> "I don't know whether or not he's a great yoga teacher," my professor replied. "I *do* know that if you take the class and spend the time worrying about whether you're getting your money's worth, you won't learn very much."

In a materialistic, individualistic society we're encouraged to worry about whether we're getting our money's worth, to ask: "What do *I* get out of this?" This can happen not only in psychotherapy, but in spiritual matters as well. If I take a week of scarce vacation time to spend sitting in a meditation retreat, I can start worrying whether I'm "wasting my time" if I don't have some "enlightenment experience." Worrying about gain inevitably involves worrying about loss, but if we spend our time trying to calculate our "net profit" from an experience we won't pay as much attention to the experience itself.

Once we start judging our experience as good or bad for us, we grasp at it or reject it. Either way, we step out of our experience and into our ideas about our experience. Then we create a separation in our lives that causes suffering as we get caught wrestling with ourselves.

> This can be seen clearly in clients who have problems with relaxation or hypnosis. Whether it be progressive muscle relaxation, meditative deep breathing, or hypnotic induction, some clients get locked in a battle with themselves. When asked to pay attention to their immediate physical sensations, they scan their bodies not in a mindful fashion that simply notices and accepts but in a judgmental fashion that assesses whether they are measuring up to some ideal image of relaxation or trance. If clients who have an image of what relaxation or trance "should" feel like encounter some internal tension or resistance, they may begin to feel they are failing or being disappointed; if they start forcing themselves to relax they run into difficulties as they try to push themselves into the shape of an ideal image rather than explore where they are. The more they try to let go, the more they tighten up; the more they try to gain, the worse they feel.

Therapists can encounter similar problems:

> I mentioned previously that when my colleagues and I did our project on single-session therapies and videotaped all our sessions, the more we tried to be brilliant,

the more we stumbled. The problem was that the videotaping activated our desires for personal gain: We wanted to show off how good we were as therapists. In our fantasies, a videotaped record of a good therapy session could be used on the workshop circuit to gain fame and wealth; if not that, at least a good session would make us feel like good therapists and give us a little puff of self-pride. Our attempts at brilliance were intended for our own benefit as much as for the clients.

Somehow it always seemed the sessions with clients that we *didn't* get around to videotaping were the sessions that blossomed. I remember one time a colleague coming out of a session saying what each of us had thought one time or another: "Boy, I wish I had that one on videotape! I could show that session around on the circuit and retire!" Then he asked, somewhat plaintively, "Why can't those sessions happen when we are taping?"

Our desires for personal gain (and fears of personal failure in looking bad on tape) were getting in the way of meeting our clients eye-to-eye. These desires led us to anticipate each session with both hope and fear, and we experienced what people who have a fear of public speaking or taking tests experience: Anticipation about performance interferes with the performance itself.

It took us a while to let go of our fantasies, but once we stopped being invested for our personal benefit in making the sessions turn out spectacularly, the sessions flowed more smoothly. We were able to accept that some sessions would have good outcomes, some would not; that some clients would need to be seen for more sessions, others would accomplish what they needed in a single visit. When we were able to forget about the videotape, how we'd look, and how things would turn out, we were more able to pay attention to what was going on right in front of us. We began to adopt a curiosity about what each session would hold, without any personal agenda: However and whatever we and our clients did, we were interested to see how it worked itself out. Each session was ordinary, nothing special, and therefore fascinating: delightfully itself.

Zen students also get caught in ideas of gaining some kind of attainment; enlightenment is the ultimate carrot held out to the donkey. Students sometimes mistakenly think the goal of zazen is to produce enlightened Buddhas; then they ask questions like the following:[22]

A monk asked the priest Ch'ing-jang of Hsing-yang, "The Buddha of Supremely Pervading, Surpassing Wisdom did zazen on the Bodhi seat for ten eons, but the Dharma of the Buddha did not manifest itself and he could not attain Buddhahood. Why was this?

Ch'ing-jang said, "Your question is exactly to the point."

The monk said, "But he did zazen on the Bodhi seat; why couldn't he attain Buddhahood?

Ch'ing-jang said, "Because he is a nonattained Buddha."

In zazen, our practice does not *attain* anything but *expresses* our sincerity and compassion in the midst of the darkness of delusion. In psychotherapy, our practice does not create health but helps us rediscover our fundamental sanity and wholeness in the face of the crazy fragments of our lives.

> I happened to be writing this at a time when meditating was not getting me anything. Quite the contrary; I sat on the cushion rocked by depression, anger, and physical pain. Zazen was a rather grim business and I got tired of it. I talked to my teacher about it, and he reminded me: Don't expect anything from zazen. When it's painful, it's painful. Just stay with whatever's happening, and find how to settle down in that spot.
>
> "But," I objected, "this has been going on for a year. I'm stuck. I don't know where I am or what to do."
>
> "Well," he replied, "If you don't know where you are or what to do, you're not stuck."

Not-knowing helps to free us so that we are not stuck in our preconceptions. But this is easier to see from the outside. The teacher can see that the puzzlement and confusion are part of the learning. The therapist can see that the client's anxiety and depression are part of the process of change. The supervisor can see that the therapist's frustration with the client's "resistance" provides important keys to the unfolding of the therapy for both client and therapist.

But when we are the one who is frustrated, confused, or in pain, we can lose sight of the larger picture. The more we are focused on "getting something" to escape our distress, the more we are blinded by the anguish that seems to be standing in our way. If we are trying to head in a particular direction to gain something and come up against an obstacle, our disappointments and anger, our fears and depression loom close and release seems far away.

> Aitken Roshi likes to tell the folk story of a ship which suffered through a bad storm off the coast of South America.[23]
>
> Its water kegs were smashed, and the crew was parched with thirst. Encountering another vessel, the captain signaled a request for water. To his surprise, the signal came back, "Let down your buckets." He did so, and found the seawater was fresh. For though he was out of sight of land, the ship was off the mouth of the Amazon River, where the water was sweet for many miles.
>
> "Let down your buckets where you are," concludes Aitken Roshi.

In zazen and in psychotherapy, if we keep looking to attain something, so long as we keep searching for gain we won't be able to see what's right at hand. We need to fully embrace our lives as they are in order to see they are not frozen, but fluid fresh streams.

But there is a somewhat subtle potential snare here. Sometimes we might say to ourselves "I'll let go of trying to attain something," but harbor a secret hope that *this* will be the secret to attaining the peace or security we want. It doesn't work.

> During one intensive meditation retreat, I was suffering intense physical pain. This came as something of a surprise; in the previous few retreats, I had learned ways of

relaxing body and mind that had let me sit zazen for long periods of time in comfortable enjoyment. This time, however, no matter what I did, the pain steadily intensified.

When I had an interview with my teacher, I told him I'd gotten to a point at which there didn't seem to be anything to do about the pain. "I just sit there and try to accept the pain and make an offering of it."

"That's a good thing to do," my teacher said. "So long as you don't think it's going to make the pain any better!"

The fact is that sometimes when we accept things as they are, we still will be in pain. Sometimes our lives are bitter to our taste and difficult to swallow. When we are in the midst of difficulties we may not be sailing in the Amazon River but may be sailing blindly in a brackish or even a polluted ocean. In the larger scheme of things, the ocean is the source of all fresh water. But seeing the grand scheme of things doesn't always offer much consolation when you're thirsty. The fact is that sometimes when we let down our buckets where we are, what's at hand is not cool refreshing water but the salt of a vast sea.

There is only one answer for this I can find: I look at my teachers, fellow students, fellow therapists, and my clients, and I remember: Everyone's tears are salty.

We carry the sea in our blood, our veins, in every cell of our body. Our clients' and our tears both have their source in an ocean of water that rises into the air through evaporation, then falls in torrential rains into some particular high mountain stream, travels over streambeds and becomes the water imbibed by an individual human being shedding tears to a personal grief. Once shed, our tears rejoin the vapors of the air we breathe and eventually find their way back to the sea.

We're all connected to each other and to the larger world: We thirst for this sense of connectedness. The key to Aitken's story lies not just in the fresh water under the boat, but in the connection that comes in one captain's calling to the other and the other captain answering.

When Zen practice closes down to a preoccupation with personal liberation and practices meditation to achieve enlightenment, it forfeits that connectedness and becomes restricted by the very greed and pride from which it is seeking liberation. When psychotherapy increases a client's preoccupation with himself by focusing on gaining satisfaction of personal wants and desires, it isolates the client from the larger context of his or her life and casts both client and therapist adrift. Sometimes it is not our or our client's happiness that is redeemable, but that of a child, a parent, or lover: Even a pet or a tree may be the tie that binds.

When they follow their true nature, both psychotherapy and Zen inherently place us in a wider context. The world is too big for us to restrict it to our personal rules of gain and loss. We are embedded in the world and depend for our very existence on all around us: all our ancestors before us, all that follows, all who coexist with us. We are not alone. We practice not for ourselves, nor even for others, but *with* everyone. The antidote to neurotic ideas of gain lies not in finding some personal gratification but in discovering the satisfaction inherent in our connectedness with others; the antidote to Zen sickness is not to obtain enlightened bliss, but to realize our interdependence with all beings.

We get isolated and blinded if we practice psychotherapy or Zen to gain something for ourselves, but we keep falling into the trap. Fortunately, there is a simple antidote: to practice giving. Giving transforms us by taking us out of ourselves: it inherently connects us to others. Giving is the foundation of both psychotherapeutic and Zen practice. Dogen reminds us that although

> ... the mind of a sentient being is difficult to change, you should keep on changing the minds of sentient beings... This should be started by giving.
>
> Mind is beyond measure. Things given are beyond measure. Moreover, in giving, mind transforms the gift and the gift transforms mind.[24]

Many clients come to psychotherapy hoping to get something out of it: Some love or validation they feel they have not gotten from their parents, some recognition or appreciation that they have not gotten from their employers or children. If the therapist responds to this just by giving to the client, it only teaches the client about getting, not giving. Often what is equally or even more healing for clients than being given to is to have an opportunity to give of themselves to others. Sometimes clients need to learn how to give genuinely of themselves to others in order to give to themselves; sometimes they need to learn how to give to themselves in order to give genuinely to others. They are two aspects of the same thing. As Dogen says,

> If you are to practice giving to yourself, how much more so to your parents, wife, and children. Therefore you should know that to give to yourself is a part of giving. To give to your family is also giving. Even when you give a particle of dust, you should rejoice in your own act.

In psychotherapy and Zen practice we learn the mutuality of give and take. We are always receiving from others and always giving to others. We may, however, have the illusion that giving is unidirectional: that we must give to benefit others and deny ourselves, or conversely that we are entitled to be given to without any obligation of returning the favor. If we think we deserve to be given to or must be given to, we will feel either helpless despair or righteous anger if we don't get what we want. On the other hand, if we think we can give to others without being given to, we will put ourselves in a position of feeling one-up on the person we see as needy and dependent on us. Therapists are in real danger of this, because illusions of both the profession and our clients can pull for this kind of giving. Feeling one-up can be temporarily gratifying, but ultimately it proves draining.

There are many different kinds of giving. There is giving in which we give in order to feel good about ourselves. This is hardly ideal, but often we have to start learning about giving from this point. The process of giving in itself helps us learn about the selfless pleasures of generosity. This can lead us to the kind of giving in which we give in order to help another person. There, the process of giving teaches us empathy as we sorrow at the other person's pain and rejoice in their happiness. But as we practice giving more and more, it becomes as natural as respiration, with as little thought of gain and loss as breathing in and breathing out. In this giving we simply rejoice in the act of giving itself, as a simple expression of our true self.

At this point, we begin to realize that giving always involves a mutuality: The giver offers a gift to the receiver, but the one receiving gives the gift of allowing the giver to give. The teacher learns from the student; the therapist learns from the client. Although it may not be obvious if we look at giving and receiving from either side, when we look at the whole process we can see its interactive nature.

> Yesterday we were driving through some woods when my twelve-year-old daughter said, "You know, some people think trees were put on earth to serve us and provide oxygen for us to breathe. They're wrong!
>
> "But you know, there are also people who think we were put on earth to serve it and to provide carbon dioxide for the trees to breathe. I think they're wrong too.
>
> "Trees and us, we just go together with each other and give each other what's needed."

Giving transforms the mind by helping us see how we go together with each other. This is the great advantage of group psychotherapy: It allows clients an immediate chance to give and be given to. Most therapists have had the experience of saying something to a client with no effect whatsoever, and then seeing a client become profoundly moved when a fellow client in a group says the same thing. These days, the HMO at which I work strongly encourages us to refer clients to groups because it is economically efficient. If we shove a client to a group to "get rid of them" so that our caseload doesn't fill up too fast, we will send a message that group is a second-best treatment for the mass delivery of psychotherapeutic techniques that we don't have the resources to deliver individually. It's important that we don't fall into this trap, so that we can foster the healing value of mutual giving that groups can provide.

> During the holiday season, the discussion in our stress-management group turned to grief. Several clients had experienced death during the previous few months. One of the women in the group talked about her father's death, and how she would "never get over it," that it seemed it would be a betrayal of her father for her to be happy.
>
> Another group member, a man, said: "But do you think your father would want you to be so unhappy?" The client admitted her father would want her to be happy, but clearly this was just an intellectual understanding. I thought to myself, "That's something we say as therapists; it doesn't usually have much effect."
>
> But then the man told the story of his own father. His father grew up dirt-poor, a sharecropper. He sacrificed everything for his family. My client was his oldest son, and he spoke with tears in his eyes of how his father had taught him to fish, encouraged him to go to school, and took pride in his son's accomplishments. His voice choking, he said that the only thing that got him through his father's death was the

knowledge that his father got happiness from his son's happiness. "I'd have gone crazy otherwise."

As this man told of his life, the other client listened and something eased in her own grief.

When this man gave of himself to the woman in the group, he helped transform both her and himself. All he needed to do was share of himself, by telling the truth about himself. When this kind of giving happens, as Dogen points out,[25] "The truth can turn into valuables; valuables can turn into the truth. This is all because the giver is willing." This man willingly offered his own life to another person in a form of beneficial action that is "an act of oneness, benefiting self and others together."

I think my seventeen-year-old daughter expressed how giving benefits self and others together when she wrote, in her college entrance essay,

It means a lot for me to help other people and often, through them, help myself. I learned this probably the most from a man named Fredrick R———. Fred is a patient at a convalescent home, and I began visiting him in my Junior year. Going in at first to see Fred was very hard, and very scary. The building he lived in stank of urine and hopelessness and every time I entered it I received in turn a kind of deep sadness for all living there. It was this sadness I had to put aside to laugh with Fred, talk with him of his past and my future, and listen to him play oldies on his stereo. It was my fear of death that I had to put aside when he told me that his wife, asleep in the next bed, had suffered a heart attack the other night and was not recovering well. And it was strength that I had to come from instead. I went to the convalescent home to help Fred, but he helped me out probably a lot more than he will ever know. For I watched him continue to fight and to live and from him I learned about love and gratitude.

Giving without thought of name or gain is a form of sharing ourselves with others and thus is the ultimate antidote to separation and loneliness. Our pain comes from our sense of isolation, but our experiences of suffering and joy bind us all together. When we share, although we are not trying to gain anything, we wind up widening the field of experience. To give, we pull our hand back from our eyes, where it restricted our vision: Then we can look into another's eyes, and see our own.

> Those who long to leave the world and practice buddha-dharma must study Zen
>
> The dharma turns you, and you turn the dharma. When you turn the dharma, you are leading and the dharma is following. When the dharma turns you, the dharma is leading and you are following. These two aspects are always present.

Psychotherapy and Zen take the personal world in which we all feel confined—the preoccupation with *my* thoughts, *my* feelings, *my* desires—and unlock our prison doors through mutual giving, taking, and sharing. The client re-treats from her life in the world to focus on herself in psychotherapy but can only focus on herself by sharing her life with the therapist. As therapists we share our lives by giving our full attention to each client, devoting our life to the client for the minutes we are together. As meditators we share our lives with the sincerity of the person sitting next to us and the annoyance of their noisy breathing, with the light filtering through the window and the buzzsaw cutting lumber next door. When we practice, we are always practicing together with everyone and every-thing else.

A lot of people initially come to Zen and to psychotherapy, however, to get away from other people and the demands of the world. We become dissatisfied with our lives, and long to leave the world in which we live. So we go off to look for satisfaction someplace else, only to find we bring our unhappiness with us.

At one point I felt my life was getting stale. I'd been working as a therapist for a number of years, and the initial excitement had worn off as I saw client after client. I'd been a father for some years, and the initial wonder of having children had settled into the monotony of reading the same bedtime story time after time. Marriage had settled into an unexciting familiarity as, thinking we knew each other, we began to take each other for granted. In my Zen practice I'd gotten stuck on a koan for a long time; instead of energizing or frustrating me, being stuck had become simply boring. I found myself meditating less and less and eventually stopping altogether.

I felt a nagging, chronic sense of dissatisfaction. I thought I needed some ex-citement in my life, so I applied for and received a Fulbright fellowship to teach psychotherapy in India.

My family and I went to India and it was fabulous, in the horrible sort of way that only India can encompass: filled with dirt, disease, discomfort, color, life, and won-derful people. Each day I would take a motorized rickshaw to the National Institute of Mental Health and Neurosciences in Bangalore, where my duties were light. I had the opportunity to sit in on fascinating clinical cases and visit with warm and intelligent Indian colleagues, and I had plenty of time left over to spend with my wife and two children in novel surroundings that helped us see each other in new ways. Life was ideal.

Yet I still did not feel satisfied. Surrounded by stimulating, even exotic, surround-ings, immersed in the love of my family, some part of me still was not happy. I had brought my staleness with me to India, and no external wonders were sufficient to freshen it.

I began to realize I was looking for happiness outside myself: I'd thought having a happy family, a good job, an exciting journey would solve the riddle of my life, especially if I added the spice of solving a koan and obtaining enlightenment. In my search for satisfaction, I was grasping at the things around me. It wasn't working.

I was stumped and didn't know what else to do. So I began sitting zazen again. I had been stymied by my koan, I was far from Zen books or training centers, and didn't have any guidance what to do, so I wasn't able to "correct" my zazen and try to "do it right." I could no longer use my meditation to search for something special, because I didn't know what to search for or how to search. I could not escape the reality of my life by distracting myself with some romantic Zen Quest.

Not knowing what to do, I began sitting shikan-taza: no goal, no technique, just sitting, being open to whatever came, letting myself become aware of what I was bringing to the bare experience of just sitting and what the bare experience of just sitting brought to me. I was surprised at how hard I found it to just sit and accept my life moment-by-moment, and how many expectations, hopes, and fears I brought even to the simple act of sitting quietly breathing in, breathing out.

Although I'd been practicing for some years, this was really when my practice began.

In the hectic life of juggling clients, insurance companies, and our family life, going off to a distant country or a remote monastery to escape can sound quite appealing. In the pain of unhappy relationships, job stress, illness, and the misery of anxiety and depression, going off to a psychotherapy to escape can sound quite appealing. But when we sit zazen, we find we bring our misery with us: If we're high-strung, we bring our striving to our zazen; if we're lazy, we bring our sloth to our zazen. When we come to a psychotherapy session, we think we'll leave our relationship problems behind, only to discover that we repeat them in our relationship in the therapy, whether we are clients or therapists.

The fact is, there's no escaping ourselves. There's no escaping our lives. Realizing this is the first step in practice. Going off to a monastery and sitting on a meditation cushion or going off to a psychotherapy session and sitting in a chair can provide a respite, an opportunity to step back from our lives and look within. But monasteries and psychotherapy clinics are not paradises we can escape to: They have their share of greed, hate, and delusion: sexual misconduct, embezzlement, and jealousy are all well known to both spiritual centers and consulting offices.

All the therapists in our clinic were sitting in a staff meeting. People began to get upset about an administrative issue, and one of the staff began making disparaging remarks about another member of the team. The other person argued back, and the conflict escalated: Suddenly one of them sprang up, fists clenched, and challenged the other to a fight. The other started to lunge back. Both had to be physically restrained from hitting each other.

Each of these therapists led a group in anger management.

When the Fifth Patriarch of Zen sought to find a disciple to transmit the authority of his teaching, he held a competition.[26] Whoever wrote the best poem would receive his robe and bowl (symbols of the transmission of the teaching) and become the next teacher, his dharma-heir.

The head monk wrote a good poem that was pasted on the wall of the monastery, but an obscure unlearned kitchen helper wrote an anonymous poem that showed even deeper understanding and placed it on the wall next to the head monk's poem. The teacher guessed who had written the poem; in the dead of night he snuck off to the kitchen helper (Hui-neng), gave him the bowl and robe, and told him:

"You're my true dharma-heir. I transmit the light to you. But there are many people here who will be jealous that I give this to you, an obscure unlearned monk. They'll want to kill you.

"You better run like hell."

Hui-neng fled, but he couldn't run fast enough. Another monk, a former warrior, pursued him with sword drawn, ready to kill. Hui-neng saw him and tried to hide, cowering behind a rock, but the other monk found him out.

No matter how far and fast we run, the world comes with us. So when Dogen says "Those who long to leave the world and practice buddha-dharma should study Zen," though he may seem to be saying "drop out, leave your life, enter a monastery" (and Dogen certainly believed in and encouraged monastic practice), his words can also have another meaning. Dogen is also telling us we can't study Zen by leaving the world. He is saying if we believe that we can leave the world to practice Buddha-dharma, we are sadly mistaken: If we go practice Zen, we will discover that we can only practice buddha-dharma right where we are, in the midst of our messy lives.

Clients often come to psychotherapy seeking to escape from their lives, or at least to escape from their problems. It doesn't work. Clients can't get better in the consulting room; they have to get better in their everyday lives. Our job is not to help clients escape, but to help clients find themselves. Leaving home to go to psychotherapy ultimately is about coming home to one's self.

A man came to me when his girlfriend of three years had broken up with him. He found that whenever he was at home by himself he obsessively telephoned his friends to have their voices drown out the surrounding silence. He also couldn't resist repeatedly calling his girlfriend on the telephone. He said he was coming to psychotherapy because he wanted to learn how to feel comfortable being alone.

He was amenable to learning some relaxation and meditation techniques he could do to calm himself down and seemed to derive some benefit as we practiced them in the session. However, at the end of the session, when it came time to set up another appointment, he became very anxious. He said he didn't want to have too long a gap between appointments: He wanted to be seen frequently, and to be able to call me if necessary in between appointments.

I usually encourage clients to call me between appointments if something comes up. In this case, however, it seemed counterproductive.

"I'm sure that it will be difficult at times when you're alone in your empty house." I said to him. "You'll feel uncomfortable. But does it make sense for you to call me or a friend at such times? How can you learn to feel comfortable being alone," I asked him, "unless you spend time by yourself and stay with the uncomfortable lonely feelings which come up?"

Coming home to one's self is, ultimately, discovering that our house houses the whole of our experiences, including unpleasant ones. If we flee our unpleasant experiences, we feel herded in a particular direction: The unpleasantness we avoid determines the direction of our life. When we sit down to do zazen or come to psychotherapy, even as one part of us is trying to escape, another part of us has decided to stop running and face our lives. This is a potential turning point in our life. If we stop running from ourselves and instead allow ourselves to dwell mindfully with whatever experience comes up, we see how an experience turns our thoughts, feelings, and sensations this way and that. We see our reactions to our experience as intertwined with, but separate from, the experience itself. Then we gain some flexibility in our reactions.

When our experience turns us, if we turn *to* it rather than away from it, we turn even as we are being turned. When clients with panic attacks can tune in to their experiences, they may discover that in the midst of their fears of death and rapid heartbeats they can also pay attention to the sensations in the soles of their feet; then they discover that both feet are still planted firmly on the ground. Turned and tumbled by the panic attacks, when they turn their bare attention to the experience and drop their preconceptions and ideas about the experience, they discover that their thoughts about their symptoms ("it's a heart attack") are just thoughts, their fears about what the symptoms mean ("I'm going to die") are just fears. Turning towards their experience and allowing themselves to go deeper, clients begin to realize they include their fears, thoughts, and sensations but are also larger than them. They discover that their fears, thoughts, and sensations arise in their body and mind and pass away in their body and mind: that after the turmoil, body and mind naturally gravitate and settle down to a more balanced state.

To paraphrase the old Shaker hymn, when we find the gift to be simple, to meet our bare experience as it comes regardless of our likes or dislikes, we discover the gift of being free. We are free to turn this way or that, so that "turning, turning, we come out right."

> *You should find a true teacher to practice Zen and learn the way*

> *A true teacher has to be free from egocentric views and not fettered by emotional feelings; his practice corresponds to his understanding.*

In zazen and in psychotherapy, we turn to ourselves. When we turn to ourselves, however, we find that we are constantly being turned by all around us. In the midst of this swirl of motion, it is natural to turn to others: to seek a guide, a therapist or Zen master who we hope can point out the way.

When we seek a teacher, we let go of our view that we know it all or know enough to manage solely on our own. Seeking outside ourselves for a teacher, we have some presentiment that what we can know about ourselves is intertwined with what we can know about others. As we listen and take in the perspectives of others, letting our own and others' perspectives interact, we expand a bit and realize our interbeing; when we seek a teacher this way, we are letting go of self-centered views and becoming a teacher ourselves.

In contrast, when we seek teachers with the idea that they know it all, or we idealize their wisdom as superior to our own, we run the danger of just swallowing another's self-views and pasting them onto our own. Then there is no teacher and no learning, only the passing of dogma from one person to another.

Clients often ask therapists to be experts, to tell them what to do. Yesterday, one client asked me whether she should stay in her relationship with her boyfriend; another client asked me whether I thought he was getting better. As therapists, we sometimes shake our heads at how "dependent" our clients become. But we do the same thing: We go to a conference and hope the "master therapist" will tell us how to treat that difficult couple we saw yesterday; we ask our supervisor whether we are doing a good job. As Zen students, we often ask our teacher to approve our understanding. All these questions can reflect a sincere desire to learn and be part of the process of discovery: They become problematical, however, if we are seeking to imbibe some authoritative dictum which will assuage our insecurities. If we seek a teacher, we must be careful not to alienate ourselves from our natural talents; the purity of intention that underlies our seeking can get lost if we locate teachers only outside ourselves. We will wind up not trusting ourselves if we don't recognize the teacher that lies at the heart of our, and our clients', seeking.

Most often, we cling to experts and preformulated answers as a way of escaping from suffering. The client clings to the therapist as an expert in the hope of being given a powerful solution that will alleviate his or her ills. As therapists, we cling to our expert role to insulate ourselves from our clients' suffering. Sometimes there is so much pain in our clients' lives that we seek to step back from it and hold it at arm's length by thinking of a diagnosis or formulating a treatment plan. If we can fall back to a position of superior knowledge, we can stand "above" the client and be more protected from their pain than if we stand side by side and share their discomfort.

A friend of mine (who is not Buddhist but has some familiarity with its teachings) had just seen a harrowing case, a fifty-five-year-old woman in a wheelchair with so many physical ills my friend felt he needed a wheelbarrow just to carry this unfortunate woman's medical chart.

She was immersed in her misery. She had a disease similar to that of "the Elephant Man," and her weight fluctuated wildly between 350 and 95 pounds. Once in the office, she started disrobing to show my friend the ungainly flabs of skin that hung loosely all over her body. She was in constant pain in her joints, despite all the medical treatment she had received.

On top of this, she was depressed. Several family members had died recently. A son had AIDS; a daughter was addicted to drugs and stealing from the patient. Her husband was diagnosed with terminal cancer. She also experienced dissociative states in which she relived the traumas of being ritualistically abused as a child, and she went through one of these during the interview.

My friend had been upset by this litany of horror, combined with the impossible pressure of having only a few sessions of brief therapy that he could offer the client. When he ran into me in the mailroom of our clinic immediately after the session, he was still shaken. He told me how difficult the session had been: "It was just so awful, so horrible, I tried to calm down by saying to myself over and over: 'I am the Buddha. I am the Buddha.'" He laughed uncomfortably.

I felt sad at this client's plight and my friend's discomfort and moved by how he had been moved. But I also felt somewhat uncomfortable about his response. I empathized with how hard it must have been to be with that client. I said to him it's true, he is the Buddha. But our challenge is to look at her and say: "*She* is the Buddha. She is the Buddha."

It is a basic tenet of Buddhism that all beings possess the heart of enlightenment. Every being—every client, colleague, friend, family member and acquaintance—can be our teacher and help us realize our enlightenment together. I am not enlightened if I say, "I am enlightened and you are not." I am also not enlightened if I say, "You are enlightened and I am not." When Gautama had his great realization and became Shakyamuni Buddha, he did not say: "I'm enlightened!" Instead, after a long night he saw the morning star and said:

I was, am, and will be enlightened, together with the whole of the great earth and all its sentient beings, simultaneously.[27]

The heart of enlightenment involves interbeing, being together with the whole of the great earth and all its creatures. In contrast, the heart of suffering involves being apart, imprisoned in self-views and the pain of disconnectedness. Clients increase their sense of disconnectedness if they place healing outside themselves. As Zen students, we increase our sense of disconnectedness if we think we lack something that our teachers can provide. As therapists, we increase our sense of disconnectedness if we use a diagnosis to place a client over there in one part of the room and ourselves over here in a different, more comfortable place.

True teachers help repair the sense of disconnectedness by constantly alerting students to the teachers all around and within them. Pain and discomfort are teachers, as are peace and joy. Dogs and cats, roses and weeds are teachers. Divorce and marriage, birth and death are teachers. Clients and therapists are teachers of themselves and each other.

Who is the teacher in psychotherapy? To single one person out is to get confused. If we say the client is the teacher we abrogate our role as experts with something to teach. If we say the therapist is the teacher we can fall into arrogance and stop listening to our clients. Clients come to psychotherapy to learn something from the psychotherapist, but this learning is facilitated if the therapist is also learning from the client. Each client has special knowledge gleaned from his or her unique experience of the world. This doesn't mean that a therapist needs to deny her or his expertise; it simply means that the therapist needn't treat her- or himself as the only expert in the room. Both therapists and clients practice acccording to their own understanding.

As therapists we have professional experience and skills that we need to acknowledge; it doesn't work if we pretend that client and therapist are both in the same spot. Every school of therapy and every therapist has particular views that can be helpful to a client so long as we are not overly attached to those views. We cannot be teachers if we don't have some way of viewing things that can prove helpful to a client; the trick is to acknowledge our expert views and our position as teachers without treating our views or position as anything special.

> Recently, at Berkeley Zen Center, we had sho-san ceremony. This is a formal question-and-answer in which the teacher sits up front of the assembly in a chair, the students sit on the floor and one at a time come up, bow to the teacher, and ask a question in front of the whole community.
> One student asked our teacher, "If there's nothing special about enlightenment and we're all Buddhas, why did you take on the role of teacher?"
> The teacher replied, "Because my teacher asked me to."
> The student asked, "Who teaches the Dharma?"
> The teacher replied: "Everything is always teaching the Dharma. Trees, rocks, and rain; bodies and mind; everyone and everything is always teaching the Dharma."
> The student asked "If we're all and everything is teaching the Dharma, why are you sitting up there in that special chair?"
> The teacher replied, "I'm a special-chair teacher," and laughed.

It is not a chair that holds the teaching, but how we sit in it and laugh. When I do psychotherapy, I have one chair that I sit in, and my clients have their choice of several others. I am, like most of us, a "special-chair" psychotherapist. There's not much more than that separating myself from my clients. Of course, I have some years of experience that are different from my clients' experience: This is why they can learn from me. But there's no need to get puffed up about this. My clients also have years of experience that are different from my experience; this is why I can learn from them. All psychotherapies have ways of learning from clients, whether it be the psychoanalyst examining his projective identifications and countertransference, the cognitive therapist interested in the outcome of an experiment in alternative thinking, or the narrative therapist curious about the client's next reply to a question about the experience of an experience.

All psychotherapies also have ways of teaching clients. It's important to offer the professional skills we have, but we need to guard against our tendencies to get attached to our expertise and think we know what's best for a client. If we make a psychodynamic interpretation, we may run the risk of thinking we've got the right view of what's "really" going on. Then the interpretation may be perceived as an invasion rather than an invitation to an intimate relationship. If we devise a homework assignment we may run the risk of getting attached to having it turn out the way it's "supposed to." Then we may lose the information that can be derived from how it actually turned out. If we pose a "paradox" to a client we may run the risk of using it to try to get him or her to act the way we want. Then we may not enjoy the intertwining, recursive relationship that provides the basis for a therapeutic interaction.

If we don't get caught in one-way relationships and can learn by teaching and teach by learning, the question becomes not so much who is the teacher in psychotherapy, but rather "How do we teach each other?"

Sarah was going through a divorce. She was intelligent, psychologically minded, creative, and insightful. However, she felt guilty about leaving her husband after many years, even though she had previously made numerous requests to him to deal with his alcohol problem and emotional withdrawal.

Sarah intellectually knew her guilt was not particularly rational, but whenever her husband bemoaned her leaving and told her she had ruined his life, she became convinced she was responsible for him and felt guilty. Initially we attempted to work with this guilt as an old habit, an automatic way of thinking that would respond to cognitive or strategic interventions.

But I felt a lot of sadness in the room. Sarah acknowledged and expressed this feeling as soon as I mentioned it. I found myself thinking of her father, who had been physically abusive; she talked of how she mostly felt scared of him but acknowledged that a part of her saw him as pathetic and may have wanted to cure him. Then she paused and said thoughtfully: "You know, when he died, I never felt anything. I always felt guilty that I didn't feel more when he died." Sarah had wanted to love him more. She felt guilty she didn't love him more.

Guilt is not a stranger to me. When Sarah said this, I had a flash of insight into my own family dynamics: Sometimes I would feel guilt as a *substitute* for love, a way of "paying back" the person I felt I hadn't been loving enough to. We began discussing guilt as a substitute for love. I had never thought about it that way before, nor had she, but it made sense to both of us. We became fascinated by the ideas and feelings which emerged as we explored this.

I suggested that the next time Sarah felt guilty when her husband complained to her, perhaps she could take some of that energy and use it to express some love to someone else. She quickly agreed she could think of people in her life who needed some extra love and ways she could express that love... but then she paused. She said at first she felt excited by the idea, but then she started to feel guilty about feeling good about herself giving to someone else. Maybe this meant she just wasn't capable of loving fully; maybe this meant she was not capable of intimacy.

At that very moment, however, I felt Sarah and I were very "connected" to each other. I asked her whether she felt there was an intimacy now, between us. Sarah agreed yes, she felt this sense of intimacy. I told her I felt the same thing and pointed out it was rather clear: She is capable of intimacy. It was happening right now.

This stimulated more curiosity and more dialogue. We explored how intimacy in the therapist's office is different from intimacy in everyday life. It's harder day-by-day in a relationship, in which you get bogged down in the details of who's washing the dishes and taking out the garbage. But the fact that you get lost sometimes doesn't mean you're incapable of intimacy. It just means that intimacy involves a lot of mundane work. To think that intimacy is something apart from the daily struggles of life is like thinking that just by talking to the vegetables in your garden they'll grow, without your getting down in the mud and doing some weeding. Intimacy involves some mucking about with compost.

We continued to explore the feelings of guilt as a substitute for love, guilt at not giving, guilt even when you are giving. I found myself thinking of a homely example. It was Christmas time and Salvation Army volunteers were out ringing their bells, asking for donations. I noted that most people closed themselves off and just walked by; some people would become defensive at the implicit demand and get annoyed. Others would walk by, feel guilty, then go back and put money in the pot. Sarah agreed that was what usually happened. But then we both became intrigued by the idea: Why not just *enjoy* donating the money?

We discussed how much we both enjoyed ourselves when we did volunteer work. Sarah talked about the homely pleasures of sharing time with others doing concrete, helpful activities. Then Sarah looked at me and said:

"So intimacy doesn't have to be something deep? It can be as simple as that? I don't have to feel all vulnerable and hurt to be intimate?"

I replied, "It seems that way, doesn't it? Maybe intimacy is just enjoying being with each other and sharing some of our lives together."

That's what we were doing. We were just enjoying each other's company. In the process, my pleasure at learning and teaching her helped call forth her pleasure at learning and teaching me. We thanked each other for the mutual lesson.

Who was leading who here? In psychotherapy, sometimes the therapist is leading and the client is following; sometimes the client is leading and the therapist is following. Sometimes the therapist makes a mistake, and the client corrects the therapist; sometimes in correcting the therapist's mistake, the client corrects herself. When we practice psychotherapy *with* each other rather than "on" each other, we immerse ourselves in the process of psychotherapy rather than in any one particular technique. Then we ride the flow of the therapy.

The process of psychotherapy is like a stream that carries us along, sometimes buoying us up, sometimes carrying us away; we learn how to sometimes swim in a particular direction and sometimes to just float. We are swimming in a very deep river with wild currents, so sometimes we catch each other swimming together, sometimes we catch ourselves swimming apart. Dogen's "Mountains and Waters Sutra"[28] says:

> From ancient times wise people and sages have often lived near water. When they live near water they catch fish, catch human beings, and catch the way. For long these have been genuine activities in water. Furthermore there is catching the self, catching catching, being caught by catching, and being caught by the way.
>
> Priest Decheng abruptly left Mt. Yao and lived on the river. There he produced a successor, the wise sage of the Huating. Is this not catching a fish, catching a person, catching water, or catching the self? The disciple seeing Decheng is Decheng. Decheng guiding his disciple is his disciple.

To paraphrase the Mountains and Waters Sutra: "The client seeing a therapist is the therapist. The therapist guiding a client is the client. Is this not catching a fish, catching a person, catching water, or catching the self?"

The activities of Zen monks

Please try releasing your hold. Open your hands. Just let everything go, and see: What is body and mind? What are daily activities?... Ultimately, what are mountains and rivers, the great earth, human beings, animals, and houses? Take a careful look at these things again and again: it is clear the dichotomy of movement and stillness does not arise at all. However, at this time, nothing is fixed.

In psychotherapy and in our other most intimate relationships we catch each other and catch ourselves. This is wonderful but incurs its own problem: once we catch someone or something we tend to hold on tight. If we hold on too tight, however, we lose what we hold on to. If we try to catch a fish and don't release the reel, the too-taut line will snap. If we try to catch a bird and hold too tight, we crush its fragile feathers and it can't fly. If we want life to flow fully, we need to find a way of catching our experience even while letting it go.

In psychotherapy we encourage our clients to let go of their usual habits, their usual ways of thinking and acting, their usual ways of "being themselves" and observe with a fresh mind, asking in effect: What is this? Who am I? Who are you? As clients, therapists, and Zen students we try to let go in order to give ourselves and the people we encounter the freedom to be who we and they are. This often is not easy.

I find it interesting that Dogen doesn not say, "Please release your hold." He says, "Please *try* releasing your hold and see what happens." We learn to let go little by little. Anyone who has sat zazen knows that when we sit, as soon as we try to let go we come face to face with all our constrictions, all our fears and attachments. The same thing happens in psychotherapy; when we start to let go, we discover where we are hooked and learn something about ourselves. This is true for therapists as well as clients.

I was seeing a client who was dying of cancer.[29] She had worked hard on coming to peace with her condition and cultivated a spiritual awareness that helped her to enjoy each moment of life that remained to her. She had mentioned that she had conflicts with her grown daughter who had severe, long-term drug and alcohol problems. My client had adopted her daughter when she was around eight years old, not knowing how severely she had been abused in her prior family. Perhaps in part because of this, the mother-daughter relationship had always been a stormy one. The daughter was demanding and entitled; she rarely showed consideration for her mother, and was generally a drain. She had repeatedly stolen from and lied to my client. After many years of struggling wholeheartedly to achieve a more intimate relationship, my client had achieved an uneasy truce with her daughter by setting rather rigid boundaries. They saw each other seldom and kept a distant politeness.

One session, my client told me she was nearing her end: It would be but a few months before she died. She said she felt she was achieving serenity as death approached; as an aside, she mentioned that she had decided she would not speak to her daughter again, even if the daughter called her.

This tugged at something in me. It seemed discrepant with her overall acceptance and spiritual openness; it didn't gibe with what I thought was "spiritually correct." There are traps of "spiritual correctness" as well as traps of "therapeutic correctness" and "political correctness."

I inquired about her decision not to talk to her daughter again, suggesting it might be a pity to end a lifelong difficult relationship unharmoniously. My client became angry and told me I had no right to question her about this; she was at peace. I told her I accepted her decision but commented on her agitation and said I was just trying to find out if there was some more work she wanted to do on this issue. She told me, in considerable distress, that she felt my questions implied she was not good enough or reconciled enough. I backed away from the issue with her daughter but then tried to get her to look at her reactions to me. The client told me her reactions were not the question: that I ought to look at whether I had my own agenda here that I was imposing on her.

After the session ended, I realized I had been harboring high hopes for this client, whom I admired sincerely. I had an image that she could attain enough serenity that she could end her life on a loving note with her daughter, no matter how badly her daughter behaved. I realized I had once again been caught by my perfectionistic tendency to push for what "should" ideally happen, rather than accept the human limits of our actual life situations.

So at the start of the next session, I told my client I had thought of what she'd said, examined myself, and realized I had been pushing her. I apologized, and said I could understand how she would have felt unaccepted and unsupported. I could see how this was, indeed, my own and not my client's agenda.

Or was it? My client replied she had been thinking, too. She felt she did have work she needed to do regarding her feelings about her daughter. This work, which she proceeded to do in the session, was something different than either of us anticipated. It involved acknowledging her sadness at the lack of connection with her daughter, her pain at seeing her daughter's suffering, and her grief at her inability to ever have mothered a biological child. This in turn connected naturally with her grief about how her own mother had never wanted her or loved her.

With this mourning process, my client said she felt she was learning something about letting go of these old hurts as she approached her death. I also was learning something about letting go, about how I needed to let go of my own perfectionistic ideas in order to accept my client and trust her own path to wholeness.

It's not so easy to let go. We hold on to our ideas of what should happen. We also hold onto our old hurts. Perhaps we do this as a kind of protest against how life tosses us about, a defiance of the lack of control we have over our lives.

A client came to me several years after I had seen her for a few sessions of hypnosis that had cured her until recently of trichitillomania. She was tearing her hair out again now, but that wasn't what brought her to therapy: She said she realized she was pulling her hair because she was mad all the time. She wanted to stop feeling constantly angry.

For several years she had nursed her father through his terminal illness. When he died, she mourned him and it was some time before she let herself get involved in a relationship. Eventually, however, she developed a good friendship with a man; they had similar interests and spent most weekends together. Gradually the relationship became more intimate and seemed to be developing into a long-term commitment. Then he suddenly, without warning, went and married a mail-order bride. Shortly after that, her brother died unexpectedly.

She said, "I know why I'm angry. It's because I feel life's out of my control. Why should I stop being angry when life treats me this way? Whenever something good starts to happen to me, something always goes wrong. Awful things keep happening. It happened with my friends, it happened with my father and brother, it happened with the man I'd been seeing. I *know* the rest of my life will be this way. I won't accept that I can't control what happens. I know thinking this way makes me depressed, but I'm not going to stop thinking this way: It would only open me to disappointment again, and I'm not willing for that to happen."

It's hard to come to terms with our lack of control over the events that come to us. We get mad that we cannot control our lives beyond a very small margin, that life isn't going the way we want it to. So in reaction we hold on tight to the small areas we can control. There are many ways of holding on. We may hold on to an emotion, to a way of thinking, or to our hair, like the client above. We may also try to get control of our lives by trying to control others.

We see this most readily in couples' therapy, in which the poisonous game of controlling oneself through controlling the person nearest to you takes on variegated forms. I feel overwhelmed and unable to keep up with the demands on me, so I yell at my wife for not completing one of her tasks. It happens all the time, yet we often have troubles seeing ourselves do it when we are enmeshed in the process. Sometimes the inability to stop trying to control the other person leads to separation or divorce. Then it is often the client who has been most rigidly controlling of his spouse who turns into a quivering mass of jelly when his spouse leaves; without her as a convenient host for his projections, he cannot calm himself and often becomes obsessed and haunted, unable to let go even though holding on is no longer a realistic option.

The client-therapist pair is another kind of couple, and therapists also have their projections and difficulties getting control of their own feelings and reactions. For many of us, it was in part our very helplessness over ourselves that led us into therapy and eventually into becoming therapists. Not being able to fully control our own lives, how much less can we control our clients': Yet in some ways we hang on to the illusion that we can control others even if we can't control ourselves. In order to feel on top of things, we look for techniques of influencing clients, we craft interventions,and formulate our therapeutic plans. As therapists it's our job to engage in a relationship in which we influence our clients in helpful ways, but if we make this influence unilateral—if we are unwilling to be influenced in turn by our clients—we may become attached to the illusion that as therapists we're in control of the therapy and become angry if that is challenged.

> When I was a freshman in college, there was a period in which I became depressed. I saw a psychiatrist who, after a few sessions, told me he thought I should take a leave of absence for a semester. I disagreed, because I was feeling much better, but the psychiatrist told me that it wasn't my decision to make: Whether I wanted it or not, he would recommend the school put me on leave for a semester.
>
> I tried to argue with him but he told me his decision was final. I felt shocked, dismayed, betrayed. I told him I would appeal his decision. He told me there was nobody to appeal to: The school would abide by his decision. I felt he was becoming antagonistic and started to get up, saying I thought I'd better leave.
>
> He sprang up from his chair, swiftly walked over to me and prevented me from standing up. "You can't leave yet!" He snapped. "I'm not finished with you!"

Although this is a rather dramatic example of a therapist trying to hold on to his position of being "on top of" the therapy, there are many instances in which therapists may have troubles letting go. Therapists sometimes try to hang on to a client when the client feels she's ready to stop therapy; in the not so distant past, a client's desire to terminate therapy was routinely interpreted as a form of resistance. This kind of refusal to release our hold can undermine the client's autonomy and confidence in himself. In extreme form, holding onto control of the therapy can take the form of undue influence, abuse of the therapist's position of authority, and even sexual seduction. More subtly, any time we repeat an intervention even after the client has rejected it, we are holding onto "our way" even at the expense of being unresponsive to the client. If we cling to our therapeutic plan as if it were a life raft, however, we won't be able to release our hold and swim in the currents that the client is presenting.

The problem with holding on tight is that it undermines our ability to trust in the natural flow of our lives. A lot of our clients, because of painful past experiences, have difficulties trusting that when everything is falling apart, someone or something will be there to catch them. So they hold onto ways of protecting themselves from hurt. We cannot rediscover trust, though, without letting go and allowing ourselves to experience whatever there is to be experienced.

When our clients are faced with emotional pain, if they are unable to trust themselves, their first impulse is to *do* something about the pain rather than just experience it and see where it leads to and what can be learned from it. Therapists face a similar problem in psychotherapy: If we are unable to trust the process of two people sitting down and meeting each other, we may feel we have to *do* something quickly about a client's problems to take the pain away.

> A psychiatrist colleague referred a sixty-eight-year-old man to me whom she had been medicating for depression because he was still having problems sleeping. The man had recently suffered a heart attack, his wife was dying of Alzheimer's disease, and he readily admitted to depression. His chief concern, however, was the lack of sleep.

When I inquired about his sleep habits, he told me when he woke up during the middle of the night he stayed in bed awake for several hours. Because I "knew" this could cause sleep problems, I suggested some behavioral sleep hygiene interventions. They helped a little, but not much. I suspected he might suffer from sleep apnea; a workup confirmed the diagnosis. I "knew" treating the sleep apnea would help, but a mechanical device (c-pap) aided him only a little. He clearly had a biological depression, which I "knew" caused sleep problems, so in consultation with the psychiatrist we tried varying his medications by adding a more sedating antidepressant. I also had done hypnosis for sleep problems with many clients, and "knew" it could help, so we did hypnosis. All of these interventions helped a bit, enough for him to get by, and I did not see him for a while.

Six months later he came back complaining he was sleeping worse than ever. He was drained and exhausted; both he and I felt we had to do something. But I had exhausted most of my interventions. There wasn't much I could do except just listen and empathize with his suffering.

So he talked about his life. He told me he continued to suffer terrible feelings of guilt for putting his wife in a nursing home a few years ago. He had nursed his wife at home for a long time and only put her in a nursing home when her Alzheimer's was quite advanced; she had ceased to recognize him, was verbally and physically abusive, and incontinent; physically he was no longer able to move her enough to bathe her, feed her, and prevent her from getting bed sores. But even though intellectually he recognized the wife he knew was no longer "there," he felt so guilty for abandoning her that he had been unable to get on with his life during the years that followed. He visited her almost every day, taking on the responsibility for her care without any help from her family, who lived in the area.

Recently, the nursing home had told him that his wife had stopped eating and that the end was approaching. He now spent all day every day at the nursing home, hand-feeding his wife bit by bit. She rallied a little at this, and he felt that if he didn't continue feeding her she would die and he would be responsible. At the same time he felt resentful about spending all his time nursing her without any help from anybody else. He was getting old and ill himself; his heart attack and back pain made him feel time was running out on his chances of making a new life for himself. He felt torn between wanting to let go of and wanting to hold on to his wife: He saw his only choices as abandoning her or being in constant attendance on her.

As he talked about the situation it became clear that neither fleeing from her (and his sense of responsibility for her life and death) nor trying to take on an impossible control for her living and dying was feasible. He acknowledged that the problem was how to let go and allow the process to take its course, but he didn't know how to do this.

Although I hadn't realized it, I had felt similarly in the therapy, torn between feeling responsible to help him overcome his symptoms and wanting to tell him I had done everything I could and had nothing left to offer. My task, like his, was to find a way to trust that if he and I let go and let the process take its course, some healing would occur. To do this, I had to be willing to sit with him through his suffering rather than cure him.

I suggested that he go visit his wife every day, because he felt he had to do this, but to stop feeding her, stop taking responsibility for keeping his wife alive. Instead, I suggested he spend the day there holding her hand lightly. Sometimes she might drop his hand and wander away; sometimes she might hold on tight. His job was just to attend her and allow her to hold on or let go of him as needed. I mentioned he would probably have a lot of feelings as he did this; he should notice them, but just continue stroking her hand when she let him, letting go of her hand and just sitting there when she pulled away.

This was a form of zazen, of "just sitting," just being there with his wife without doing anything in particular. It frightened him but he had the courage to see it through. He went to the nursing home and neither shouldered nor rejected responsibility; he just sat with his dying wife and in so doing he held his, and her, pain in his hands.

Doing this brought up many issues for him. Now it was my turn to "just sit" and be there with his pain. He had a history of horrible physical abuse as a child. When he was about six years old he had been attacked with a blowtorch and suffered terrible burns over most of his body. He almost didn't survive but eventually was sent home from the hospital and was bedridden for months. During this time of horrible suffering his bandages were changed daily, a terribly painful process; in the midst of his agony his mother would yell at him and threaten to beat him if he cried. He had reacted to this with the thought: "It's all my fault." He had dealt with this by devoting most of his adult life to taking care of others, including his wife, without complaining.

The course of the therapy shifted to examining his unresolved feelings about his mother, who had been unavailable and cruel to him in many other ways. He sought to find ways to forgive her or at least find some peace in his memories of her. It was a challenge for him to do this, but he had courage to sit not just with his dying wife but also with his grief, guilt, and anger. Soon he was able to let go of his wife enough so that he did not have to visit her every day. He was also more able to visit the memories of his mother without being trapped by guilt or anger.

He started sleeping well and waking up refreshed. He said he felt like he was no longer living in the past but was able to let go and start making a new life for himself.

My client and I each tried to take responsibility for something beyond our control; our sense of responsibility initially got in the way of our ability to accept the situation and meet it where it needed to be met. It's good to take responsibility, but we have to acknowledge that this is sometimes a screen for trying to control a situation for our own ends. When we try to mold a situation to the way we think it "ought" to be without accepting the situation as it is, we usually have some agenda of our own, however benign it may be. To really take responsibility, we have to be willing to face what is actually happening regardless of our efforts, whether it be the death of our wife or the continued suffering of our client. We have to sometimes "lose our grip" of a situation in order to experience the situation itself.

Our fixed ideas about what things are can get in the way of discovering the things themselves. Zen practice encourages us to look at things without preconceptions, to let go of our mind's hold on things and experience them as they are. "Ultimately, what are mountains and rivers, the great earth, human beings, animals, and houses?" What, in the end, are the mountains of our defenses, the rivers of our suffering, the earthiness of our joys? What, in the end, are we as therapists, clients, and human beings?

When we release our hold and let go of our old views, we are more able to experience things as they are. This is the only way to discover that if we release our hold on our protective defenses and experience our hurts, even though there's hurt, it can still be all right; we can make our peace with the totality of our lives. Then we discover the things and beings of the world are not something fixed, something we can capture in a name, a diagnosis, a picture or an idea. We cannot grasp life to control it because life is always moving. We cannot make life stand still by our attempts to command it: The only place we can encounter life is as it is moving this moment, right now, right here.

> You should practice everywhere toward the way, immediately hitting the mark.

> The Buddha-Way is right under your feet. Immersed in the way, clarify it right on the spot. Soaked through by enlightenment, you completely become yourself.

> To be immersed in the way means to forget any traces of enlightenment... let body and mind drop off; throw away delusion and enlightenment.

> To realize buddha directly through nothing other than your body and mind is to accept the Way and hit the mark immediately. Not trying to change your body or mind, just following the realization of the true teacher completely, is called being here or settling down.

> To follow buddha completely means you do not have your old views. Since you just settle down right here, you do not seek a new nest in which to settle.

Catching ourselves letting go, every moment of a therapy can point to *releasement*, in which we and our clients can more fully actualize our true selves. Psychotherapy is about helping people let go of fixed ideas they have about themselves that get in the way of their current experience. Once we let go of the *ideas* we carry about what our "self" is and the *ideas* we carry about what an "experience" is, we simply become our experience. We can only do this "right on the spot" in the immediacy of each moment.

What is this spot, this moment where client and therapist meet each other and themselves? We have very naive views of time and place. In our search for stability and control over our lives, we try to hold onto a frozen self-image that is timeless and placeless; we then view time and space as something outside us and separate from our selves. We see our selves as traveling "through" time and space but not being "of" time and space. One form this takes is to think to ourselves, "It takes time for a person to change."

If we think of time as some thing that exists "out there" that is measured by clocks, then "it takes time for a person to change." If we think of place as some thing that exists "out there," then I have to get from one place to another. If we think of change not as a constant flow, but as some thing which has a beginning point and end point, then "it takes time for a person to change."

If we think of time and place in the conventional way, we break them down into a linear "before and after," a "here and there." In linear time and space, we mistake ourselves for our memories of our desires. We think we keep telling ourselves who we are, but in fact are telling ourselves who we've been or where we hope to be. It is hard, when we are prisoners of our old views, to find room for anything startlingly different, discontinuous or qualitatively new.

If we are attached to our old linear views, each second the clock ticks we can feel like we are losing time; each place we are at can seem a long distance from our goal. In this view, time and space are outside of us: We pass through and displace them, we live "in" a time and "at" a place. Time elapses; things take time. I was this; I want to become that, later. As far as therapy is concerned, I come to therapy in one place and want to use therapy to get to another place; there is a gap between the therapy office and the rest of my life, there are a certain number of sessions I must have or I will not get well. The Zen student experiences this as a gap between life in the Zendo and life in the "real world," as a feeling that there is life "before" and "after" enlightenment. Time and place become amounts of things rather than living, breathing experiences.

Compare this to Dogen's description:

> Even though you do not measure the hours of the day as long or short, far or near, you still call it twelve hours. Because the signs of time's coming and going are obvious, people do not doubt it. Although they do not doubt it, they do not understand it....
>
> The way the self arrays itself is the form of the entire world. See each thing in this entire world as a moment of time. Things do not hinder one another, just as moments do not hinder one another. The... mind arises in this moment; a... moment arises in this mind.
>
> Thus the self setting itself out in array sees itself. This is the understanding that the self is time.
>
> Since there is nothing but just this moment, the time-being is all the time there is.... Each moment is all being, is the entire world. Reflect now whether any being or any world is left out of the present moment.[30]

Whether it be the first session of a crisis intervention or the six-hundredth session of a psychoanalysis, the first time we sit zazen or the thousandth, we always realize ourselves at this one place at this one point in time. Being our self does not "take" time, because it is not being *in* time: Rather, it is time being.

Psychotherapy does not occur *in spite of* time that is measured as short or long, space that is measured as large or small; psychotherapy *depends on* the space of time being. Therapy can only take place a session at a time; each session can only take place a moment at a time with client and therapist each sitting in their own spot. When we settle in to one spot and one moment, we don't measure the time or place but simply experience it. So in therapy, we need to pay attention to what the client and ourselves are *being* at this very moment right here.

We tend to ask our clients, "What have you been doing? What do you want to be doing?" but all the time we are implicitly asking, "What is our being, now?" We don't ask this explicitly, because the client probably would not know how to answer in words. But we ask it implicitly with our gaze, our listening, our every interaction with the client. In this way we join with our client, practicing mutually with each other, and we become the session's time being. We find ways of bringing all of our and the client's life into this place and moment: Role plays, transference, hypnosis are not so much techniques as *invitations* to be fully present. Our task is to bring our clients' lives into vivid relief in the moment of this session.

> The importance of making the client's experience present in the session was brought home to me some years ago when I was talking about a case to my friend and colleague, Eric Greenleaf. An extremely obsessional client of mine complained of inhibitions in completing projects and being successful. He felt paralyzed.
>
> In one session he described a memory of being ten years old, on a baseball diamond playing second base. His team was about to win the championship if they could only get the last out. The batter hit the ball to the shortstop, who was the team coach, whom my client described as a "father-figure." My client described how he could still see the coach cock his arm and prepare to throw the ball to the patient to win the game: He remembered becoming numb, paralyzed, and seeing the ball approach him in slow motion. He remained immobile; the ball hit him and bounced off his chest. His team lost.
>
> I had listened raptly and been touched by the story and how it embodied my client's present difficulties. Eric listened and remarked, "If I had been there I would have..." and then reached down, picked up a piece of paper, crumpled it into a ball, and threw it at me.
>
> So now I throw client's dropped balls back to them. If the client is talking about the difficulties of relaxing, I ask them to show me what they look like as they struggle to relax. If they are talking about regret for the past, I search for ways to express that regret concretely now, whether it means a letter of apology or a visit to a dead parent's grave. If a client is anticipating the future, I invite the client to stop waiting and to take a step into the future right now. When I throw a ball to my client, if the client catches it, she or he can have a healing experience. If the client drops it, the old awkwardness is summoned to a possible exorcism or healing. Either way brings matters to a head in the immediacy of the moment.
>
> Our clients are always throwing things at us. Sometimes we catch them, sometimes we drop the ball. We are always throwing things at the client, some of which they drop, some of which they catch. We play catch with each other: Each pitch is an entire lifetime, but the game has an infinite number of innings and never ends until called for rain, darkness, or death.

When we find ourselves in this moment completely, something opens up. The paradox is that to fully open up to the moment, we must let go of both ourselves and of the moment. So long as we are concerned about enlightenment and understanding we stand apart from our experience and can only see a part of the picture. When we forget about enlightenment and understanding and simply immerse ourselves in the situation at hand this moment, right here on this spot we experience some sense of wholeness.

When we bring our entire self to bear on each place each moment, what does this point consist of? How can we possibly hold it? The more we try to catch hold of time, the more it slips away. As we reach out to it, it is already gone. Yet even as we try to catch it and think it slips away, we are immediately embodying it.

Your existence here, in this space, reading, on this chair, is an expression of time being. Our clients' existences in their chair, at the moment of a session, are the time being. Or, another way of saying it: We *are* time. Change does not *take* time: Change *is* time and time *is* change. So long as we stop looking ahead or gazing behind us, time and self become both infinite and infinitesimal in the moment and we and all our clients experience complete freedom.

If the bottom-line question in therapy is, "Who am I?" ultimately, the answer has to be:

"Here I am."

If this leads us to ask, "What or where is 'here?'" we must answer:

"Now."

We *are* the expression of here-and-now. *We* are the expression of here-and-now. We are the *expression* of here-and-now. We are the expression of *here-and-now*.

We cannot make here-and-now into a nest, settle in, and build a permanent residence. This is closing rather than opening. If we hold on to our thoughts and feelings about who we are and what this is, we form little nests to settle in. In these small sanctuaries, we may feel complete. In the nest of the Zendo we may feel enlightened; in the nest of the psychotherapy office we may feel we understand ourselves. But then we may run into troubles dealing with the daily events of our lives, when somehow we and the world fail to act according to our understanding of how things "should" be.

In contrast, if we let go of old views and avoid settling into stale nests, then when we sit down to do zazen each morning and greet a client each hour, we can experience it anew every time with wonder. Cultivating the moving enigma of our lives, when a client says to us, "This is who/how I am," we can compassionately respond: "Don't be so sure." Complete enlightenment and full understanding know they can never know anything fully or be complete by themselves: They know that because of the constant movement of interbeing, all we touch and are touched by must remain mysterious. Then whatever we experience, in therapy or outside of it, we can greet it with an open smile rather than a settled idea.

So good psychotherapy and zazen are unsettling. Psychotherapy and zazen remove the nests so that we may perch in the trees, forage on the ground, and fly freely through the skies.

Each place in our lives creates the time to be ourselves. Each moment of our lives creates the space that shelters us. We are continuously uprooted and replanted in the soil of our living and dying: The sky is our ceiling and the earth below us our foundation.

> As the World Honored One was walking with the congregation, he pointed to the ground with his finger and said, "This spot is good to build a sanctuary."
>
> Indra, Emperor of the gods, plucked a blade of grass, stuck it in the ground, and said, "The sanctuary is built."
>
> The World Honored One smiled.[31]

We don't need to go anyplace else but where we are; we don't need to look to anyone else but to ourselves. We and our clients are complete in our incompleteness: We need not search for something special. Because our lives are not caught between the future and the past but are a continuous current flowing, there is no need to wait for a particular "now." *This* is the time and place to realize our true selves. Each session of psychotherapy and every moment of zazen provides the opportunity to make each spot a sanctuary: We need only pluck and replant our impermanent existence as it is, where we are, and consecrate it with a smile.

Evolution

time time time time
The fourth is different from the first.
Evolution is the clock in which
Continue and Invent will dance
forever? Maybe not, because
the brand new glancing back
pursues directions limned by melodies:
Starfish cannot see the ocean roar,
Porpoises leap forward to a silent echo.

The Metta Sutta[1]

This is what should be accomplished by one who is wise
Who seeks the good and has obtained peace.

Let one be strenuous, upright and sincere, without pride,
Easily contented and joyous.
Let one not be submerged by the things of the world.
Let one not take upon oneself the burden of riches.
Let one's senses be controlled.
Let one be wise but not puffed up, and let one not desire great possessions, even for one's family.
Let one do nothing that is mean or that the wise would reprove.

May all beings be happy.
May they be joyous and live in safety.

All living beings, whether weak or strong, in high or middle or low realms of existence, small or great, visible or invisible, near or far, born or to be born, may all beings be happy.

Let no one deceive another, nor despise any being in any state; let none by anger or hatred wish harm to another.

Even as a mother at the risk of her life watches over and protects her only child, so with a boundless mind should one cherish all living things, suffusing love over the entire world, above, below, and all around, without limit; so let one cultivate an infinite good will toward the whole world.

Standing or walking, sitting or lying down, during all one's waking hours, let one cherish the thought that this way of living is the best in the world.

Abandoning vague discussions, having a clear vision, freed from sense appetites, one who is made perfect will never again know rebirth in the cycle of creation of suffering for ourselves or others.

Chapter 3

Happiness, Suffering, and Psychotherapy: The Metta Sutta

We would all like to consecrate our lives with a smile. In her college entrance essay, my daughter wrote:

> There is something very beautiful and simple about a smile... often I feel it says so much more than words. You can look at a person, smile at them, and already you have opened a window into your heart. Maybe that's what makes people smile back, because when you offer someone a smile you offer them yourself. You say, here, this is me and I am happy as I am and how do you do?
>
> I believe that one smile, from any person, anywhere, can change the way you're feeling, the day you're having, or even, your life. I can recall numerous times in *my* life when I was struggling beyond belief and someone smiled at me, I looked at their smile and thought, how can I learn to smile like that? How must I change in my life to be so full of smiles? And so I have changed, and now I offer my smiles to other people. I also continue to learn about smiles from other people, especially children.

We sense how wonderful it would be to make each spot of our lives a sanctuary, to smile gently and open the windows of the heart. In the rough and tumble of everyday life, though, it is sometimes hard to remember happiness. It is not always easy to smile at the person who cuts us off on the freeway, at the bureaucrat delaying us with extra paperwork; it is not always easy to be happy when a family member seems to be ignoring our needs, or when we come down with a virus that weakens us and makes it difficult to breathe. For psychotherapists, it is not always easy to smile when confronted by the sea of troubles clients bring to our consulting room.

Our efforts to protect ourselves from the pain of life sometimes can lead us away from not only pain, but also happiness. Therapists sometimes try to avoid drowning in the sea of clients' (and our own) suffering by retreating to a safe "clinical" distance; clients sometimes flee from pain into a frenzy of hectic, busy activity; Zen students sometimes retreat to the illusion of a safe haven in a monastery where suffering can be pared down to trying to manage the pain of in our knees, sore from long meditations. All of us struggle to cope, but too often our work—and our life—becomes a process of simply struggling to get by.

Getting by, however, is not very satisfying. If we close ourselves off to suffering, why did we become therapists? Our job requires an empathic immersion in suffering, together with a commitment to find some genuine release from suffering. But how can we remain open to our own and our clients' suffering without becoming subsumed by it? How can we approach our work and our lives in a way that will promote true happiness and peace? Can we, can our clients, feel happy in the midst of suffering? Or do we need to distance ourselves from suffering, capture it in some diagnosis or case formulation, in order to get a handle on it and remove it? Must we cure our ills before we can be happy? What, after all, is happiness?

Ignoring these issues is perilous. If we don't come up with some answers to the above questions, our actions threaten to become mere reactions to events that come up. If we are not clear about the basic intention that guides our work as therapists, we have no internal compass to serve as a beacon when we feel lost. It is surprising, however, how little time we spend examining these questions thoroughly. Our lives are busy: We feel that we don't have time to step back and take stock, that asking these questions is faintly embarrassing and smacks overmuch of adolescent earnestness.

Fortunately, though, life is difficult. We can count on life to illuminate our absent-mindedness and raise these questions again and again. Life brings us incidents that, if we face them without any guiding attitude, are sure to leave us feeling frustrated, dissatisfied, angry or generally unhappy. In these days of managed care, we are asked to see more clients in less time than seems possible. Perhaps a client fails to come in or comes in and makes difficult demands. Perhaps our car breaks down and requires more money for repairs than we have at our disposal. We go on a beach vacation and it rains. We get caught in a traffic jam on the way to an important meeting. Someone we love spurns us. Our family refuses to go along with what we want. Dinner is undercooked or overdone. We don't get a good night's sleep. Perhaps we catch a cold. Perhaps we pull a muscle. Perhaps we get cancer.

> I met with a husband and wife today who had spent the last nine years undergoing fertility treatments. About a year ago, they started to accept that they would never have a child. The wife had felt depressed about this, particularly because the doctors never

were able to determine a reason why the couple was infertile. Through a previous psychotherapy, she had largely resolved her grief.

Six months ago, at Christmas, the couple suddenly were given an opportunity to adopt a child who was yet to be born. This seemed almost a divine intervention to them; they were elated and eagerly awaited the birth of the baby. A month later the child was born with severe birth defects. The baby had an unusual physical condition that would require special care, and the doctors told my clients the child also had neurological impairments that would lead to difficulties that could range from mild learning disabilities to possible severe mental retardation. The couple, however, fell in love with the baby boy whom they described as "something special." They spent a great deal of time learning how to take care of the baby's special physical needs and brought him home from the hospital.

Four weeks later, the baby was in distress. The couple brought him to the hospital, where they were told the baby was dehydrated. There was some confusion in the hospital, and the baby never received an intravenous line. The baby's condition deteriorated and the baby had to be hospitalized but was not put on the pediatric intensive care unit (which would have been merited by his condition) but placed in a regular hospital room. His parents, my clients, were at first trusting of the doctors but became progressively more alarmed as they saw their son's condition deteriorate. They were by the baby's bed when he went into a seizure.

Because the baby was on a regular hospital ward rather than a pediatric unit, a nightmare ensued: When the couple frantically summoned a nurse, the nurse said she "didn't know how to deal with babies" and ran away. Someone brought a cart to try to provide respiration for the baby, but the equipment was meant for adults and wouldn't fit the baby. By the time a pediatric cart was provided, twenty minutes later, the baby had died in his parents' arms. They were holding their dead infant when a doctor came by with a form to sign to give their permission to cremate the baby; the doctor asked them what kind of urn they wanted.

This had happened only a month before. When I saw them they were filled with grief and rage. They couldn't understand how this could have happened. They were angry at themselves for not being more assertive with medical personnel at the outset of the hospitalization. They were furious with the doctors and nurses for not providing adequate care; when they tried to find out exactly what had happened medically, they felt the hospital administration stonewalled them. They were making inquiries about a possible malpractice suit, not for financial remuneration, but because they wanted answers to their unanswered questions about how this had occurred. They mourned the loss of their hopes and dreams. They tried talking to friends but felt hurt and rejected when friends, overwhelmed at the pain and loss, backed away or shut down.

Through all this, they supported each other. When one of them cried, the other found strength to be supportive. They took walks by the ocean, holding hands. They decided to adopt another child. But they often felt lost and confused.

I was profoundly moved by their story and impressed by the way they were dealing with the tragedy. It felt like we connected emotionally. Toward the end of the session, when it came time to talk about what they wanted from therapy, I told them that of course I'd be glad to meet with them, but I also wanted them to know that as far as I could see, they didn't have a psychiatric problem: They had a real-life tragedy, and everything they told me indicated that they were dealing with it with just the right mixture of grief and anger, love and despair.

They looked surprised for a moment. Then the wife said: "That's really reassuring to hear. We sometimes feel so lost." I replied that feeling lost was part of dealing with grief and a loss of this kind. The question was, when lost, how do you find your bearings? Lost in the woods at night, you might look up to the sky and find the north star to guide you. It seemed to me that the grief was still very fresh and at the moment they were doing well to just ride the waves of their reactions, but ultimately the issue would be: what would they rely on to find their way, and how would they determine in what direction they wanted to go?

They discussed this at some length. They felt they faced a real challenge, but they wanted to find a way to deal with this so their lives would not be poisoned by bitterness, anger, and disappointment, and instead find a way of restoring their faith in life and facing the future with hope.

We all need to find a way to deal with disappointment and hurt without being subsumed by bitterness. Paradoxically, in some ways it is easier to face the question, "How can I be happy?" when a tragedy clearly forces us to confront the problem directly. The issue is not always so clear-cut. In the absence of dramatic traumas, life brings so much nagging unhappiness on a daily basis that we need to be careful not to become overly accustomed to being unhappy and adapt ourselves to chronic mild misery. We can easily get inured to a routine, numbed to the point at which unhappiness seems "normal," until we just resign ourselves to life as a kind of endurance test.

When this happens, it's important to pay attention to unhappiness as a signal: "I'm off track! I need to find and return to my original intention!" Otherwise we will keep doing what we're used to doing, and even though we may appear to be coping well and seem outwardly successful, something important will be missing. We can respond empathically to clients, make transference interpretations, reframe clients' narratives, help them search for solutions, make a paradoxical intervention, educate them about automatic thoughts, and the therapy will move on and even look like it's working. A lot of therapy works simply if both client and therapist show up for the meeting. But some vital spark, some essence to the meeting, will be lacking so that over time we will exhaust the fire of our original intention and, failing to renew it, "burn out."

This doesn't happen just to psychotherapists. It happens to teachers, parents, factory workers, and executives. It happens even to people who devote their lives to a spiritual vocation. Monks and nuns, priests, ministers, and rabbis, all can lose track of the basis of their spiritual practice: We all run the risk of having rituals become rote, faith turn into fear, and spirituality become soulless if we are unable to rediscover and reignite our original intention.

The Metta Sutta is about intention. The issues it touches on are not restricted to Buddhism; it is broad enough to serve as a guide for anyone who is perplexed or unhappy, not just clients but also psychotherapists, not just students but also teachers. But the Metta Sutta is not a "how-to" guide: To have the Metta Sutta assist us as a guide to happiness in our daily life and our work as therapists, we must treat the Metta Sutta not as a set of commandments but as a koan.

Koans are Zen Buddhist tools for learning the essential nature of our existence. They are "public cases" that Zen practitioners study, which often take the form of an anecdote or story. Usually they pose a particular question, but it is a question that cannot be solved like an arithmetic problem. Instead, koans depict some dynamic interaction of student and teacher, person and circumstances, happiness and suffering to reveal multiple sides of some fundamental issue. Koans do not lead us to "right" and "wrong" answers but into a shimmering process of wrestling with our lives from many viewpoints. In psychotherapy, too, we entertain multiple perspectives and risk altering the basic way we relate to our self, to others, and the world. Then psychotherapy also becomes a koan: an opportunity for some particular point to provide the focus for becoming more one's self.

Put another way, then, whether it be in Zen practice or psychotherapy, koans are tools for realizing our essential nature. If we approach our unhappiness as a koan, it stops being something to be "fixed" and instead becomes a gateway to our lives. We begin to see that happiness and unhappiness, health and sickness, are not only related to each other: They are inextricable from who we are and how we live. Thus the following koan:[2]

> Yun Men, teaching his community, said,
> "Medicine and disease subdue each other:
> The whole earth is medicine; what is your self?"

We can hear the above koan speak to the Metta Sutta. Faced with lives that seem divided into medicine and disease, good and bad, joy and sorrow, we can only be happy if we heal this split. If we can find out how each of our experiences is valuable, then the whole world will be medicine. But we can find this only by recognizing our whole self in each and all of our experiences.

The koan the Metta Sutta poses could be put variously as: How is happiness connected with my self? What is happiness? Where does happiness come from? What kind of intention should guide my practice and my life? What relationship does my happiness bear to the happiness of others?

The Metta Sutta poses the question: How can I *realize* happiness?

This is the central subject matter of all koans: *realization*. Realization does not mean understanding, although it includes understanding. Realization does not mean awareness, although it includes awareness. Realization does not mean you "get" anything. Realization is the activity of making real, or perhaps better phrased as bringing what is real forward: real-izing. So the Metta Sutta's koan of "how can I realize happiness" translates to: How can I make happiness real? How can I *become* happiness? In traditional Buddhist terms that echo the concerns of psychotherapy, the question is often phrased: "How do I real-ize my true Self?"

We, and all that surrounds us, are always completely real: How can we be anything else? But although we do not need to *become* real, we often fail to recognize that being real means being complete and whole exactly as we are, this moment. Although most of us can accept we are "real" in the sense that we exist tangibly, it is more difficult to real-ize ourselves and the world as Real in the sense of being complete and whole. We all get trapped in illusory appearances and start feeling we are missing something; we start feeling separate and incomplete. We feel fragmented, thinned out like butter that's been scraped over too much bread,[3] conflicted, phony, unreal. Then it is hard to be happy in this moment without wanting something else.

Unhappiness and restlessness come from our alienation from our lives, from our missing some sense of wholeness. People who come to Zen meditation or psychotherapy usually are acting from an implicit sense of feeling alienated from themselves: "I'm not enlightened," says the Zen student; "I'm not myself," says the client. We feel frustrated at our sense of disconnection, our separateness, at the gap that springs up between ourselves and the completeness of our lives.

Zen practice, psychotherapy, and the Metta Sutta all are about closing the gap. In order to do this and realize ourselves completely, however, we need to understand not just happiness but also suffering.

THE INEVITABILITY OF SUFFERING

Therapist: What brings you here?

Client #1: I'm almost fifty years old. For the first time in my life, I'm living with a woman. I had a girlfriend a long time ago, but it didn't end well, and we had to call it off. Since that time I haven't been involved with anyone on an ongoing basis. But a little while ago I met this woman, and something opened up in me, and there's a strong connection there. So we've been together. But I also worry that maybe I'm settling for something - I have a tendency to settle for less than I can achieve. Like in my job. And this woman, she's wonderful, but I don't feel like we can communicate on an intellectual level. So sometimes I think how can I get out of this relationship without anyone getting hurt. Then other times I think it's important to go ahead.

I'd like to be of one mind.

Client #2: I never had to deal with death before. Then, two months ago, one of my uncles died. Shortly afterwards, my grandfather died. While I was home for that funeral, after the funeral, we got a phone call from a friend. He had been watching the TV and told us he'd seen my brother had been shot and murdered, I couldn't believe it. And then I had to take care of things, and everyone relied on me, and I didn't feel there was anything I could do, I felt helpless.

I haven't been sleeping well lately. And I can't turn to any of my boyfriends, because they don't like to see me looking needy.

I feel so lonely.

We feel isolated from others and fragmented within ourselves. Clients come to psychotherapists because they are suffering, and psychotherapists tend to become psychotherapists because, having had some experience with anguish, we want to help others and ourselves in the struggle with suffering. It's odd, then, that although there is a great deal written about symptoms, interpersonal problems, and "affective experiencing," the psychotherapeutic literature rarely uses the word "suffering" or approaches the issue of suffering directly.

There are many different approaches to psychological misery. Perhaps the most common view in psychotherapy—and certainly the view espoused by professional societies, insurance companies, and all who embrace the medical model of treatment—is that clients' suffering is a by-product of "psychopathology." In the name of finding a cure, a client's suffering is objectified and encapsulated; often the cause of the "psychopathology" is seen as "inside" the client. The client who can't commit to relationships may be seen as fixated on some early childhood experience; the distress of the client whose brother was murdered may be formulated as a reaction to a trauma that does not fit within her existing psychological schemas. Biological psychiatrists, meanwhile, may suggest that in both instances the cause of suffering lies at least partially in some neurotransmitter imbalance.

Such diagnostic formulations can be helpful in guiding treatment but sometimes lead to more suffering than they ameliorate. If the client who comes to therapy in an unhappy marital relationship is diagnosed as being the "adult child of an alcoholic," it tends to focus the client's attention on the label rather than her or his life. This can have the unhappy effect of making a client feel that the label constitutes a kind of badge of identity that defines who she or he is, something she or he may need to spend five years in therapy to escape. But therapy will never make the client an "adult child of a nonalcoholic."

Some therapeutic schools make a diagnosis but attempt to avoid pejorative labels by talking instead about "problems in living," "maladaptive behaviors," "dysfunctional patterns," or something similar. However, these still treat suffering as a definable *entity*, a sort of unwelcome alien intrusion. There are also therapists who are uninterested in diagnosis, eschew any focus on pathology, and concentrate instead on promoting growth. Humanistic and existential therapists attempt to value and embrace whatever experience the client brings; narrative and solution-oriented therapists focus on clients' unique strengths and abilities. Even with these therapies, however, suffering is viewed basically as an unpleasant feeling, as something we may have more or less of, as something avoidable if only we can remove the "glitches" in our lives.

Clinicians have theories of intrapsychic conflicts, irrational beliefs, interpersonal patterns, biological imbalances, or problem-saturated narratives. Clients have their own theories. Both therapists and clients tend to think of suffering as arising from one of three causes: There's something wrong with *me*; there's something wrong with *them*; or there's something wrong with the way the *world* is. Both clinicians and clients tend to view difficulties as somehow extrinsic to existence, something that can be isolated and separated from the overall scheme of things. Suffering is viewed as an intrusion on a person's life, unnecessary baggage that can be jettisoned; if only we had the proper medicines, therapeutic techniques, interpersonal tools, or self-help skills, we could effect a cure.

If we think of suffering as an avoidable "glitch," this encourages us to think: "I will be happy if only I... " Then the search for happiness becomes a process of filling in the blank. A client thinks, "I will be happy if only I become more lovable and attract the right partner"; a therapist thinks, "I will be happy if only I learn the right technique and get a chance to practice it without intrusions from managed care"; a Zen student thinks, "I will be happy if only I... meditate correctly and become enlightened."

Clients, therapists, Zen students, we all tend to share an illusion: that suffering is somehow an aberration in the fabric of life. If suffering is an aberration, then it can be avoided or, if necessary, fixed. This illusion seems particularly strong in America, where an open frontier and a "can-do" attitude often leads us to think that inventiveness or technology can fix anything. If told their back pain is chronic, untreatable, but manageable by daily exercise, patients sometimes become outraged and file for disability; if told the surgery was unsuccessful and the illness is terminal, in disbelief and anger they may file a malpractice suit. Many of us spend years grappling with the unhappiness we experienced in our families of origin, thinking in our heart of hearts that we can somehow repair the pains of the past. The illusion that suffering is an aberration contributes to the glorification of youth culture common in "advanced" industrialized societies, because it feeds our denial and fear of death and old age. Beyond these larger trends our denial of the inevitability of suffering can permeate both the large and small affairs of our daily experience:

> There is a story[4] that a person consulted a Zen teacher to help him feel better about his life. He told the Zen teacher he had many, many problems and proceeded to enumerate them: His wife had left him, his daughter was on drugs, his boss was a tyrant, his parents demanding, his health was poor.... As he listed his problems he counted them up, and at the end he said, "No wonder I'm miserable. Look, I counted that I have 39 problems!"
>
> The Zen teacher disagreed, replying, "No, you have 40 problems."
>
> The person asked, "Did I miscount? I thought it was 39."
>
> The Zen teacher replied, "Your 40th problem is that you think you should have no problems."

> I grew up in an urban environment. When I was in my early twenties, a friend introduced me to backpacking. We hiked to Flower Dome in the Cascade mountains. After a long hike uphill, we came to a beautiful meadow, filled with wildflowers, looking across a valley to stunning views of a glaciated peak, I sat down and prepared to enjoy myself. Yet soon, black flies started feeding on me. The sun beat down; there was no shade. Sitting on the ground was uncomfortable; ants were crawling around, and I worried they'd crawl up my leg. "This would be wonderful," I thought, "if only it were a little cooler, and there were no bugs."

I wanted to be in a mountain meadow without bugs or excessive heat (a nice easy chair would have been good, too). I ascribed my dis-ease to things outside myself (the ants, the prickly ground, my aching body), but in fact the dis-ease was a product of my mind, my failure to accept fully that mountain meadows don't come with easy chairs and without bugs any more than life comes without painful experiences, disease, and death.

We all know, at least intellectually, that there's no escaping death. More to the point, there's also no escaping life, and life is full of "glitches." It is not the unpleasant glitch that causes suffering, though, but rather the relationship we form with the glitch. The same holds true for all dis-ease. We tend to view disease as an aberration, as something "wrong" or "bad." Disease, however, is as inevitable as death, and as inescapable as breathing. Presumably if we never breathed in, we would be less subject to bacteria and viruses. It is very hard, though, to live without breathing in. We all know we will get sick and die, but somehow we all feel we will be an exception: We are always slightly surprised whenever disease and death come to visit us personally, so when they pay us a call we try to run away. Running away, however, we unwittingly run into what we are trying to avoid.

This brings to mind the classic Sufi story[5] of the man who was in the marketplace in Cairo and saw the Grim Reaper. The man knew that you only saw Death when he was coming for you: Terrified, he tried to escape by running away. As he bolted from the market, he looked back over his shoulder and saw Death looking at him with a surprised expression. That encouraged him: Maybe he had done something Death didn't expect and could escape. Once home, he grabbed a few clothes, some money, and fled to Mecca, where he assumed a new name and a disguise.

A week went by in Mecca, and the man began to relax. He was lonely without his friends and family, and bored without his work, but at least he was alive. He had been able to outwit Death. He went out to the market to buy some provisions, and someone tapped him on the shoulder. He turned and saw it was Death, who had come to claim him.

The man said, resigned, "Well, at least I escaped you for a while, I managed to get another week of life. I saw how surprised you looked when I got away from you in Cairo."

Death replied, "Yes, I was surprised. You see, I didn't expect to meet you in Cairo last week, because I knew I had an appointment with you today in Mecca."

There is no escape from death, disease, and suffering. Disease is the counterpart to health: There can be no health without disease. There can be no joy without suffering, and no life without death. If we open ourselves up to one, we must encounter the other; their interplay is the woof and the weave that constitutes the basic fabric of our life.

If we reject or deny suffering, it will pursue us as surely as death itself and we will continue to squirm in fruitless attempts at avoidance. The paradox is that freedom from suffering lies in first accepting suffering fully. The First Noble Truth of Buddhism says: "Life is suffering." Although the Third Noble Truth of Buddhism teaches there is release from suffering, we cannot realize this without planting our feet in the firm ground of the First Truth.

In Buddhism, we say, "The lotus flower blooms in the mud." We acknowledge that our lives are inherently messy. The roots of the Metta Sutta's prescription for happiness lie not in the heavens but in the muck of our pains and delusions.

Psychotherapists know the necessity of acknowledging problems and facing suffering head-on if a client wants to change. But the First Noble Truth, taken in its most radical form, is still hard to swallow. Even if we accept that some suffering is inevitable, we still tend to think we can avoid or ameliorate suffering at least some of the time. If we are therapeutic optimists, we might say, "Suffering is unnecessary, or at least can be kept to a minimum," and emphasize the solutions and strengths in our clients' lives. If we are therapeutic pessimists who subscribe to a "tragic" view of life, we might say, "Suffering can't be avoided, it's part of life, but let us, as Freud suggests, replace neurotic suffering with common human misery." Implicitly, in either view, suffering is seen as somehow "bad," a misery that must be eliminated if possible, tolerated if necessary.

We discriminate between feeling unhappy and happy: We see happiness as one thing and suffering as another, thinking they mutually exclude each other. We may penetrate further and realize that our unhappiness comes from trying to avoid suffering, and that it is necessary to be "open" to suffering and face it squarely. But behind this statement we have a kind of sneaky hope: that if we don't look away from our suffering, if we look our suffering in the eye, we'll become transformed and somehow suffer less.

We tend to hold on to the idea that there is life *outside* of suffering. We deny we are suffering all the time. We may acknowledge that there is a lot of inevitable suffering in life, but we do so from a perspective that insists that there can be times in our lives when we will be able to avoid suffering and just feel good. We believe our lives can stand apart from and somehow exist separate from our sufferings.

Buddhism, in contrast, insists that our lives are inseparable wholes. The First Noble Truth does not say life *contains* suffering but that life *is* suffering. Because life is an inextricable whole, if we separate ourselves from our suffering, we begin to separate ourselves from our joys as well.

To say that life *is* suffering does not mean that life is unpleasant: It means that suffering, like any experience, has a simple facticity to it that joins it with every other aspect of all existence. The existence of suffering is no different from the existence of the sun, the moon, the tides. Life is suffering, is the arising and passing away of our experiences. There is joy, and there is sorrow, and both are suffering, expressing the momentary flow of existence. The baby being born is suffering. The stream's rushing water meets the solidity of stone: Rock and river suffer together in this meeting and make a vast song. Love and death, birth and peace, are suffering, joined in the fact that all experience is impermanent and ungraspable.

All of us are looking to find a certain ideal state that would bring eternal happiness. Therapists and clients strive for some particular state of "well-balanced adjustment"; Zen students strive for some particular state of "enlightenment." If we are seeking some special state, however, we may not find a way to enjoy the state we are in. Furthermore, if we have not come to terms with impermanence, we may begin to either fear things ending (if they are pleasant) or hope things will end (if they are unpleasant).

The seed of our unhappiness lies in our wish to control how things will be. When this wish ceases to be a transitory feeling or impulse and we become attached to our desire to the point where we have troubles letting go of it, the desire starts running the show: It becomes a craving that pushes us this way and that.

CRAVING

The Second Noble Truth teaches us that the root of suffering is desire. The word "desire" can be misleading, however. Desire does not in and of itself result in suffering; all human beings are subject to desires and urges. Hunger and thirst, hope that our loved ones will be happy and healthy, wanting the world to be a better place: Desires like these are part of being in contact with the world. If I touch a hot stove, I want to pull back; if I feel a cool breeze, I want to move forward. If I am hungry and eat just enough to satisfy myself, the hunger is not a problem.

Wanting something is not a problem, but becoming *attached* to what I want leads to suffering. If I cling to self-centered desires, they become stronger and stronger until they are running me. If I am hungry and for some reason cannot eat but keep thinking about eating, I get miserable. (I remember one meditation retreat during which most of one day was spent lusting for a Ben & Jerry's New York Double Fudge Crunch ice cream bar). If I am hungry and I eat too much, I also feel miserable. (My stomach is still a little bit upset from that bag of Doritos I ate last night). Hunger (and all desire) becomes a problem if it transforms from a natural urge into an unhealthy Craving.

Craving may not necessarily take the form of an obvious wish or a want. Sometimes it may take the form of fear or aversion, such that we *don't* want things to be a certain way. This is still Craving, it is just taking the form of rejecting what we have instead of reaching for what we don't have. A client comes in complaining that his girlfriend is too dependent, and he wishes she'd give him more "space." Very often this is the same client who, when his girlfriend leaves him, comes in obsessed about getting her back. Either way, he feels Craving tugging at him. The hallmark of Craving is its restlessness: feeling "jerked around," feeling that we are being pushed or pulled toward or away from something.

Craving doesn't let us relax and devote our full attention to the present moment. In this way, Craving hinders us from realizing our true selves; it clouds our vision by setting up some ideal image of life-the-way-I-want-it-to-be until it is all we can see, obscuring the actual lives we have. Craving then becomes the central character in the story of our lives; it appropriates past, present, and future, where we came from and where we are going.

Craving involves a nagging sense of feeling unhappy, of feeling unsatisfied, of being ruled by momentary wishes, impulses, and wants. Craving is that gnawing feeling that something is wrong with us, that sense of internal dissatisfaction, that yearning to fill up some inner emptiness by taking something into us. Craving is partly a physical sensation, partly a psychological process, and partly a spiritual seeking. Craving often hides behind a smokescreen, speaking in a language that alternates between self-indulgence and self-loathing.

> Take the example of a client who is consumed by longing for the girlfriend who left him. He craves her: He remembers what it was like being with her as if it were an ideal time; he thinks of the future, reunited with her, as if it will be paradise; he devotes all his time now to obsessing about whether he should phone her, or write her, or leave her alone, or change something in himself to please her. It seems to him that his whole life led up to this relationship, that his life is only meaningful in terms of the relationship. He feels all previous relationships were mere preludes to this one; any subsequent, different relationship becomes unthinkable.
>
> Perhaps my client's girlfriend has told him she "needs space" to sort out her feelings and asked him not to call her for a month. My client obsesses over whether she "really means it" and debates with himself whether he should call her.
>
> When Craving speaks to our bereft lover with words of self-indulgence it might say things like, "Oh, go ahead, indulge, a short phone call won't hurt... I'll be able to talk to her without getting too upset... I've been good, I haven't talked to her for five days, I deserve to call her now... this is just her testing me, if I don't call her she'll think I don't care... let me call her now and tell her I've seen the light, I won't act that way any more, she'll change her mind."
>
> When Craving speaks to our bereft lover with words of self-loathing it might say things like "I was so bad to her before... I'm really lonely... I'm so weak.., I can't even get along by myself.., I have no self-discipline.., I didn't treat her well enough, I don't deserve her... how could anyone respect me, if they only knew how I can't control myself and my need for her... "

When Craving whispers in the language of indulgence and temptation, it tries to deceive the client by convincing him he'll be happier, if only for a moment, if he gives in. Craving also speaks in a language of self-hatred, punishment, and denial: It uses a language filled with "should" and "shouldn't," constantly judging the client according to idealized standards that don't allow any room for natural human wants or wishes. But even as it judges incessantly, Craving is not interested in learning from experience. The client who is obsessed with regaining his lost love rarely takes time to listen to the lessons of the relationship but instead frantically seeks a way to undo the past or dictate the course of the future. Either way, the client flees the taste of the present.

Notice that in a way, Craving is always saying the same thing: "Don't feel content this moment! Don't feel happy with what you have! Want something else!" This is the message virtually every television commercial sends us. Whether it is tempting us with a new car, a new lover, or a new self, Craving tries to convince us that we're missing something. From Craving's point of view, it really doesn't matter whether what we're missing is more companionship or more self-reliance, a faster computer or a bigger house, more food or more thinness, more strength or more love or more money.

The fundamental problem of Craving is that, although Craving can be satisfied for short periods of time, fundamentally, *Craving does not know how to be content.* This is because Craving is tied up with illusions and fantasies. Craving daydreams about how it wishes things were, but doesn't deal well with the reality of how things actually are. So if Craving gets what it thinks it wants, it starts daydreaming about something else. Craving is always yearning for what it doesn't have or yearning not to have what it does have.

When Craving succeeds in paralyzing someone by pulling him with forbidden or unavailable wants and wishes on one side and harsh "shoulds" and "shouldn'ts" on the other, people often retreat into the fantasy land of "if only:"

> My client thinks: "If only I had been more thoughtful, she'd still be with me... If only she came back to me, things would be different, I'd be more attentive and she'd nag less... if only she came back to me I'd never hit her again, no matter what... if only she loves me then I'll feel some self-respect and confidence in myself... "

Some of us chase ideal girlfriends or boyfriends, some of us chase ideal jobs, some of us chase ideal selves. Whatever we are chasing, if we daydream about some ideal existence, Craving takes us away from the reality of our lives this moment. Craving places happiness in some far-off heavenly nirvana, that time when psychotherapy (or meditation practice) is "completed" and we're healthy and enlightened.

This is delusion. This is looking for the mountain meadow in our heads rather than on the hill: This may offer a meadow without bees and prickles but also a meadow in which the colors are less vivid and there are no flowers. This is the *idea* of the meadow, perhaps gained from looking at picture books, but it is not the meadow itself. If we let Craving rule our lives, we look for satisfaction from the air-brushed photo of the magazine model rather than from the imperfect body lying next to us in our bed. But the body lying next to us is warm: Its pimples are three-dimensional and alive, while the magazine is a thin piece of perfect paper.

Craving convinces us to be unhappy about who we are at this moment. When it substitutes the Heroic Quest for the mundane pleasure of the life in front of us, it sometimes leads to obsessive addictions: gambling, drugs and alcohol, computer games, compulsive exercise, overworking. Endless psychotherapy and excessive meditation can also become self-centered activities in which we neglect ourselves and the people in our lives in favor of seeking some ideal state. In any of these addictions we are kept busy chasing happiness and don't ever stop to face ourselves and the people around us to create happiness from the flawed, but real, materials at hand. Craving is subtle and can even take the form of self-denial:

> In ancient days, an old woman gave housing and food to a hermit over a period of twenty years. One day she sent her sixteen-year-old niece to take food to the hermit, telling her to make advances to him to see what he would do.
> The girl laid her head on the hermit's lap, and said, "How is this?"

The hermit said, "The withered tree is rooted in an ancient rock in bitter cold. During the winter months, there is no warmth, no life."

The girl reported this to her aunt. The old woman said, "That vulgarian! To think that I have made offerings to him for twenty years!"

She drove away the hermit and burned down his cottage.[6]

In his comment on this case, Robert Aitken notes that the hermit was not responding to the real human being who laid her head in his lap; he was attached to his own self-centered craving for ascetic accomplishment.

Whether it be through attachment to daydreams of gain or attachment to dreams of purity, all attachment is a form of addiction. Ultimately we all are addicted to our ideas about our selves and our ideas about the world; to say it another way, we are all attached to the narrow self-centered ideas we form about who we are or ought to be, about what the world is and ought to be. When our vision is constricted in this way, Craving narrows our apparent options down to just a few limited possibilities and robs us of the fullness of our lives. Craving seduces us with a dream of happiness and traps us in this dream. Buddhism (and psychotherapy) are about waking up from our fantasies and instead finding happiness in who we are, where we are, in the reality of this moment.

SEEKING THE GOOD

The Metta Sutta turns us towards finding happiness in who we are this moment, but it is easy to take a wrong turn. When we feel unhappy we're often like the drunkard who lost his glasses in a dark alley but looks for them under the streetlamp on the corner because "that's where the light is"; we look for the good someplace other than where we are and seek out advice on how to find it. Buddhists seeking "the good" often turn to the Metta Sutta for advice on what we should do to become wise and peaceful, much as clients often come to therapists for advice on what they should do to become free of their misery. Even if they don't give specific advice about how to handle a particular situation, both therapists and the Metta Sutta point people in a certain direction, and in doing so two potential problems arise.

The first problem is that as soon as we start looking for what we "should" do it is easy to get caught in striving for perfection. This is a common and very perilous trap for anyone who devotes much energy to either a psychotherapeutic or a spiritual calling, because it appeals to our pride. Once we start thinking we know what "should" be done—whether it be what "should" be done to lead a good spiritual life or what "should" be done to pursue psychological health and happiness—we become susceptible to the diseases of self-criticism and perfectionism as we measure how close we come to the ideal. Striving to be flawless, however, easily can turn into striving to be faultless, and excessive self-criticism in the service of seeking the good can become converted to sanctimony or arrogance whether we are Zen students or psychotherapists.

I have a friend who tells me that she likes what she reads about Zen, but often feels uncomfortable around her Zen practitioner friends; she feels they carry excessively large superegos and obsessively self-scrutinize. A common unwanted side effect of trying to be good is that it tends to insidiously promote intolerance and irritation. If we are trying hard to be good, peaceful, and wise, and we encounter someone who seems to be barreling along, acting immorally or aggressively, it becomes difficult to not to get annoyed at that person—especially if he seems to be enjoying himself!

When we are trying very hard to be "good," there is a tendency to reject what we see as our "bad" traits. Psychotherapists know that the more a client rejects or disowns "bad" traits in him- or herself, the more intense is the tendency to project those "bad" traits onto others and become upset with the other person's "bad" habits. Therapists and Zen students are not immune from this. Intimate relationships—with partners, parents, therapists, and religious teachers—offer fertile opportunities for such projection. There is a tendency to see our "good" self as somehow different from that "bad" person over there. This tendency to attempt to be "good" by pointing a finger at "bad" becomes a particularly nasty problem if the "bad" person my "good" self is mad at happens to be me.

The second problem that arises if we seek the good is that it is easy to fall into the trap of thinking that wisdom, goodness, and peace are things we do not currently have and must be pursued somewhere outside of our current experience. The danger here is that we may implicitly put off happiness to some future date, feeling first we must do what "should" be done in order to eventually earn our way to happiness. Zen students often feel they "should" meditate and become enlightened in order to seek the good and obtain peace. Psychotherapy clients and their therapists often feel there is something they "should" do to be happy, that happiness is somehow outside themselves. For both the Zen student and the psychotherapy client and therapist, this usually involves a sense that something is wrong with them, or with their current life, that needs to be "fixed." We start to feel we need to do zazen to get somewhere; we feel we need to have psychotherapy and repair ourselves to be less miserable.

When we pursue goodness or happiness outside of the present moment of our lives, it is like chasing the end of the rainbow, always just out of reach. What is it we must grasp or seek? If we do not already have some sense of goodness and happiness, how could we recognize it when we encounter it? If happiness lies somehow outside us, we feel it is separate from us: We think to be happy we must acquire something we don't yet have. If, on the other hand, happiness is inside ourselves, we often feel that it is somehow hidden from us: We think we cannot be happy as we are but must change something inside ourselves.

Most therapists and clients initially approach therapy feeling there is something missing from the self that needs to be acquired, or some conflict or impulse that must be resolved, before they can feel happy. Similarly, most Zen students initially approach meditation feeling they must "polish their minds" before they can realize Buddhahood.

> One day Nangaku visited Baso's hut. Baso stood and greeted him. Nangaku asked: "What have you been doing recently?"
>
> Baso replied: "I have done nothing but sit in zazen."
>
> Then Nangaku asked: "Why do you continually sit in zazen?"
>
> Baso answered: "I sit in zazen in order to become Buddha."
>
> Then Nangaku picked up a tile and started to polish it using a tile he found by the side of Baso's hut. Baso watched what he was doing and asked: "Master, what are you doing?"
>
> Nangaku answered: "I am polishing this tile."
>
> Baso asked: "Why are you polishing the tile?"
>
> Nangaku answered: "To make a mirror."
>
> Baso said: "How can you make a mirror by polishing a tile?"
>
> Nangaku replied: "How can you become a Buddha by doing zazen?"[7]

Like Nangaku, in seeking peace we feel we must do something special to realize ourselves and find peace: we think we must find the "real" me, but that somehow the "real" me is different from the "me" that is here right now. This can be exacerbated if psychotherapy and Zen urge clients and students who seek peace and happiness to practice certain techniques in order to find the "true" self.

Many clients when they are given good therapeutic advice get worse: They not only feel bad about what brought them to therapy in the first place but also feel bad because they're not able to fulfill their (or their therapist's) advice of how they "should" act to be psychologically healthy. Therapists berate themselves for not being good enough; Zen students torture themselves for being "bad" Zen students. It seems that injunctions to "be Good" often result in an interior battle between "good" and "bad"; we can become morbidly self-conscious, self-righteous, conflicted, or alienated if we strive to make ourselves ideally good and perfectly healthy. This leaves peace always out of reach.

If we take the Metta Sutta as a kind of laxative to purge us of bad habits and lead us to perfection, instead of feeling better we can fall ill if excessive cleansing leads us only to be more preoccupied with our remaining impurities. But even as it tells us that "this is what should be accomplished," the Metta Sutta subtly provides the antidote to this poison. For at the same time that the Metta Sutta tells us what should be done, it tells us this is done by "the one who *is* wise and *has obtained* peace." It doesn't say, "This is what should be accomplished by one to become wise, so you can find goodness and obtain peace." It implies that the person seeking the good has already obtained wisdom and peace. In fact, seeking the good *comes from* wisdom and peace. The Metta Sutta's prescriptions are not what we need to do in order *to become* happy: Its mode of being is happiness itself.

What we seek is always already right here, in the seeking, inextricable from us as we are. When we feel that there is something flawed in our current life or self and start to look for "the Good," as the Metta Sutta enjoins, it is important to ask ourself: Where does this impulse to seek the good come from? At this very moment that we seek the Good, the face of "the Good" appears; Goodness is seeking goodness. Zen calls this "the Fire God has come to seek for fire."[8]

This is very helpful for therapists to remember when working with clients. A client often will say, "I wish I could be more loving toward my spouse... there's something in me that just doesn't know how to love." What the client doesn't see is, if he didn't *already have* the ability to express and value love, he would not be wanting to become more loving toward his spouse. His already-present love is simply seeking to actualize itself; love has come to seek for love.

> In the previous chapter we met Tom, the thirty-five-year-old man who through much of his life had struggled with self-doubt and had problems accomplishing his goals. Although intelligent and creative, while still young he had decided that if he could not be immediately brilliant at something, he was a stupid failure. During the therapy Tom had found a way to work at projects one step at a time and subsequently did well professionally.
>
> He came back to therapy several years later because he and his wife were considering having a child. He very much wanted to have children but tortured himself with the idea that he wasn't capable of love, wasn't a good husband, and wouldn't be a good father. The situation was complicated by the fact that Tom felt wounded in his relationship with his own father. He had loved his father, but when he was a young boy his father had developed a serious alcohol problem and had rapidly deteriorated, become a skid-row bum, and died just when Tom needed someone to look up to and mentor him. Tom felt he had never received the fatherly care and instruction he needed. Now, when his wife was attempting to convince him to have a child, Tom felt terrified that he'd be an unfit father.
>
> Tom felt sure he was incapable of love. He gave his relationship with his wife as an example: He often found himself wanting to withdraw from her in order to take time for himself. When his wife pursued him, he would feel resentful but also feel guilty that he wasn't a more loving husband. Tom acknowledged that he was supportive of his wife's career, listened empathically to her, respected her wishes in matters of joint concern, and shared household duties amicably, but he didn't see these things as evidence of his loving her. He felt his wife was a wonderful woman and wanted to raise a family with her but felt he wouldn't be able to provide the kind of emotional atmosphere he thought would be best for a child.
>
> I asked Tom, "You regret not being more loving?" He answered yes.
>
> "So you have some image of what being more loving would look like?" Tom answered yes and was able to elaborate what he would be doing: He would be paying attention to his wife, enjoying her company, remembering little things she liked, and so forth. On careful questioning, it turned out that some of the time he was already doing these things, acting in accordance with his vision of being more loving. However, he continued to berate himself for not doing this more of the time.
>
> "So some part of you *wants* to be more loving? It's not just that intellectually you think you 'ought' to be that way?" Yes, Tom really wanted that. "And you can recognize love when you encounter it?" Yes, he could.

I asked Tom, "How can you recognize love if some part of you isn't already capable of loving?" He didn't know how to answer that. I said, "It seems to me the part of you that wants to be more loving is the part that has love to give."

This was a novel idea for Tom, and he couldn't accept it immediately. But he began to have a little less certainty that he was incapable of love, and what had been self-defeating doubt became doubt about the negative images of himself. We worked together for a number of sessions while he considered this.

Tom went ahead and had a child with his wife. He was ecstatic about being a father, filled with tenderness for their child. When I saw him some years later, the joy he felt being with his son continued to teach him how to love life, even in the midst of some difficult circumstances.

An unloving person can't want to be more loving any more than a twelfth-century European peasant can want to immigrate to an America he doesn't know exists. Therapists need to ally themselves to the client who is *already* fundamentally whole, fundamentally loving. Fortunately, all people are born fundamentally loving, however much deprivation they have suffered. However much trauma has warped the ability to love, we are born with an innate ability to not only breathe but to laugh, smile, cry: We are born attending more to human faces than to other stimuli; we are born connected to our world and the people in it.

GRASPING

We may be born enlightened and whole, but we are also born screaming at the top of our lungs. We are born with the ability to love but are also born with primitive desires and a grasp reflex that does not know how to let go. Suffering comes from our being misled by Craving's urgings to grab hold of our experience and control our selves and our lives so that they fit the image of how we want them to be. But grasping too tightly can become a problem. In grasping, the world becomes experienced as a thing, an object to be possessed or rejected, but also one that can be lost. Our ego may then feel a sense of excitement or self-centered pride when it is able to obtain and hold on to the things it likes, but it will also feel a sense of depression and loss when it cannot hold on to the things it desires.

We try to hold on to what we like and fight against impermanence. But we cannot make the impermanent permanent. This is a simple truth for all life, but it doesn't seem to stop us from trying to stop the world and get a grip on our lives as we want them to be. If I cannot accept the transience of life, I may become upset if my new car gets scratched; perhaps I'll even try to avoid getting it scratched by keeping it in the garage under a tarp. But then I won't enjoy driving; I'll fail to realize that the only way for something to remain new is for it to renew itself each moment. If I hold on too tight, I separate myself from what I try to grasp and turn it into an object. Then I am like the jealous man who attempts to control his lover by insisting she never leave the house without him: The tighter he tries to hold on to her, the more she will withdraw. The more attached I get to holding on to keeping something a certain way, the further away I'll be from enjoying it as it is.

If we can't enjoy things as they are, Craving suggests we pine for some better state. In the midst of our yearning, however, often we are unwilling to let go of the unsatisfying state we currently are in. Oddly enough, we tend to hold on to our unpleasant experiences just as much as to the pleasant ones. We just grasp them with a different valence, a more painful affect.

We may have a lemon of a car but keep trying to repair it, unable to accept that it's a lemon. We may have an abusive spouse whom we keep trying to reform: He or she may not be much, but at least she or he is ours. We may know that our tendency to be perfectionistic or overwork is causing us insomnia, weight gain, or high blood pressure, and yet we have troubles letting go of our trait because "that's me.., I have to do it that way." We hold onto even extreme hurt in many ways: through unwillingness to accept it and fighting it; through rehashing it and revisiting it time and time again; through blinding ourselves and denying what's happening.

A colleague came to me rather astonished after a session with a client, a man who was married to a woman who was physically abusive. This had been going on for many years; his wife periodically would fall into a rage and attack him not just with her fists and nails but also with whatever object came to hand. The client had suffered many bruises and had often come in to therapy, sometimes in attempts to improve the relationship, sometimes just for emotional support. His therapist had warned him the violence might escalate and had been urging him to consider what kept him in the marriage, and whether he should consider leaving.

Then several months passed during which the man didn't come in to therapy. Today was the first session after a long hiatus; the man had been in the hospital. He told his therapist that the last time his wife had attacked him, she had taken a large kitchen knife and plunged it up to the hilt between his ribs. He had been recovering from the attack ever since. He was still with his wife, however.

His therapist was somewhat dumbfounded, and said: "I don't understand. How can you stay with this woman, after she's stuck a knife in you?"

The client answered: "Well, she didn't hit anything vital."

We cling to our current state sometimes from fear, sometimes from greed. Therapists often see clients who seem "stuck" in their problems and wonder why, once they have other options and become aware of alternatives available to them, they don't change the things they are doing that lead to their suffering. There are many psychological theories about this, ranging from psychoanalytic resistance and secondary gain to reinforcement contingencies and systemic homeostasis. But it's not really much different from what most of us do in our daily lives. We enjoy telling the story of our surgery and pointing to our scars. We enjoy complaining of our misery or, for those of us who are more attached to being stoic, we enjoy holding onto our pride and not complaining of our misery.

We identify with what we have and make it our own until we are unwilling to part with it. We become attached even to our misery. It may be misery, but it's *my* misery and at least has the virtue of being familiar. My misery fits me.

About an hour ago, I watched an interaction between my daughter and my wife. My daughter was wearing her favorite shirt. She likes wearing this shirt and is very attached to it; she'd had the shirt on for several days.

"Mom," she said. "I'm getting a rash on my shoulder, where my shirt rubs. It really bothers me."

My wife looked at the rash, which did look red and angry. "Well, Bekka," she said, "sometimes if your shirt is dirty, or if it had too much detergent left on it, it can cause a rash when it rubs against your skin. Why don't you take your shirt off, if the rash is bothering you?"

"I *love* this shirt, Mom," my daughter replied. "I don't *want* to take it off."

This is Buddhism's theory of suffering in a nutshell.

In psychotherapy we sometimes see clients who have shirts they refuse to take off despite the fact that the shirts are rubbing them the wrong way: the man who is enraged at his critical boss but who is unwilling to look for another job; the woman whose promotion makes her anxious about performing but who doesn't want to settle for less pay and prestige; the spouse who loves his partner but complains she gets under his skin. Sometimes we see clients who have lost their shirts: The person who has been laid off and cannot find work; the woman who has lost her child to drugs; the man whose house was swallowed by an earthquake. If we've lost our shirt, we want it back; if it is rubbing, we don't want to give it up but wish it would stop irritating us. Whether the shirt has been lost or is rubbing, it arouses a desire that life be different than it is.

Here is where the seed of suffering takes root: in our Craving for life to be other than what it is, in our attachment to being able to pick and choose from what life offers us on the basis of our personal preferences. All sentient beings have a tendency to move toward pleasure and avoid pain, so naturally we are constantly making choices, but in the process we sometimes lose sight of the fact that *both* pleasure *and* pain are part of the wholeness of life. If we lose sight of how each moment of our experience has an essential connectedness to life, regardless of whether it is pleasant or unpleasant, we may feel we're not getting what we want and always be yearning for something else.

We want to choose what shirts we put on. We've all been dressed at some time in clothing that grew confining; we've all had clothing which disappointed us by wearing out too soon or by not helping us make the impression we had hoped for. We even get tired of the clothing that once pleased us but is no longer in style. So we go shopping for a better shirt. Having learned to be dissatisfied, we become very careful in our shopping. We cultivate our tastes as an expression of who we think we are or who we want to become.

I tend to identify who I am according to which things I like and which I don't like: which I hold on to, and which I reject. I define who I am by my preferences and discriminating tastes. But when instead of accepting each experience for what it is I judge an experience according to whether or not I feel comfortable with it, rather than appreciate the object, the person, the feeling or the relationship for what it is, I look at it only in terms of what it is for *me*. In this way I set myself apart and fail to see the connection that already exists between my self and the rest of the world.

As soon as I start judging experiences from this self-centered perspective, relating purely on the basis of what I like and don't like, I become attached to some things and reject others, I label some things "good" and others "bad," but rejecting the bad and pursuing the good splits the wholeness of life: It makes both "bad" and "good" separate from an "I" that stands apart from my moment-to-moment experience. In the process I create a division not just between good and bad but also between me and it; I create a boundary between the judger and the experience being judged. A split arises between "me" and "my experience," between "the world out there" and "the I in here."

If I feel the experiences of my life are somehow separate from me, I'll try to grasp them, to force them to be the way I want them to be to satisfy my Craving. But the origin of my dissatisfaction comes in the separation of "me" from the impermanent, fluctuating flow of experience. Once an "I" exists separate from the world, separated from the rest of all being, existence becomes inherently fragmented and unsatisfactory.

The solution cannot lie in having more good and less bad, because in the act of choosing good or bad I isolate myself from the circumstances of my life. Even if I then encounter the "good" things, they will appear as objects outside of me and therefore always just beyond my reach, the elusive ideal shirt that will bring love, peace, and happiness. The alternative Buddhism offers to the impossibility of grasping at such straws is to become aware that our separateness is an illusion. Perhaps the central teaching of Buddhism is that we are always connected to everyone and everything that was, is, and will be in the whole world: a reminder that our boundaries are not inert material but a living, breathing skin that, wrapped inseparably in the world, is responsive to its touch.

"LET ONE'S SENSES BE CONTROLLED... "

Despite being embedded in the world, the illusion that we are separate comes up incessantly because we can only see a little bit of the picture and because language tends to objectify our experience. We eat a peach and say, while we are eating it, "That's a good (or bad) peach," as if the taste of the peach is something outside ourselves. The peach's taste, however, arises in the eating; we "create" that taste and in the process are created as peach-eaters; we and the peach arise together with the sunshine that helped it grow and the farmer that raised it for us. It doesn't really matter whether the peach is ripe or sour, "good" or "bad"; the point is that we and the peach form, for that moment, a complete experience of life itself. This is true for each object we encounter: how much more so for sentient beings. Birds and birdwatchers, spouses and their lovers, clients and their therapists, we are always inextricably linked in our wholeness.

We rarely see it that way, however, because we think Reality is something outside us, solid and graspable. We can only apprehend things through our senses, but our senses provide only fleeting glimpses of ourselves and others because everything is constantly changing. Because of the inherent fluidity of experience, we can only "capture" it with ideas that synthesize the transient sensory impression into a more enduring concept that can be more readily grasped.

Ideas are interpretations of experience, not the experiences themselves. We think how something looks to *me* is how it is; we tend to mistake our ideas for the real thing. Our senses bring us warmth, and different colors of light, and sounds, but it is our conceptual mind that tells us that this is "a meadow." I think I see a mountain meadow that is "really" out there, "outside" me, but "a meadow" is only an idea. If I get caught in my idea about what a meadow is, I can fail to realize that I am in the meadow at this moment, a *part* of the meadow, not *apart* from it.

Ideas are always one step removed from the reality of our lives, yet we get caught by them. The way sensations shift, disappear, and reappear is partially a function of our sensory apparatus, which is always looking for changes in the environment and which "tunes out" when the environment is unvarying (staring at a blank wall or a solid page of one color, or listening to white noise, makes this apparent). It is also a function of the constantly changing, ungraspable nature of experience. But without a deep understanding of impermanence, we trap ourselves in ideas that "freeze" the flow of our experience. A person who is injured looks at the wound and thinks: "This is going to hurt." As soon as we label an experience this way, we get caught by the idea of pain and feel trapped in constant misery. Yet the sensations themselves are always shifting.

One of the more interesting things that occurs during meditation is that, if one pays careful attention to any sensory impression—such as the pain in our legs—so long as we don't fight it or hold onto it, it quickly disappears or changes into something else. Sometimes the pain changes from a throb to a sharp spike; sometimes it shifts from above the knee to below the knee; sometimes it disappears as we drift into a fantasy far away. In any case, during meditation we learn not how to control our sensations of pain (or pleasure); we learn that by accepting each sensation for what it is, without holding on to it or pushing it away, sensation finds its own way to flow peacefully: We can *let* our sensations be controlled.

When we don't let our senses be controlled but instead rely on our ideas about how things should be, we give our ideas power over us. We form ideas about everything: not just about pain and pleasure, but about who we are and what the world holds for us. Therapists know how often the ideas we hold about ourselves provide as much of an obstacle to change as external factors. Many psychological techniques are ways of intervening at the level of problematical ideas, usually residues of interpretations of past experiences, in order to modify future experiencing.

Buddhists go further and say that *all* ideas interpose a division, interposing a chasm between "I" and "it," "me" and "you," "me" and "my experience." So holding onto *any* idea—not just "problematical" ones—is an unwitting form of greed: a grasping that removes us from experiencing the fullness of our lives. If we hold on to our ideas about ourselves, about others, and the world, we freeze

Table 3.1   Craving Versus Mindfulness

Craving	Mindfulness
Grasping	Letting go
Critical, Picking and Choosing	Nonjudging
Impulsive	Patient
Closed, Narrow, Bored	Open, Beginner's Mind
Distrustful	Trusting
Harsh, Pushing, Yearning	Soft, Nonstraining
Rejecting, Dissatisfied	Accepting
On-again, Off-again	Steady Practice

what was a transient experience into an enduring filter; we live according to our ideas of the past and our dreams of the future and cut ourselves off from the immediacy of how we and life are arising together in this moment.

Unfortunately, we often fear letting go of our ideas and letting ourselves come to our senses. We feel threatened by our feelings. Any intense sensation can become an addiction subject to the whims of Craving because intense feelings and sensations reinforce our ego regardless of whether they are pleasant or unpleasant; feelings seem to shout out, "This is Me! Me!" Paradoxically, however, even as this strengthens my sense of who I am, it divides me. Whether I suppress or stoke my feelings, I am treating the feelings as if "they" were somehow separate from "me," possessions I can hoard or discard. Grasping at "me" can lead to setting my self apart from my life; I start to relate to my internal feelings and to the people and things around me not as part of an integral whole, but as a means to buttress my personal sense of who "I" am, what "the world" is, and what the relationship between us "should" consist of.

The way we and our clients relate to our feelings provides a sensitive barometer of whether we are letting our senses be controlled or if we are being caught by the polar extremes of holding on or pushing away. If we suppress feelings, at some point they come back stronger than before. If we give feelings free rein, however, venting them is much like strenuously exercising a muscle; exercising it causes a feeling to subside for a while, but in the process the exercise also strengthens the feeling. Once a muscle is developed, if it isn't exercised the muscle tightens and cramps; once a feeling is appropriated as an integral part of my identity, not expressing it can lead to anxiety or depression.

There is an alternative to throttling our feelings, letting them run wild, or retreating to the world of disembodied ideas. The alternative is mindfulness, whose cultivation directly counteracts the grasp reflex of Craving. It's helpful to compare the practice of mindfulness with the habits Craving indulges (see Table 3.1).

Craving seeks control; mindfulness rides the ebb and flow of opening up and letting go. Craving stimulates our appetite with ideas, fantasies, and images; mindfulness is a reunion of sensual and cognitive modes of knowing. Psychotherapy seeks a similar mode of existence in which thinking and feeling are reconciled to each other. Just as in mindfulness practice, in psychotherapy the manner in which the feelings are dealt with is more important than the content of the feeling per se.

The issue is not whether we express our feelings or not, but rather whether we approach our feelings from a self-centered standpoint (treating my pleasure or pain as the only thing that's important) or from a standpoint of seeking connectedness (discovering what my feelings teach me about my own experience, what others go through, and how they are connected). The importance of feelings in psychotherapy does not come from venting them but from sharing them: Venting takes us back into ourself, sharing takes us beyond ourself. If we or our clients focus on expressing unhappy or angry feelings with a kind of self-justifying self-indulgence, it can actually reinforce the negative affect. In contrast, if we neither choke off nor feed our feelings but instead greet them mindfully and dispassionately, we can "ride the wave" of sensations and learn what it is the Metta Sutta is suggesting when it says, "Let one's senses be controlled," and when it says, "Let one not be submerged by the things of the world."

The Metta Sutta is not advising we purge ourselves of all feelings and disengage from the world: Isolation is not the solution to enmeshment. Some students of Buddhism confuse its teaching of nonattachment as being an endorsement of noninvolvement. In fact, though, the core of Buddhist teaching is that noninvolvement is not possible: We cannot exist apart from all the myriad things that comprise and create our lives. Such engagement is the basic ground of our existence. We are connected; when you talk, I respond, and you respond to my response. Our feelings arise with each other as surely as sounds induce vibrations in the surfaces they touch. But when we are submerged by sounds we can grow deaf to their clamor; whenwe offer a space in which the sounds of our life may resound, a greater resonance emerges.

So Buddhist practice encourages us to let feelings freely arise and pass away, experiencing them fully without grasping them or rejecting them. This is not so dissimilar from what psychotherapy aims at; in Buddhism it is called "realizing the feelings within the feelings." To realize our feelings within our feelings, to greet them with an open mind, we need to accept each feeling as it is. In order to do this, we need to stop discriminating among feelings on the basis of personal preference.

Once we get overly attached to picking and choosing our experiences we start rejecting not only some of our experiences but also some aspects of our selves. To heal the fissures that spring up within our selves and between our selves and the world, if we begin by fully accepting all of our experience without discriminating between "pleasant" or "unpleasant," the distinction between "I" and "it" also starts to drop away. Acceptance is the doorway to seeing the larger fabric of connectedness that binds world and self together. We begin to see that "good" and "bad" both present life to us, with different faces to be sure, but with the unity of life intact. As I feel less of a separate "I" and more connected to that great net of Being in which each is coexistent with all beings, it becomes easier to participate fully in each moment of life. When we plunge wholeheartedly into whatever each moment brings as it rises up and passes away, opening up fully to all the impermanence, joy, and despair of each moment; when we neither add anything to that moment nor take anything away, there is only that moment itself. Then there is no suffering at all.

SINCERE EFFORT

Although in one sense we can see there is no suffering at all, the fact is we slip again and again into a position in which we lose touch with this and fall prey to unhappiness. When we do not realize our connectedness, the path to happiness is not easy: We all get caught again and again by Craving. So we need to practice mindfulness. We need to find a practice and study a path, but we have a problem: If we don't study and practice, we remain mired in ignorance and bad habits. If we do study and practice in order to get somewhere, however, we may mislead ourselves into thinking our happiness lies in some distant time or place, coming only at the end of study. How, then, can we find a path that does not alienate us but lets us work at strengthening our ability to realize our being as we already are? Joshu, a great Zen master, asked his teacher to show him the way:[9]

> Joshu asked Nansen: "What is the path?"
> Nansen said: "Everyday life is the path."
> Joshu asked: "Can it be studied?"
> Nansen said: "If you try to study, you will be far away from it."
> Joshu asked: "If I do not study, how can I know it is the path?"
> Nansen said: "The path does not belong to the perception world, neither does it belong to the nonperception world. Cognition is a delusion and noncognition is senseless.
> "If you want to reach the true path beyond doubt, place yourself in the same freedom as the sky. You name it neither good nor not-good."

Nansen reminds us that our practice needs to be based on our everyday life; that our effort needs to come from a place of freedom, in which we stop discriminating between good and not-good; that our study needs to cultivate mindful acceptance and an ability to "think not-thinking." In Zen practice, however, this freedom comes within the context of intense hard work. The popular portrayal of Zen, attracted by Zen's enlivening embrace of the immediacy of each moment, sometimes confuses acceptance with "just letting it all hang out." So when people come to an actual Zen center, they are sometimes put off by the rigorous austerity of Zen study, the intense effort it demands, and the emphasis placed on practicing according to strict forms, I remember my initial puzzlement when I went to a Zendo and was instructed about which foot should enter the meditation hall first and where my fingers should be placed to hold the book of sutras while we chanted.

The popular portrayal of psychotherapy also sometimes confuses the importance of self-acceptance with the carelessness of self-indulgence; when clients get involved in a psychotherapy they may feel rejected or angry if the therapist provides validation but not approval or interrupts a recital of being hurt or victimized with a question about what they want to accomplish or change. I remember being a bit nonplussed once when I asked a client what brought them to therapy, and they responded "I need more unconditional positive regard." Sometimes clients feel psychotherapy is a place where an attendant can "fill 'er up" and are dismayed to discover they're in a self-service station.

Neither Zen nor psychotherapy suggest we can realize our true selves without work. There is a saying in Zen, "A day without work is a day without eating." So the Metta Sutta gives us some instructions on how to go about our task: We should be "strenuous and upright" but also "easily contented and joyous." Achieving a balance between ease and exertion is the koan of how to put forth what Buddhism calls "right effort."

How do we balance ourselves? Anyone who has sat zazen knows how easy it is to slip off the mark: If we emphasize sitting vigilant and straight, refusing to move or give in to our distracting thoughts or our impulses to shift position, our muscles may tighten up and our minds may become rigid. If, on the other hand, we sit so softly that we just let our posture slump and allow our minds to be carried away by our fantasies and feelings, then we may fall asleep, wander in dreams, and miss the opportunity to wake up. Similarly, as psychotherapists we can err on the side either of overly passive listening or of being too active with precipitous interventions. Neither one works.

So the Metta Sutta directs us to a place that evenly balances trying and tranquillity. It tells us to be "sincere, without pride." This is the middle point between being "strenuous and upright" on the one hand, and "easily contented and joyous" on the other. The key to finding our balance lies not so much in the quantity of our effort as in its sincerity. Sincerity comes from putting ourselves forth wholeheartedly while also acknowledging the truth of what we can and can't do. Anything else is a form of pride. We can puff ourselves up about how hard we are working or we can indulge pride's negative side by tearing ourselves down about not doing enough. Zen students sometimes get stuck feeling they're "bad" Zen students if they don't meditate "enough."

One time a student at Berkeley Zen Center said to our teacher, "Bodhidharma (who brought Zen to China from India) showed his sincerity by sitting day and night for seven years, I come to the Zendo when I can, but I'm always forgetting to stay mindful, and I often get so busy I just can't get here. I think I'm a pretty bad Zen student. But what makes a good Zen student?"

Our teacher replied, "If at the beginning of the year you say 'OK, this year, I'm going to sit for forty-five minutes every day at five AM,' and then for three-hundred sixty-four days you sit for forty-five minutes at five AM, but on the last day of the year you get tired and get up after sitting for only forty-four minutes—then you're a bad Zen student.

"However, if at the beginning of the year you say 'OK, this year I'm busy, but sometime during the year I'm going to sit zazen one time for five minutes,' and then you don't meditate all year, but sometime on the three-hundred sixty-fifth day of the year you sit down and do zazen for five minutes—then you're a good Zen student."

Each of us tends to lean a little off-center, toward effort or ease, depending on our psychological and physical conditioning, I tend to tilt toward the side of pushing too much: When I'm running, I often go just a little faster than is wise; when I'm screwing two pieces of wood together, I sometimes tend to turn the screw too tight. My zazen and psychotherapy sometimes push for a bit too much too soon. Some of my friends have the opposite problem: They may not run fast enough to obtain a good conditioning effect, or they may leave the screw unturned that last little bit so that it wiggles loose; their psychotherapy and zazen sometimes retreats from difficulties and settles for too little. The problem isn't restricted to our activities with ourselves but extends to our relationships with other people. If I'm a striver expecting too much from myself, I may find myself expecting too much from the people I love; if I'm a yielder expecting too little from myself, I may find myself not asking enough of the people I love. Either inclination can lead to subterranean, chronic feelings of resentment or resignation, anxiety, or depression. Thus if our feelings are not in alignment, it can be a signal that we need to address an imbalance in our effort.

Carl is an extremely well-meaning, conscientious man, a high-school teacher who is devoted to his students and a caring husband who loves his wife. He came to therapy because he had very high expectations for himself on which he didn't follow through, and because he found himself frequently having outbursts of temper with his students and his wife.

No matter how much Carl reminded himself of how he valued his students and wife, when they did something that frustrated or displeased him he would explode in angry outbursts of angry fault-finding. Generally Carl became angry when he felt that he was putting forth effort in the relationship while the other person was not reciprocating. Carl had a good deal of insight; he knew his biting censures were in large part projections of the intense self-criticism and perfectionism he struggled with himself. But he was unable to catch himself in time. He tried to suppress and avoid his angry outbursts but continued to have unexpected, uncontrolled eruption of choler.

Carl came to the stress-management group that I run and practiced the meditation and breathing exercises conscientiously. Too conscientiously: He practiced the relaxation with the same obsessive perfectionism he brought to the rest of his life. He would analyze how well he was doing the meditation and how much he was relaxing, and then criticize himself for not doing it well enough. He would go for long stretches working very hard at it, then become frustrated and avoid doing the exercises. Carl kept trying to figure out analytically what he "should" be doing.

By the end of the seven stress-management class sessions Carl had learned some techniques that helped him interrupt the cycle of his anger and frustration a little sooner. But he still felt dissatisfied with his life, his job, students, wife, and most of all himself. He continued to strive to push himself to do better. But now there was a little something different in his striving: Some gleam of bemusement or puzzlement peeked through as Carl began to realize he was working hard at something that couldn't be accomplished by working hard.

Still, he continued working hard, I saw him intermittently for several months. There were some changes in the circumstances of his life that made things a little easier, but nothing basic changed. Then a good amount of time went by and I didn't see him until he came in to my office a year or so later.

Carl walked into the office and sat down with none of the body tension that had previously held him in his grip. His face had a joyous smile instead of the sardonic grin he used to wear. He told me that he just wanted to come in to tell me how well things were going: He was experiencing the world in a whole new way. He felt much more relaxed, more accepting of his spouse, and able to appreciate his life. He had learned how to leave the disappointments of the past behind; he had become more creative, had taken out several patents, and had started marketing some products he'd invented. He was doing things he'd previously only obsessed about, but he wasn't feeling compulsively driven.

Carl told me that a few months ago, something had shifted. He had continued his meditation and breathing exercises, but basically, he just gave up trying to do them "right." He became aware he had been working at relaxing as if it were something outside him he had to wrestle with; finally Carl realized *he* couldn't do *it*, he had to just let go, find his balance, and let himself open up to something. Now he had found the knack and was experiencing a much greater sense of freedom and happiness.

I asked Carl how he had done this. He initially had troubles putting it into speech but finally expressed himself through the following words, which I took down almost verbatim during the session (the italics are my emphasis):

> I feel much more creative and am accomplishing much more since I stopped worrying so much. Worrying takes time and energy. It's amazing how much there is to balance in life. *When we try to balance, try to figure out how to balance, then it doesn't work.* You have to learn to let your subconscious intelligence do it, but we don't always let our subconscious intelligence do its job.
>
> I can't always embody these insights, but at least I can observe myself when I'm not. I've found there's some kind of reality which, even if I'm not sure if I believe in it, it doesn't seem to matter much whether I believe in it or not, whether I understand it or not. It doesn't seem to have much to do with what I want things to be like.
>
> I sometimes still have waves of anger but I have a greater perspective which seems to come from observing myself; from respecting my feelings rather than struggling with them. Even though I know the reality of my feelings are just within me, I can respect the feeling, and if I'm angry somehow it leads me to open myself up to the other person's view and still express my love.
>
> I used to be controlled by my feelings from the past or my ideas of how I should be in the future. Sometimes tried to deal with feelings and ideas I didn't like by shutting them away. But *controlling it doesn't work.* It's more like you have to be open to

> the past and to the present, but not by grabbing on to them; *it's*
> *more like... you open the doors to both at once and let go of both*
> *simultaneously."*
>
> Sometimes I find myself in a position where I can't open
> the doors of the present. Sometimes I can't let go of the emo-
> tions and expectations which catch me and make it seem only
> the feelings count. But I can accept that at that time, that's the
> door which is open. So instead of *feeling like I have to control*
> *this feeling, overcome this feeling, I just accept this as the way*
> *it is. It's like unraveling a knot: you can't undo it by pulling on*
> *it tighter.*

When we ease up on constricted personal control and face whatever door is open, we are in the balanced center: Our knot unravels and we find there was nothing at the core constricting us except the way we twined the knot around itself. To find our balance, we cannot hold on too tight to our pride: We need to rediscover that our center of gravity depends not just on us but on the mass of the earth beneath us.

GREED, PRIDE, AND POSSESSIONS

When we discover ourselves where we are, it is difficult to find our balance if we are carrying lots of extraneous objects in our pockets. So the Metta Sutta suggests that if we want to live happily we should avoid taking on the burden of riches or great possessions. This flies in the face of the predominant values of our culture, in which riches are valued highly and our net worth is calculated according to the number of things we own. Our society prizes material wealth. There is a countercurrent in our culture; it points to the poverty in much of the world and urges us to cut back on our consumption so others can have more. In a world filled with mass starvations in the midst of plenty, this countercurrent is laudable and necessary; however, it can go astray if it assumes that providing more material possessions will in itself lead to happiness. Helping Third World economies expand so that more people can enjoy automobiles and central heating has not proved, by itself, to be a viable venue to world peace.

The Metta Sutta suggests something more radical. It advises that we should not only not desire great possessions for ourselves but should not even desire them for others. It suggests that great possessions do not lead to great happiness, that they can even pose an obstacle: If we try to find happiness in what we possess, we will be unhappy if we no longer possess it. If we try to find happiness in pursuing what we do not possess, we run the risk of always seeking, never feeling satisfied. So neither having possessions nor seeking after them can provide true happiness.

The Metta Sutta doesn't say there is anything wrong with possessions per se. We live in a material world; we need food, clothing, shelter. Riches and great possessions, however, go beyond satisfying our needs and can easily form a focus point for desire: Once we start wanting things, our lives can be found wanting. If we become *attached* to having possessions, we can get trapped by them, "submerged by the things of the world." If we grasp something too firmly, it can be hard to let go of, and it starts holding on to us. We can become possessed by our possessions.

A great possession is not one that costs a lot of money: A great possession is any possession that a person greatly desires to possess–that is, any possession approached with greed. Greed is, along with hate and delusion, one of the three main "poisons" Buddhism identifies. Buddhism doesn't take a moralistic view towards greed, suggesting that we are "bad" people if we are greedy. We all are greedy sometimes. The problem with greed is the practical problem it poses: When we are greedy, no matter how much we have, it never feels like enough. We cannot be easily contented and joyous if we are always yearning for more.

A focus on obtaining possessions orients us to what we will have in the future, rather than how we are living in the present; an emphasis on possessions promotes the myth that it is what we *acquire* that will improve our lives. Life then becomes a game of gain and loss, a "possession obsession" in which we will always be worrying about losing what we have, or lusting over what we don't have. If we treat happiness as if it were a possession, we will always feel unfulfilled. We can only realize happiness not by *what we have* but by *how we live* with what we have.

This was clear during the era of the Great Depression, a time of greater economic difficulty than now but not necessarily greater unhappiness. When I work with older adults in group psychotherapy, I often hear them refer wistfully to the time when everyone was poorer but helped each other out; they compare it favorably with the economic wealth but social isolation they currently experience. The popular songs of the era may have been attempting to console people who were out of work or without money, but their lyrics also contained the kind of truth expressed by Gershwin's protagonist, Porgy, who sang of having "plenty of nothin':"[10]

> De folks wid plenty o' plenty,
> Got a lock on de door,
> 'Fraid somebody's a goin' to rob 'em
> while dey's out amakin' more.
> What for?
>
> I got no lock on de door,
> (dat's no way to be.)
> Dey kin steal de rug from de floor,
> Dat's okeh wid me,
> 'Cause de things dat I prize,
> Like de stars in de skies,
> all are free.

The Metta Sutta suggests we can more easily find happiness in this kind of freedom than in riches, which inherently stimulate a craving for more. The capitalist economic system has been a tremendously successful vehicle for producing possessions and creating wealth, but it does not lead to a balanced state of contentment; capitalism inherently demands not just a sufficiency of material worth but a constantly *growing* accumulation of assets. Companies that return a steady rate of profit do poorly on the stock exchange; to attract investors, they must show *increasing* profits from quarter to quarter. The national economy must not aim just for reaching a healthy equilibrium but must constantly expand and show some rate of growth. The basic driving force of capitalism is that "more is better," and this eventually spreads from material things to affect an everexpanding field of influence in our lives.

Under this scenario, if a little bit of pleasure is good, more pleasure must be better. If a successful (i.e., profit-making) movie has thrilling special effects or titillating levels of violence or sex, the sequels and imitators that follow must have even more spectacular special effects, violence, and sex. If one car is good, two cars are better. Even the realm of psychology is affected. At a meeting of the American Psychological Association at which I was presenting a talk on brief psychotherapy, I was bemused to discover that tapes of the convention sessions were being advertised with the motto, "More Is Better."

In an atmosphere in which more is better even in the psychological realm, people's sense of who they are tends to get confused with what they have. The car that I own becomes an expression of whether I am a swinging bachelor or a family man; its expense becomes an emblem of whether I am successful or just getting by. We may tell ourselves we don't believe that our self-worth is measured by our possessions, but the intermingling of ownership and self-identity can be subtle:

A forty-year-old client came to therapy for treatment of depression; he was agitated, couldn't concentrate or perform his usual work, and had withdrawn from his wife and small child. He told me the precipitant was that someone had stolen his 4×4 truck, which meant "everything in the world" to him. He was embarrassed to be so depressed by this, because he had a good job, a home, a loving wife, and child. But the theft of his truck had devastated him; that truck had been his symbol to himself that he was OK and had triumphed over the adverse circumstances of his life.

It turned out he had grown up poor with a violent stepfather, a "controlling bastard, a mean drunk." His stepfather had beaten him every day, always telling him he'd amount to nothing. His stepfather had never shown him any kindness, affection or praise. He only remembered getting one gift from his stepfather: When he had turned 13 his stepfather had given him a wristwatch. My client remembered how thrilled he had been not just at the watch, but at actually receiving a gift from his stepfather. But then the stepfather said: "I'm giving this to you not because you deserve it, but because now that I know you have a watch, if you're ever one minute late for anything I tell you to do, I'll beat the shit out of you."

My client ran away from home in his early teens. He spent time on the streets and became heavily addicted to drugs and alcohol. He supported himself through prostituting himself. But in his early twenties he decided he wasn't going to "piss his life away." On his own, cold turkey, he stopped using drugs and alcohol. He found himself a low-paying job. He attended night school and got his GED. He got a better-paying job, which he'd held now for 15 years, gradually working his way up to a position of responsibility. He became involved with a woman and had maintained a monogamous relationship with her for 10 years. He was proud to be raising a little boy himself, enjoyed being a good father to him. During all this time he saved his money, lived a respectable life, and never indulged himself. But he had never really thought he had "made it" until he bought his truck.

The truck was his pride and joy. Since getting married, this was the one thing he had gotten just for himself. He could afford it and enjoyed it. He described the truck in loving detail: its detailing, its color, its power. He worked on the truck several hours every weekend, polishing it lovingly, souping up its engine, enhancing its styling. The truck symbolized to him that he was defying his stepfather's predictions: that he had made something of himself that his stepfather couldn't take away.

When the truck was stolen, he went "all to pieces." He felt as if a part of his self had been amputated, that he was lost and everything he had worked for was gone, that his stepfather had been right. Although everyone told him the theft was no big deal, they didn't understand. Sure, he could afford another truck. The insurance would even cover most of it. But it wasn't the same. You couldn't count on anything. He felt as if all his work had been in vain, because someone had been able to take something precious away from him, just as his stepfather had. He felt violated and unable to protect himself.

He experienced a certain amount of relief just telling his story, but this was not a man who put much store in words. He had to do something. So after empathizing with him I said: "I think you're feeling so badly not just because you've lost a truck, but because it feels like it somehow confirms your stepfather's messages to you, I think you're right when you say that just buying another truck won't do the trick. You have to do something that proves to yourself that your stepfather was wrong, and that reminds you he no longer has control over you." I suggested the following ritual: to buy himself a nice new watch, set it to the correct time, but then, thirteen days later, plan to arrive home four minutes late. To remind him of the love he had in his life, when he came home that day he might tell his wife he was upset and ask her to comfort him. After he felt better, he could go out for a walk with his little boy accompanying him on his tricycle. Subsequently I suggested he choose a number of opportunities at which he could consult his watch and purposefully arrive a few minutes late to various obligations.

He readily accepted the rationale that he needed to remind himself of what he now had in his life, and that he was in charge of his coming and going. I suggested that after he had verified this to his satisfaction, he might drive around scanning the streets for a thirteen-year-old boy who looked like he was struggling with poverty or unhappiness; then he could take off his watch and give it to that boy with some words of kindness and encouragement.

Later, the client told me that he had gotten over his depression rather quickly. He also said that while the first part of the ritual had helped mobilize him, he had been touched by the response of the boy he gave his watch to and, in fact, had started doing some volunteer work as a Big Brother.

As the story of this client indicates, possessions are not just physical objects but also psychological ones. This being the case, when we become overly preoccupied with possessions we begin to treat other aspects of our life as if they were physical objects. We begin to think that we can acquire not just material wealth but psychological health: We begin thinking that if we buy the right house, own the right truck, marry the right person, go to the right therapy, or read the right self-help book, we can obtain the objects, traits or relationships we need to be happy. Even "self-actualization" can become subject to greed.

We have a tendency to treat even our traits as if they were objects that belong to us: We say "I *have*" a talent for singing, or playing football, or perhaps doing therapy. We also have a tendency to treat the people in our lives as if they somehow were objects we own: We say "I *have*" a son, or a parent, or a wife. Of course these can just be figures of speech, but if we treat our traits, our friends and lovers, or our good fortune as prized possessions, trophies we have bagged on our life safari, we can become puffed up and consumed by pride. If I feel I am the owner of my qualities, then I may pride myself on my strength, intelligence, or wisdom. If I view my intimates as if they belonged to me, then I may feel that what they do reflects on me: I may pride myself on my daughter's athletic accomplishments, my son's poetry, my spouse's beauty, or my father's job.

If we treat even our personal traits and our relationships with people as if they were prized possessions, we may feel proud about what we have accumulated through our efforts. The flip side of pride in ownership, however, is that it magnifies any shortcomings or losses when they occur and can quickly give way to shame or grief. If I take pride in the things I own, in the personal qualities I "own up to" and the people who are "mine," by treating them as objects I ensure that they will slip through my fingers.

All things decay and change. If I pride myself on the objects I have so that the latest model computer is an emblem of my efficiency, I may have problems when my computer quickly is surpassed by one with a more powerful chip. If my sense of self is tied up in the people I consider "mine," emblems of my self, I will have difficulties as they, I, and the world change. If I try to hold on to my lover as an emblem of my being youthful and adventurous, I may have problems dealing with the transition when my lover becomes a spouse and companion and someone must do the dishes and balance the checkbook. If I try to hold onto my children as admirers of my idealized self, I will become upset when they grow up, look at me, and see my human flaws.

If the traits I consider "mine" desert me, I may suffer if I am holding on to a cherished image of my self, wishing to be something I no longer am. If I try to hold onto my talent for the piano, or my knack for doing math, or even my ability to be compassionate and caring, I will become upset on those days when my fingers hit the wrong keys, or a problem stumps me, or I fail to come through for a deserving friend. If I try to hold onto my body and take pride in my strength or my health, I will become upset when illness and old age make their inevitable visits.

When things go wrong in our lives, one of the reasons it hurts so much is because it injures our self-centered pride. Pride involves not only the attempt to grasp onto things: It involves an insistence that things should go the way *I* want, and that if life isn't going in the particular way *I* want, something's wrong. Pride involves seeing life from a narrow, self-centered view, in which we insist life be more the way we want it. There's nothing necessarily morally bad about this; it just happens to get in the way of being happy. Looking for happiness in the way we *want* life to be gets in the way of appreciating life the way it is, whatever that may be, no matter how much it differs from our self-centered images of how it "should" be. To think that life "should" be the way we want it is an act of fundamental (if natural) hubris: the basic pride that comes of being a self-centered individual.

Therapists and Zen students have numerous ways in which we can get caught in self-centered pride. As Zen students, we may secretly boast to ourselves of the number of koans we've "solved," feel vain about our humility, or pride our selves on our selflessness. As therapists, we may be tempted to hold onto certain therapeutic techniques we are proud at having mastered. As therapists we also can be tempted to become attached to an image of ourselves as knowledgeable or wise, because clients, the popular press, and to some extent the profession itself treat therapists as if we have answers to the emotional suffering we encounter in life.

Being excessively proud leads to arrogance and unhappiness. Avoiding pride, however, need not mean we should denigrate our skills and deny whatever wisdom we have. Within the psychotherapeutic profession, there is a debate on this subject that tends to oscillate between two poles: on the one hand, those who feel therapists should be wise experts in emotional and interpersonal functioning, instructing clients in psychological techniques and providing advice with problems of living; on the other hand, those who feel that for a genuine existential encounter the therapist must eschew any pretense of special knowledge and function as a nondirective listener and facilitator of the client's own growth process.

The Metta Sutta suggests a middle way, saying we should neither eschew expertise nor be caught by it: We must "be wise but not puffed up." If we have knowledge to share, share it; at the same time, we must be aware of the vast expanse of experience that we cannot have knowledge of. As Zen students, we recognize that there are always people less experienced and other people more experienced in practice than we are. We need to teach and learn, learn and teach. As therapists, we can recognize that each of our clients has a life that can never be grasped or encapsulated; we can offer clients our insights into their lives, so long as we recognize our expertise is not privileged. Each client needs to find his or her own wisdom, which is of equal value to any wisdom we can offer and perhaps, being closer to home, more useful.

It is easier to avoid getting puffed up by pride if we can realize that none of our traits or wisdom belong to us: They're "on loan," so to speak, from the complex interactive web of our being with all other beings in the world. Any wisdom we have is a shared resource that draws on all we have read, all our teachers have conveyed to us, all our students have taught us. Our kindness is a shared resource that we owe to all the kindnesses we have ever experienced. We cannot even own our material objects in isolation, much less personal traits or people: The car we "own" would be useless without the labor of the men and women who have built the roads; we could not power our cars without the past lives of the animals that have transmogrified over millennia into gasoline and provide us with fuel. Yet we usually don't see this connectedness; we see ourselves as separate individuals.

Most psychotherapy centers on individuals. This can give rise to a false hope that we can create our own happiness, while paradoxically increasing our sense of isolation from others. This idea that we can take care of ourselves by ourselves is itself a kind of false pride that fails to see our essential connectedness. The problem with this kind of self-centered view is that it suggests we are in a kind of zero-sum game in which we have a choice between taking care of ourselves first and others later, or others first and ourselves later.

In Buddhism, however, we see self and other arising together, simultaneously. In fact Buddhism sees the root cause of suffering arising from the illusion that our selves exist as independent entities separate from the flow of all life. We cannot grow in isolation, and taking care of others is intertwined with taking care of ourselves. So in contrast to psychotherapy's centering on the individual, Buddhists begin their commitment to practice by taking a vow to save *all* beings from suffering and confusion; in Mahayana Buddhism, one puts off enjoying the complete fruits of personal enlightenment until all beings have realized liberation. This is not a martyred self-sacrifice; it is based on an acknowledgment that I cannot be fully happy while others are still suffering, simply because fundamentally I do not exist as a separate being walled off from others.

Each of us is interdependent with all life; Buddhism is about realizing that self which is always co-arising with all of life and death, inseparable from all the living beings and things self touches and is touched by. When we get "submerged by the things of the world," greed and pride obscure this self; greed confines and disconnects self from the very source of its true being. In fear of "not getting ours" or in pride in what we have, we grab onto things and try to store them in private bank vaults to hoard what we have managed to accumulate. Then we can start feeling vain about what we have managed to save, or shamed if we go bankrupt.

Feeling good about ourselves or bad about ourselves, however, is not the essence of happiness or unhappiness. Happiness has more to do with feeling whole, with feeling connected to our lives. Pride cuts us off from this connectedness by both exaggerating our virtues and magnifying our shortcomings. In doing so, it can lead to a sense of dissatisfaction that makes us envious of others' good fortune and intolerant of others' weaknesses. When our car breaks down, when our wisdom fails, when our colleague gets a bonus and we do not, when our loved ones don't give us what we feel we deserve, when someone takes away something we think of as "ours," it's easy to get angry. Anger is a close relative of pride in the obstacles it poses to fostering an environment in which we obtain peace and enjoy happiness with all beings.

ANGER

The Metta Sutta advises us that we should not wish harm to others. This moral dictum may seem so obvious it needs no comment. But if we approach the Metta Sutta as a koan rather than as a series of moralistic injunctions, we must probe deeper to find the basis for our own relationship with anger. Why should anger or hatred be obstacles to happiness? When clients tell us about a sadistic boss, a betraying spouse, or an uncaring parent, why shouldn't they be angry at the suffering they've apparently incurred at the hands of their tormentors? We talk about "healthy anger": Sometimes anger feels good, doesn't it? My enemies hate me and wish me harm: Wouldn't I be happier if I could eliminate the people who cause me problems? Why shouldn't I rejoice if my enemy suffers a setback? At the very minimum, doesn't it make sense for me to at least hate hatred?

Psychotherapy doesn't really offer an answer to this. Psychotherapy can be useful for discovering the roots of anger in our pasts and the ways we stoke our anger in the present; it can also provide some tools for coping with the internal monologues and affective rehashings that maintain the anger. However, psychotherapy does not itself offer a reason to let go of hatred. In the not-too-distant past, psychotherapists often treated anger as an unavoidable drive and sometimes encouraged clients to express anger so they wouldn't "turn it inward." Eventually, as the cognitive and interpersonal contributions to anger became apparent, psychotherapists began to help clients examine the thoughts and beliefs that led them to feel angry and could offer them a choice: Now clients often are encouraged to decide whether it is in their practical best interest to get angry. In my experience, however, if offered this choice many clients say they realize it's not in their pragmatic self-interest to get angry at their spouse, their boss, or their parent but complain that they "can't help themselves." Bankei, a seventeenth-century Zen Master, had an interesting response to this:[11]

> A monk said to Bankei: "I was born with a short temper. It's always flaring up.., I know I should do something about it, but as I was born with a bad temper, I'm unable to rid myself of it no matter how hard I try. Is there anything I can do to correct it?"
>
> Bankei: "That's an interesting inheritance you have. Is your temper here now? Bring it out here. I'll cure it for you."
>
> Monk: "I'm not angry now. My temper comes on unexpectedly, when something provokes me."
>
> Bankei: "You weren't born with it then. You create it yourself, when some pretext or other happens to appear. Where would your temper be at such times if you didn't cause it? You work yourself into a temper because of your partiality for yourself...
>
> "When you don't produce your temper, where is it? As long as you don't produce it, it doesn't exist. That's what everyone fails to realize. There they are, creating from their own selfish desires and distorted mental habits something that isn't inherent, but thinking it is...
>
> "You certainly must cherish being upset, for you to transform your mind into an angry state just so you can be upset...

"You create your outbursts of temper when the organs of your senses are stimulated by some external condition and incite you to oppose other people because you desire to assert your own preciously held ideas. When you have no selfish attachment to your own desires, there is no problem...

"All your parents gave you when you were born was an open mind. Nothing else. What have you done with it? From the time you were a tiny baby you've watched and listened to people losing their tempers around you. You've been schooled in this, until you too have become habituated to irascibility. So now you indulge in frequent fits of anger. But it's foolish to think that's inherent. Right now, if you realize you've been mistaken and don't allow your temper to arise any more, you'll have no temper to worry about. Instead of trying to correct it, don't produce it in the first place. That's the quickest way, don't you agree? Trying to do something about it after it occurs is very troublesome and futile besides. Don't get angry to begin with, then there's no need to cure anything. There's nothing left to cure."

Bankei makes it sound simple. The fact is, however, that we are partial to ourselves; we do get selfishly attached to our desires and "preciously held ideas." Many of us have not only been "habituated to irascibility" by watching and listening to people around us losing their tempers but also schooled in anger directly through its pernicious touch.

Anger breeds anger; if we experience violence it leaves us with a residue, a "hungry ghost" that only gets stronger if we give in to it, but which cannot be suppressed, exterminated, or expelled. As therapists we see this all the time. The victim of violence is troubled by violent fantasies; people who were abused as children are at risk for abusing their children or spouses, even if they have a sincere intention to banish violence from their lives. Sometimes the blame for anger gets projected outward (if the aggressor blames the victim for "provoking" him), sometimes it comes home to roost in the form of self-blame and self-loathing. Either way, it can be difficult to deal with.

If we wish to come to terms with anger and deprive it of undue influence over us, we need to first acknowledge its presence in our lives. We are always living with hatred and anger because we all do things that are mean, which the wise in us reproves. Few of us live our lives without getting at least occasionally irritable and snapping at the ones we love. We usually regret this later and feel badly about our actions; because we don't enjoy feeling guilty, we then either convince ourselves our anger was justified or tell ourselves we won't do it again, or we mortify ourselves or try to suppress our anger. None of these strategies, however, seems sufficient to consistently banish anger and prevent us from ever hurting others. Anger keeps springing up.

Even within the controlled realm of psychotherapeutic sessions in which we are being paid to treat clients with kindness and compassion, negative feelings often grip us. Every therapist has had the experience of starting a session with a sincere intention to cherish, value, and accept his client only to find himself disliking or even becoming angry at the client as the session progresses. To distance ourselves from these feelings we disown them as "not really me" and assume a "professional" attitude; we tell ourselves that, although the client is treating us badly and we feel angry, the client can't really help him- or herself and is more to be pitied than censured, and our anger represents clinical countertransference rather than personal feelings. This lets us view our hostility as if it were not quite real. Unfortunately, on our coffee break or when we talk to other therapists, the reality of our hostility often breaks through: We indulge our irritation or resentment by mildly disparaging our clients, saying,"Boy, is she borderline!" and shaking our heads.

I was seeing a client at the request of his internist. This client had multiple somatic complaints that none of his doctors had been able to pin down to a clear physical cause. He kept calling his doctors and berating them for not treating him better, filing formal complaints about them, and haranguing them when he did meet with them.

When I saw him he told me he had been in extensive long-term psychotherapy and it hadn't helped. Rather arrogantly, he told me he knew I was just seeing him as a token gesture because of his physician's request. He expanded on his miseries: His work was unsatisfying, his relationships were unsatisfying, even his hobbies were unsatisfying. Nobody appreciated what he was going through and everybody let him down. Even if things looked good for a while, they were bound to turn sour quickly.

It took some time, but by acknowledging his complaints with a combination of empathy, confrontation, and plain honest talk—for example, acknowledging that there'd be a good chance this therapy would disappoint him as well, and I hoped he'd tell me when it happened—we were able to establish a tentative working alliance. We met every few weeks (my usual custom) for a while, but the client felt he wasn't getting enough. At his request, we switched to weekly visits. But fate intervened: The next session I was caught in traffic and arrived five minutes late. The following session I was caught up in an emergency requiring me to hospitalize another client, and my client had to wait twenty minutes.

When I finally finished with the emergency and met with him, he was livid, I apologized for the inconvenience and offered to meet with him for a full session by either extending the end of the current session twenty minutes or by seeing him for an uninterrupted session later that same day: Neither was acceptable to my client, even though he told me he had nothing else scheduled, I offered to refund his money for the session: He haughtily replied that money was not the issue and refused to accept the refund. I offered to reschedule the appointment for the next day, during my lunch hour; he refused, saying, "Look, it's obvious you just don't care about me. Like all the others, you're just here to get a paycheck. Just let me see a psychiatrist and get some medicine—although he probably won't be any good either."

I tried to work with him a bit further. I asked how my willingness to meet with him the next day, foregoing my lunch hour, indicated I didn't care for him. He shrugged this off. I tried to empathize and reflect his feeling of always getting the run-around. He simply sneered at this. Finally I told him I felt a bit sad: It seemed to me that if he constantly felt nobody valued him or cared for him, even if (as it seemed to me) people tried to extend themselves to him, the source of his feelings must lie at least in part in some difficulties he had valuing and caring for himself.

This was the final straw for him. He told me coldly that he felt very good about himself, thank you, and his problem was the way people like me treated him. He stood up to leave: I told him I wished him well, got up, and extended my hand to him, but he refused to take my hand.

After he left I consciously worked at cultivating compassion for him, and in fact did feel sad for him. But I also found myself feeling quite angry. How dare he reject my best efforts and spurn the offer of my hand! A little while later I was complaining about him to a colleague. Then I had a memory of a Marx Brothers film I had seen: In the movie *Duck Soup,* Groucho is the head of a mythical country that is preparing for war with its enemy. Groucho gives in to his patron's request to go speak with the head of the other country and try to talk things over to avert war. As he walks along his way to meet with the other country's representative, Groucho soliloquizes: "I'll go over there and extend the warm hand of friendship. How nice! We'll shake hands and everything will be all right. We'll be peacemakers! Love and friendship will triumph!

"Of course," Groucho continues to muse aloud, "I could go over there and extend the warm hand of friendship, and he might not want to meet me halfway. In fact, he might not want to meet me at all. In fact, I might extend the warm hand of friendship, and what if he refuses to shake hands with me?

"How dare he refuse to shake hands with me? Who does he think he is? Nobody gets away with refusing to shake my hand! Why, he might not only refuse to shake my hand, but slap me in the face! What an insult! I won't stand for it!"

Groucho by this time has reached the residence he'd been making for. He knocks on the door: The representative of the other country opens the door, puts his head out with a quizzical expression on his face and says, "Yes?"

Groucho immediately slaps him in the face and says: "Refuse to shake my hand, will you? Think you can slap me, do you?"

"This means war!"

The fact is that sometimes we reach into ourselves for compassion and offer our hand to a client, then get mad if the client slaps us or rejects our good intentions. We're especially vulnerable to this if as we offer ourselves to a client we are secretly expecting something from them in return: some deepening of affective experiencing, or some symptomatic improvement, perhaps even a bit of appreciation. Our own self-esteem sometimes gets caught up with how effective we feel we are as clinicians; if we are overly attached to helping a client, then it's easy to get upset if things don't turn out the way we wanted, however well-meaning we may have been.

Of course, this doesn't happen just with clients. Whenever we put ourselves out for a friend, a family member, an employer, we can become angry if they appear ungrateful for our effort. As soon as we expect something in return, however—even if what we expect seems to be something good for the other person—we are doing something mean, in the sense that we are not truly being generous: We are doing good to others at least in part to bolster our own sense of feeling good about ourselves.

When we are attached to our own benefit it will be easy to get angry if we feel thwarted or injured: Self-centered entitlement is the breeding ground for animosity. If we feel we lack something that someone else possesses, we can easily feel that they are unfairly depriving us of our just dues and getting in the way of our happiness: They have more than we do (and more is better, isn't it?). Perhaps we tell ourselves the other person is stealing something that rightfully belongs to us; perhaps we convince ourselves they are selfishly hoarding what they have and refusing to share with us. We convince ourselves that we have a need for and therefore a right to their territory, so we justify invading or attacking them in order to obtain necessary "living room" for ourselves. Sometimes it does not even matter whether the other person has what we want. If we feel entitled to something, we can hate the other person for failing to be a good provider.

We do not even need to have a specific person to be angry at: We can be angry at the whole world for not being the way we want it to be and not giving us what we feel we need. As Zen students we can practice while holding on to the idea that if we are a good boy or girl, eventually we will be rewarded with the "candy" of enlightenment; when the desired "candy" is not forthcoming, we may get mad at our teacher and indignant about the way Buddhism has "lied" to us. Similar dynamics can fuel psychotherapy or any relationship in which we are trying to gain something for ourselves; if we are disappointed or our desires are frustrated we can become furious at our "betrayer" whether a therapist, client, or family member, or the universe in general. We can even get mad at our selves for letting us down. This is a common psychological sequence: blame others; then when that doesn't work, blame the world; then when that doesn't work, blame yourself.

Anyone who examines him- or herself deeply, whether through psychotherapy, meditation, or some other means, will at some point encounter personal quirks he or she does not like. Attempting to eradicate them is simply another form of intolerance and hatred, a kind of self-torture. We shake our heads when we see "borderline" clients who burn themselves with cigarettes or scratch themselves with knives: It is not always easy to see ourselves doing the same thing when we berate ourselves for not meditating "well," kick ourselves for failing an examination, plunge ourselves into depression for alienating a loved one, or lash ourselves with guilt when we make a mistake with a client.

Our inability to accept ourselves fuels our temptation to judge, reject, and "despise" others. Projecting the bad traits onto others is a way we try, unsuccessfully, to escape from the cycle of alternately rejecting and indulging negative parts of ourselves. We try to resolve self-loathing through loathing others and fight anger and rejection with anger and rejection that eventually can escalate into intense hatred.

There are various kinds of hatred. There is the consuming hatred that comes from burning hunger, from feeling unnourished in a way that no feeding will ever satisfy. There is the cold, withholding hatred that comes from feeling controlled and constricted; prohibited from expressing our natural impulses, we hate the restrictions that confine us or that demand we express ourselves only in accord with what someone else allows or demands. There is the penetrating hatred that comes from feeling belittled, defeated, or powerless to be treated as an equal.

All types of hatred involve a sense that our self (or something seen as belonging to our self or as an extension of our self) is endangered or hurt. Whether the wound is due to frustration, constriction, defeat, or deprecation, when we hate we react to some threat or insult to what we consider our essential self. Anger provides a kind of feeding frenzy that seeks to fill us, shore us up against injury and emptiness, galvanize us for battle, and give us the illusion that we are self-contained and strong. Together with their close ally fear, anger and hatred help motivate us to erect defenses; they provide energy for aggressive campaigns to cleanse the field of enemies. Because hatred functions as an attempt at self-protection and self-ownership, it always sets up a boundary between our self and others. Yet it is the very act of setting up those rigid boundaries that enhances our sense of exclusion, insecurity, and dissatisfaction.

If we set up rigid boundaries around our self, we treat our needs and happiness as separate from the happiness of others. The fundamental roots of hatred, however, can be found in this very alienation of our self from our world; if we think that what is in our self-interest is not connected to the interest of others, we lose sight of how we are all in this together. Our idea of who we are and how we exist shrinks down to a very small, circumscribed circle with ego at its center, desire as its radius, and fear as its circumference.

Self-centeredness, however, is self-deceit. If we don't see the link between "you," "me," and "the world" then we start treating our self not as a partner in a dance but as a thing that needs protection from hostile forces "out there." But the limited self that hatred pretends to protect cannot be a very satisfying self for its "owner." A self that is a thing is easily damaged or injured; a self that is a thing feels like an inert object that, lacking life, misses the ability of all living beings to heal their wounds naturally. Hatred is a sure sign that a thing-self already is feeling hurt or vulnerable: Isolated from others and the world around it, feeling itself lacking and incomplete, this self can easily sink into self-loathing. At that point we not only extend anger and blame to the people around us who we think frustrate us, we make ourselves depressed by applying blame and anger to ourselves and attacking our own flaws and shortcomings mercilessly.

Our lack of self-acceptance leads us to feel we cannot trust ourselves, that we must guard ourselves against ourselves. When we struggle with ourselves fearing and mistrusting our own base impulses—what Buddhism sometimes depicts as "hungry ghosts"—we pay a price in self-alienation. Wrestling with ourselves, we alternately reject and indulge the parts of ourselves we despise: We push them away, blame ourselves, and then, weakened by our guilt and self-recrimination, open the door for our bad habits to return. When our negative impulses overwhelm us with their return, because we are tired of fighting we sometimes "give them their due:" We surrender to them and act them out; then we blame ourselves for doing this, and the cycle continues.

Buddhism's suggestion for escaping from this cycle is to follow the middle way when our "hungry ghosts" knock on our door: Invite them in, but don't feed them. In other words, we must acknowledge and accept our demons without indulging them. Therapists know that if we wish to exorcise our hungry ghosts or even transform them into helpful allies, we must start by accepting them as part of ourselves. This is not always easy.

Clients often say they wish to "have more self-esteem"; they usually mean they want to accept their "good points" and rid themselves of their "bad points." They may be dismayed if we suggest that anyone can accept their good points: The real challenge for all of us is to learn how to gently tolerate ourselves when we fall short of what we want to be. To develop tolerance and compassion for ourselves, we must cultivate compassion for others. To develop tolerance and compassion for others, we must develop tolerance and compassion for ourselves. Anger is often the byproduct of our difficulties doing do this.

Yet anger is not necessarily a bad thing; it has its redeeming qualities and can be a source of considerable potential.

Stan was a depressed middle-aged man who stated clearly that he was angry at himself for letting himself be taken advantage of. He had worked many years as an engineer for a company and had invented a number of useful things. Each of his inventions, however, had been appropriated by the company, and usually his boss had taken credit for the innovation. Rather than praise or reward him, the boss apparently felt a certain jealous rivalry and went out of his way to denigrate and demean Stan. He was passed over for promotions and made the butt of jokes at company meetings. He wanted to quit and start his own business but never felt confident enough about his own abilities to do so. He also felt a general lack of energy; he would come home from work too drained to work on any of his own projects. By the time he saw me he thought he was too old to leave the company and felt mired in self-disgust and despair.

Despite our being able to develop a sense of intimacy in the therapeutic relationship, psychotherapy didn't seem to be helping Stan get out of his depression. Eventually Stan dropped out of therapy, and I didn't see him for a while. Several years later, however, Stan contacted me because he was having some family difficulties.

When I saw him, he was frustrated at his marital difficulties but remarkably free of depression. I asked him what was going on at the job, and he told me he wasn't working there any more but had started his own business. I was pleased but somewhat surprised and asked him how he had done that.

"Well," Stan said, "after a while my boss's son started to throw his weight around, and he treated me like shit. There was incident after incident, and I just kept getting more mad and more depressed.

"Then one day, after another humiliating incident, I really could feel myself getting angry. And I could visualize the anger building up and building up, and so I took my image of the anger and I *squeezed* it. I squeezed it and compressed it until it was a cold black thing, a lump of coal. And after that, every time something happened that made me mad, I let myself be aware of the anger and I squeezed it into another lump of coal. And then in my imagination I built a storeroom, and I started piling up the lumps of coal and saving them up."

As Stan told me this, I was concerned: This didn't sound all that healthy. But Stan continued: "And eventually, when I had enough coal stored up, I pictured myself building a steam engine. It was my 'start-your-own-business' steam engine. And I used the coal to power it. And suddenly I found I had more energy, so when I got home at night I worked on my own invention, and I finished it. And I used that steam engine to give me the energy to go out and market my invention, and I sold it to a couple of places, and that gave me the courage to quit the company.

"Now I work for myself, and my old company calls me and wants to hire me back as a consultant."

This illustrates the fact that ultimately, the problem with anger is not that it is immoral or "bad," but that it is mistaken: It seeks satisfaction in ways that hinder feeling true contentment. For anger to be helpful it needs to be, as in Stan's case, not only accepted but transformed so that it no longer is mired in despising life. Anger finds its roots in a form of self-centered preoccupation that cuts us off from connecting with the true possibilities of our lives. So the Metta Sutta steers us away from anger not in the service of an abstract morality but in the service of a practical transformation. By itself, anger simply does not lead to happiness, because when we despise any being in any state or wish harm to another, we wind up despising our current state and cause harm to ourselves.

DEALING WITH ANGER

Couples' relationships often provide an arena in which we start to approach intimacy and connectedness but get waylaid by anger arising from self-centered concerns. Sometimes the hungry ghost of anger comes from past hurts experienced in the family of origin that now haunt the present; sometime the anger arises from disappointments or betrayals experienced in the current relationship; sometimes it is a combination of the two. Regardless of its source, if members of a couple hold on to anger it can lead to escalating quarrels or frozen silences that separate people who have cared about each other. Because anger breeds anger, a major goal of couples' therapy is to shift the focus from anger to love, from resentment to compassion, and from revenge to forgiveness. This can be aided through an adaptation of a classic Buddhist Metta meditation:

I frequently run couples' therapy groups. Most of the couples I see are feeling very angry and hurt with each other. Although they frequently want to put the past behind them, they often have difficulties doing so. To help them, I invite them to perform a little ritual.

Everyone takes a sheet of paper and individually writes down the past hurts and disappointments suffered at the hands of his or her spouse and then seals the paper and writes his or her name on it. Everyone then closes his or her eyes and holds the list out at arm's length: They are instructed to keep their arms out and feel the weight of these old hurts and the associated anger; when they are ready, but not before, they can let go of them by dropping the papers. The group leader collects the lists and deposits them in a bin for safekeeping with the following agreement (discussed before starting the exercise): for the next eight weeks group members will do their best to put the negative experiences behind them. So long as they do not have the list in their possession, they agree to not refer to the items they've written down in arguments or discussions with their spouse. They also agree to try to let go of those past hurts in their private thoughts. If, however, they find they *need* those past hurts to fuel their anger (if, for example, they want to separate themselves further from their spouse), they can do so by recovering the list from the therapist, who agrees if requested to return it with no questions.

This enumeration of old hurts followed by disposing of the list physically seems to help clients relinquish some of the painful past. Clients rarely ask me to return their list of old hurts, but many come back the next week and say, "I want to let go of that old stuff, but I find I can't. It keeps coming back up, no matter how much I try to push it away."

So I usually start the second group session with a guided imagery exercise. I have people relax, get comfortable, take some deep breaths. Then I suggest people remember incidents in which they felt kind, forgiving, enjoying the happiness of another person, concerned for the welfare of someone they've loved. After anchoring in these feelings, I ask people to strengthen them by exercising the feeling: I suggest they remember some stranger they saw that day and extend the feeling of kindness, acceptance, compassion, good-will to the stranger. After they do that, I ask them to remember a casual acquaintance and extend similar feelings to that casual acquaintance. Then I ask them to extend the feelings to someone like a coworker, cousin, or sibling who they basically like but with whom they've had some disagreement. Next I ask them to work on extending feelings of kindness, forgiveness, understanding, and good-will to their spouses, together with compassion for whatever suffering they know their spouses have experienced in their lives. Finally, I ask people to extend the same feelings—acceptance, compassion, kindness, and joy—to themselves.

The emotional climate of the group usually deepens a great deal at this point as group members discuss both their positive feelings and the difficulties they encountered extending these feelings to people at whom they felt angry. Participants are often surprised to discover that they have the most difficulties extending acceptance, compassion, and kindness not to others but to themselves. They often talk about how much happier they feel trying to cultivate kindly feelings, even if they have difficulties doing so, then they do stoking their anger.

One of the advantages of an exercise such as this one is that it builds on some positive feelings that already exist in the relationship; in addition, each member of the couple knows that while they are cultivating compassion and acceptance for their spouse, their spouse is doing the exercise cultivating compassion and acceptance for them. When someone displays good will toward me or toward others, it is relatively easy to respond with good will in turn. However, when someone seems to be wishing harm to me or to someone I care about, it's easy to get self-righteously angry:

A friend of mine was in the car with her six-year-old son, her eleven-year-old daughter, and her daughter's friend, driving them to a party. The six-year-old kept tattling on his sister, telling her friend every incident he could think of that would embarrass his sister. His sister was on the verge of tears. My friend kept telling her son to stop, but because she was driving, she was unable to intervene very effectively.

My friend found herself getting angrier and angrier with her son for being so mean to his sister and treating her so badly. Finally, steaming mad, she stopped the car. She grabbed her son by the hand, dragged him to the side of the road, and wagging her finger in his face told him: "If you don't stop saying all those things about your sister to her friend, then the next time you're in the car with one of *your* friends, *I'm* going to tell your friend some things you'll feel embarrassed about!"

Her six-year-old-son looked up at her, wide-eyed.

"But Mommy," he said. "Two wrongs don't make a right!'"

Realizing the truth in her six-year-old's words, my friend was able to laugh, realize the silliness of self-righteous rage, and let go of her anger. But even when we know two wrongs don't make a right, the tendency to fight anger with anger can be very strong. When we take to heart the Metta Sutta's injunction to avoid anger and hatred, we can become incensed at others who do not act as if "this way of living is the best in the world." We can run into the trap of feeling our anger is justified: Our very embrace of the principles of the Metta Sutta can lead to angry indignation at its violation, even for people who have made their life one of being peace:

> Thich Nhat Hanh, a great present-day Buddhist teacher, described how he once was preparing to visit the United States and received news that the President had ordered the bombing of one of the Arab nations.[12] Thich Nhat Hanh became very angry at this warlike act that would rain death on many innocent people; the United States seemed to him to be morally bankrupt. He decided, in a fit of self-righteous virtue, that he would cancel his trip.
>
> After a while, however, Thich Nhat Hanh had a painful insight: He realized he was waging war in his own way and was not himself so different from the President of the United States. Once he saw he was requiting hostility with hostility, he began to feel a connection with the President and the soldiers enforcing his decision. He began to realize how the soldiers involved in the war would be carrying their guilt, their anger, and their violence back home with them when they returned to their native country. This made it possible for him to feel compassion for how the soldiers would be harmed by their own violence, which would infect their relationships and their country like a virulent virus.
>
> He went through with his visit and continued his task of spreading peace. But it took him several days of meditation to calm down from his initial anger.

When we feel another person is evil or harmful, we easily respond with re-flexive anger. Even if we know that meeting hatred with hatred can be coun-terproductive, we often convince ourselves that our anger is justified if it arises defensively. If someone is attacking us or if they are threatening to hurt someone we love, we tell ourselves not only that our anger is reasonable but that we *should* and *must* be angry in order to be strong enough to protect ourselves and our loved ones. We do this even if this contradicts our moral ideals.

> I was recently talking to one of my relatives. He was upset; some peeping Tom had re-cently opened his young daughter's bedroom window and spied on her while she was

asleep. This normally peaceable man was incensed: "If this guy comes back again," he said, "I'm going to break both his knees."

I could understand his feeling, but after empathizing with him I tried to engage him in a conversation about the problems of requiting hate with hate. He agreed it was not a good idea but said, "It doesn't matter that this anger doesn't fit with my Christian ideals. This is my daughter we're talking about. If that guy comes back, I know how I'm going to react: He's going to get hurt."

I let the matter drop, but privately I sanctimoniously shook my head. Then a year later, someone got into my twelve-year-old daughter's America Online account and altered her profile so that it was sexually obscene, soliciting sex with older men. They added her home phone number and address, and they posted it on some bulletin boards and chat rooms. We did not learn about this until our daughter started receiving obscene phone calls and her e-mail account became the recipient of pornographic pictures. It looked like this was the work of some adolescent prankster, the electronic equivalent of graffiti on a bathroom stall, but we feared that some pedophile could come across the information and begin stalking her.

I was furious.

When someone we love is threatened, we tell ourselves the person who is doing the threatening is morally despicable and has no right to exist. We feel we must return anger with anger to remove the threat and teach the other person a lesson. But although we think the anger that arises in these situations comes from love, we are mistaken. Love engenders good will, not hate; something else is at work here.

The Metta Sutta suggests we cherish all living things and suffuse love over the entire world, but usually we care more for some people than others. This is natural, but if I discriminate according to how close or distant a person is from me, I can easily confuse proximity with possession. Sometimes I subtly treat the people I care about as if they somehow belong to me: Then I get angry if somebody hurts them not just because they are being harmful to the one I love but because they are taking something away from me. I see them as trespassing on "my" territory.

This air of possessiveness can be seen in how we often act as if we have the right to hurt our loved ones, but nobody else does. We will fight people who insult our spouse, then turn around and insult our spouse ourselves. We are ready to kill someone who hurts our daughter, but we allow ourselves to spank her when she misbehaves, injure her with harsh criticism, or wound her with neglect. If I see a person as being "mine," then I can do what I want with him or her, can't I? But if *you* try to do something with her or him, I see it not just as a danger, but as a theft. So I will try to punish the perpetrator and put the thief behind bars.

I can feel virtuous meting out punishment if I justify it as a way of protecting society against some evil beast. But this virtuousness is a bit shaky: Sometimes satisfying angry desires for revenge becomes more important than whether our harsh reprisals are actually helpful. Behavioral research shows clearly that punishment does not work very well; clobbering and condemning an assailant will not make him more loving and caring. We keep putting people in prison despite ample evidence that prisons do not stop crime but provide an incubator for it; we build prisons for the people we fear, but in the process we imprison ourselves behind walls and security systems that only retain the poison of our own hatred.

If somebody is hurting me or someone I love, of course I must do what I can to stop them. It does not follow, however, that I must hate them while I do this. If some burglar comes in and looms over my daughter, I may feel justified in breaking his kneecaps, telling myself that this will ensure he will never get a chance to bother another person's daughter. If I do this, however, he will never be able to rescue another person's daughter from a burning building should the need arise. There is also the chance that if I try to shoot the burglar or break his kneecaps, he might shoot back and in the process kill my daughter.

It is not always obvious how to respond to violence and threats. Sometimes it is best to confront it forcefully and directly; sometimes it is best to stand aside or yield in a way that transforms the violence without giving in to it.

During the 1960s, a college friend of mine named Roy was traveling with another friend, John, in the South. They were dressed as hippies, hitchhiking in decidedly unfriendly territory. A man stopped and gave them a ride in the cab of his pickup. It was tight quarters, with my friend sitting by the window and John sitting next to the driver. As they were driving along, the man reached under his seat, pulled out a gun, cocked it, and placed the muzzle against John's temple. There was a moment of petrified silence. Then Roy leaned over, looked at the driver, and said: "Wow! That's a *really nice* gun! What make is it?"

The driver laughed, put the gun away, and proceeded to have a long discussion with his passengers, eventually going several miles out of his way to drop them off at a convenient spot.

I suspect that if my friend had started cursing or attacking the driver, the outcome of the above story might have been very different.

When dealing with someone who is violent toward ourselves or others, many times the best course is, as in the case above, to find some way of connecting with the other person. This is not easy. Therapists know that if a client is hostile and potentially dangerous, we often can defuse the situation if we manage to find a way to help the client feel we are an ally and not an enemy; despite knowing this, we often are pulled to respond to a client's hostility with fear, self-righteousness, or anger. Remaining calm in the face of violent emotional storms is hard enough in the controlled setting of the therapy office; when we are faced with situations in which we or the people we love have been harmed, it is difficult to maintain compassion for the person who has harmed us.

The idea that force must be met with force is often defended by alluding to the experiences of World War II. In this century, one of the great symbols of violence and hatred is the Nazi effort at exterminating the Jews. It is hard, faced with the Holocaust, to feel compassion for the Nazis. Yet the Metta Sutta does not suggest that we avoid wishing harm to *some* others, or just to the people who are good to us; it does not advise us to extend good will to some people, but to all living beings, even to Nazis.

Being Jewish, I had problems feeling compassion for the Nazis until I recently visited the Holocaust Museum in Washington, D.C, I went there with some trepidation. I had been brought up to feel anger at the people who had embarked on a course of exterminating my relatives. Many of my family held a great deal of anger not only at Germans but at everyone whom they held accountable for failing to prevent the Holocaust. Many of my relatives nurtured their anger to a point where they lived with a level of bitterness that I found quite terrifying.

As a result, I tried to avoid thinking about the whole issue. This didn't work, however, I found I would often feel overwhelming feelings of sadness, depression, and despair when I thought about the Holocaust. The same feeling came up when I encountered other contemporary events around the world—the fratricidal wars among Serbs, Muslims, and Croats; the massacres in Africa; the mirrored violence of Israelis and Arabs—that amply displayed the horrifying ability people have to slaughter and torture, usually with righteous indignation, their enemies who "deserve" to suffer. Former victims often seemed to feel they had a right to torture their torturers. It seemed that hurt created hurt and suffering engendered suffering, with no solution in sight.

There was a great deal of suffering on display at the Holocaust Museum, but I was particularly struck by how the Nazis, despite dominating and brutalizing their victims, did not seem particularly happy. They could be seen laughing, joking, displaying bravado and even a sense of self-righteous virtue, but there was not much evidence of Nazis exhibiting a sense of peace or satisfaction. I began to suspect that the Nazis might not be purely evil, sadistic people who tried to exterminate other races for fun and profit: They appeared profoundly embittered and unfulfilled in the midst of their anger. Their projection of blame for any unhappiness they felt onto the Jews and the other groups they persecuted did not appear to have worked very well.

As I read through the Nazi proclamations I saw how they justified their racist policies as necessary to "protect" Germans, I had always discounted these statements as mere excuses to be self-indulgent beasts, but in the Holocaust museum I suddenly realized that many Germans actually *believed* what they were saying. At that point I experienced a profound shock. I realized that at least some Nazis had acted in the way they did because they genuinely felt that to protect their loved fellow-countrymen and their families, they *needed* to round up and exterminate the Jews. Their motives were, in their own minds, noble. However wrongly they felt persecuted, however much they had been deceived by propaganda and by their own fears, the fact was that at least some of them felt they needed to respond to an "unfair" persecution by sinister Jews with a "just" persecution of their own. Were they so different from the father who shoots the burglar to "protect" his daughter? Was my fury at failing to protect my daughter from the perversions of the Internet so different from the Nazis' fury at being powerless in the face of the political and economic forces they felt had buffeted them?

As I struggled with this question, I remembered the Metta Sutta's prescription for happiness: to cherish *all* living things, to cultivate an infinite good will toward the *whole* world while not wishing harm to *any* being in any state, I realized the problem with the Nazi's "noble" effort to help their constituents was that the Nazis were trying to help only *some* people and in the process gave themselves license to harm others.

Once we start picking and choosing who to like and who to feel "justifiably" angry at, we run into trouble. Once the Nazis said, "*We* are good and *you* are bad," they isolated themselves from a substantial part of the human race. Once they rejected some people, some aspects of experience, they unwittingly cut themselves off from any possible sense of wholeness and doomed themselves to unhappiness. Hatred feeds on hatred and when it eventually turns on its creator, as it inevitably does, hatred destroys the destroyer. The frenzy of the Nazi effort, being based on anger, hatred, and wishing harm to others, inevitably lacked any sense of true joy. No matter how many enemies they defeated, they could never find peace.

Hatred does not lead to peace. Yet much of our life feels like it takes place in the midst of war. Seeing others hurt, feeling attacked ourselves, how can we avoid bitterness and find peace in the midst of horror?

One way of doing this is to return to the simple basics: that our lives are connected to everyone else's. In order to do this, it helps if we follow the Metta Sutta's advice to "abandon vague discussions," to eschew the ideological arguments and theoretical purities that lead to holy wars. If we indulge in our ideas about how things ought to be, we get confused: A disagreement about whether the Godhead is transubstantial or consubstantial in the Host can lead to 100 years of war; disagreements between Liberals and Conservatives, Communists and Capitalists, can obscure the fact that my opponent breathes the air I breathe and that we both share blood whose saltiness comes from a common sea.

When we come back to the concrete reality of being connected, living beings, we have a clear vision of what constitutes right action. I was impressed, when I visited the Holocaust Museum, that most of the people who lived in Germany who had helped rescue Jews had no particular ideology; faced with the Nazi extermination program, regardless even of whether they liked Jews or not, they simply had responded, "This is not the way to live," and proceeded rather matter-of-factly to save whoever they could, even if it involved some risk to their own safety. Most of them, when interviewed, said that it ultimately boiled down to the fact that they would not feel like a human being if they allowed other human beings to be brutalized; they saw their lives as connected with the lives of all, rather than some, other people.

When we feel our lives connected to everyone else's, it creates the possibility of meeting violence and anger not with fear or hatred but with its antidote, compassion. It can be very difficult to find compassion when we feel hurt, angered, outraged; at such times it helps to have some inspiring examples. Recently, I learned a great deal when one of my students decided to do his dissertation on people who had suffered a severe trauma.[13] He investigated whether it was possible not only to recover from the trauma but actually to find a gift in the trauma that allowed them to grow in some significant way. He chose to work with parents who had suffered through having a child murdered.

Somewhat to my surprise, he found a good number of people who clearly had experienced some positive transformation in their lives after the murder of their child. Most of the people he interviewed talked at some length about how they had needed to overcome the destructive influence of hatred, as can be seen in these quotations:

> "Being angry and vengeful could really, really consume you, if you are just out for revenge. That doesn't help you. So I had to figure another way... "
>
> "I didn't know that I was capable of... such emotion, of such anger, all the ugliness, you know... I was being rendered impotent in a sense... and I knew that it would do me in, if I didn't do something about it... "
>
> "What I see over and over again [in parents of murdered children who come to support groups] is that those who retain a vindictive mind in the end give the offender another victim, however justified they feel about their anger. Their health deteriorates, their own peace of mind, their relationships... "
>
> "Hate is not for me, because it destroys me. If I hate somebody, I am not destroying that person, I am destroying myself."

All of the participants who found a way of transcending the murder of their child reached out to others in compassion. The experience of their own pain led them to reach out to help others. Several of them found, to their surprise, that their compassion eventually reached out even to the murderer. One mother said,

> "If he were to come to my door right now, I would not be afraid, not at all, I would open the door to him. And I would say, 'Come in, Tom, I have been waiting to talk to you. Let's sit down and talk.' He needs to hear that from me, I told his mother that. 'Please tell your son I don't hate him.'"

In another case, compassion helped solve the crime. The murderer had been calling the parents of the child he had murdered to taunt them. The mother described how one day, while speaking to the anonymous killer on the phone,

> Feelings began to arise in me, to my own surprise really... feelings of genuine concern and compassion for this man, and he wasn't expecting it. And he was really taken aback by it, I was surprised myself... but I desperately wanted to reach this man... At one point I said to him, "What can I do to help you?" And he broke down and he wept and he wept and he wept... And... in that milieu of concern and compassion he stayed on the phone for over an hour and so let down his guard, that he inadvertently revealed enough information about himself that the FBI was able to identify him.
>
> I got a chance to meet... the mother of this young man. You know, I have an ongoing relationship with her. I know how she has suffered, I know her headaches and her pain and... whenever we kill somebody, that person... not only is that person a human being who has a right to life... that person has family too, who will grieve his loss. And it is like, I don't want any part of that, in contributing to that, I want the violence to end, whether it happens in the streets, or in the homes, or in the death chambers, you know. I want the violence to end.

LOVE

If we want the violence to end, we cannot move in this direction by forcefully suppressing our rage or angrily choking off our hatred. Instead, we need to strengthen our ability to feel compassion and cultivate our aptitude for love.

Love is a universal emotion that reaches out expansively, seeking to dismantle the boundaries between self and others; we sometimes run into problems when we try to reconcile these universal, transcendent aspects with the needs of a bounded personal ego. When the Metta Sutta teaches us that the way to be happy is to care for others, "suffusing love over the entire world," it poses the koan of love, of how we balance the intimacy of connectedness with the needs of individuality. How can we love each other? How can we love ourselves? As therapists, how can we love our clients?

Psychotherapy deals with the problems clients have in forming emotional attachments, and virtually all schools of psychotherapy emphasize the importance of establishing a caring therapeutic relationship. This being the case, I've always been puzzled by how little the psychotherapeutic literature talks about love. We have devised numerous euphemisms for the "L-word:" transference, attachment, cathexis, bonding, and the like. It seems that in the quest to become a respectable social science, we have become afraid to use the word "love." For a healing interaction that, from the time of Freud, has been recognized at least in part as a "love cure," this is a major gap. We need to learn how to love our clients.

Many people reading this may instinctively shrink back. Wouldn't loving our clients be dangerous? Couldn't it unlock unruly passions, foster dependency on the part of the client, and open the door to sexual misbehavior by the therapist? Is it realistic or even *possible* to love all our clients? Wouldn't it be exhausting? Wouldn't we lose our objectivity and be unable to help?

Loving our clients requires that we accept our lives, our selves, and our clients with perhaps a more encompassing embrace than the usual "warmth, acceptance, and positive regard" prescribed in basic counseling classes. The kind of love described by the Metta Sutta is unattached to any particular goal, feeling or sensation; it is a love that greets everyone we encounter without any purpose beyond the simple joy of connectedness, the pleasure inherent in self meeting self.

Our fears of loving clients arise if we confuse the selfless love of the Metta Sutta with the pseudolove that arises from self-centered desire. We all know the ravages false love can wreak. Every therapist has seen a client who professes love for his partner, but who reacts with rage, jealousy, or despair when his partner exercises her autonomy and acts in ways that don't conform to how the client feels his partner should act "if she really loved me." These clients are trying to fill up some sense of personal emptiness through grasping the other person's affections. We all do this to some extent, but love becomes twisted if it is marked primarily by personal possessiveness; if our desires and senses are not controlled, we may attempt to control the other person in order to gratify what we call our "love." If we are trying to satisfy our egos' hungers through this kind of "loving," it feeds our personal cravings in ways that inflame both our physical and psychological appetites.

The question in all our love relationships is: How can I transform self-centered desire into unselfish love for another person? The question for therapists is not *whether* but *how* we can love our clients so that our needs don't mar the meeting.

The Metta Sutta suggests a way when it encourages us: "Even as a mother at the risk of her life watches over and protects her only child, so with a boundless mind should one suffuse love over the entire world, above, below, and all around, without limit." Suffusing love over the entire world extends love to every manifestation of life. This means we seek to love each thought, each feeling, each sensation, each perception, each impulse, each psychological state that arises from our selves and our clients.

This kind of attitude, of course, is crucial to psychotherapy, but it is important not to misconstrue the implications of this kind of love. Loving is not the same as liking. Loving an impulse does not necessarily mean giving into it; loving a thought does not necessarily mean agreeing with it; loving a person doesn't mean we need become involved in an enmeshed relationship. The loving balance the Metta Sutta leads us toward involves full engagement without excessive attachment. The Metta Sutta advises us to watch over each being as if he or she were our only child, but the Metta Sutta also advises us to avoid grasping at great possessions.

If we treat our only child as our possession, we might overprotect or smother our child. The same can be true of our attitude toward our thoughts and feelings, our clients and our families. To avoid the trap of possessiveness or indulgence, the Metta Sutta advises us to extend our love equally toward *all* living things. By balancing the universal (loving *all* beings) with the particular (treating *each* being as our only child), love can avoid getting stuck in any kind of excess.

If we treat each being as if he or she were our only child, this means that we will cherish each being for who he or she is. A parent watches over and protects his or her only child not by pushing the child to grow in a particular direction, but by recognizing that the child has her or his own tendency toward growth. The parent attempts to provide a nourishing, safe environment that makes it possible for the child to develop, at the same time maintaining a willingness to let go and allow the child to realize her- or himself.

In order to move toward love and away from self-centered desire, the first steps involve cultivating acceptance of other people for who they are, rather than who we want them to be. This is facilitated by understanding. Faced with a trait we find harmful or repulsive, whether the trait be in ourselves or in a person with whom we have a relationship, if we can understand and recognize the suffering that lies at the root of the behavior we often begin to feel compassion. Such compassion is a step on the way to love. Therapists struggling with "countertransference" often find it eases as they understand more about their client; spouses who resent some behavior of their partners can sometimes ease their resentment by understanding more about the motivations and struggles (often coming from their partners' families of origin) that underlie their partners' behavior. Often I begin couples' therapy groups with the following quotation from Thich Nhat Hanh,[14] where he suggests that

> Love cannot exist without understanding. Love *is* understanding. If you cannot understand, you cannot love. Husbands and wives who do not understand each other cannot love each other. Brothers and sisters who do not understand each other cannot love each other. Parents and children who do not understand each other cannot love each other. [Therapists and clients who do not understand each other cannot love each other.]
>
> If you want your loved ones to be happy, you must learn to understand their sufferings and their aspirations. When you understand, you will know how to relieve their sufferings and how to help them fulfill their aspirations. That is true love. If you only want your loved ones to follow your own ideas [i.e., conform to your expectations of how a client "should" behave] and you remain ignorant of their needs, it is not truly love. It is only a desire to possess another and attempt to fulfill your own needs, which cannot be fulfilled in that way.

When we try to understand someone we put aside some of our self-centeredness and feel solicitude for the happiness and welfare of the other person. This loving concern for the other is a form of unstinting, bountiful giving that does not deplete the giver: This love is something when you give it away, you end up having more.

When love is generous, good-willed, and eschews greed, it is not concerned with possessing others or getting anything for one's self; directed toward giving, not getting, such love does not focus on receiving personal physical satisfactions, so its senses are naturally controlled. This love, wishing no harm to any other, has nothing to do with hurt; this love, cutting through delusion, does not see separate people but sees us all as intimately interconnected.

When we love someone, we hope they will be happy. The Metta Sutta extends this wish to *all* beings: Weak or strong, small or great, may *all* beings be happy. Not only those beings who are currently alive; not only those beings in our realm of immediate contact; not only human beings; may *all* beings who are living, who have ever lived, or who will ever live, in any realm or any form, may they *all* be happy. The Metta Sutta does not say "love people who agree with you." It does not say "love people who need you." It does not say "love the clients who respond to therapy." It says to love everyone. This love extends to include not only our easy clients, but also our difficult clients; not only our helpful family members, but our problematical ones; not only our sympathetic colleagues, but also our competitors, our antagonists, and the administrators who monitor our managed-care contracts. The extension of love to all beings is crucial: As soon as we extend our love to some but not others, we begin the cycle of suffering. Hitler very much wanted *some* beings (Aryans) to be happy: That is what led to the Holocaust. The

Metta Sutta tells us that to find peace, we must suffuse love over the *entire* world, without limit.

The key to unselfish love lies in applying it universally; in its use of the key word "all," the Metta Sutta points us to the source from which this love derives both its protection and its power. The love the Metta Sutta teaches as a gateway to happiness is a love based on nondiscrimination; it is not aimed at acquiring something for myself or idolizing a particular person or thing. If as therapists we exercise this love for all our clients, we will be less likely to become ensnared in a perversion of love through a sexual relationship or a selfish desire for a particular client.

As Buddhists we take a vow to save all beings. Not some beings; not those beings that we can manage to save: We vow to save *all* beings. This may seem like a tall order. It is. Such a vow may also seem arrogant, if we don't realize that the vow is based on the goodness of interbeing rather than the narcissistic satisfaction of being good. If I think I am ultimately separate from you, then saving you means I am powerful and must rescue you because you are weak. If I realize that we are all fundamentally connected, saving you means that together we save each other again and again. This is closer to another way in which the vow to "save" all beings is sometimes translated: We vow to *awaken with* all beings. Whether we vow to save each other or awaken with each other, both are a form of love.

It may be impossible for any human being to save, awaken with, or completely love even one other person, let alone all beings. But by taking this formal vow we cultivate our intention to live our lives this way; the vow is a way to reinforce our resolution to make our best efforts in this direction. As therapists we make a commitment in our hearts to help our clients, but our vow is implicit rather than overt. When we get lost in the interpersonal mazes of psychotherapy, we do not have something akin to formal Buddhist vows or the fine old Hippocratic oath to fall back on. A formal vow taken in the company of others who witness and affirm the vow might help remind us of our original intention and provide support for our actions when we get tired, waver, or fall short.

Some people might object that taking an idealistic vow to love, save, or even help all beings is dangerous, arguing that because we are sure to fail we will run the danger of becoming discouraged or acting out our frustrations. I think we will not be in danger so long as we realize that taking a vow need not involve building a cross of high expectations on which we must crucify ourselves: It is more like having a map to consult when we inevitably get lost.

When we take a vow to save all beings we realize we will always fall short. So taking a vow is not something we do once and then it is over and done with; once we take a vow, we have to continually renew it, time and time again.

Love is a matter of waking up and seeing each other. When we take a vow to save all beings, we take a vow to love each other. Then every time we sit zazen, every time we sit down together as therapists and clients, we have a fresh opportunity to wake up to one another anew.

HAPPINESS IS NOT A FEELING...

Every moment we have an opportunity to open our eyes and experience the joy of being. Sometimes, however, when we wake up we don't like what we see. When we wake up after the honeymoon and find we married not our idealized lover but a flawed human being, we may make ourselves unhappy. Sometimes when we wake up we may feel we are in a nightmare: If we get up and are greeted by intense pain radiating from our spine, or by a message our daughter has been severely injured in a mugging, or by a telephone call telling us the routine laboratory tests on our wife came back indicating cancer, it may be hard to be happy. But just as love is of limited value if it only extends to loving the traits we like in the other person, the Metta Sutta's prescriptions for happiness are of limited help if we can apply them only during the good times of our lives. Life is not a grab bag from which we can pick and choose at will.

> My aunt was a travel agent in the days when people usually purchased tours that were complete packages; they would include airfare, hotels, meals, buses, and guides for sightseeing. Inevitably, many people called my aunt asking if they could change part of the tour and stay at a different hotel or go to some different spot than the ones included on the itinerary. She would have to tell them they were getting a good deal precisely because the tour was all-inclusive; they couldn't pick out one part to eliminate or substitute something else. This didn't stop people from continuing to try to wheedle some special accommodations and, when they failed, complaining vociferously to my aunt.
>
> When my aunt died, she left instructions in her will for what she wanted inscribed on her tombstone. If you go to the cemetery and find my aunt's grave, you'll see inscribed there a travel agent's motto: "Life is a package deal."

Our challenge is how to embrace the whole package deal of our life, to find love even in the face of disappointment and anger, to find happiness and peace even in situations of pain and loss, violence, and hurt.

The Metta Sutta is a prayer for all living beings to be happy whatever their circumstances: that they be happy whether they are in "high or middle or low realms of existence," in heaven or hell or someplace in between. The Metta Sutta is saying, "May all beings realize their being in happiness *right now*," finding the perfection and completeness of each moment, of every situation. It doesn't matter whether or not our circumstances conform to our ideas of what happiness "should" be: The challenge the Metta Sutta sets forth is to realize the happiness of enjoying being who we are *right now*.

Running after some mental image of satisfaction keeps us from understanding that there is no special form of "true" happiness outside of that which occurs in each instant of our lives, moment by moment. If we seek for happiness outside of our immediate experience we are like a fish in the ocean searching blindly, endlessly for water. As Zen Master Dogen says: "If you cannot find the truth right where you are, where else do you expect to find it?"

We can only be happy with the truth of our existence through a radical acceptance of *all* the circumstances of our lives, equally accepting all our faults and the idiosyncrasies of others, all our virtues and the benevolence that is extended to us. This kind of acceptance is not easy. We often find it hard to accept not only our situations but also our selves, our loved ones, and our clients just as they and we are. We find it hard to believe life is complete and perfect at this moment, so we keep seeking. Feeling incomplete, dissatisfied, and flawed, we feel we have to add or subtract to ourselves and our experiences to make things turn out as we wish, rather than accepting what is for what it is.

We are not too sure what would happen if we let go of our striving, our expectations, our defenses and our hopes, so we hold on tight. But in doing so we hold on to our unhappiness. We all feel we are somehow lacking perfection and are separated from wholeness. We all feel ill, and like the monk in the following story we seek to discover the secret of one who does not get ill.

> When Dongshan was unwell, a monk asked, "You are ill, teacher, but is there anyone who does not get ill?
>   Dongshan said, "There is."
>   The monk said, "Does the one who is not ill look after you?"
>   Dongshan said, "I have the opportunity to look after him."
>   The monk said, "How is it when you look after him?"
>   Dongshan said, "Then I don't see that he has any illness."[15]

We look for someone who is not ill to take care of us and make our selves happy, but in so doing we lose sight of "the one who does not get ill." The Metta Sutta directs our attention to "the one who does not get ill" when it mentions the "one who is made perfect."

We can read this part of the Metta Sutta in two ways. One way is: Make yourself more perfect. This way can lead to frustration at our continuing imperfections and yearning for some special state of attainment. If we are looking to make an individual ego—ours or our client's—perfect, we are in for a lot of frustration. The natural state of an ego is not wholeness, but separation; not undividedness, but fragmentation.

But another way of reading this section of the Metta Sutta is to realize that every ego-fragment arises from and is embedded in a wholeness that is originally made perfect. That wholeness does not *become* perfect: It does not go from imperfection to perfection. That wholeness has always existed as perfect; all the bits and pieces of life appear as expressions of that perfection. Regardless of whether we are good or bad, skillful or clumsy, sick or well, Buddhism teaches us that such wholeness is our natural state of being.

All of us, when we are born, are made perfect. It doesn't matter if we are born with ten fingers or eight; with a tin ear or perfect pitch; with an irritable nervous system or a placid disposition. We are all born exactly who we are, complete and perfect in ourselves, expressing the universe in our particular way. Each moment we are completely ourselves. When we seek the good, when we cultivate peace, we are returning to ourselves: Goodness is seeking to express itself. Where else can the motivation to get better, to realize happiness, come from?

Most of our clients don't trust themselves enough to rely on their natural state of being; they feel they must look for something outside themselves and their present lives for happiness. If, as therapists, we in effect agree with our clients that they are incomplete and lack what they need to be happy, we reinforce their idea that the "one who does not get ill" must be sought someplace other than where they are. Then we may be able to help our clients search for peace, but we will not be able to help them discover the completeness already available right at hand; we may be able to help them tolerate their sorrows but will not be able to help them realize how happiness and peace can be present even in the midst of intense sorrow.

To find the health that exists in the midst of illness, it is important for us to keep sight of that one who does not get ill, the wholeness that supports every moment of our own and our clients' lives. In the midst of suffering and confusion, we cannot base our therapeutic work on suffering and confusion; we cannot base psychotherapy on psychopathology, but rather on the clarity and joy that lie at the heart of every moment of our existence. We have to take care of "the one who does not get ill" in our clients, that basic impulse for self to return to true Self that brings our clients to therapy. We have to cultivate their and our hearts' intention, our basic impulse, to be fully human and whole.

Born human, we have the ability to return to who we really are: not someone who looks out for "Number One," but some One who looks for its Self in all the numberless beings. Born human, we have the ability to remind ourselves how we are connected to all other beings, to let go of some of our self-centered concerns and devote our energies instead to appreciating and taking care of the universe as it expresses itself in each person, each living creature, each hunk of rock and bit of earth that presents itself to us. When we do this, we return to our true selves, appreciate and take care of our selves together with all beings; in doing this we begin to find a way to love the world and realize happiness each moment, whatever it may bring.

The Metta Sutta is about how to realize happiness each moment, not some moments. But every-moment-happiness is not some *particular* feeling. If we iden-tify happiness with the feeling we think of as "happiness, a pleasant feeling" we will quickly become frustrated and dissatisfied. Happy feelings, like sad, angry, or scared feelings, are ephemeral; they rise up in reaction to some thought, per-ception, sensation, or memory, run their course, and pass away. We sometimes try to hold on to our feelings: We reinforce them by rehearsing them in our thoughts, by doing things to stimulate certain feelings and not others. This is natural. If we try to grasp at happiness, however, it is like caging a wild animal; restricting it in a predefined container deprives it of the quality that made us seek it in the first place. Happiness needs to be free to come and go, to take unexpected byways. Happiness is not a tame tiger.

If we are to realize the happiness and peace offered by the Metta Sutta, we must make friends with the wild but wonderful tiger of impermanence. If we try to hold on to some pleasant feeling, to some comfortable existence, or to some idealized image of ourselves or the people we're involved with, we will think we must be unhappy when the pleasant feeling fades, the comfort gives way to difficulty, the ideal turns into mundane reality. But if we stop trying to hold on to temporary appearances and accept in our bones the fleeting transience of our lives, we can become open and consoled to each moment, even though it occur in the midst of civil war, as this poem by Ho Chi Minh attests:

> After the rain, good weather.
> In the twinkling of an eye, the universe throws off its muddy clothes.
> Bright breezes
> Sparkling flowers
> All the birds sing at once.
> What could be more natural?
> After sorrow comes happiness.[16]

This is the truth of human existence: Sorrow and joy are *connected*. Each provides some aspect of the whole; when one is there the other is implied. Although we say "after sorrow comes happiness," it is not just that happiness follows sorrow; sorrow also follows happiness. Although one follows the other, both are present at the same time, because each is present in the other. So seeking one and rejecting the other doesn't work: If we fail to see the essential connection, then when we are happy we will be fearing it will fade, and when we are unhappy we will feel weighed down.

We cannot find happiness by fending off discomfort and grasping at pleasure; we can only find happiness by embracing the totality of life, the completeness that comes with storm clouds and sun, the knowledge that they are joined at the hip in their shared impermanence. Happiness comes in the knowledge of the inevitable linkage of each experience to the totality of life. Then the knowledge that each experience will pass leads not to despair but to an appreciation of the experience for what it is.

Everything in life dissolves but as it dissolves, it shimmers with its own particular light. If we accept impermanence, let go of our personal preferences, and meet each experience as it comes with total acceptance, then when it's raining we can sing in the rain. If we reject rain we'll get sodden and soaked by showers; if we enjoy rain it will water us and provide refreshment. Greeting the world with innocent enjoyment, when it's muddy we can laugh like a child who, not "knowing" mud is "dirty," enjoys mud's texture and the pleasures of molding it into the shape of pies. Joy and sorrow are connected as surely as rain and good weather, light and dark, birth and death.

Ultimately, happiness comes from finding a way to renew our wonder and find our connection with each moment of life, regardless of its pain and pleasure.

Ultimately, suffering comes from rejecting impermanence and trying to live in an illusion that, picking and choosing, clutches at some particular feeling or life circumstance. When we try to grasp at happiness this way, it disappears.

When instead we see that every thing is ephemeral, ready to dissolve at a touch, we gently greet each experience—regardless of whether it is pleasant or unpleasant—as a precious fragile moment that has never existed quite like this before and will never exist quite like this again. Once we stop grasping and meet each experience as it is, everything and everyone becomes a precious multifaceted jewel: not the kind of jewel that is kept always out of reach behind glass show-cases, but the kind of jewel we see whenever sunlight passes through water vapor to produce a rainbow. If we recognize that we meet ourselves and our clients at the end of the rainbow, we can meet our clients and our selves moment-by-moment at the place they and we are right now. This place, being beyond grasping, beyond judgments of "good" or "bad" or "like" or "dislike," offers a field in which we can realize and appreciate the joy of being.

Happiness is not a state, but a way of being. Perhaps better said, happiness is the ground of being: It is the completeness of existence, which appears moment-by-moment. Each instant life is expressing life, death is expressing death, pain is expressing pain, and joy is expressing joy; each is Being Itself. At the same time, because each is connected to the other, life provides the field for death to express itself just as death provides the field for life to express itself; sadness provides the opportunity for joy, and joy for sadness. Happiness lies in the very foundation of existence, in the natural state of each being expressing itself and realizing itself in all other beings, in Being being its Self.

As therapists, as clients, we must rely on this fundamental foundation. We do this by throwing ourselves fully into all aspects of our lives: into hurt and sickness, healing and health; into separation and loss, reunion and reconciliation; into fear and sadness, courage and joy. If we treat each of these as our brothers and sisters, we appreciate the whole family of experience; in doing so we make our lives real: We *realize* our selves as we realize the universe to which we are connected. This realization is the happiness and peace the Metta Sutta teaches us.

If we set ourselves apart by our personal preferences for one place or another, one person or another, one feeling or another, we restrict ourselves and narrow our field of play. But if we can let go of saying to the universe, "Be what I want," we can appreciate the universe when it says to each of us every moment, "Here we are."

Happiness involves experiencing the universe as an indivisible whole and at the same time realizing the universe is composed of billions of separate foci. Happiness involves being completely ourselves by discovering each moment how our self and the universe are not so far apart as we might think. Finding our-selves at the center of the universe while realizing that each being is the cen-ter of the universe, we realize happiness itself. Then happiness is not something special, found only in some particular mental state or psychological experience. Happiness becomes the harmony of our life's music: Harmony includes discord and resolution, movement and stillness. Happiness encompasses joy and sorrow, life and death, pain and pleasure. If we realize this we can see happiness is present in each moment of every one's life, and "May all beings be happy" means:

> be happy when you and your client shake hands in the waiting room
> be happy when you and your client have some realization
> be happy when you and your client are at an impasse
> be happy when you are tying your shoes
> be happy when you are washing the windows
> be happy when you are struggling with your daughter, son, or spouse
> be happy when your loved ones go away to be themselves
> be happy when your loved ones return to be with you
> be happy when you are breathing in
> be happy when you are breathing out
> be happy when you are listening
> be happy when you are thinking
> be happy when you are quiet
> be happy when you are tense
> be happy when you are feeling well
> be happy when you are feeling miserable
> be happy when you are living
> be happy when you are dying
> be happy this moment, while you are reading this

May you and I and all beings be happy together. When as therapists we work with clients, let us enjoy our work together. When we enjoy the work, we appreciate our clients; enjoying our selves, we help clients appreciate their selves. By enjoying life we are actualizing the Metta Sutta.

Just as the Fire God seeks fire, happiness seeks to find itself at all times and express itself through all beings. Happiness seeks itself, and in doing so happiness seeks happiness for all. Happiness cannot be a *personal* attainment, something we accomplish and possess: I cannot be happy without all beings being happy. Happiness is freedom from self-clinging, liberation from greed, hate, and delusion. Happiness involves finding our place in the vast net of interbeing, realizing our essential connectedness, and so "suffusing love over the entire world."

The Metta Sutta is a love song, not a prescription for purging ourselves into purity or for obtaining some state of eternal bliss. The Metta Sutta simply describes the forms of action happiness takes as it actualizes itself, and it encourages us to cultivate these forms. If we see actualizing happiness for all beings as the foundation of our existence rather than our goal, the Metta Sutta becomes not a series of rules but a sort of poem of thanksgiving, a guideline to appreciating everything we meet, each moment of life.

The Metta Sutta's advice and directions point out a path that leads us back to our original selves. The Metta Sutta gently urges us to constantly remind ourselves, our clients, and all we encounter that happiness is being wise; that being wise is being peace; and that being peace arises from loving all life, whatever it brings.

Tides

Just now
My daughter found Orion's belt on her right wrist:
Look, she says, I have scratches on my arms.
Are these questions? - she asks, and looks for Truth,
then worries about wars and Hitler.

How do I show her these scratches are no other than herself
Except by showing her my scars and laughing at past pride of
ownership?

But the coastline is always good,
singing the tide in her veins, mine, yours.
If our back is to the breeze we do not feel it on our face;
Turning, tears anoint our desiccation
For all eyes are opened in that perfect mirror, Death.

How wonderful that there are things one cannot grasp
despite a self that, striving to let go, grasps the firmer.
Folding the laundry, carefully,
Making such straight lines I double back upon my self
a wave watching waves create a beach
of footsteps, salt and stars.
Breakers never reach the shore;
sloughing their crests in sprays of light
with the world moving, with the waves standing still
an old rock welcomes lichens, mosses, moons.

Each strand of seaweed can only be itself,
one word in conversations between tides and land
where wind becomes the ocean disappearing into sand.

The Sandokai of Sekito Kisen Daiosho[1]

The mind of the great sage of India was conveyed intimately from West to East.
There are differences in human personality;
Some are clever and some are not.
The teachers of North and South are but different expressions of the same reality.

The spiritual source shines clearly in the light.
Branching streams flow in the darkness.
To be attached to things, this is delusion;
But just to understand that all is one is not enough.
Each and all the elements of the subjective and objective spheres are interdependent,
and at the same time independent;
Related, though each thing keeps its own place.
Form makes the character and appearance different;
Pleasure and suffering appear unrelated.
The dark makes all forms one;
In brightness dualistic distinctions become apparent.

The four elements return to their nature like a child to its mother.
Fire is hot, wind moves, water is wet, earth hard.
Eyes see, ears hear, the nose smells, the tongue tastes salt and sour.
Each is independent of the other,
But the different leaves come from the same root.
Cause and effect both necessarily derive from the great reality.
The words "high" and "low" are used relatively.
Within the light there is darkness, but do not be attached to that darkness.
Within the darkness there is light, but do not be caught by that light.
Light and darkness are a pair,
Like the foot before and the foot behind in walking.
Each thing has its own intrinsic value,
And is related to everything else in function and position.
Ordinary life fits the absolute as a box and its lid.
The absolute works together with the relative
Like two arrows meeting in mid air.

Reading the above lines you should have grasped the great reality.
Do not set up your own standards.
If you do not see the way, you do not see it,
Though you are actually walking on it.
When you walk the way it is not near, it is not far.
If you are deluded you are mountains and rivers away from it.
I say respectfully to those who seek the way:
Do not vainly pass through sunshine and shadows.

Chapter 4

Intimate Relationship: The Sandokai of Sekito Kisen Daiosho

The mind of the great sage of India was conveyed intimately from West to East.

When we practice loving all life, we begin our lessons in relationship. Everything we learn we learn intimately, whether it be in psychotherapy, in spiritual practice, or in our family life. True learning is not a matter of a neuron registering some fact with no involvement from ourselves; in order to know, we always must participate in the act of knowing. Learning takes place not by acquiring something, but from opening up, dropping self-centered concerns, and meeting each other.

If when we encounter each other we wish for a true "meeting of minds," we can only accomplish this through intimacy. Learning or teaching, we exchange not just information but also something essential of ourselves. We try to do this in many ways with the people we care about. We lecture, we question, we listen, we talk. With our clients we hold conversations, offer interpretations, reframe symptoms, and prescribe interventions. With our loved ones we tell, ask, plead, command. We write letters, make phone calls, even put down our thoughts on paper or write a book chapter. Throughout all this communicative activity, however, the fact remains that I am over here in the West, and you are over there in the East. If I want to bridge this gap from me to my client, from me to my loved ones,

I must open a door in order to let myself touch and be touched intimately. What is this intimacy?

> There are differences in human personality;
> Some are clever and some are not.
> The teachers of North and South are but different expressions
> of the same reality.

The first step to intimacy is acknowledging that others are different from me, accepting those differences completely without regard to my own preferences. This is sometimes difficult.

Each of us is a little bit of humanity, expressed in a slightly different way. The problem is that when I discover you are different from me, I also discover I am not all-encompassing, that there is something, someone other than myself: I discover my limitations.

As a limited being I often feel like I am missing some vital parts: I start wanting the other person to fill in those blanks or fearing that the other person will threaten my vulnerabilities. So I start to pick and choose among the differences and say, "This is good" or "This is bad." If I have to bear the insult of having limitations and you being different than I, then at least I want to retain my pride by deciding whether or not I like those differences. Reacting to things as good or bad seems so natural we hardly ever think about it. When I say, "This is good," it sounds as if this thing is objectively, really "good," as if goodness is some quality I can point to as impersonally as if I were saying, "This is pink." Really, however, what I mean is that "this is good for *me.*" When I say, "This is bad," really I mean, "This is bad for *me.*" I treat differences in human personalities the same way: I like some people and not others. I like this trait in my client but not that trait; I admire this quality in my spouse but wish my spouse would eradicate the traits I don't like.

Ultimately however, differences in personality have very little to do with my likes or dislikes: They are just what they are. Clever is clever. Not is not. I may have certain reactions to encountering a clever client: I may feel stimulated, or challenged; I may feel competitive, or intimidated, or overjoyed. I may feel I can relax and let the client do the work, or I may feel I need to look especially brilliant; I may get exhausted or enjoy the back-and-forth of the exchange. When my lover is being clever, I may run through a similar gamut of feelings, ranging from idealized admiration to humiliated rage, depending on whether I feel my lover's cleverness is likely to provide something to me (fill up my limitations) or likely to demand something from me (expose my limitations).

All this is just adding complications to something basically simple: meeting the other person directly. If I get caught up in the layers of how I want or fear people to be, I may miss seeing them as they are. If I miss seeing them as they are, I may lose sight of the fact that *every* person is a particular expression of human being. Each of our lives recites a tale that contributes its own legend to the larger story of humanity: Therapists and clients, husbands and wives are all always teaching each other what it is to be human. I don't know quite what it means to be human, but I'm sure it includes more than just my particular way of living life.

If I pursue some traits in the people around me but reject others, I may close off to seeing other human possibilities. Trying to pursue a particular vision of a therapeutic or loving relationship, I may lose an opportunity to learn something about how to engage in a relationship in some bigger, wider, more embracing way than I could possibly have envisaged though my own, necessarily limited, viewpoint.

> *The spiritual source shines clearly in the light.*
> *Branching streams flow in the darkness.*
> *To be attached to things, this is delusion;*
> *But just to understand that all is one is not enough.*

In the myriad details of our everyday lives, interacting with countless people, we can lose sight of our common source. We all have a common source: We are united in our humanity, in our rootedness in life-and-death itself. The sun shines on us all with an equal light. Yet we are also all branching streams: Concerned with following our own particular course, we are in the dark regarding the experience of others. We can never quite know another person's life. There are differences in human personality, and each of us is an individual, different from anybody else dead, alive, or yet to be born.

It is precisely this individual who seeks intimacy and connectedness, and precisely this individual—this collections of fears and hopes, love and anger, wisdom and ignorance—that gets in the way. We are inextricably linked to each other, yet we are separate; we are different, but the same. This is the problem we have to resolve; this working out of sameness and difference is what causes relationship difficulties, and what moves them along.

Yesterday I saw a couple.

The woman said, "I like some order in my life. I know Saul doesn't feel the same way. I've accepted the fact that when I go to the kitchen cupboard, I won't find all the cans of soup organized according to whether they're celery, chicken noodle, or split pea. But at least he could put things away instead of just leaving them lying around."

The man said, "I need to be able to feel like I can relax a bit. I understand she has a right to have the house be clean, and I usually mean to put things away but sometimes I'm tired after work and want to rest a little; then she comes across what I've left out before I can get back to it. She could at least give me a little more time and loosen up a little."

When I asked them what they wanted to get out of their meeting, each agreed: "We want to stop fighting and be more of a partnership instead of getting on each other's case."

In the course of the session, each was able to summarize the other person's point of view. But each of them held on to their desire that the other person would not only understand their view but agree with them that their way was really better. In fact, even when they came up with a compromise for how to handle the issue of putting things away, they didn't feel satisfied. Each wanted the other person not only to do things more their way but also to *like* doing it their way.

We are all alike in wanting the other person to be more like us (even though we married our lover because we want to be more like them). Either way it's as if we have a myth: Love should eliminate our differences or at least somehow merge them. At the same time, we don't want our personal uniqueness erased, so we usually want the *other* person to do most of the merging. We get attached to "my way" and try to direct the course of the branching streams of our lives. By building reservoirs and dams we may temporarily override the natural ecology and limit our streams' flow into predefined channels. But periodically floods overwhelm us; in time all dams crumble; eventually all rivers rejoin the sea. The natural order of being is wider than our personal plans.

To the extent that therapy helps people widen the field in which they dance out the balance of individual existence and immersion in relationship, all psychotherapy is couples' therapy. Within myself, there is sameness and there are differences. I am myself all through, and yet I have different parts. I am married, polygamously, to all my selves, and it is difficult and probably inadvisable to try to obtain a divorce from any part of myself. Even "individual" psychotherapy is couples' therapy, reconciling our selves to ourselves.

Spiritual practice, psychotherapy, and couples' relationships all offer a greater understanding of life, but we cannot take advantage of the offer without realizing intimacy. When we seek to understand someone or something, we cannot comprehend without touching and being touched by whoever or whatever we are seeking to understand.

When my wife and I were first married, we came to the relationship with very different experiences of anger. I had grown up in a New York Jewish family where if the soup was too cold, you'd express your displeasure with a loud voice and large gestures; my parents argued frequently and vociferously. My wife had grown up in a small desert town in a family where anger was never expressed; she had never seen her mother and father get mad at each other or raise their voice.

So when we got together, I would pound the table with my fists when I was unhappy with minor matters. I didn't think much about this, but unbeknownst to me she experienced each such incident as if we were teetering toward divorce. Meanwhile, she would sometimes express dissatisfaction with something I was doing by mentioning it in a quiet sentence or two; because she wasn't shouting or waving her arms, I assumed she wasn't particularly upset and this wasn't an important matter.

Over time, we learned each other's language. As we shared our hurts and hopes, we forged an intimate bridge that allowed us to touch each other, even when we seemed strange and foreign to each other. Gradually I stopped losing my temper and shouting. Gradually she became more overtly assertive and expressive. We began to appreciate that each other's differences were not just frustrating but also intriguing.

Our differences gave us a precious gift: the ongoing opportunity to learn more about ourselves by discovering each other.

We learn through meeting. This is why couples have an opportunity to grow through relationships: Intimate relationships offer a ground for meeting each other again and again. In meeting the other, we have an opportunity to come to know our true selves: We learn that knower, known, and knowing are inextricably linked. Who I am only arises with who you are: We are alone, but connected, one yet two, neither one nor two.

> *Each and all the elements of the subjective and objective*
> *spheres are interdependent, and at the same time independent;*
> *Related, though each thing keeps its own place.*

"One" and "two," "same" and "different," "separate" and "connected" are just words. They are concepts pointing at understanding, not understanding itself. Spouses complain of a lack of communication, and try to resolve it through arguing.

In couples' therapy with John and Mary, John says: "I really try to listen to Mary and do what she wants. But I have ADD [attention deficit disorder], and I sometimes start to do one thing, and then something else comes along, and I get distracted, and do something else. Then she gets mad, and it just seems like nothing I do will satisfy her. So I try to keep the level of conflict down by just keeping quiet and staying low-key."

Mary says: "I just can't trust him. He's promised and promised to do things, and he may start them, but he won't follow up without my nagging him. Then as soon as I try to tell him what needs to be done, he clams up. He won't talk with me, so I feel lonely and depressed."

Each member of the couple sees a different reality and fights over whose version of reality is right. We run into problems whenever we fail to see that each "take" on reality, each piece, each person's version, has its own validity but is dependent on all the other versions of reality. John's version of reality doesn't exist in a vacuum: It depends on Mary's version of his version. John takes what he thinks she thinks about him and creates a vision of himself for himself, herself for himself, himself for herself, and herself for herself. Mary does the same. The therapist joins in.

Although our clients may get caught up in fighting about which reality is "right," therapists sometimes get caught up in the question, "Are any of these realities really real?"[2] Is there a True Reality out there? Zen practice answers clearly: "Yes—it's just not what you *think* it is."

Reality is not our ideas about reality. Our ideas overgeneralize and trap us into pictures of ourselves and our loved ones that are timeless and therefore false. If I think I'm a good wife, but when my husband talks about his troubles with his boss, my mind wanders to whether that means he won't get his pay raise and I won't be able to go on vacation—in other words, to my own needs—then at that moment I'm not a good wife. The key words here are: "at that moment." When I say, "I'm a good therapist," it obscures the fact that at one moment I may be a wonderful therapist, in touch with my client; at another moment I may be way off base. Each member of a couple holds ideas about what their relationship is like, and these ideas influence how they act. Each member of a couple may think the other doesn't care about them, yet each is engaged, many moments of each day, in the myriad cooperative acts—washing the dishes, bringing home the paycheck, feeding the baby—that sustain the relationship.

Our ideas about our relationships are always more limiting than the acts of the relationship itself. Our ideas form pretty (or horrifying) pictures, but our lives take place moment by moment according to how we act, what we think, feel, and sense each moment. Reality is a momentary affair.

Reality manifests complete each moment. When the client pauses and looks at the therapist, and the therapist looks back, at that moment there is nothing else and the therapy is complete. When one spouse sighs and the other shakes his head, there is nothing else that moment: The whole relationship is there, each person separate but connected. Perhaps a better way of putting it is that each of us is constantly expressing Reality, *being* Reality.

Because you are, this moment, expressing Reality, I must acknowledge you. Anything else is either ignorance or denial. If I want to be happy, I need to find a way to appreciate, rather than avoid, this Reality in front of me. If a therapist does not appreciate a client, this is a kind of denial of Reality. If a spouse does not appreciate a spouse, this is a denial of Reality. If I do not appreciate myself, this is a denial of Reality. If I don't appreciate my cup of coffee, this is a denial of Reality.

Practice is simply appreciating Reality. Couples' therapy is learning appreciation of the whole in each part, each part in the whole, the whole wholly itself, and each part completely itself as a part.

Bob and Jane have been married over 20 years. They have had a commitment to each other but a stormy relationship. Bob's patriarchal background has led him to regularly demand control of the relationship; Jane has been mostly willing to accede to his dominance, so long as he provided her security. However, there have been occasions on which Bob failed to provide that security. He had an affair (a long time ago), and he has had chronic financial problems. Whenever Jane feels Bob lets her down, she gets anxious and panicky, remembers being abused as a child, and starts feeling bad about herself. Replaying a scenario from her past, she feels responsible for rescuing her irresponsible caretaker while simultaneously feeling resentful at his betrayal and failure to provide security for her. More recently, however, she has started wanting to detach from this pattern and work more autonomously: She started attending school and wants to get a job of her own.

Bob has always insisted on running his own business, but he is not good at financial statements, bookkeeping, and organization. He expects his wife to do his secretarial work and accounting. She did this, but Bob's generosity and excessive trust in others has left him bankrupt. This activates all of Jane's old issues. She doesn't want Bob to run his own business any more, but she has resigned herself to the fact that this is important for him. At this point, she mostly doesn't want to work for him and get stuck in an impossible position, trying to provide organization to the unorganizeable. She is sure, however, that Bob will see her reluctance to work for him as disloyalty. Thinking about working for him again, she gets panic attacks and depressed.

They've run through this pattern many times. In today's therapy session, Jane is talking about how she just can't work for Bob but fears if she "lets him down" by following her own inclinations to get a job with someone else it will destroy their relationship. But this time Bob responds to her differently than usual.

Bob turns to Jane and says, "If you want to work for someone else, go ahead."

Jane says, "You're just saying that here; when we get home you'll be angry and hurt."

Bob says: "No. I know last night I said I wanted you to work in my business and help me out. I know I've been saying that our whole life. I've always *felt* that our relationship should be a partnership, and if you didn't work in my business something was wrong, and that it meant you didn't respect me. I felt that was how Our Heavenly Father really wanted our relationship to be. But I was sitting here in the waiting room today, and I realized: *You're a separate person and I can't make you do anything and that's OK."*

Bob looks a little surprised at what he's just said. He pauses, and seems to think this through and elaborates it out loud. "It doesn't work for me to force you to do things. I'd love it if you wanted to work for me, but you need to do what you want to be happy. That way, I'll be happy. I have to appreciate and accept you for who you are, not for what I want you to be. Actually, you know, I realized, if you go to work and earn money—that'll actually take some pressure off me [smiling]. But more important, I realized that for our relationship to work, I have to give you your freedom, even if sometimes you don't do what I want. But we'll still be connected; our relationship is for all time, even after we die. It feels weird, but that's the way it seems to work."

Bob had expected that work and marriage "should" be a certain way, but he has discovered that Reality has nothing to do with what we *want* it to be. Accepting this is a difficult lesson for couples to learn: Each wants his or her partner to fulfill some ideal image that will somehow heal his or her injured self. Often each spouse subtly coerces the other to be the way he or she "should" be. Healing, however, can never come through force; healing always begins with acceptance.

When I am able to let go of my desires for my spouse to fit my preconceived notions from the past, then I can see who she is right now. This opens up a whole new world with infinitely more possibilities than I had previously thought of. To be open to the possibilities my lover offers to me in the present, I must first begin with accepting her as she is, different from me and from what I think of what the world "must" consist of. Acceptance begins when we see that there are many separate parts, each related to the others, each an equal link to the whole.

This lesson applies to all the "couples" in our lives, including the relationships between different parts of ourselves. A loving, kindly part of me looks at an angry, critical part of me and asks: "Am I *really* so selfish?" If I answer yes, I may despair. If I answer no, I may try to fight the "negative" part of myself, or deny it, or eradicate it. Answering either yes or no misses the mark and falls into the delusion that my altruism and my selfishness are unrelated to each other. Altruism and selfishness each come from the fact that I am both a separate person and inextricably linked to all the people and all the things that constitute the world.

> *Form makes the character and appearance different;*
> *Pleasure and suffering appear unrelated.*
> *The dark makes all forms one;*
> *In brightness dualistic distinctions become apparent.*

The varieties of my experience appear unrelated to each other. Happiness and sorrow seem like different worlds; freezing ice seems unrelated to hot steam. Yet ice, steam, and fluid water all are forms of H_2O; grief, anger, and joy are all expressions of our humanity.

The varieties of myself also can appear unrelated to one another: What I like about myself seems very different from what I don't like about myself. I often feel differently in the various roles I play as lover, husband, father, worker; it's sometimes hard to accept that *all* my actions show different aspects of me, especially if some of them don't mesh with my image of myself. However, if I cannot embrace all the variegated forms of myself and try to disown my despised pieces, I will feel fragmented within.

The same applies to how I view other people; when my spouse is doing something I don't like, I may ask myself: Is this really the same person I loved and wanted to marry? If I'm feeling angry or disappointed, my spouse may appear to be a different person from who I thought she was. It may be hard for me to connect the person who makes me laugh with the person who makes me cry, especially if I get attached to my idealized image of my spouse-as-I-want-her-to-be. Then it is harder for me to embrace the actual person in front of me, who exists quite separate from my desires and fears about her, who simply is herself in all her multifaceted glory.

Just as it can be hard for me to see the connection between the liked and disliked aspects of my lover, so I may sometimes be ignorant of how the actions I take to gain happiness often lead to suffering. I know that I am happy and proud to get a job promotion to be a supervisor; I know that I am irritable and anxious dealing with difficult subordinates. However, I may have difficulty seeing that these are two parts to the same whole. I know the rapture of witnessing my child's birth and the joy of having her nestle in my arms; I also know the frustration of dealing with my teenager's anger and depression. Can I see the two as connected in a larger relationship? I know that I love life and don't want to die: Can I let life and death shake hands, two sides of one coin?

To do this I have to find a way to avoid getting caught in any one partial view. I need to cultivate a wide field of acceptance that makes room both for the bright light that distinguishes between what I know and what I don't know, and the deep darkness that equally embraces both knowing and not-knowing.

As I go through life, I gain knowledge. As I gain experience as a therapist, after a while I learn to distinguish between what works and what doesn't work with different kinds of clients. As I gain even more experience, however, I start to become aware not only of what I know but also what I don't know. As a therapist, when I encounter clients who don't conform to my opinions and the textbooks' descriptions, I start to realize the mystery each individual client presents. The same is true in the rest of my life, in my relations with my loved ones and even with my self: Just as I think I'm getting to know them intimately, I discover I can never know another person completely, not even myself. At this stage it's easy to become fearful of not-knowing and try to master uncertainty by pretending to know more than is possible; it's also easy to despair of ever knowing anything, shut down, and make a virtue of ignorance.

At this point if I can let go of a bit of my wants and fears, I may start to realize that knowing and not-knowing are just two faces of the same coin, just one small dimension of a larger relationship. Therapist and client, lover and beloved are also just different faces, partners allowing the magic dance of autonomy and connect-edness to express itself in concrete forms. Once we can accept this, a space opens up in which everything the client does simply expresses the client, everything I do simply expresses myself as a therapist, and everything we do in psychotherapy we do simultaneously separately and intimately linked. At least for a little while we're just here, now, alive with each other and there is no wall, no blockade to the flow of the therapy.

In the field in which knowledge and discriminating judgment meet all-embracing innocence and complete acceptance, a tree stands forth between heaven and earth; wisdom and joy celebrate leaves opening to the bright sun and roots drinking deeply of the dark soil.

> *The four elements return to their nature like a child to its mother.*
> *Fire is hot, wind moves, water is wet, earth hard.*
> *Eyes see, ears hear, the nose smells, the tongue tastes salt and sour.*
> *Each is independent of the other,*
> *But the different leaves come from the same root.*

When innocent acceptance meets knowing judgment, child and parent meet. Each of us is a child feeling separate from our parent; each of us is a parent feeling separate from our child. At the same time, this separateness creates the basis for relationship.

The relationship of parent to child to parent is impossible and essential. All of us and all of our clients bear the imprints of this in our mind-bodies. We experience our separateness as a void, a yearning; we experience our connectedness as a confining straitjacket. Some of us have had particularly difficult times growing up, and this often makes it harder for us to trust ourselves and to trust the foundation of existence that cradles us. Then we get certain ideas about the kinds of people we "must" be in order to avoid further pain. We turn ourselves into self-sacrificing caretakers or into hurt orphans; we turn ourselves into shielded strongmen and volatile volcanoes, and we invite others to join us in reinforcing our false images of relationships. If we let go of these images and return to ourselves things become much simpler. If I'm hurt, I cry; if I'm happy, I laugh. I begin to realize you do the same. I begin to realize that each of us is a twisted branch on a very big tree, begin to accept your contortions and my own and let my leaves open to the sun.

> I was meeting with a client who most therapists would label as borderline. She complained of feeling a great emptiness within. She said her mother had hated her, physically abused her from the time she was an infant; as a child she had been regularly sexually abused as well as physically beaten to the point at which she sustained a skull fracture when she was four years old. She was frequently depressed, and very sensitive interpersonally: Small incidents could leave her crying for days.
>
> Yet this same woman had been married to one man for over 20 years. She worked hard on the relationship, seeking intimacy. She had a daughter with a severe congenital physical illness: She had cared for her daughter (and her other children) under very difficult conditions, doing her best (and being quite successful) to provide them with warm love and appropriate boundaries. She had worked a long time in psychotherapy to get over the felt lack of love in her own life. She had done guided imagery in which, as an adult, she mothered and nurtured herself as a young child.
>
> But she was tired of having to do all the work. She said, "I'm tired of going to that old well of sadness and emptiness [the depression at feeling unloved]. I wish it would dry up. But I'm getting better. I am taking care of myself now. I am telling myself I'm worthy of love." After a recent incident, she had started crying, then (using some tools gained in the therapy) she had comforted herself by picturing herself as an otter, teaching her baby otter (also herself) to swim. She was happy at this image, but somewhat disbelieving, because she thought of herself as basically deprived and miserable. She *knew* she had received poor parenting, and could not have a deep well of positive health. So she asked: "Where do these images I create come from?"
>
> I answered: "From the universe's love for you."
>
> I don't usually say things like this to clients. Brought up in New York with a somewhat hard-edged personality, I find such sayings seem a bit mushy and I fear they will be unbelievable to my clients. Yet I had a feeling of empathy and caring, and this "popped out" as if it needed to be expressed at the moment.
>
> My client stopped short suddenly. She took a breath, seemed to absorb this a bit, then shook her head as if trying to shake off something that felt foreign but which could not quite be dislodged. She finally said: "I can't hear that yet... but tell me again next week. I'm getting closer."

She is learning not just that she is worthy of love, but that she is, simply by being alive, buoyed up by the universe, shined on by the sun. She is not separate from the fabric of life. She does not need to be worthy. We're all loved and none of us deserve it. Love is just the way things are. Limitless love, unborn and undying, is at the root of all existence; its self-expression is at the very base of all causes and all effects, all life and all death.

Cause and effect both necessarily derive from the great reality.
The words "high" and "low" are used relatively.
Within the light there is darkness, but do not be attached to that darkness.
Within the darkness there is light, but do not be caught by that light.
Light and darkness are a pair,
Like the foot before and the foot behind in walking.
Each thing has its own intrinsic value,
And is related to everything else in function and position.

The universe is not just love. There is cancer and hatred, ignorance and despair. A ten-year-old boy is out delivering papers on his bicycle when he is struck by lightning. Spouses cheat on each other. Parents devour their children, who respond by murdering their parents. Therapists consign patients to hopeless diagnoses and involuntary hospitalizations. Spiritual masters have sex with their disciples. If we ignore any of this, we're incomplete and dishonest. I cannot say to a client that her healing images are rooted in the universe's caring unless I stand on the impersonal destruction of exploding stars. I cannot love my wife without realizing the deep hurts we can and do cause each other.

If we wish to bring our whole self to our relationships, we need to look without blinking at our wishes about who we'd like to be and our anxieties about who we fear we are. As therapists, we must be honest about our own pain and yearning; we must acknowledge the selfishness within our need to help others. As Zen students, we must be honest about our delusions of seeing clearly. In our close relationships, we have to be able to acknowledge our angers if we wish to express our loves.

Some years ago I tried to stay always calm, accepting, and loving when dealing with my family. In the process, I put on a rather sanctimonious mantle and detached myself overmuch from the people I loved.

I didn't wake up from this dream until one day when my ten-year-old daughter was giving me a hard time, purposely provoking me. I maintained an artificially placid posture through deep breathing and "active listening." I projected calm until my daughter couldn't stand it and burst out: "Dad, you don't understand! Sometimes I want to feel that I *can* get you angry!"

She taught me how I'd been holding back, depriving the relationship of something necessary instead of really opening up to it.

If we bring just the "nice" parts of ourselves to our relationships, our connection cannot be very deep. Intimacy needs room to embrace our own and others' imperfections and faults. Zen and psychotherapy are not about never getting angry, but about smiling at our anger. They are not about being constantly enlightened and healthy, but about finding light in darkness, darkness in light, health in sickness, and sickness in health. Our relationships require that we do not restrict our travels to one particular shading but be able to stumble together through the dim forest and burn together on the bright beach, comfort each other in the night and encourage each other to get up and greet the rays of dawn.

Experiencing the darkness of life is crucial, but there is a romantic current in psychotherapy that sometimes overvalues the shadow side. This view holds that plunging into the disowned, disturbing parts of our lives results quasiautomatically in the integration of those parts into some healing wholeness. However, it is easy to get lost in the dark; the very limitlessness of its embrace, in which "all forms become one," is powerfully attractive. Once we stop rejecting pain, if we're not careful, we can become fascinated by the infinite varieties of suffering and the illusion that we can become masters of the dark. This road can lead either to sadistic pleasure or to being attached masochistically to our agonies. We can learn from the dark, but it is important not to get caught by it and become lost.

> During a question–answer period at Berkeley Zen Center, a student asked Sojun-sensei, "Many spiritual teachers seem to live wonderful lives, but then wind up doing terrible things: having sex with their students, running off with the donations believers sent them, betraying their followers and getting lost in the dark alleys. You don't seem to do that. How do you avoid getting lost in the dark alleys?"
>
> Sojun-sensei replied, "By knowing the dark alleys like the palm of my hand."

We illuminate the dark alleys not by avoiding them but by exploring them with a lantern in our hand.

Experiencing the light of life is crucial, but there is a rationalist current in psychotherapy that sometimes overvalues the bright side of things. This view holds that we are masters of our fate so that identifying our past solutions, answering back to our negative thoughts, and reinforcing our strengths will result in the subjugation of our hurts. But we've all met people who seem to cling to a brittle brightness, a fragile optimism that simply denies anything unpleasant. Someone who is always smiling makes us uneasy. But although it is easy to see the problems of being caught by the light in door-to-door proselytizers and Little Mary Sunshines, it's sometimes harder to acknowledge how I can cling to false purity. We can learn from the light, but it is important not to get attached to it or take the light for granted.

One of the wonderful teachings of the Sandokai is its ability to be evenhanded in all matters. There are differences in human personality, some clever, some not. There is light, and there is dark. There is salt, sweet, sour, bitter: The taste of life is simply what it is. Good and bad, light and dark are twin siblings: They alternate being the foot before and the foot behind in walking. Each highlights the other so we can deepen our appreciation of life itself.

My eleven-year-old daughter one day struck up a conversation that dealt with the connection between light and darkness. Struck by her insights, I recorded what she said: "You know, Dad, I used to like take for granted that life would always be there... everything was safe and I felt like I won't ever be hurt and nothing bad could ever happen, but then bad things started happening."

(We'd had a hard, dark year. My father, who was living with us, died of cancer: My teenage daughter had significant emotional difficulties and eventually went off to a boarding school. Then my sister came down with cancer.)

"I feel like I see things differently now... Now I notice more when things die, and really when things live too... I think it's because I don't take things for granted after last year. The little things in life that I took for granted... um, I really think about them more now... Like a flower with the light shining on it a particular way, I used to just dismiss it as well, that's beautiful, but now I really think about it and enjoy... like how's the light shining on it and the color against the trees and the sky especially blue that day."

I asked how she went about doing this, and she replied, "I realized... [you're not] going to be secure forever and protected for your whole life because one day you're going to have to go off too and it won't be perfect. But then you can enjoy the little things you wouldn't even notice otherwise, little things which make life better, bearable.

"It comes naturally sort of, you don't really have to think about it, *you just look at it and you see the good and the bad side and just decide whether you want to enjoy this or just let it pass.*"

Our relationship to what we see as dark and light determines whether we're walking with it or standing still. If we get stuck in either, we can't move our feet. If we reject either, we won't be able to take a step. If we can be engaged but nonattached, we can "just look at it and see the good *and* the bad"; then we begin to see that darkness and light are *connected.*

Light and darkness form a pair. It's not enough to acknowledge darkness, and acknowledge light: We must see that they are related to each other. It's not enough to acknowledge how wonderful my spouse is and overidealize her; that will preserve a surface harmony that may not leave room to air dissatisfactions in the turmoiled arguments that lead to growth. It's not enough to acknowledge that my spouse is not everything I want her to be and that I'm not everything she wants me to be: That will lead to resignation, but not necessarily to joy. I can, however, discover the very basis of our relationship in both its limitations and in our being enough to each other, limited though we are. Not being enough, we change and grow to deal with our conditions: Being enough to each other, we can tolerate the changes and growth that create new ways of being with each other that still remain not enough. This way we endlessly renew ourselves and each other.

This holds true not just in couples' relationships but also in psychotherapies and spiritual practice. Each school of psychotherapy is limited and will inevitably fail with some people at some times while helping other people at other times. Each spiritual practice will have its limitations and its liberation, its traps and its revelations. Each has its own intrinsic value, and none functions alone. All paths are connected.

Faced with the frustrations of incomplete or unsatisfying relationships, struggling with the difficulties of the path we're on, the temptation is strong to move from relationship to relationship, from therapy technique to therapy technique in endless eclecticism, from spiritual practice to spiritual practice in endless search.

> I remember once hearing a friend ask our Zen teacher: "There was a tradition in ancient times, where students wandered from teacher to teacher. But there also seems to be a tradition of apprenticing yourself to one teacher. Which is better?"
> Our teacher thought for a while, and then replied: "Maybe better to stick to the poison that you have." And laughed.

The great advantage of being in a relationship is that we're stuck with each other. The great advantage of being a person is that we're stuck with ourselves. We can't move away from ourselves but are stuck with the poison that we have. Our antidotes are paired with our poisons; our perfection is the twin of our flaws.

> Last night I had a conversation with a deeply religious friend about being perfect. I maintained there is perfection; he disagreed. He asked me if I knew anyone perfect, and I answered: "You." He replied, "But I don't think of myself as perfect." Of course I replied: "That's where you are perfect." He thought about this a little while and then said, "Yes. I can accept I am a part of something perfect."
> But anything perfect is perfect in all its parts: Each ordinary part—which only exists in relation to all the other parts—is perfection itself.

> *Ordinary life fits the absolute as a box and its lid.*
> *The absolute works together with the relative*
> *Like two arrows meeting in mid air.*

There is nothing special about perfection: If we reserve perfection for some rarefied, unusual occurrence, it becomes imperfect in its very restrictiveness. We lose perfection if we look to something beyond our immediate experience. If we focus overmuch on our vision of how we want life to be and ignore the mundane details of life itself, we may fail to realize how the special qualities of life are founded on our ordinary acts.

If we want our spouse to be something special, he or she will always fall short. If we are attached to some vision of ourselves fulfilling a grand ideal, we can easily despair at our shortcomings. In contrast, if we find the specialness in our spouse and ourselves in the daily acts of tying shoelaces, changing diapers, and washing the car, each ordinary act fulfills ourselves and each other.

Couples often have some vision of how they want things to be with their partners but get into difficulties when they try to "work on the relationship." They may reserve some time to sit down and have a serious discussion, but even if they adopt an attitude of flexibility and good will, somehow they often get into an argument that merely rehashes old hurts and disappointments. Partially this happens if each member of the couple is too attached to his or her own way of looking at things. More fundamentally, however, "working on the relationship" can be frustrating because relationships are elusive: Relationships can't be grasped and won't sit still to be worked on. You cannot grasp the moon by reaching out to its reflection in the pond: You cannot heal yourself by projecting some image of yourself into your spouse and insisting that your spouse do what you "need," and you cannot change a relationship just by talking about it.

We can't work *on* a relationship, but we can *engage in* a relationship through the ordinary acts that constitute it. It's not enough to have an idea about being a good husband or wife: You must *act* like a good husband or wife. In the abstract a relationship can be too amorphous an idea, too big a commitment, too fearful an intimacy. So it's better to just do the little things that make up the relationship. If you want to work on your relationship, go for a walk with your spouse. Wash the dog together. Listen to what your lover is saying. Cook something. Have an argument.

Couples often come in to therapy wanting to "work on their relationship." Consistently, however, I find that the hardest thing to get couples to do is to simply spend time together, one with the other. Something—work, the kids, the household chores—always seems to get in the way. They want to work on their relationship, but they don't *do* anything together. So recently I've worked less on devising fancy interventions for couples and more on getting couples to just spend time together doing whatever they like. I don't know how to work on togetherness, but perhaps I can learn how we can tend our garden together.

The same is true for the relationships at the heart of psychotherapy. I don't know how to do psychotherapy. It's too big for me. I am learning how to sit down in my office and listen to someone. Each client teaches me a little more about how to listen. Every once in a while I even have something to say. But the therapy arises in how we look at each other, how we shake hands in the waiting room, how our eyes meet as we leave each other or share our lives together.

I also don't know how to meditate or walk a spiritual path. So I just sit down on my cushion each day, and I bow to my friends, and to my family; I bow to my anger and suffering; I bow to my clients. As I bow, something seems to be moving.

Our lives are not a series of grand gestures, but the moments in which we make coffee, go to the bathroom, wash our hands, kiss our loved ones goodbye, work, play, and go to sleep. The sun does not set out to give forth glory: It simply burns itself up doing what's in front of it, and in the darkness of that destruction light streams out.

Our relationships are not made or destroyed once and for all, but over and over. In the humble tasks that actualize our lives, however many times we take out the garbage or make the bed or prepare dinner, all these tasks will need to be done again the next day. Whether it is with my spouse, my patient, my children, my parents, my sister, or my self, however many times I struggle with them over some issue—how much I can depend on you, how much I will let you ask of me, how much I can quiet myself to really listen to you, how close I can let myself be to you, how much separateness I need to be intimate—there is one thing of which I can be sure: However we resolve the issue, the next time we meet we will dance again.

The dance of frustration and satisfaction, sameness and difference, closeness and separation, may take many different forms: arguing about where we'll spend our vacation or why one of us was late; worrying together about the illness of someone we love; making love in the leaves beneath a pine tree. But the dance itself is eternal. Our lives transcend ourselves in each mundane act. Our lives are absolutely relative:

> Hunting meteorites
> An ordinary piece of granite
> Stubbed my toe
> Advising me
> We both must be
> Shared fragments of the sun.

> *Reading the above lines you should have grasped the great reality.*
> *Do not set up your own standards.*
> *If you do not see the way, you do not see it,*
> *Though you are actually walking on it.*
> *When you walk the way it is not near, it is not far.*
> *If you are deluded you are mountains and rivers away from it.*

The solution to the impossible riddle of relationships is simple: Don't set up your own standards. If I try to make a relationship run according to my ideas of what the relationship "should" be I will be blinded by my own desires, needs, and fears. Relationships take a great deal of courage and faith, so we usually qualify our commitment by saying inwardly, "I'll love you *if...* " As soon as we do this, however, the relationship becomes unsatisfying because a part of me is standing apart, setting up my own standards, evaluating whether I'm getting what I want from the relationship. This sounds sensible, but while I'm standing apart from and judging the relationship, I can't be fully *in* the relationship. I cannot be fully engaged and intimate while simultaneously holding some part of myself back.

This is true not just of our relationships with our loved ones but also of our relationships in psychotherapy. For a long time, therapists lived under the illusion that somehow the patient could be in a relationship with the therapist without the therapist being in a relationship with the patient. That has largely changed, and most modern schools of therapy do not adopt a surgical model in which therapists operate dispassionately on suffering patients.[3] There remains a seductive lure, however, that somehow we have some technique that will cure people or at least help them realize themselves. Then we get attached to our ideology,[4] set up our own standards of health and sickness, and get lost.

We all constantly set up our own standards. We discriminate and make judgments. We say to ourselves, "That person was nice to me/mean to me" or "I'm not attracted to him/her because he's fat/she's thin." Therapists are not immune from this, but we clothe our standards in an air of technical virtuosity. We say, "That patient is a good candidate for insight psychotherapy," or "That patient is borderline." We say, "I enjoy working with that patient, but I dread seeing that other one," according to our standards of who fits our treatment model or who we find interpersonally appealing.

Do we have the courage to let each patient teach us how to do psychotherapy anew? The challenge for us as therapists is to find a way to genuinely enjoy meeting *each* patient who comes, to allow ourselves to learn, teach, touch, and be touched in each intimate encounter whatever it offers, moment-by-moment. If we allow ourselves to let each client teach us how to do psychotherapy anew, however, how do we maintain the necessary boundaries required to keep an edge to the relationship? How do we avoid falling into haphazard "anything goes" therapies and respect the knowledge we have of what is necessary to be helpful?

This is the same question that we must ask ourselves in any relationship: How can I surrender completely to the relationship without setting up my own standards but still stay true to my self? Unsure about such matters, at times we may not see which way to turn. We may not know how to respond to our loved one or even to our own needs. We may not know what to say to our parent, child, or lover. We may not know how to intervene with our client.

Even when we are confused, however, there is a true ground to being that underlies the needs of each moment. We lose sight of this ground if we try to control it too much; we trip over our own feet. We have to get out of the way in order to find the way; we have to drop our expectations and personal desires to let the need of the moment make itself known. If I let go of my personal concerns, I am more able to engage in whatever I'm doing with you, this moment, with every fabric of my being. If we let go of our own narrow standards and open ourselves up, something clarifies itself. Then whatever is necessary to do to meet the relationship in that moment emerges in spontaneous activity.

> I was working with a couple I liked very much. They were intelligent, articulate, caring people who kept getting into the same basic argument that kept their relationship from becoming fully committed and satisfying.
>
> We had worked together for a number of sessions and apparently made no progress. Over the course of the therapy I had tried most everything I knew: behavioral practice tasks, psychodynamic interpretations, strategic interventions, solution-focused inquiries, relative influence questioning, and so forth. Nothing had budged the couple, and we appeared to just be repeating the same old stuff over and over.

I had exhausted all my ideas, and in the middle of the session I confessed I was stumped and asked if they minded if I consulted with a colleague. They gave their permission and I excused myself and walked around the corner to a friend and highly valued colleague, an expert in working with couples. I spent twenty minutes going over the case with him, and after some hard work on both our parts we had come up with an intervention that seemed to show some promise. I rehearsed the exact words of the intervention carefully, then returned to my office. I sat down and opened my mouth to offer the intervention when the wife interrupted me:

"Excuse me," she said. "We both are interested in what you have to say, but we felt we should tell you what we talked about while you were out of the room. We both agreed you're working way too hard, and all we really need is for you to sit back and listen and give us a chance to talk with each other."

I thanked her, expressed my appreciation, closed my mouth, and listened. They moved on and the relationship changed.

You would think I would have learned my lesson from this? But a few years later I was having repeated run-ins with my teenage daughter who was depressed, angry, alienated. I had tried listening and repeating back what I heard her saying; I had tried setting firm limits; I had tried writing letters to her; I had tried negotiating behavioral contracts; I had tried getting mad; I had tried staying silent; I had tried talking about my own experiences. Nothing worked.

A few months after she moved out to attend a boarding school we were attempting to have a conversation. She was angry at me, and we cycled through all the interactions mentioned above. I tried hard to find a way to relate to her, but it seemed whatever I did or said, the gulf only became wider and wider and the pain intensified.

Finally I cried out: "I don't know what to say to you. I don't know what you want, I don't know how to relate to you."

"There!" she said, with some triumph and some relief. "At last! That's the best thing you've said. Maybe now we can get somewhere."

Later, we were able to cry a bit together about how we'd both hurt each other; Burdened by fewer assumptions and expectations and assisted by forgiveness, we began to find a way of rediscovering each other.

> *I say respectfully to those who seek the way:*
> *Do not vainly pass through sunshine and shadows.*

We are always passing through sunshine and shadow, knowledge and ignorance, togetherness and separateness. Our lives are short, but each day that we wake up we have a new chance to practice our love affair with the world. The more we can let go of our self-centered concerns, the more we can distill this love's unselfish root. Each session with each client we have a chance to meet them and let the encounter transform us both. Each moment with our loved ones offers an opportunity to communicate intimately, to touch and be touched by something greater than either one of us alone, yet which still preserves and values the uniqueness each of us contributes. Reading and writing, talking and listening, we are seeking the way together. I say respectfully to me and to you: Let us not forget to treasure our selves. Let us not forget to treasure each other.

Dust

Dust on the mat.
Fragments of some star which, dying,
Found itself in light.

Seeking searched transparently
'til no thing interposed itself
between the sky and earth except
time resting in a moment.

I brush the mat clean:
Ten thousand motes sparkle in a sliver of the sun.

Dust on the mat.
No dust?
No beam of light...

Great Wisdom Beyond Wisdom Heart Sutra[1]

Avalokitesvara Bodhisattva, when practicing deeply the Prajna Paramita,
Perceived that all five skandhas in their own being are empty,
and was saved from all suffering.

"Oh Shariputra, form does not differ from emptiness,
emptiness does not differ from form.
That which is form is emptiness,
that which is emptiness, form.
The same is true of feelings, perceptions, formations, consciousness.

Oh Shariputra, all Dharmas are marked with emptiness.
They do not appear nor disappear,
Are not tainted nor pure,
Do not increase nor decrease.

Therefore in emptiness
no form, no feelings, no perceptions, no formations, no consciousness;
no eyes, no ears, no nose, no tongue, no body, no mind;
no color, no sound, no smell, no taste, no touch, no object of mind;
no realm of eyes until no realm of mind-consciousness;
no ignorance and also no extinction of it until no old-age-and-death
and also no extinction of it;
no suffering, no origination, no stopping, no path;
no cognition, also no attainment.
With nothing to attain
a Bodhisattva depends on Prajna Paramita
and the mind is no hindrance.
Without any hindrance no fears exist.
Far apart from every perverted view one dwells in nirvana.

In the three worlds all Buddhas depend on Prajna Paramita
And attain unsurpassed complete perfect enlightenment.

Therefore know the Prajna Paramita
is the great transcendent mantra,
is the great bright mantra,
is the utmost mantra,
is the supreme mantra,
which is able to relieve all suffering
and is true, not false.

So proclaim the Prajna Paramita mantra,
proclaim the mantra that says:
ga-tè, ga-tè, pa-ra-ga-tè, para-sam-ga-tè!
Bodhi! Svaha!"

Chapter 5

Empty Self, Connected Self:
Great Wisdom Beyond
Wisdom Heart Sutra[2]

We assume we exist: that we were born and will die. We assume we have our own existence, living alone encased in bags of skin. You assume you exist separate from me, separate from the chair in which you are sitting, separate from the book that you are reading. It looks like things are either outside you or inside you: Material objects, therapy clients, lovers are outside you; perceptions, thoughts, intentions, feelings, and consciousness are inside you.

At this moment, however, are these words "inside" or "outside" you? This vision of a page that you see: Is it inside you or outside you? Right now this book is part of your experience: Can you continue reading while remaining completely separate from the book? When a client speaks and you feel moved, and the client feels moved by your feeling moved, are the two of you separate or connected beings?

You tend to assume, unquestioning, that you exist, separate from me. I tend to assume, unquestioning, that I exist, separate from you. This, however, is a fundamental error, perhaps *the* fundamental error that creates our suffering. Psychotherapy cannot be truly transformative and pierce the heart of what is the matter so long as it remains burdened by this mistaken view.

The Heart Sutra directly addresses this: When we come right down to it, what is the essence of what makes me me, you you, and things things? It asks us to look deeply to discover what is at the core of everything's and everyone's existence. We concluded the previous chapter by saying that we must remember to treasure our selves and each other. But what does this "self" we treasure consist of?

This question, of course, is at the center of psychotherapy. "What is the problem?" is another way of asking "Who am I? What is the world? What is life? What is the core of my existence?"

The Heart Sutra has a surprising answer for us: Avalokitesvara, the Buddhist figure who personifies compassion, tells us that when we go deeply to the very core of our existence, we don't find any particular thing to hold on to. There is no special essence that sets me apart from you, you apart from the chair, the chair apart from the earth, sky, and stars. Instead, we find that our being is interbeing:[3] We only exist in relationship to everything and everyone else. Prajnaparamita is the great transcendent wisdom that, in holding us, lets us know through its touch that we are not separate from the universe. Suffering comes from looking selfishly for something special onto which I can hold and proclaim: "This is my own being, *my* essence." Release from suffering comes from the discovery that we exist in the act of touching each other: Essentially, *I* depends on *us*. We're all in this together.

It is not just that we are dependent, that we need others (although this is true); the Heart Sutra reminds us that we actually do not exist except through our interlocking, interdependent, interbeing.

You are a particular person, holding a particular book, at a particular time. If you close this book you cannot continue reading; your reading depends on the book. While the book is open your thoughts, feelings, sensations, impulses, and consciousness at this moment are intertwined with the physical paper and ink in your hands and before your eyes. As you hold this page, you are connected to the tree that gave itself up to become paper; to the sun and rain that helped the tree grow; to the people who worked the wood, printed the print, made the book; to the earth whose mass keeps us all from spinning out into space. Each contributes some of his, her, or its life to this book: You are holding pieces of life, packets of energy, in your hands.

You cannot be reading this without light; your vision, your seeing-consciousness, is a transformation of light. Whether that light is streaming through your window direct from the sun or comes indirectly from the sun in the form of electric energy powering a lamp, the sun is helping us communicate with each other. Scientists tell us the very minerals of our body are composed from other suns that exploded long ago and made the journey across interstellar space to wind up in the cells of your body and mine.

By virtue of the sun and stars, the printer's sweat and the editor's emendations, you and I are communing at this moment. Your thoughts, feelings, sensations, impulses, and consciousness as you sit reading are interacting with my thoughts, feelings, sensations, impulses, and consciousness as I write this to you. But we are not alone. Besides those who contributed to physically making the book, our families, our clients, our students and our teachers are all here now as well; they contributed to the thoughts we think and the feelings we feel, which are born through the intercourse of all the other thoughts and feelings that have embraced and fought with each other. As you experience this, we are all meeting each other: You are touching me and allowing me to touch you. I thank you for this.

The same kinds of intertwining are at work when our client sits down in front of us. Generations past and present, whole ecologies of current and potentially future existence, are meeting. Powerful forces are at work here.

Where does "I" fit in to all this? This is what our clients are asking when they feel out of sorts, alien to themselves and to the lives around them. We need to respond to them not so much with an answer as with a greeting.

We do not usually think of ourselves, our clients, or our problems as so inherently interconnected. We have a tendency to assume that we each have some core identity that underlies our existence and defines each of us. We usually think of ourselves as the repository and integrator of personal experience as represented in our thinking, feeling, and actions. In doing so we think we are living out who we are: Actually, however, we are living out our *ideas* about who we are. Too often our underlying (usually unstated) assumption is that the self is, ultimately, a thing: an object with some "essence."

If we think selves have some underlying unchanging essence, we begin to assume selves and objects can be characterized with fixed qualities and measurable quantities. We believe that real objects actually exist "out there" and can be discovered or interacted with by a separate, real observer "in here." Our observing self then becomes not a living, breathing, unfolding mystery, but another object that we place inside "me" instead of outside "me." Then if we try to face ourselves to discover the truth of our existence, we become confused about who we are.

Emperor Wu of Liang asked Great Teacher Bodhidharma, "What is the highest meaning of the holy truths?"

Bodhidharma said, "Empty—there's no holy."

The emperor said, "Who are you facing me?"

Bodhidharma said, "Don't know."

The emperor didn't understand. Bodhidharma subsequently crossed the Yangtse River, came to Shaolin, and faced a wall for nine years.[4]

When the Emperor asks his question about truth while he and Bodhidharma face each other, each is also facing his true self. But the Emperor takes it for granted that there must be some "thing" that gives meaning to Truth and some "who" that constitutes the person who faces him. Bodhidharma tries to shake him free of these assumptions. He fails. It would be easy to think the fault lies in the obtuseness of the Emperor Wu, but this misses the point: Truth is not a thing, but rather the vibrant emptiness of interbeing. Bodhidharma knows he cannot knowingly say who he is in this meeting independent of the Emperor's questioning. This is like psychotherapy: When knowing and not-knowing meet, who is it that truly comes forth?

The emptiness of the Heart Sutra is not an emptiness of gaping holes: It is the emptiness of nothing-getting-in-the-way, the emptiness of points of intersection at which there are no blocks to meeting each other. If our physical hearts were not empty, they could not be constantly pumping blood to all parts of the body. When our physical hearts have some thing in them, we get a blockage: a heart attack. The emptiness of the Heart Sutra is the emptiness of a healthy heart.

QUANTITIES AND QUALITIES

If therapists treat the self as existing with real characteristics (or deficits) "in" it, we collude with our clients by implicitly treating the client's self as a thing. A thing-self is an object, a residue that contains certain "amounts" of feelings, traits, or residues of past experiences. Then there is a danger that therapists will share their clients' delusion: that a client's problems come from having either "an excess of bad stuff" or "insufficient good stuff" "inside" them, or perhaps "not enough harmony" among the client's internal states. Then the solution to suffering appears to depend on having more or less: more good stuff, less bad stuff.

This is very much an economic view of mental functioning. Although virtually all therapeutic schools have rejected Freud's original formulations of the economics of mental or instinctual energy, we still tend to be subtly bound by a therapeutics of gain and loss. Perhaps this is inevitable living in a capitalist culture that measures happiness according to the amounts of things accumulated. But we make a fundamental mistake if we apply accounting ledgers to organic being. It is not possible to quantify harmony, touch a bad introject, or fill up a self that contains gaping holes in some tangible, impoverished structure.

If we treat our feelings as things, then we develop therapeutic strategies for clients to have more good feelings and less bad ones. This seems natural. We can treat depression by increasing the number of activities a client performs from a Pleasant Events Schedule; we can treat anxiety by decreasing the amount of muscle tension a person holds on to. These are useful strategies, but not if taken in isolation. If a depressed client's favorite pleasures are gambling or shopping, doing more of these and running up debts may not be so helpful; if an anxious client decides to relax by neglecting household chores and sloughing off at work, his or her tension level may go up when spouse and boss put in their objections.

More pleasure and less pain are not necessarily solutions to suffering. What is crucial is not the quantity but the quality of the experience; honesty, sincerity, and wholeheartedness cannot be measured with a ruler and a watch. Our experiences and feelings cannot be predicted in terms of physical magnitude. A firm but gentle touch that is reassuring does not become more reassuring with "more" touch (which may be experienced as pain or intrusion) and may not become less reassuring with "less" touch (which may be experienced as a caress or a playful tickle). Feelings and relationships are not quantities, but qualities.

Self is not a quantity. Yet most of us feel as if we have a certain amount of "self," and virtually all of us feel that the amount we have is not enough.[5] Feeling this way, we act as if we have some quantity of self that can be gained or lost. We may try to get "more" self by borrowing or stealing it from those around us, or we may try to hoard the inadequate amount of self we have by pulling back and distancing from other people. In either scenario we may feel threatened in our relationships, worried we might "lose ourselves" if we have too much or too little intimacy. We can easily make the mistake of grasping for more of someone or pushing someone away, when a shift in qualitative "feel" is what is needed:

> A couple came in contemplating divorce. She insisted that her husband would have to spend more time accompanying her and her friends on the activities she enjoyed if the marriage were to survive. He felt she was pulling away from him: He wanted her to spend less time in her activities and more time with him, being *his* friend, if the marriage were to survive. As she started to do more without him, he withdrew by working longer hours at work; as he withdrew, she felt abandoned and spent more time with her friends.
>
> Each was able to acknowledge the other's point of view. When I had them talk with each other during the session, they were polite but distant. They each felt sad, separately, but they were not able to empathize with each other or feel a sense of shared intimacy.
>
> I had them both stand up. One at a time I asked each of them to position themselves and their partner so that their physical distance and the way they faced and touched each other illustrated first how close they felt to each other in their current relationship and then what their "ideal" closeness would look like. They agreed on a picture of their current situation and stood side-by-side, holding hands. However, whenever the husband moved closer, the wife sidled further away; as the wife sidled away, the husband started moving in the opposite direction and dropped his hand. The dynamics of "more" and "less" were leading to a push-me-pull-you oscillation that threatened to break them apart.
>
> They were being frustrated by their impasse until they discovered that if, as they held hands, they used their touching as a pivot point, they could step around and face each other rather than stand side-by-side. Once they were facing each other, they were able to experiment with different positions, each of which had a different "feel" to it.
>
> The solutions they began to evolve during the session involved getting out of the plane of "more" and "less" time together. Instead, they began exploring what the quality of their relationship was like during the time they actually spent together.

The amount of time we spend with each other can be important, but it can also be a red herring. There are people whom we see every day as we commute to work or walk through the halls of the office building; although we bump into them every day, this is not the same thing as truly *seeing* them. We may see our spouse every day, but sometimes familiarity breeds contempt or, even worse, the absent-minded ignorance that takes the other person for granted. Then we talk at each other rather than listen to each other.

QUANTITY AND QUALITY IN THERAPY: A CASE EXAMPLE

The same thing that holds true for clients' relationships in their lives with their partners also applies to the relationship between client and therapist. Emotional distress generally cannot be alleviated by providing a certain amount of a missing emotion; a client who feels unloved does not need a certain number of hugs or nods of approval, but rather a certain quality of experience within the relationship.

We cannot rely on quantity. Even if we meet once a week with a client for a year, fifty-two hours measured against the hours in a total lifetime may seem a small amount indeed. Based on a twenty-four-hour day with 365 days in a year in a life of seventy years, a year of weekly psychotherapy occupies .00008 of the person's time in life; a twelve-session psychotherapy takes up .00002 of the person's total hours. Is this a critical difference?

In these days of managed care, we often get caught up in the issue of the number of sessions the client and therapist will be able to see each other. This is not unimportant, but it is not the whole story. I work in a health maintenance organization where clients often come for therapy concerned that they will be short-changed by the health care plan and not get what they need. Sometimes they ask me how many sessions they can have; sometimes they know they have twenty sessions and tell me they want to "ration" them. I usually address their realistic concerns first, assure them that I will meet with them as much as is necessary within the confines of the situation, but then ask them, "Wouldn't you like to feel differently as soon as you can?" and echo Hillel's question: "If not now, when?" What's getting in the way of making a shift today? This often helps us get down to the core of an issue rather quickly.

Nevertheless, as therapists we often see clients for whom the amount of deprivation in their early home life is so great that it seems they must require lengthy treatment. We may even feel we will never be able to provide them enough of a psychological structure for them to settle in securely. To feel at home with ourselves and the world, however, the issue is not the size of our house but the quality of its comfort. The following extended case example illustrates some of the issues involved.

Laura had a neurological diagnosis of idiopathic autonomic insufficiency: Basically her nervous system would sometimes "shut down," leading to hypotension, problems in changing position (getting up from a sitting position, sitting down from a standing position), fainting spells, and irregular heartbeats. She had had this condition since early childhood and needed a pacemaker.

Laura had originally been referred to me by her neurologist for an unusual reason: She would come in to doctors' offices and fall silent. Although she could (and did) talk normally in her everyday life, in the doctor's office she would be mute. Every once in a while she would force out a few words; sometimes she would bring a written list of questions. If asked questions directly, she would start to reply, shake her head, shrug her shoulders, and fall helplessly silent. However, she communicated with her neurologist by writing him long letters. She was very appreciative of her neurologist's help and expressed her appreciation through generous gifts in ways that seemed to presume too much of a personal relationship and made him feel somewhat nervous. At their last meeting she had hugged him, and he had felt compelled to put the relationship on a more distant, "professional" level. He referred her to me.

When we first met, we experienced the same problems. She arrived late, and when she came into the office she did not sit down or talk. It is hard to form a therapeutic contract with a client who doesn't express herself, but I suggested that she might want to meet with me so that she could feel free to talk or keep silent whenever she chose.

A few days later I received a letter from her that eloquently portrayed her current and past struggles. By way of background, here are some portions of her initial letter and my subsequent written reply:

> I am now going to share with you my intellect... Imagine your brain as a house in which you live. There are many rooms in your house. There are two stories. Have you been in all the rooms in your house?... My medical problem is in the lower story of my house. There is as you could say, damage to the lower story. In where the conscious and unconscious do not work in conjunction together....
>
> I feel much sorrow for people.... I have seen people who simply lack the will to be, others who are trapped within certain rooms within their house, either due to damage, or to simply not knowing how to leave the room, so to speak. I know this, understand this, but with my own lack of intelligence am unable to help them.
>
> I would also request of you that when you are with one of these people who are, as I say, neither here nor there, that you show respect. These people do exist. What could help these people? Talk to them, touch them, bring animals to them, play music. All of these things appeal to the most simplistic part of being.
>
> The reason Dr. X [her neurologist] has, what you would say, an "in" with me is because I know him to be true of heart. True of heart finds it difficult to deceive. I revealed myself more to him than any other, and then was somewhat chased back in, so to speak. This was not the fault of anyone, but of all of us.
>
> I know that I am safer within the boundaries of my house. It is easier to write because the paper is not prejudiced. I can be safe here. I can come out, and not be sought as different or strange. I am not different, I tell you.... I am the same.... No one is any more, or less, than another.
>
> [She described some of her early history. Her mother's pregnancy and her birth were difficult, and she was born underweight and jaundiced.] After my mother was allowed to take me home [from the hospital] she was very saddened because, as she maintains today, she knew when she held me that something was not right. She says that I was like a little rag doll.... My brother hated me. On one occasion my mother had left the room to go wash the dishes. She was alerted to me screaming out. She ran to see what had happened and found that my brother had removed me from my crib and placed me on our floor heater....
>
> [As she grew older her disability became more pronounced. She had difficulties sitting up and standing, moving her arms and legs. Her family was unable to deal with it and restricted her to

one room in the back of the house where she would be out of the way.]

The household grew very sad. Life in my house was very quiet. My father and mother grew more and more distant as issues were not addressed and not allowed to be discussed. My father began to turn to alcohol as a way to escape this. He began boxing with me and forcing me to learn to not cry or show pain. I learned.... [T]he pain, by the way, is not caused by him but by my constant hiding it; it hurts badly but I look at you and show nothing. This is the evil. The denial. I have denied my true self.

My father became an alcoholic. My mother would always tell me that if she just hadn't of had me, "then everything would be O.K., there wouldn't be these problems between me and your dad, and your brother would be happy too, we'd all be better off." My father began to be truly cruel to me, saying things like "You know, if there is something wrong with an animal, the other animals kill it. To keep the herd healthy." I was treated badly by my family, and rarely was I spoken to, or even touched. They forced me to hate my disability. My family still doesn't have anything to do with me for the most part. They don't touch me....

I saw the outside world to be a hostile place. From my first memories, I recognized that my difference to what you call normal was grounds for discomfort, fear, confusion, and a basic separation from the world as we know it and its inhabitants. I knew without being told that I was "different."

Was I lonely? Yes, in many ways I was, and still am....I will ask you, would you be lonely if you weren't able to share yourself with someone else?... If I know so much about myself, why can't I correct the emotional dysfunction that I am struggling with?... My need to protect my innermost self is stronger than my need to step-out, shall we say, and share with you.

I have recognized myself to be safer within the boundaries of my house. Your house is not free from damage. True, it is safer but, well, imagine outside forces as.... like someone throwing rocks at your windows. Your windows may, or may not be broken, but certainly there are going to be scratches. I have sustained scratches on the windows in the room in which my emotions lie, and because of this I have become too afraid to, as you said, Dr. Rosenbaum, willfully come out of my house when I want to and to stay in my house when I don't.

What I want for my life is the most basic and simplistic of needs. I would like to be recognized as being the same as you. I would like to share totality with someone, that is, to share all of my being with them. I would like to help as many people as I can, in whatever way I can. More simply put, what I want is to be a wife, mother, friend, to work with people, animals, nature, to share love of life and everything that exists in it. To not have to fear that coming out of my house will bring harm to me....

My letter in response:

I was very moved in reading what you sent me, and your sharing your intellect with me. It is clear to me you have sometimes had to struggle hard to satisfy some of the most basic and simple needs: the need to be recognized and accepted. To be accepted as the same, and as unique. Despite being scared, and tired, you were willing to share your insights with me....

Of course it is safer within the boundaries of your house. You have acknowledged the importance of being able to come out of your house, and go back into it, as needed. It is good to have a refuge, and also good to explore the world. When you come out of your house, in order to avoid feeling like you're being treated as different or strange, could it help to remind yourself, as you say, that "we are all capable, and no one is any more, or less, than another?" How could you go about reminding yourself of this during difficult times?...

I know you feel there is some problem between your conscious and unconscious, due to some damage to your lower story. Is it possible that the simplest, most basic parts of your being provide a foundation that is deeper even than conscious or unconscious stories? Perhaps you have explored the basement, but what do you need to do to fully appreciate—or, if necessary, shore up—the foundations of your house? How do you go about appreciating the simple solidity of the earth your house rests on?

You have been treated cruelly, and learned to not show pain.... You have written of your loneliness, and the conflict between your need to protect yourself and your need to step out and share; to work with people, animals, nature, and to love life. You have asked why, if you know so much about yourself, can't you correct the emotional dysfunction you are struggling with. Don't you think your writing is a step in the right direction?

Nobody's house is free of damage. The nature of a house is that, as time goes by, it weathers and sometimes needs maintenance. Sometimes this involves putting on a new coat of paint; sometimes it involves shoring up the foundation. I used to live in a house which was built around 1917. We later found out that, because it was built during the war, the concrete that was used in that house and many of the houses around it was "softer" than most concrete, and we were told it had a high chance of collapsing under stress and should be replaced. And yet, when the earthquake struck last year, that house and the others like it were left undamaged, while some of the other houses with supposedly "stronger" foundations suffered significant damage. Do you think that sometimes, when a house has some flaw, after a period of time it adjusts to its weaknesses and that this can give it greater flexibility to withstand stress than houses which rely on strength alone?...

We can all help each other. As I ponder how to help you, I come back to the fact that one of the most basic and simple of human needs is conversation: to speak and to be listened to, to be spoken to in a respectful manner.... As I read about the sadness in your life growing up, your quiet, and the petrified stillness of your family, I found myself thinking of your problem as the Tyranny of Silence. Silence can be a peaceful companion, but it can also be a cruel jailer....

I really appreciate your writing me. If this letter to you has
been at all helpful, I would be very interested in your responses
to my questions.

We established a rather intimate relationship through an ongoing exchange of
letters, and she soon became much more comfortable during office visits. After just a
few sessions she experienced a rather dramatic cure. She told me she had "found her
voice." She felt many of her physical symptoms were psychological. She became free
of both physical and psychological complaints, felt happy raising her boys, and began
taking some classes at a local college. She talked freely in both my and other doctors'
offices.

I did not see her for a while. Then she returned and again spent most of the
sessions in silence. She seemed in some distress but could not express it. At the end
of one session, when I told her we were about out of time, a tear trickled down her
cheek. Very quietly, she said: "I have to go home but I don't want to."

I wasn't sure what she meant. It was the holiday season and I knew she was
planning to visit her parents' house, something she always dreaded; was this the home
she didn't want to go to? Was something happening at her own home? Or was she
saying she didn't want to leave me today? Maybe it was some combination of them
all? But she stayed silent and didn't answer my questions about what she meant. So I
said,

"What do you mean when you say 'going home?' Do you mean your real home?
Because, your *real* home is always welcoming, a place of support and comfort and
acceptance of being yourself,... I know you grew up in a place which looked like
home but wasn't, that you were relegated to a room to be not seen nor heard, that it
was cold and unaccepting, a place you could comply with others but not find yourself.
This was not home,.. but how do you find your real home? Whenever you feel warmth
and peace, those are signposts,..."

When my client got up from her chair to leave, she was trembling. She extended
her hand to me: I took her hand in both of mine, and she gripped them tightly. Seeing
her tremble, I suggested that she could anchor herself now, standing up... that a little
human contact helps, too... that she could notice where she was trembling and also
notice that while one leg was trembling, one wasn't. So she could attend to how the leg
that wasn't trembling was firmly rooted... and let some of its calm spread throughout
her body and she could find her balance. I suggested that she could pay attention to
her strong grip, be aware of her strength, and let that, too, spread evenly through her.

She stopped trembling. Her body became balanced and calm, and she seemed
more peaceful. At her own time and pace, she let go of my hand.

I said to her, "Good work. Welcome home." We paused for a moment, looked at
and acknowledged each other. She smiled gently and left in apparent peace.

Is it more useful here to think of the *quantity* of comfort or the *qualitative*
"feel" of the encounter? Is the essence of this or any meeting between client and
therapist a matter of the number of minutes we spend with each other, or does it
lie in the nature of our mutual horizoning to each other?

This client had experienced considerable "emptiness" (as understood in the
conventional sense) in her life. At times during the course of the therapy I was

concerned that she might have some psychotic process; sometimes I felt that no matter how many sessions we might have or how much effort I might exert, I would not be able to fill her up. But filling up is not the issue: Our human challenge, rather, is to find a way to fulfill our lives. In order to fulfill ourselves we need space to meet each other: space within ourselves and space to hold us.

When we are not filled with ourselves but clear an empty space to touch each other, we create a stage on which intimate, even magical transformations can occur.[6] The number of contacts is less important than the kindness of the touch. Most of us have had the experience of being profoundly touched by someone in our lives whom we knew only for a very brief period of time.

> When I was perhaps four years old, my parents took me to the beach. I discovered a delightful game: I would close my eyes and roll in the sand first in one direction, then another. Each time I rolled a little further. Finally there came a time when I felt particularly bold, rolled away, opened my eyes—and discovered I couldn't find the blanket on which my parents were. The beach looked very crowded with big, strange people. I was lost and scared and started crying.
>
> Two of the big, strange people got up off their blanket, came to me, and asked whether I was lost. When they discovered I could not find my parents, this man and woman took my hand and brought me to the "lost and found" area of the beach. I remember they bought me an ice cream.
>
> My parents soon came and retrieved me. They were somewhat surprised that I was not upset. But those strangers had helped me find my way home. I never knew their names, but I remember the kindness with which they held my hand. Isn't their kindness present in the psychotherapy office whenever I work with someone who feels lost?

NO TRAITS

When someone touches us with kindness, we are touched forever. But there are no kind people. There also are no unkind people; rather, the fact is that everyone is kind some times and not others. We don't harbor a certain amount of kindness within us as if it were a measurable constituent of our personality. The same is true for all our personal characteristics; they come and go. Yet we tend to label ourselves and others as if we were constant "types." We devise names for different kinds of personality and see how we and our acquaintances measure up to them. Even when we devise tests and questionnaires to measure "personality," however, we cannot measure our living selves. We can measure our height and weight (although even these are always changing throughout the day), but the qualities of self are not capturable quantities that can be doled out in a cook's teaspoons and half-liters, nor in a psychologist's Likert scales.

There is self as measured and self as lived. Self is never half-measured nor half-baked: It is always complete each moment. But we like to label ourselves, so we tend to enumerate our traits and feel they constitute us, as if we were some food composed of a number of ingredients. If that is what we are, however, who's the cook?

Still we persist in our attempts at self-measurement. For measurement one needs a ruler, some standard of comparison: The only way to measure ourselves is to compare ourselves to someone else or to some abstract standard. When we do this we treat ourselves as objects. Something measured is either big or small, good or bad. So when we measure ourselves, our self-judgments tend to lead to either pride or guilt, arrogance or depression: Whether the judgment leaves us feeling good or bad about ourselves, however, the inflation or deflation is of some image of ourselves as an object rather than the moving reality of self Its-self. We think we can "really" be a particular kind of person, but to the extent that that person is only an idea rather than a living, breathing being, we confuse the images of ourselves with the reality.

But what are the images that comprise our selves? Experiences. Fantasies. Memories. Feelings. Habits. Thoughts. Sensations. Awareness. The Heart Sutra reminds us that these are all empty. This does not mean they don't exist: It means that if we try to pin any of these down in isolation they will slip through our fingers.

Our experience is always in flux; there is no unchanging essence that we can grasp. Our memories, feelings, thoughts, sensations, actions, impulses, physical being, and consciousness are always moving. If we look at them closely, they do not stand on their own: Each thought, feeling, sensation, and so forth exists only in relationship to other thoughts, feelings, sensations, and states of mind. If we try to hold on to any one of them, it dissolves and something else comes up.

Life is always changing. This means that we, too, are always changing. But we don't like feeling unstable, so we try to hold onto our selves. Even though it be an illusion, we fill ourselves up with our images of ourselves and hold on tight. Then we are all in the position of the university professor in the following story:[7]

> Nan-in, a Japanese master... received a university professor who came to inquire about Zen.
>
> Nan-in served tea. He poured his visitor's cup full, and then kept on pouring.
>
> The professor watched the overflow until he no longer could restrain himself. "It is overfull. No more will go in!"
>
> "Like this cup," Nan-in said, "you are full of your own opinions and speculations. How can I show you Zen unless you first empty your cup?"

When self "empties out its cup" so it is not full of defining opinions and speculations about itself, self gains considerable freedom. As therapists, this is what we hope for our clients; as Zen students, this is what we hope for all beings. Yet we all fear freedom. We seek to confine ourselves within familiar boundaries, where we can feel unsurprised by ourselves: We seek security. In the process of seeking security, however, we can turn ourselves into things.

Self is not a thing but a process. This process is constantly shifting; self is a work in progress rather than a set piece. Even as we breathe in and breathe out, the atoms that comprise us are changing. Self is not unitary but the product of multiple drafts. When seeing clients, therapists may bear in mind something Milton Erickson said:[8]

> "Your patient is one person today, quite another person tomorrow, and still another person next week, next month, next year. Five years from now, ten and twenty years from now, he is yet another person. We all have a certain general background, that is true, but we are different persons each day that we live."

In the face of the chaos of our lives, in an attempt to maintain some inner stability, we and our clients clutch at some image of ourselves as a coherent, fixed personality. All stability, however, is maintained by change, just as all change relies on stability.[9] We rely on activity to support our stillness: In order to stand very still for more than a few seconds, to maintain our balance we must allow ourselves to sway slightly. We also rely on stillness to support our activity: It is hard to step forward on slippery ice. To go forward, we must first find someplace that does not slide beneath us. We must support our movement on something that does not move.

Now, we usually think that what doesn't move is *us*. Careful observation, however, reveals our self-identity to be fluid and constantly changing; the stories we tell ourselves about ourselves vary according to the contexts and relationships involved. At work, we may be decisive and authoritative; when out to dinner with our spouse, we may be hesitant and deferent about what to order for dinner. In the face of a financial success, we may feel confident; in the face of a bankruptcy, we may feel worthless. Yet we believe our selves should be the "same" person, even in the face of events which radically alter our perceptions of ourselves.

Jill, a psychotherapist, had just quit her job working at a shelter for battered women. After ten years in the field Jill no longer enjoyed her work, even though she was good at it. She felt a strong commitment to social activism but was tired of working in social agencies in which the pressures of operating with reduced funds and sometimes poorly trained personnel often led to interpersonal difficulties. Jill had no desire to go into private practice. In fact, Jill was realizing she had no particular desire to continue being a therapist; she was more interested in her political activities advocating for women. I had been impressed by the sensitivity of Jill's writing in the letters we had exchanged and by the sincerity of her work for women.

However, Jill felt depressed. She thought her change in interests showed she never could complete anything, that she'd always be "flighty." She was also terrified of changing professions. In the decade of her twenties, Jill had a successful career as an editor, but decided after a while that she wanted to do something else. When she quit her job as an editor, however, Jill had fallen into a deep depression, and she feared this would happen again. She scolded herself for not having a stable career, although she realized such stability was more her mother's goal than her own.

I said to Jill, "You're a narrative therapist. Haven't you shown your clients how they can write different stories about themselves? For that matter, in your letters to me, haven't you shown the many different aspects of your evolving character? You've told me how your relationship with your mother has changed over the past ten years and given me numerous examples of how you're no longer bound by that. Besides, you've also been an editor, and you still like to write. Haven't you told me how you sometimes like to rewrite multiple drafts and make changes to your stories?

"You're a feminist. Isn't the idea of fitting people into defined roles part of the patriarchal, capitalist ideology to maintain a certain kind of order? Is it possible that a feminist vision involves more fertile possibilities, cycles of multiple births and re-births?"

Jill began to laugh. She acknowledged her many strengths, and said, "I know how to avoid getting depressed. I know how to catch it and keep it from imprisoning me. My depression wants me to be the same all the time—the same misery. When I laugh, when I am creative, I can let myself change. I can even let myself enjoy it."

When we are able to laugh and be creative we can enjoy letting ourselves change. While we do this, however, we usually are holding on to the idea that there are some things about ourselves that stay the same. We discriminate between what we think of as the essential versus the nonessential parts of ourselves, our core versus our superficial traits. Most people feel they may change certain aspects of themselves, but not others. The therapist suggests a new course of action; the client replies, "I can't do that... it's not me." I try to hold on to my self by enumerating my traits and telling myself that they are stable and constitute "who I am." The nature of what is "essential" to the self, however, is very much a matter of perspective.

Most of us feel that we can put on a different sweater and not change our essential self. Yet a teenager may be afraid to wear a new sweater for fear of how it will alter her image and influence both how others treat her and, through that, how she sees herself. We smile when we see teenagers do this, but most of us have some kind of clothing we wouldn't be caught dead wearing. Some people can lose a limb and still think of themselves as basically the same (albeit altered) self, but this will be harder for a pianist than for a singer.

We know we can lose a favorite sweater and still be ourselves. We know we can lose an arm, and although we may have to mourn the loss and alter how we do things, we usually sense we can still be ourselves. But how far are we willing to take this? Most of us feel there is some point at which, if we take away too much, the self disintegrates. If a spouse leaves, a child dies, or a serious illness makes it impossible to perform the work that gives us a sense of personal identity, we may feel we lose the "essence of me."

If in order to be myself I must have some core "essence of me," it follows that I must have certain core traits that function as stable defining characteristics. So I construct a description of myself. Perhaps I tell myself I am of average intelligence, kind but timid. But when we label ourselves, in the process of defining ourselves we exclude some of our possibilities in exchange for maintaining a stable image. Circumscribing myself under the rubric of average intelligence, I may have difficulties accepting the full range of my abilities: I may lacerate myself for "stupidity" when I make human errors and discount any good ideas that I have. If I have a good idea, I tell myself it can't be that good, because it comes from somebody who is only "of average intelligence."

We bind ourselves by our names and limit ourselves in our labels. Because we use language, we have a tendency to name things: We go hiking and a pile of stones reminds us of some familiar image, so we christen it "the washerwoman" even though this cliff never has done and never will do laundry. We call a tall mountain Everest, but the name of a thing is not the thing itself. The map is not the territory[10]; our names are not our selves.

Nevertheless we mistake ourselves for the names we call ourselves. We label our selves as having certain traits: Someone tells us we are lazy, and we try to live up to the label. If we feel defined by the roles we have adopted, the traits we carry around in our minds as self-labels can weigh heavily on us.

A twenty-nine-year-old woman came to me asking for hypnosis to lose weight.[11] She mentioned that she had recently moved back in with her parents and felt her mother was scrutinizing her weight "for her own good." The client mentioned she had one brother, a drug addict. She, on the other hand, was the responsible one. This was her defining trait and her role in the family; sighing, she remarked she had "always had the weight of being the ideal child."

Her mother nagged her to lose weight, but the client felt that this was something she wanted to do for herself. It was a little difficult to do this autonomously; because she was living at home, her mother would notice as soon as she went on a diet. It would be hard to diet without assuming the weight of being the ideal child.

So I suggested she tell her mother up front that she was going on a diet and post a chart on the refrigerator of her daily caloric intake; however, to facilitate her doing this on her own, without having to conform to her mother's expectations about how she should or shouldn't "ideally" diet, I advised her she should, without her mother knowing, put *inaccurate* figures on the calorie chart. She was greatly amused at the idea of misleading her mother and taking charge of her diet herself.

During the formal hypnosis, I helped her imagine that she was going shopping with her mother for clothes and went into a "changing room" by herself. Within the changing room, the client took off layers of clothes and put them on, repeatedly, until she reached a point at which "having found what's comfortable to take off, from now on you can keep it off."

On follow-up, a year later, the client had moved out of her mother's house, had gone back to school to get a graduate degree, and had lost weight and kept it off. She had resumed singing and dancing. She said that what had been helpful in the single session of therapy was realizing that she had her own choices to make, independent of the images her family held of her. She no longer felt constrained by the role she had maintained in the past.

Whether we adopt the name of "ideal child" or "incest survivor" or "intelligent therapist," living our names becomes tiresome. Emily Dickinson expressed this well:

How dreary—to be—Somebody!
How public—like a Frog—
To tell one's name—the livelong June—
To an admiring Bog![12]

We bog ourselves down in our labels and run the risk of freezing our selves to fit our words. When we do this we ignore the episodic nature of our lives and substitute frozen images. Our lives consist of discrete actions, but we abstract from the choices we make and think they describe us as having enduring attributes. We say, "I am a Democrat," instead of, "I voted Democratic in the last election." Then, attached to the label rather than the reality, we may feel that if we want to maintain our identity as Democrats we should vote for a candidate who bears the party's imprimatur even if we don't like her or him. We say, "I am kind," instead of, "I helped that little girl who was crying... but I didn't give any money to that bum on the street." Then we can excoriate ourselves with guilt, rather than being generous to the next person we see. We box ourselves in to maintaining a fixed attitude and then get upset if our fixed attitudes don't fit our changing circumstances.

Furthermore, if we feel filled with substantive traits, we tend to judge our traits as good or bad. Then we do an accounting. Maybe we have more good traits than bad traits, or vice versa; we add up the totals and think we must be good or bad people. We can become quite neurotic about this.

If we are collections of traits and we have a problem, we may begin to think that our problem lies "in" us; we may even believe that we cannot "be" ourself without having the problem. In our attempts to maintain a stable picture of our self, if we cannot be consistently "good, successful, and competent," at least we can think of ourselves as consistently "bad, defective, or impaired." A negative identity seems preferable to no identity at all.

Ted, a young man, came to therapy complaining he was depressed and suicidal and couldn't control his temper. He had lost his job about a year before during a layoff in the aircraft industry. Because of money problems, Ted, his wife, and their young infant were forced to live with his mother-in-law. He had been severely physically abused as a child and felt this had scarred him forever.

Ted described himself as full of bad characteristics. He felt his present dilemma proved he was worthless; he "never did anything and never will do anything" and felt that he didn't even help out around the house. Ted had a fixed idea that he had been and would always be a "loser." He said that even in high school, when he'd been on the football team, he hadn't lived up to his potential; he downplayed the injury that had sidelined him and blamed what he felt was the feebleness of his own efforts.

After spending some time empathizing with Ted's situation and feelings, I attempted to discover whether there were any exceptions to his overgeneralizations about himself. It turned out that when Ted had been laid off, he had not only contacted every single one of the airlines in the area looking for employment; he had done this every week for six months. I asked whether this was a profile of somebody who "never did anything"—it sounded more like the actions of someone who didn't quit easily. Ted did recall, then, that in high school nobody had ever thought he'd make the football team to begin with; he persisted, however, and became a starter.

I said I found it hard to believe that someone who could be so persistent, even if he would occasionally get discouraged, never did anything now. Ted did admit he sometimes helped out around the house—it just seemed that he never could do anything to his mother-in-law's satisfaction. Ted had continued to look for work and found a part-time but dead-end job, and the changing shifts he worked left him tired. This made it hard for him to look for other work; it also made it hard for him to exercise as much as he wanted (Ted lifted weights) and left him little energy to do housework. We discussed the family situation in more detail; it wasn't easy living with a mother-in-law who criticized him for not providing adequately for his newborn and nagged him to do more household chores.

I asked whether Ted ever felt, after lifting weights for a while, that the weights felt heavier than at the start of the session. Sure, Ted said, that was when he just would reach inside himself and make an extra effort. That's how he got stronger. I suggested that next time he was exercising, Ted pay attention to how he"reached inside himself" to lift those weights just when they felt heaviest.

By the end of the first visit, Ted remarked on how he'd been treating himself like a "piece of garbage" but realized he was a person who had his ups and downs. On his next visit, several weeks later, he reported that his depression had remitted almost completely. He was doing more around the house and felt more optimistic and generally better about himself. He resumed looking for work and soon found a job in an entirely new field about which he was excited. He promptly moved his family out of his mother-in-law's house; when I contacted him a year later, he and his wife were enjoying raising a family together.

In these days of economic insecurity we often see clients who have lost their jobs and with that loss, lose their sense of themselves: Like Ted, they tell themselves they're worthless, filled with bad traits. To the extent that we conceive of self as having enduring traits, however, the fixed nature of these characteristics gets in our way. These traits are, after all, only our ideas of what we think we should be. If we hold onto ourselves as fixed ideas, the chimera elbows aside the reality: we don't "have" a self, we are "had" by our self, by our need to be Somebody. Emily Dickinson expressed not only the problem with this, but also a solution: to say,

> I'm Nobody! Who are you?
> Are you—Nobody—too?
> Then there's a pair of us!

When we can recognize we're Nobody, that we only exist together with others in interbeing, we can begin to let go of what we think are the traits that define us. This helps us become curious about what else we are and can become. If clients let go of overgeneralizations about themselves, they can start to notice times in their life that are problem-free and may begin to experience themselves differently.

When Ted came in to see me he thought he knew who he was; had he known the lingo of psychotherapeutic discourse, he probably would have self-critically diagnosed himself as having some kind of "loser" personality disorder. Ultimately, however, there is no personality "disorder" other than the disorder of thinking we have a fixed personality. Our "personalities" are temporary, partial expressions of a wider, constantly changing potentiality.

In reality, Ted was neither the best parent and husband in the world nor the worst, the most responsible wage earner nor the most irresponsible, neither worthy nor worthless. He was, like all of us, neither essentially good nor essentially bad. The Heart Sutra reminds us that all things are empty, so there are no ultimately defining, essential qualities: In emptiness, we are not tainted or pure. We're all just doing the best we can as we swim in life itself. In Zen, as in psychotherapy, we come to terms with our selves and find that we are both more and less than we thought: less magnificently bad, less sickeningly good, more surprisingly ourselves.

Usually as therapists we attempt to restore hope to our clients who have suffered some loss—a stolen truck, a bankrupt business, the loss of an eye or a lover—by implicitly saying, "That was a sad loss, but it's not the core of who you are; you can still be you without it." Our clients don't believe us, however, because in fact what they lost *was* a core part of them. So we cannot reassure our clients by insisting that they retain the most essential parts of their identity even in the face of loss. A deeper comfort is available for our clients who come in complaining "I'm not myself" or "I'm losing my mind": The Heart Sutra reminds us that in emptiness there is no self to not be, no thing-mind to lose. If we can realize there is no fixed, "core" identity to the self, we begin to recognize that ultimately self cannot be damaged or mislaid.

On some level, therapists are aware of this. Whether through making disowned, unconscious parts of the self conscious or through discovering "exceptions"[13] or "unique outcomes"[14] that contravene the problem-saturated descriptions of clients' lives, as therapists we labor to increase the flexibility or broaden the scope of our clients' overly restrictive definitions of their selves. But if we only substitute one story for another we are just helping clients relabel themselves in a way that later may turn into another pigeonhole. There is no single story that tells the truth of our lives and binds us to live out its legend; we cannot even hold too tightly to the role of narrator, lest we isolate ourselves by standing "above" our experience. Freedom lies in realizing the ever-changing, interconnected nature of story *telling*. There is no fixed storyteller "behind" the stories who stands apart from the ongoing novel of the universe.

NO BODY

We may recognize that our ideas about ourselves are illusory; because they are abstract concepts, they feel somewhat insubstantial when we step back from them. We may be intrigued by the flow of thoughts without a thinker[15]; we may be attracted by the image of being Nobody. Yet our body feels like a solid fact. If our true self is not confined to what we *think* it is, can we find the reality of our lives in our physical sensations?

We usually feel we have a fleeting mind-consciousness that is housed in a "real" body. We experience desires and our impulses to give in or not give in to our desires. We experience pain and pleasure that, in their intensity, seem very "real" in and of themselves. The Heart Sutra's revelation of emptiness, however, asserts that no thing exists in and of itself: When it says "no body, no mind" it is, among other things, reminding us that there is no body without mind and no mind without body.

This is familiar terrain for psychotherapists. From the time Freud[16] argued that the ego is first and foremost a projection of bodily experience, we have recognized that the way body and mind present themselves to each other constitutes a critical area for defining self-identity. If we try to get to the bottom of the mind, we find the body; if we try to get to the bottom of the body, we find the mind there waiting for us. Clinical examples abound:

A seventy-year-old man was referred to me by his exasperated physician. His physician told me that ever since a heart bypass operation eighteen months previous, the man had been to the medical center several times a week with a virulent dermatitis. He had received every treatment known to medicine; he had been to an experimental teaching hospital at which his case was presented for grand rounds; he had been given every medicine and salve under the sun. In desperation, his physicians had even tried antidepressant medications, to no avail. The man continued to suffer and scratch, and he wasn't doing it quietly; he would call his doctors almost daily and complain angrily about the treatment he was receiving. His physician asked me if I'd see him for hypnosis on the off chance I could help him.

When I phoned the patient to make an appointment, he was brusque and irritable. He told me how all the doctors "weren't worth shit" but agreed to come in and see me: "I'll give you guys one last chance," he said.

When he came in to my office the next day, he refused to sit down. He couldn't sit still: He itched too much. He undid his shirt and pants and showed me the red, inflamed skin. He spent fifteen minutes on a long tirade about how awful the doctors at the medical center were and how all the medicines that he'd been given had just given him terrible side effects without helping the problem. I mostly just listened and empathized.

When he paused, I told him that given the magnitude of his problem I couldn't promise much, but, because he was fed up with doctors and medicines, it might be worth trying hypnosis. He agreed it probably wouldn't work: He couldn't concentrate enough to do it, the itching would get in the way. But he'd try.

I initially used a standard eye-fixation technique. He kept his eyes fixed and open throughout, but there was never any hint of a trance state. He stayed alert, tense, and vigilant. I tried a utilization technique for an open-eyed trance induction; he kept up a running commentary on how it wasn't working. He kept reverting to his bodily discomfort, so I tried suggesting that he focus on the bodily discomfort and transform it with mental imagery; he readily reported the discomfort but never formed an image nor did he report any change in sensation. I tried droning on in the hopes of boring him into a trance: He droned back. I tried interweaving direct and indirect suggestions, embedded metaphors, and the like; he kept repeating that nothing would work.

We kept on like this for an hour or so, him with his eyes open staring at the ceiling and itching, me trying every hypnotic technique I knew. I was exhausted. Just as I was about to give up and end the session, the man said, still staring at the ceiling,

"Doc, I think this is going about things the wrong way. Doc, let me ask you something. Do you think a guy's wife can get him so upset that he breaks out in a rash?"

"Well," I said. "Women have been known to get under a man's skin."

"Shit, Doc," he said, "I know what this is all about. I just can't talk with my wife. She drives me crazy. You know, if I go over to a buddy's house and we play some cards or something, I won't itch for the entire time. Then I go home, try to talk to my wife, and she just turns on the TV and watches her soap operas, and I feel like my skin's on fire."

"I'd leave her, but I've been married to her for 50 years. What's a guy to do?"

We talked about his marital problems for a while. It turned out that after his heart surgery brought home to him his mortality, something had shifted in his relationship with his wife. He could express this not with his tongue, but only through his skin.

We feel we live "inside" our skins; our bodily sensations lend substance to the "I" who seems to be experiencing them. When we experience pain or intense body discomfort, the "I" that is hurting feels very real. Yet people get under our skin and into our hearts and minds. Sensations do not constitute the core of our being.

The Heart Sutra reminds us that reality is not what we *sense* it is. For one thing, our senses miss a lot. If we are talking during dinner, we may not taste our food. If we are concentrating reading a book, we may not hear a bird sing or feel the chair beneath us, but this does not mean the birdsong and the chair are unreal. On the other hand, our senses provide us with "false-positive" impressions. Cut off an arm and phantom pain will tell you years later that the hand is still there. Interview a schizophrenic with auditory hallucinations, and the voices will seem genuine representations of the way things actually are. Look at a photograph made from polarized and nonpolarized black-and-white images, and colors will emerge although there is no color "in reality."

Our senses are always creating images of things that are not there. The image of the book you see is not the book itself; the weight of the volume in your hands is your feeling of its substance, not the thing itself. Reality is not a thing: It cannot be confined to being touched, smelled, seen, heard, or tasted.

This does not mean that reality does not exist and our senses are liars. When the Heart Sutra says that form is emptiness, and therefore in emptiness "no eyes, no ears, no nose, no tongue, no body, no mind," it does not mean that there is no experience. We experience reality through our senses; every moment we are fully immersed in our seeing, hearing, smelling, tasting, touching. So the Heart Sutra not only says "form is emptiness," it also reminds us that "emptiness is form." This is how we experience the world, through tangible forms and sensations. In the "no non-sense" words of the Sandokai, "eyes see, ears hear, nose smells, the tongue tastes salt and sour." The emptiness of sensation does not mean that there are no sensations, it means we cannot *grasp* our sensations. Our sensations are not things any more than outside objects are things.

Living is not a thing. Our selves are not things living but living beings. Each moment we have a direct experience of our lives. By reminding us that form is emptiness and emptiness form, the Heart Sutra brings us back to our true being, our life beyond form and emptiness. Our immediate experience is beyond sense or non-sense, as the following case from the *Book of Serenity* reminds us:

> *Introduction:* When there is seeing and there is not seeing, this is lighting a lamp at midday; when there is no seeing and no not seeing, this is pouring ink at midnight. If you believe seeing and hearing are like illusion-creating cataracts, then you will know that sound and form are like flowers in the sky.
>
> *Case:* The Surangama scripture says, "When I don't see, why don't you see my not seeing? If you see my not seeing, that is naturally not the characteristic of not seeing. If you don't see my not seeing, it's naturally not a thing—how could it not be you?"
>
> *Commentary:* To discuss it thoroughly, one should say, "If you don't see my not seeing, then you don't see my seeing either. Since you don't see my sight, my seeing is naturally not a thing. If my seeing is not a thing, your seeing is not a thing either. Since your seeing is not a thing, how could it not be your true seeing?[17]

Seeing is not a thing. You cannot grasp your sight; you cannot tell your eyes to see this book. Yet at this moment, as you read, you not only are seeing, you *are* your Seeing.

We are not separate from our bodies. We do not "have" sensations and thoughts and feelings: We *are* sensations and thoughts and feelings. This is our direct experience, even though there is no "substance" to it. We cannot grasp our sensations, because the hand that grasps cannot hold itself. We cannot grasp the world "through" our bodily sensations, because we are not separate from the world; the world constitutes our body.

The Heart Sutra's teaching of "no body" simply means that the body does not have an existence outside interbeing. No body stands alone without the earth; our bodies are comprised of the earth's elements and are always responding to the world's touch: In the warm sunshine, muscles stretch out and we become factories for Vitamin D; in the arid desert, our throats become parched and we realize our links to water.

The Heart Sutra's teaching of "no body" also reminds us there is no single core "piece" to the body that constitutes our essential selves: All its pieces are connected. Take out a wisdom tooth, and the whole body aches; let the big toe relax, and the corners of the mouth curve into a gentle smile. Our eyes rely on a skull to house them; our skull relies on our muscles to support it; our muscles rely on our mouths to take in sustenance to give them energy; our mouths rely on our brains to help them know what to say to get a job to earn the money to obtain food. Our bodies rely on our minds, and our minds rely on our bodies, and both touch and are touched by the natural world in which we are immersed. Mind-body-nature form a necessary unity.[18]

Because mind-body-nature are interconnected, each is empty: The physical world that gives rise to sensations, the sensations themselves, and our ideas about our sensations are all interconnected and always moving. This means that if we can help a client alter the quality of his or her awareness of body sensations, the body sensations shift; if we can help a client have different body sensations, the quality of consciousness shifts. If we are working with clients with panic disorder, we may try to shift their awareness by encouraging them to become curious (rather than fearful) about the perceptual qualities of the sensations; alternatively, we may encourage them to alter sensations by doing deep breathing, or by relaxing their muscles so that the weight is born by the soles of the feet. Either approach usually leads clients to notice the shifting qualities of the sensations, become more flexible in the ideas they have about the sensations, and create space for a new view.

Discovering this can be very liberating, especially if we are in great physical or emotional pain. If we are in agony we may wish for nothingness as a substitute for pain; we may seek to take refuge in a numbness that, devoid of sensation and feeling, might seem to promise some relief. This is not the kind of emptiness the Heart Sutra proclaims, however. The price of this kind of "vacant" emptiness is high, because it involves shutting off the experience of life.

To say that self is empty is not to say that it is void; this would imply self is marked by a particular quality of nothingness. The emptiness of the Heart Sutra, in contrast, reminds us that self has no permanently fixed "thing-like" characteristics. This helps us avoid getting stuck in some particular sensation or some particular idea; by reminding us of the fluid, interconnected nature of our physical hurts, it fosters a wider awareness with which our relationship to our experience can shift.

A fifty-eight-year-old woman was referred to me by her physicians. For the past year, she had been complaining that there was something wrong with her tongue. It was numb, stiff, sometimes sore; her speech was sometimes not fluent; she feared she had a stroke or some kind of nerve damage or possibly even cancer. She had been given every medical test her doctors could think of, all of which turned out negative. Her doctors told her it was "all in her head" and referred her to me.

She was quite angry about the referral. She *knew* that there was something physically wrong with her. She didn't want to talk about her childhood, or her relationship with her husband. She wasn't depressed, just uncomfortable and worried about her medical condition.

I assured her that, as a neuropsychologist, I often worked with people with "nerve difficulties." I told her, however, that I needed more information about her problem. I asked her a series of very detailed questions: Was the numbness greater on the left posterior or the right anterior side of the tongue? When there was numbness, were the tingling sensations directly next to the numbness or were they at some remove, in another area of the tongue? Did the stiffness get worse or better with exercise, such as pressing the tongue against the tip of the teeth ten times in a row? Were the sensations influenced by other muscles, say the tightness in the jaw or throat? Were the sensations worse in the morning or the evening?

She didn't have answers to most of these questions. I composed an extensive list of questions and suggested that over the next week, she spend ten minutes an hour observing the sensations from a detached, objective viewpoint so that she could fill me in when we next met. In order to assist her in getting a clear view, I gave her some relaxation instructions, concentrating in particular on the facial muscles.

When she came back the next week, she told me that she had tried to carry out the task. She found, however, that when she concentrated on her tongue for 10 minutes, the sensations kept changing. In fact, her tongue felt much less stiff, and she hadn't really had the symptom there in a stable enough form for her to be able to answer all the questions I put to her. In fact, she said, this was the first week in a year during which the symptom really hadn't bothered her very much: She wasn't sure she needed any more treatment but would call me if the symptom recurred.

I had a colleague follow up on her a year later. She remained free of physical and psychological symptoms.

The paradox here is that by attending to—by minding—her body, the odd sensations disappeared and the self-conscious worries eased. This is the paradox of "no body, no mind" that applies to both Zen practice and psychotherapy. When we plunge deeper into our bodies and our minds we forget ourselves and some split or separation heals. Then there is no body and no thing to get in the way. We stop tripping over our own feet and can mindfully appreciate whatever sensation is suffusing our universe of right here, right now.

NO CONSCIOUSNESS

If shifting our awareness can lead to some freedom from suffering, we may feel puzzled when we read the Heart Sutra advising us there is "no mind, no consciousness." Many therapists see their work as one of increasing awareness and may feel uneasy at the Heart Sutra's exposition of "no consciousness." Not only therapists, but virtually all of us, regard our consciousness as the essence of our selves. During our lives we fear "losing our minds"; in the face of death, we are terrified at the prospect of the cessation of consciousness.

When the Heart Sutra says "no consciousness" it means that consciousness, just like sensation, is empty: That is, there are no fixed, essential qualities to distinguish it. Consciousness depends on all the other skandhas—form, feeling, perceptions, impulses—to constitute it and has no existence apart from its composite existence. When we are infants, we see our hands waving about in front of our eyes and begin to realize that our sensation of movement is connected to our sensation of vision; we feel the air on our skin and the touch of the people around us and begin to become conscious of both mental and physical boundaries. We become able to identify objects: my crib, my bottle, my mother, my self. Even when our consciousness is aware of objects, it does not stand alone; it is dependent on the existence of the object in order for consciousness of the object to arise.

All the forms of consciousness arise in a relationship; consciousness is a way of mentally touching the world "within" and the world "without." As "I" touch "the world," it may appear that there is a boundary with "my" self on one side and "the world's" selves on the other side. In fact, however, the selves on either side of the boundary only exist by virtue of their interdependence, by virtue of their touching each other. When I bump up against you, I discover both you and me bumping each other: I find my self in the act of touching and being touched. I may touch myself touching myself[19] (consciousness being aware of sensation, feeling being aware of thought) or I may touch myself touching others (my feelings and thoughts leaping alive in response to yours).

Our touching self is an experiencing, self-reflecting self but need not stand apart as a separate observer; the kind of consciousness involved in touching is not consciousness *of* an object, but rather consciousness *with* a coparticipant.[20] This is what happens when we touch ourselves touching a client. The hypnotist enters trance along with the client; the teacher enters learning along with the student; the therapist winces at the client's pain and smiles at his or her joy. If we allow ourselves to touch and be touched, we lose ourselves and find ourselves in loving contact. Where am "I" as I touch you touching me touching you? It all happens very fast, too fast to separate into a separate "me" here and a separate "thing" there. Touching is a horizoning of each with the other: It generates an awareness of self and other, not as entities separate from each other, but as coparticipants.

We touch others and also touch ourselves. When our body and mind meet each other, consciousness touches itself touching; when consciousness takes itself as an object it becomes recursive, self-reflective, and self-conscious. At that point, it looks to consciousness as if a "true self" is there. But if I take myself as an object, "who" is it that "I" am conscious of? This is an infinitely recursive road: We can be aware of being aware of being aware of being aware...

Buddhism does not deny that we have the conscious experience of being aware of our selves. The Heart Sutra's "no consciousness" simply is a reminder that consciousness cannot stand alone. Our self-consciousness seems to like to think that, because it is aware of our thoughts, feelings, and sensations, it somehow stands above them and is running the show. In fact, our consciousness is dependent on the rise and fall of all the other realms of experience.

We often confuse the consciousness that is aware of objects with the essence of me. When this kind of consciousness asserts its self as "essential" and assigns itself the primary place in the universe, it becomes self-centered. Then, despite the interbeing of our consciousness, we set our selves apart. Such self-consciousness can become morbidly absorbing; it runs the risk not only of interposing a division between ourselves and others but also of separating ourselves from ourselves.

A twenty-year-old woman came for psychotherapy saying she had been depressed most of her life, but what really bothered her most was her self-consciousness. She had been born with spina bifida and walked with a lurching, awkward gait. Although she felt her external life circumstances were fine—she had graduated from high school, married a man who was loving and accepting, and was raising a child—she still felt embarrassed every time she went out. She felt people stared at her; she felt ashamed of what she saw as her disfigurement.

She knew all the arguments of why she "shouldn't" feel this way but rational self-talk didn't help her. We discussed various ways of desensitizing herself in order to become less self-conscious (for example, a program of drawing attention to herself intentionally in a controlled fashion, e.g., by wearing an unusual earring or bright scarf, and then practicing relaxation and self-soothing), but she said she was unable to even consider such a program. She just couldn't tolerate people looking at her at all. She couldn't even tolerate looking at herself, either in a mirror or in her mind's eye; whenever she got to her deformed legs she would inwardly recoil.

She was particularly distressed by how irritable she had become. She felt it was sensible to be irritable with herself, but she didn't feel it was fair to be irritable with her family. With a combination of psychotherapy and antidepressant medication she was able to become much less irritable with others rather quickly. She continued, however, to feel ashamed and irritable with herself. She wanted to be able to ignore other peoples' stares and what she imagined them thinking about her, but she "just couldn't."

I inquired about how she was able to be less irritable with others. She initially waved this off as something she "ought" to be able to do anyway. I persisted, however, in asking her to describe to me what it felt like when her kids or husband did something that she'd formerly found irritating. Was she simply not finding it irritating any more, or were there still occasions when if something went wrong, she started to feel irritated, and she did something instead of indulging her irritation?

It was the latter. As we explored this together, it turned out that when she started to feel irritated, she intentionally cultivated a different feeling to contravene the irritation. I asked her what this different feeling consisted of. She was unable to describe it, so I asked her to try an experiment: to close her eyes, now, in the session, remember a recent incident that could have been irritating, and then remember what she brought up in its stead. Did she talk to herself, giving herself messages such as, "It's no big deal?" Did she have a particular physical sensation?

She closed her eyes and we explored this together. It turned out the thought/feeling/sensation was something akin to peace, calm, and centeredness. In response to my questions, she was able to identify it as being in her chest... it had a vaguely circular shape... it wasn't a smooth circle but had wavy edges.

I had her open her eyes and discuss her experience. She was intrigued but still somewhat self-denigratory; she had experienced difficulty because other thoughts and images came up and interfered: She kept thinking about her children. She also felt self-conscious about my looking at her. I reassured her that the distracting thoughts were natural and commented on how she was experiencing with me the symptoms of being self-conscious of being looked at. But I also noted that as far as I could tell despite this, she had continued the exercise successfully. I asked how she had managed to deal with the intrusive, self-conscious thoughts and feelings.

She said she just noticed them, let them go, and brought herself back to what she was focusing on. I complimented her on this, and asked whether she was aware that she was doing naturally what other people struggled to learn through self-hypnosis or meditation. This surprised her. I simply encouraged her to do more of this and added a few suggestions about using her breathing as a way of centering.

We then resumed the exercise. This time the peaceful feelings were in two places: two spheres, one each on either side of her collarbone. She was able to let her breathing and gravity do the work and let the two sink down until they touched each other in the center of herself... somewhere around her heart... she could imagine a gentle smile in her heart... it was easy to bring the "intrusive" thoughts of her children into that space, because they also were a source for the smile and the warm feelings... practicing that, she was able to do something similar with other intrusive thoughts; some of them she could let "slide" off that interior space and dissolve; others she could take in and surround with that gentle smile. Her hands found each other and touched each other, relaxed. She could feel her hands cradling the feelings in her mind... or perhaps it was her mind cradling the sensations of her hands and heart... I gave her some straightforward suggestions that each time she practiced this, it could become more familiar and easier, sometimes different from this experience, sometimes seemingly the same.

When we discussed her experience, she was smiling slightly. She found the whole thing surprising, a little odd, intriguing. She said that as she became absorbed and curious about the process she had "lost track of herself" a bit. She stopped being concerned about whether or not she was being observed by me and "forgot" to be self-conscious.

When we are conscious *of* ourselves we can feel divided and awkward. This is because although thought is a useful analytic activity, too much disembodied thought interferes with our lives. If we start overanalyzing we feel divided and doubtful because we are separating ourselves from immediate experience. When we cogitate this way we re-present an experience to ourselves and in depicting the experience, limit it. Our self cannot exist as pure thought; we cannot exist except through our active experience.

When we are conscious *with* ourselves we enter a partnership in which different modes of awareness can enhance each other. We are not just thinking *of* something but are letting our minds participate *with* our experience. In the activity of mindful experiencing we become aware of the fluidity of consciousness and open a larger "space" in mind-and-body that gives us room to be more free to entertain new experiences. Here experiencing does not involve discrete stages of perception, cognitive representation, decision, and action, but rather a total immersion in being alive. Realizing emptiness we engage in wholehearted activity in which we plunge in and forget ourselves.

After a session of hypnosis or of deep relaxation, when clients focus "with" immediate body or mental experience they often spontaneously comment, like the client above, "I lost track of myself." Sometimes they are surprised to find themselves doing things that had previously felt difficult or even impossible. When a client says, "I lost track of myself," who is "the self" here?: the person losing track, or the person being lost track of? When a client says, "I lost track of myself," "full-self" theory might suggest that the client is "dissociating" or "regressing." An empty self instead finds the fluid boundaries of unselfconscious action natural; when we are deeply absorbed in an experience, deeply touched and touching deeply, we don't have to bother to keep track of where we are: We know we're right here.

At this empty point we rediscover that, at heart, we are whole, and that our self is undivided activity. Consciousness always arises through activity; experience is not a noun but an ongoing activity of experienc*ing*.[21] As embodied minds we come to know ourselves through our actions, which reflect our selves back to us. Mindfully engaged through our physical liveliness we can let go of the illusion of separateness and drop our self-consciousness. When we do this we do not lose ourselves but rather the opposite: We find ourselves in an essential unity. When we leap clear of our concepts into undivided activity, we are free to discover ourselves in a process of constantly adjusting to what is happening this moment. Then we are moving, finding our path not by consulting a map but by reconnoitering the territory.

As we do this, we "lay down a path in walking"[22] and become more interested in walking than in formulating theories about how we walk. Experience becomes more important than explanation; action brings forth outcome brings forth action in a continuous dance. Laying down a path in walking we are always choosing, but without a separate chooser or chosen: the path, path maker, and the path making, all dance with each other. As Yeats[23] put it:

> O chestnut tree, great rooted blossomer,
> Are you the leaf, the blossom or the bole?
> O body swayed to music, O brightening glance,
> How can we know the dancer from the dance?

Zen practice and psychotherapy are forms of dancing. We may sometimes have to strain to hear the music, we may sometimes trip over our own feet, we may sometimes not even like the tune that is playing and want to sit it out. Still, we are always dancing. Zen practice and psychotherapy help us learn to dance with ourselves and the world around us. The Zen student dances with the cushion, the wall, the broom that sweeps the sidewalk. The therapist dances with the client, the client with the therapist. In this kind of activity the "doer" and the "deed" are not separate from each other but meet in the dance: Physical body, thoughts, feelings, perceptions, impulses, and consciousness respond to and actualize each other.

NO ATTAINMENT

When our consciousness is centered on ourselves, we often get attached to our personal agendas and focus on where we are heading. We then respond to the events of our lives as if they were either obstacles or opportunities for accomplishing our cherished goals. In contrast, if we can let go of our self-conscious concerns, life becomes less a matter of making something happen and more a matter of dancing with the music that is currently playing. When we are dancing, we are not trying to get any place in particular.

"Empty" interbeing has a lively spontaneity to it, but even though its dance has no particular purpose or goal, that does not mean that there is no need for "formal" preparation or planned study. As the Heart Sutra tells us, form is emptiness, emptiness form. In order to dance, we need to be free to respond to the rhythm of the music, but it is also helpful to know the various dance forms; it will be awkward to foxtrot to a waltz. There is no contradiction between the "natural" spontaneity of movement and the need to learn the techniques for executing specific dance steps; each relies on the other. There is no contradiction between the freedom of zazen and the need for a strict adherence to the forms of right practice in a particular posture, breath, and mindful attention. There is no contradiction between the creativity of psychotherapy and the need for a familiarity with the forms of therapeutic technique.

The path of Zen is to find freedom of action within form. Dancers, Zen students, and therapists all need to use technique; technique gives us a language for communication, a method to practice. A thorough familiarity with technique can also help bind our anxiety, relieve us of the need to think overmuch about the mechanics of action, and thus facilitate a deepening of experience freed from distractions. We should not avoid technique; however, neither should we get trapped in it. An excessive reliance on formal techniques can lead to stereotyped gestures, manualized treatments, and oversimplified prescriptions of how we are "supposed" to treat not a person but a diagnostic label. On the other hand, insisting there is no need to study traditional forms and relying only on our intuitive responding can lead to wild irresponsibility.

Buddhism seeks the middle path, the path the Heart Sutra sets forth when it speaks of "no cognition, no attainment." "No cognition" does not mean "don't think" but rather, as Dogen advises, "think not-thinking." "No attainment" does not mean "don't try to master the forms of skill" but rather "practice without being fettered by any hopes for attaining something through mastery." So long as we hold onto an idea of getting what we want from our action, we can get caught by our desires. Anticipating gain and fearing loss, we are no longer free to move and we easily stumble.

If baseball players or golfers do not try to improve themselves and do not put in hours of practice, they will not master their craft. But golfers or baseball players can get stuck if they worry too much about achieving a particular effect. The golfer who is very invested in having her drive carry far hooks her shot; the batter who is very worried about striking out swings at a bad pitch and pops up. If they don't think about their swings, they'll never improve; if they do think about their swings from the standpoint of excessive desire, they'll get caught by anticipation, worry, and hope. If we drop our pride, our hopes of achieving greatness, and our fears of humiliating failure, we can also drop our excessive self-criticisms and our worries about whether we are doing well or doing poorly. If we forget ourselves and just do what is necessary for each moment, we can swing freely and hit the mark.

The same applies to active techniques in psychotherapy and to actualizing our selves. The key to uniting spontaneity and formal technique is to act without any expectations or hopes of gaining something in particular. The Heart Sutra's "no attainment" reminds us: Self and object, "doer" and "deed" are empty. No "thing" exists as a goal separate and apart from the ongoing activity of living. If there is no thing to attain, the mind is no hindrance: We don't get in our own way of doing whatever is needed to meet the moment.

Reaching for enlightenment, long hours of meditation heighten our frustration by showing us the vastness of our ignorance and desire. Realizing self as empty, we simply sweep the Zendo's path and sit on our cushion. We spend a lot of time in Zen practice doing household tasks: washing the dishes, cleaning the windows. But we don't do this to attain some state of pristine spotlessness. Rather, we have a saying: We clean the windows because they are already clean. They may look awfully dirty, but no matter how much dust accumulates on the glass, the basic ability of glass to let light pass through is not something that we struggle to accomplish but rather something we can rely on.

Reaching to cure our client, we strain for a technique that will produce a certain effect and feel frustrated if nothing seems to change. Realizing self as empty, not a thing but a moving music, we can approach each meeting with our client without memory and without desire.[24] Then the hard work of psychotherapy becomes indistinguishable from free play. We spend a lot of time in psychotherapy utilizing whatever techniques are at hand to help clients "clean up their act." But we don't do this to create some perfect person or attain some special state of psychological health. Rather, our technique relies on our human nature to provide a fertile, empty field for growth. We can have faith that as we work in psychotherapy something will start to move, even if it is not necessarily in the direction we expect. Technique becomes a way of being responsive, of expecting the unexpected, of "calling" our client and "clearing" our self so that we do not force the therapeutic process. Then therapy becomes a form of play.

Even in free play, however, we need rules to structure our activity. Practicing psychotherapy and Zen from the perspective of "no attainment" does not mean "anything goes." Some people mistake emptiness for aimlessness, thinking that if you are fully absorbed in your activity, it does not matter what the activity consists of. But the fact is, in our activity we are always making choices; even if our choices take place on constantly shifting sands, all our volitional actions produce consequences.

> Once when Pai-chang gave a series of talks, a certain old man was always there listening together with the monks. When they left, he would leave too. One day, however, he remained behind. Pai-chang asked him, "Who are you, standing here before me?"
>
> The old man replied, "I am not a human being. In the far distant past, in the time of Kasyapa Buddha, I was head priest at this mountain. One day a monk asked me, 'Does an enlightened person fall under the law of cause and effect or not?' I replied, 'Such a person does not fall under the law of cause and effect.' With this I was reborn five hundred times as a fox. Please say a turning word for me and release me from the body of a fox."

He then asked Pai-chang, "Does an enlightened person fall under the law of cause and effect or not?"

Pai-chang said, "Such a person does not evade the law of cause and effect."

Hearing this, the old man immediately was enlightened.[25]

Many people have difficulty understanding how Buddhism can reconcile its teaching of emptiness with its doctrine of karma. If there is no substantial thing that exists, no "doer" behind "deeds" but only "doing," how can we be bound by the law of cause and effect? They look at a swordfight and say, "Because sword and swordsman are empty, when one person thrusts a saber through the other's heart there is no one who kills and no one who is being killed." This ignores a simple fact: Ripping somebody with a slashing blade will produce a lot of blood stains. Karma is a shorthand for reminding us that volitional actions produce repercussions. Zen archery teaches us a way of shooting in which there is no separation between archer, arrow, and target, but the arrow still goes somewhere. Buddhism is not aimless but devoted to saving all beings. In psychotherapy clients and therapists meet in undivided activity, but this process is directed toward an outcome that ameliorates suffering.

In order to reconcile "no attainment" and purposeful action, psychotherapeutic and Zen practice can be approached as if they were a kind of gardening. In this kind of gardening, we seek not to control nature but to participate in its actualization. If we seek to attain a perfect garden conforming to some prefabricated ideal vision, we may need bulldozers and chain saws to force the land to our will. If our Zen and psychotherapeutic practice consists of this kind of gardening, we will treat psychological symptoms or errant desires as if they were our enemies, weeds to be uprooted. This kind of gardening is hard work, because it does not appreciate the potential in the current landscape. If we work to eradicate the "bad stuff" in or around our client's land or to eliminate the thoughts and feelings that come up in the vegetable patch of our meditations, we may see only the weeds and not the flowers or the healthy deep roots. If we use strong chemical weed killers, we will need to wear protective masks and gloves.

Suzuki Roshi, the founder of San Francisco Zen Center, once said: "Pulling out the weeds we give nourishment to the plant. We pull the weeds and bury them near the plant to give it nourishment... you should rather be grateful for the weeds, because eventually they will enrich your practice."[26] If we approach psychotherapy in this fashion, we need not feel discouraged by the dense undergrowth on the acreage of our practice and wish for a better piece of land. We can realize that the terrain on which all growth occurs, the ground on which client and therapist meet—and the space on which we meet ourselves—is not a fixed plot of land but an empty field. This field has no ultimate identity but arises together not only with what is visibly growing, but with the worms that turn the soil, the animals that fertilize it, the gardener who plants it, the birds and insects that carry its seeds to new places. Tending the garden becomes a matter of joining with all its parts.

A little while ago I was trying to weed my front garden, to make the yard presentable before having a group of friends over. Despite my attempts to cultivate nonjudgmental acceptance, I was feeling annoyed with both myself and with Nature for letting the weeds grow so high (three feet tall!). They had already gone to seed, so I knew they'd be back again next year; I felt the weeding was an exercise in futility. The sun was hot, the ground was rocky and hard. The weeds' roots went down deep. I kept attempting to dig down as far as I could but couldn't get very far; I would grasp the weed's root and pull, and the root would break off in my hand.

After an hour or so of fighting the weeds, making little progress, it came to me that I could help myself relax by using a different kind of "technique." I got off my hands and knees and planted both feet firmly on the ground. I reached down as far as I could, and took hold of one weed's root. I closed my eyes, and stopped opposing myself to the weed. Instead, I let myself "feel" the weed's root all the way down to its deepest tip, appreciating it fully. I let myself feel the soil surrounding the weed, and the whole earth under foot. The activity shifted from extirpating something bad to encountering the root in its present place, acknowledging, meeting, and cherishing it; then to help it move to another place where, becoming mulch, it had an opportunity to join with the garden in a different way.

I let my whole body join with the root, the earth, and sky. With all involved fully engaged, pulling in one direction, the root came up effortlessly. The remainder of the weeding became a joy.

NO ORIGINATION, NO STOPPING: MOMENTOUS HISTORIES

When we are absorbed in joyful weeding, the time does not seem short or long. The empty field in which we harvest our selves does not appear and disappear. It does not come forth with the sunrise and then vanish at dusk: It abides eternally each moment. A garden includes not only what is currently blooming; it rests on past growths whose death and decay provide their nutrients to this moment's soil; it relies on seeds and bulbs that, presently quiescent, hold future blossoms.

Our lives flower moment-by-moment. As the Buddhist sutras teach us, in the immediacy of our experience the past is gone, the future is not here yet, and the present cannot be grasped.

This does not mean, however, that we have no personal history. Although the Heart Sutra says that there is no birth (no origination) and no death—seemingly implying that there is no history, no development or "course" to our lives—it also says that there is no extinction of birth and death. Thus the Heart Sutra affirms both "no birth-and-death" and also "no 'no-birth-and-death.'" In doing so it points the way to freedom: We cannot evade the law of cause-and-effect, but we need not be bound by it. We cannot deny our history, but we need not be prisoners of our past and slaves to our future.

In psychotherapy, we frequently see people who feel that their past will always shadow their present with an indelible brand. People who have suffered horrific early childhood experiences or appalling traumas sometimes seem trapped in their memories of old fears and hurts. This imprint can be very powerful. But the fact is that our pasts, being past, can only influence us through our calling them up in the present. We cannot be frozen in the past unless we keep refreezing, putting forth some energy to keep the temperature cold, although it makes us rigid and set in our ways. We do this all the time. We recall our painful old images to our selves by bringing them up or acting them out again and again. Painfully heavy though they may be, we carry our pasts around with us, holding on to what has gone before like Ekido in the following story:

> Tanzan and Ekido were once traveling together down a muddy road. A heavy rain was still falling.
>
> Coming around a bend, they met a lovely girl in a silk kimono and sash, unable to cross the intersection.
>
> "Come on, girl," said Tanzan at once. Lifting her in his arms, he carried her over the mud.
>
> Ekido did not speak again until that night when they reached a lodging temple. Then he could no longer restrain himself.
>
> "We monks don't go near females," he told Tanzan, "especially not young and lovely ones. It is dangerous. Why did you do that?"
>
> "I left the girl there," said Tanzan. "Are you still carrying her?"[27]

We cling to our past conditioning and carry our burdens around with us. When we do this, our vision is restricted. Zen uses the metaphor of carrying a board on your shoulder: If you carry a wide board of lumber on your shoulder, it will be hard to look to one side, or to turn easily. The problem is not so much the board as in the restriction of vision that does not even let us entertain a life without it. Both psychotherapy and Zen are about dropping the board and looking around.

Our pasts are often long planks that we carry in the form of images of who we are: This heavy lumber burdens us, but because it seems integral to our identity it can be hard to lay it down. It is odd, though true, that sometimes we cling the most to experiences that were the most painful and traumatic. Traumas present us with history as a nightmare that we are trying, and failing, to escape. It seems that there is something about traumas that freeze us into an apparently timeless "loop" in which we replay the trauma over and over again, then push it away, then take it back and replay it. We seem to relive traumas in some attempt to relieve and master them.

Traumas violate our image of ourselves; they remind us that we are not invulnerable, permanent, or infinitely resilient. To the extent that we try to cling to a particular image of what my self "must" be, the trauma seems to threaten not only to hurt us but to tear our very self apart.

If we treat our self as if it were a stable object that holds residues of a past "inside" us, it decreases our ability to cope with traumas. If we treat our self as an object that has things happen to it, we stop being active participants in a life lived moment-to-moment and become recipients and repositories of experience. Then the self must be either an active agent or a passive recipient: If it is an active agent, somehow we feel (no matter how unrealistic it may be) at fault for what happened; if a passive recipient, we feel like a frighteningly helpless victim. Faced with this unpalatable choice, sometimes we remove ourselves to a safe distance; we step out of our lives as an ongoing being-in-the-world and instead become observers of both life and ourselves as separate objects. However, if what we observed in the past was horrifying or traumatic, we can become trapped in a helpless voyeurism in which we feel distant from the scene we are condemned to watch again and again, frozen in an unchangeable time.

Paula was a thirty-year-old woman who came to see me because she heard I had special training working with clients who had post–traumatic stress disorders. She had experienced a terrifying trauma about nine years ago. Although she had been in several psychotherapies since then, she still did not feel free from the effects of the trauma; she often felt scared, had nightmares and intrusive thoughts. Whenever the anniversary of the event came around, she would experience two months of sadness, tearfulness, and low energy and would withdraw from her activities as a mother, wife, and worker.

She described the trauma. She had been working in a responsible position for a nationally prominent company. They had just moved from one office building to another, and she had gotten behind in her work. Because there was a three-day holiday weekend, she decided to go in to work to catch up. She had dressed casually, because there was no one else going to be in the office other than a lone security guard.

She worked in the office for several hours. Just as she was preparing to leave, the security guard came to her office and put a gun to her head. He forced her to disrobe and spent the next four hours raping her and torturing her. Early on in her ordeal, he told her that he was sorry, but he was going to have to kill her when they were done. He would alternate among brutality, apology, tearful crying, and rage. She was so terrified that she soiled herself, but this only seemed to excite him more.

Throughout her ordeal she kept thinking that if she could only get to the door, she might make a run for it. Yet she feared he'd kill her if she attempted to escape. At the end of several hours, her tormentor was momentarily distracted after raping her yet again. She seized the moment to fling something at him, stun him slightly, and flee. She described how she ran out of the building "naked, covered with my own shit, crying, terrified." She was able to make it to a house where people took her in and called the police, who were able to capture her assailant. He was convicted and sent to prison.

She had never been able to fully resume her business career and felt awkward about being a housewife. She was tired of having her tormentor continue to ruin her life. She also felt that her intermittent symptoms made her overly dependent on her husband, whom she described as loving and supportive. Her daughter's birthday was right around the same time as the anniversary of her assault; she didn't feel it was fair that she would be distracted and depressed at a time when her life should be joyful. Her feelings of shame and humiliation at having "lost control" and shit on herself were particularly troublesome for her, as was her sense of naked vulnerability. She had tried everything she could think of but was still unable to shake this trauma from her past.

When I saw her, the issue was particularly acute because her assailant was scheduled to come up for his first parole hearing in six months, right around the anniversary date of the assault itself. We set up a twelve-session therapy contract. Paula was initially worried about having a fixed number of sessions: How could we be sure she would be better at the end of that time? I assured her that she would be feeling differently and more free; that making a commitment to complete the work in a certain amount of time would help her feel that she really was putting an end to this.

In the course of the twelve sessions we revisited the trauma several times. I followed the psychodynamic format with which I was most familiar[28] but also augmented it with some hypnosis. She experienced significant improvement, especially from a hypnotic visualization technique in which she would review the traumatic event but alter some insignificant detail—for example, the color of the assailant's shirt—to give her some sense of influence over the intrusive images that had previously seemed to her to be unalterable.

However, she continued to worry about whether she'd ever really be able to get over the trauma: Maybe her improvement was only temporary. She was particularly concerned about whether she would have a recurrence of symptoms a few months after the therapy ended, when the anniversary of the assault, the parole hearing of her assailant, and her daughter's birthday all would occur within a week or two. As the final few sessions of the therapy approached, she was anxious and obsessed about whether she could ever shake off the past.

A turning point came during some hypnosis in the tenth session. She was able to imagine a long corridor lined with doorways. Using various techniques of hypnotic time distortion, I suggested that because she already knew that she could alter details of her images of the event, she could now use this time to open doors to explore alternative pasts: pasts in which the traumatic event had not occurred, pasts in which it had occurred but turned out differently. As she opened doors to alternative pasts, she could discover that they led to alternative futures, and trace the futures back to alternative presents.

She spent some time doing this and had many strong emotional experiences. She was able to realize a certain psychological truth to each doorway: Some held her fears, some her hopes; some her courage, some her vulnerability. Each time, after exploring to where a doorway led, she came back to her central "choosing place." I emphasized her ability to come back from whatever doorway to her "choosing place." I then suggested that because she was in a "choosing place," she could now choose to close or open any of the doorways: She could choose the past that gave the most meaning to her life. She made her choices and seemed to experience a sense of relaxation and peace.

She later told me that she chose the doorway into the past in which the trauma had happened pretty much the way she remembered it. It was good to feel the freedom to choose, she said. But she realized that perhaps if the trauma had never occurred, for all she knew she would still be a single professional woman. The chain of the past led through trauma, but it also led to her marrying her husband and having her daughter; she would not exchange this love for anything and would not allow anything to stain it.

The final few sessions of the therapy involved some painful work around termination. We discussed altering the treatment contract so that she could feel control over how many sessions we would meet: She chose to stick to the original twelve sessions. She subsequently contacted me and told me that the anniversary of the trauma and the parole hearing came and went accompanied by normal emotions but without any recurrence of her depressive or post–traumatic stress symptoms. She was even able to feel some pity for her assailant, rather than pure horror and hatred (although she was relieved to have his parole denied and have him still behind bars).

She was able to fully enjoy celebrating her daughter's birthday and to love and be loved by her husband, and she also was doing some personally meaningful part-time work. She had been raped, threatened, and nearly killed, she said: This didn't mean that her assailant could have a hold on her. She had decided that her personal identity was not just what came to her, but what she made of it. She said that now, instead of feeling lost in the past, she felt reconnected to what was going on now in the world around her and the people she loved and who loved her.

Most psychotherapies suggest that after a trauma a person needs to process it to either accommodate his or her self-schemas to the trauma or to assimilate the traumatic event into the self-schemas. This kind of therapeutic strategy can be helpful, but it does not fully address the core incorrect belief: that both self and world are things. If the self is a thing, it may be lost, damaged, or hurt. If the world is a thing, it can be quite threatening: It can rape us, invade us, disappoint us, or overwhelm us. If self and world are things, our life experience consists of photographs of our past that we carry in the albums that define our selves.

The snapshots of our experiences, however, are not the experiences themselves; photographs always lie. Life is always moving. Time is not linear, but lived. Our lives occur in the "choosing place" of this moment, where we exist in relationship to all the empty potentiality of being time. Our histories are not our fates. Zen practice opens a window to a different view of history than the one to which we are used, a view in which we are not statues molded from our pasts, but rather living organisms in constant development.

If we think that we are the sum of what we have experienced in the past, we have an idea of self-development that is essentially one of self-by-accretion. In this view, we do something or have something done to us; we then encode it in some form of representation that we remember later, and our self gradually becomes an accumulation of all that we have previously thought, felt, and done. We think we have residues of the past that lie "within" us and determine how we will react to new experiences. We say, "I am the adult child of an alcoholic," or, "I am a good son." This is an edited version of ourselves that leaves out much of our past: It also leaves out all of the present.

If we see ourselves as the products of our pasts, we confuse who we are with who we've been. This closes many of the possible doors to who we may become. In contrast, the Heart Sutra's description of "no origination and no stopping" reminds us that *our self is not an accrual of experience but an ongoing, ever-changing manifestation of potentiality.*

As we develop, we are constantly changing and transforming. Our pasts are not "back there" behind a boundary and our futures are not "ahead" of us across some gulf. Our personal history is not bounded in this way. We do not touch our pasts and future: We live them, now. As we live our lives touching ourselves touching and being touched, we are centered in the immediate moment. But we live our lives not just as isolated points in time, but as time lines: We span developmental histories. Our history is defined by the seamless absence of boundaries that marks continuous transformation.

If one examines a growing child, you can say that she was four feet five inches tall last month, and is currently four feet six inches tall. You can never say, however, at what precise moment she passed from being four feet five to four feet six because it did not occur as a discrete quantum jump but rather in a constantly ongoing process of growth. So although we live moment-by-moment in the immediacy of present-time touching, these moments have no boundaries that set them off from each other: They are an ongoing, indivisible flow. This flowing growth in which we experience our individual history is a "proceeding-from becoming," it has a quality of being past-future-in-the-present. In Zen it is sometimes called "the going-to within the coming-from, the coming-from within the going-to."

We make our pasts and our futures in the present. Modern historians recognize that there is no single "reality" in the past that can be captured and codified: Rather, each history text constitutes a particular present-time reconstructing, another version of the story. Neither our personal nor our collective histories can be reduced to mere collations of more-or-less accurate recollections of "real" past events that happened to us.[29] Our individual self develops not by accruing experience but by eliminating certain possibilities. Our history as an individual is not what we have done or what has happened to us. Rather, our history tells the story of what we have excluded—sometimes from convenience, sometimes from fear—from our set of possible actions. I may be used to saying of myself, "I am a psychotherapist," but this is shorthand for saying "I do not choose to act like a carpenter, candlemaker, or so forth even though I potentially could."

We are back to the problem of mistaking the label for the reality. Labels can be convenient and efficient; by restricting our realm of possibilities when we face a decision, labels save us time. But language creates a dangerous illusion when it assigns labels: We start thinking there is a "thing" called "being a psychologist," which is "in" me. Then eliminating possibilities can shift from a convenience to a confining role. If I can recognize that my "identity" is not a characteristic "in" me, but merely a tag or a marker, I can recognize that my self faces a wide range of potentialities. I may have previously excluded or not utilized some of these abilities, but many of them remain potentially available.

The Heart Sutra reminds us "all Dharmas are marked with emptiness. They do not appear nor disappear, are not tainted nor pure, do not increase nor decrease." When our self experiences this freedom our personal history does not involve a self that either vanishes or accumulates; we need not "erase" the bad nor even pile good on bad to change, because we are *always* changing. If we conceive of our self as the collection of our past experiences it can be hard to find new paths. If in contrast we conceive of our self as a nexus of potentialities, with certain ones being manifested at a particular time, then changing our self does not require subtracting from or adding to the self. Self-change only requires a turning, a rediscovery of potentialities that have always been there but have been temporarily excluded. The self as an accumulation of experience is a prison; the self as empty, as shimmering potentiality, is a prism that, depending on its turning, gives forth many different colors.

> During the course of the couples' therapy of Bob and Jane described in the chapter on the Sandokai, as Jane's husband's obsessive self-recriminations lessened, Jane began to feel flooded with painful childhood memories of sexual abuse and humiliation and asked to be seen individually. She told me how when she was growing up her parents, both nudists, would embarrass her if she brought friends home; they forced her to pose for "cheesecake" photos and conspired to give her sexually to their friends. Jane's primary feeling was one of self-disgust; she felt as though she had an indelible "stain on her soul." She felt that she had been treated like shit, and that made her feel like a piece of shit on the inside, no matter how competent she appeared on the surface.
>
> After several sessions she remained mired in self-disgust. I looked for some way to both acknowledge her terrible experiences and free her from them and said, "You know, when you take a mirror and hold it up to a piece of shit, it looks like the shit is in the mirror. It's easy to believe this illusion. Imagine what it would be like being a mirror, if you believed you were everything you reflected. But you are making this mistake here. You look at yourself and see the shit in the mirror, but fail to see that *you are the mirror*, and the mirror isn't sullied."
>
> Jane stopped. She looked transformed, as if a great weight fell off her shoulders. "I'm me," she stated, in some wonder, "I'm not what *happened* to me."
>
> Jane subsequently became much less anxious, more able to laugh, less reactive to her husband's emotional swings. She went back to school and finished her degree.

When the past is a fact, it can be a ball and chain around our ankles. When self is empty, it finds freedom. Because "the" person doesn't exist except as an ever-changing flow of experience, history becomes a participatory dance, not a collection of facts apart from us that weighs us down. We discover we realize our past in our present, and life becomes not a calendar of events but a fluid experiencing. In Jane's words, "I'm *me*; I'm not what *happened* to me."

We are not what happened to us; we are always recreating our selves. We do not "have" a past: We have a *relationship* to our past.

SELF AND RELATIONSHIP

We do not "have" a past, nor a future, nor a present; we do not "have" a lover, or a child, or a job, or even a self. Instead, we have relationships to our selves: Our relationships to our past, present, and future intertwine with our relationships to our families, our work, our physical environment. The central message of the

Heart Sutra is that we exist not in things but through dependent co-arising: We live our lives through interbeing with our selves, the selves of others, and the world its-self. We are not alone.

If I feel isolated and do not realize my intrinsic connectedness with other beings there will be times when, feeling scared, sad, or overwhelmed, I will look for my self and not be able to find it. If I feel I must have a unique, special self that I can grasp firmly, I may become defensive if my self seems to slip away. The insecurity of an isolated self can be felt by individual people, or by nation-states. In the effort to hold on to the security of a narrowly defined self-territory, we sometimes define a person or groups of people "outside" us as the Enemy, and create ourselves by saying "'We' are not 'Them.'" This is a self based on isolation and fear; it leads to antagonism, prejudice, and persecution. In my effort to shore my self up, I may try to do so by elevating myself as more special than others; in extreme cases I may deny that others have a self at all and assert that my enemy is soulless.

Even if we do not treat others as enemies, if we feel we stand alone we may treat other people as objects. My boss, my employee, my spouse, or my client may not be seen as a complete living being but only as a stereotype; if we approach people only as representatives of their roles, our relationships with them are governed not by the excitement of mutual discovery but according to principles of gain and loss. The question, "Who are we in this relationship?" is replaced by, "What do I get out of this?"

If "my" self is not empty, if I have a core existence, I may feel I must be "true to myself" to live a good life. This viewpoint leads inevitably to conflicts between selfishness and altruism, because when I look to my own being, I become self-centered and assume that when you look to your own being, you become self-centered. Then we may get into arguments about who gets their way, rather than looking to discover what is *our* Way. We may start to argue whether "my" self's needs are somehow more valid than "your" self's needs.

This jousting over the validity of individual needs is a frequent topic for arguments, whether they be between conflictual couples or warring neighbors. Sometimes what underlies these conflicts, however, is not so much a fight for scarce resources as a fear of sharing. Sometimes we run into difficulties not from standing too far apart but from our fear that we will lose our distinctive elements as we get sucked into a relationship in which you and I merge in an amorphous fusion. If we conceive of our selves as insecure self-contained entities, intimacy can be a threat: "I" fears "us." If we don't understand the freedom and security that is inherent in the emptiness of interbeing, we may fear we can be absorbed or subsumed by another person. When we get confused about this, meeting can turn into merging, and connectedness can give way to emotional reactivity. The fact is, however, it is only "full" selves that can be dissolved or taken over by another; "empty" selves have no-thing to lose.

As soon as we assume that a substantive identity exists that has an intrinsic essence separate from its interactions with the world, then a chasm intervenes between "I" and "it," "me" and "you." If I feel that you and I are each ultimately separate, each of us holding some private, core existence, then *I* can never know *your* experience. Yet if our selves are not separate, how can they remain distinct? How can I respond to your pain without either becoming overwhelmed by it or coldly closing myself off and standing apart from your suffering? How do I navigate between the Charybdis of isolation and the Scylla of symbiosis?

Therapists sometimes try to resolve the issue by adopting an "interpersonal" perspective, acknowledging that much of our sense of our selves comes from our interpersonal experience but still reserving some fundamental essence for the individual self. In this view, interpersonal relationships are something like a stock exchange on which images of self and other are traded back and forth; the challenge for "maintaining healthy self-esteem" lies in ensuring that we balance giving and taking in proper amounts as we interact with each other.

Stating that the self "interacts" with others, however, doesn't really resolve the issue. The interpersonal standpoint perceptively states that the self consists of the reflected appraisals of others.[30] But if this is true, we must then consider that the other's self is also a reflected appraisal. Then our selves are reflections of reflections. This kind of circular causality—mirrors within mirrors, in which my perception of you is affected by your perception of me, which is affected by my perception of you—can be dizzying and confusing if we are still, in the midst of all this, trying to hold on to some core essence of ourselves. If "I, the therapist," am inherently separate from "you, the patient," at best, I can empathize only through an act of imagination, rather than through participating in a shared experience.

The Heart Sutra offers us a way out of this dilemma. In the emptiness of interbeing, everything and everyone exists *only in relationship*.[31] We can only know ourselves in the process of experiencing others knowing us, but in this knowing we know no-*thing*, because there is no such "thing" as self and no such "thing" as other outside of their constantly changing interdependence. Essentially, the Heart Sutra suggests that rather than starting with "me" and trying to find "you," we start out from the basic fact of connectedness and proceed to find our selves from there. Love and compassion arise in the joy of inherent connectedness:

> Chuang Tzu and Hui Tzu
> Were crossing Hao river
> By the dam.
>
> Chuang said:
> "See how free
> The fishes leap and dart:
> That is their happiness."
>
> Hui replied:
> "Since you are not a fish
> How do you know
> What makes fishes happy?"

Chuang said:
"Since you are not I
How can you possibly know
That I do not know
What makes fishes happy?"

Hui argued:
"If I, not being you,
Cannot know what you know
It follows that you
Not being a fish
Cannot know what they know."

Chuang said:
"Wait a minute!
Let us get back
To the original question.
What you asked me was
'How do you know
What makes fishes happy?'
From the terms of your question
You evidently know I know
What makes fishes happy.

"I know the joy of fishes
In the river
Through my own joy, as I go walking
Along the same river."[32]

There is a space between us and simultaneously an unbreakable link: Form and emptiness, emptiness and form together make relationships possible. We do not exist independent of each other, but neither do we merge together in an indistinguishable blur. This is the Zen heart of psychotherapy: Touching and proceeding-from meet for a moment at an empty intersection that does not make self or other into an object but which realizes our life together. The meeting point is infinite and instantaneous: a "singularity" that cosmologists tell us created (and is constantly creating) a universe from nothing: a moment of vast, dimensionless emptiness.[33]

With all Dharmas marked by emptiness, we find our way together as individual members of a pair, as the foot before and the foot behind in walking. Self meets self and other in shared activity, sometimes strolling, sometimes running through our lives. Other times we bring both feet together, stand still and gaze with wonder at the unexplored frontiers that spring up and surround us with every step we take.

PROCLAIMING THE MANTRA

The mantra "ga-tè, ga-tè, pa-ra-ga-tè, para-sam-ga-tè" is usually translated something like "gone, gone, completely gone, gone completely to the other shore." It is the very existence of the shore, however, that makes the journey to "completely gone" possible. We find our selves at horizons[34] at which other people and the world at large arise to greet us as we greet them. Shorelines are meeting places in which fluid oceans and firm land realize themselves at each other's boundary.

Boundaries are always expressed in constant interaction with a world from which they are not separate. The infinite world within, the infinite world without, and the infinite line between them all arise and define each other through necessary boundaries. So an empty self does not mean an egolessness of diffuse boundaries and confused pseudofreedom that seeks to abandon all constraints. We must give self-identity boundaries, but not the rigid boundaries of penned-in lines on a political map. Wars are fought over such boundaries, despite the fact that if you stand on the land itself, these map lines cannot be seen, smelled, heard, tasted, or touched. Our boundaries must rather reflect living shores on which sea and winds constantly change the form of cliffs and cove, inlets and jutting rocks.

World and self mutually influence and create one another; self and other arise to meet each other in each moment. In this flow of experience, self does not subsume other nor other subsume self, nor does self exclude other or other exclude self. Separateness and oneness are not mutually exclusive: Buddhists say that the vast sky does not hinder the white cloud.[35]

Part of being human is that we can only approach the limitlessness of experience from a particular perspective. Recognizing, however, that each particular perspective has no ultimate constraining characteristics, that it has the freedom and fluidity of emptiness, can liberate us from the trap of a "full" self who feels inherently isolated. Emptiness brings us together; banishing illusory obstacles of "I exist here, you exist there," it offers a field for healing our divisions, for melding unity and uniqueness.

When both self and world are empty, they embrace each other fully. If we meet each other wholeheartedly, we are open to each other without thinking of personal gain; if we do not hold anything back to protect or defend some small illusory territory, the universe opens up and embraces us. We can then immerse ourselves in each act, each moment so that washing our car, hugging our child, tying our shoes, reading a book all become different expressions of our life's practice. Such acts of daily life provide the medium for ongoing, healing psychotherapy and moment-by-moment meditation. This is proclaiming the Prajna Paramita mantra.

When the Heart Sutra tells us to proclaim the mantra, it tells us we cannot rest in empty silence but must actualize its wisdom. Stepping back to emptiness, we must step forward into form; we must find stillness in motion and movement at rest. We must not get stuck on the shoals of any one partial view. That point at which history and immediacy meet, boundary and infinity intersect, touching and proceeding-from dance is our original existence its-self.

Each person constantly expresses his or her original self, and this original self has no unchanging characteristic that brands it permanently. That being so, original empty self has no surfeit or lack; to call it perfect is not right, but it cannot be blemished. It is like when the wind strikes the water: Water and wind meet for a moment in a wave, which crashes on a shore that is then wiped clean by the wind. Therapist meeting client is like this.

Fundamentally, *empty self is connected self.*Looking deeply into emptiness reveals that each can only interbe with all the others. Because identity is empty, there is room for wood and woodcarver, individual and family, self and society. Each realizes his or her self in the other, the other in his or her self, the other in the other, and the self in the self. Zen students stare at the wall, and the wall stares back. A reader picks up a book: When eye and word meet, "self" and "other" vanish in the act of reading. The therapist realizes himself or herself touching the client and the client realizes himself or herself touching the therapist.

Coming from and going to each other, we constantly die and are recreated anew on a field of no-birth and no-death. Freed from clinging to an illusory fixed identity, self and world arise to meet and actualize each other. We cannot find happiness in going our own way alone. In the intersections of the lines forming patterns that connect, and in the space between the lines that makes such intersections possible, we can find the joy of true freedom.

Freedom

Eating dust makes one hungry.
The wise fish bites off
Bait, hook, line all at once.
Swimming free of the light
Swimming free of the dark
The joy of fishes.

One may die in the shallows as well as in the depths
But following one's nature
Swimming up waterfalls
Opening the heart to strew
Birth and death glittering jewels
glacial pebbles on smooth sands' beds
One inch of water will suffice

Lightning strikes the mountains with laughter
Aspens whisper to life,
drop their leaves—
an offering to moonlight.

The "Song of the Jewel Mirror Samadhi"
by Tozan Ryokai[1]

The teaching of thusness has been intimately communicated by buddhas and ancestors.
Now you have it, so keep it well.
Filling a silver bowl with snow, hiding a heron in the moonlight—
When you array them, they're not the same;
When you mix them, you know where they are.
The meaning is not in the words, yet it responds to the inquiring impulse.
If you're excited it becomes a pitfall;
If you miss it, you fall into retrospective hesitation.
Turning away and touching are both wrong, for it is like a mass of fire.
Just to depict it in literary form is to relegate it to defilement.
It is bright just at midnight; it doesn't appear at dawn.
It acts as a guide for beings—its use removes all pains.
Although it is not fabricated, it is not without speech.
It is like facing a jewel mirror; form and image behold each other—
You are not it—it actually is you.
It is like a babe in the world, in five aspects complete:
It does not go or come, nor rise nor stand.
"Baba wawa"—is there anything said or not?
Ultimately it does not apprehend anything, because its speech is not yet correct.
It is like the six lines of the double split hexagram;
The relative and absolute integrate—piled up, they make three;
The complete transformation makes five.
It is like the taste of the five-flavored herb, like the diamond thunderbolt.
Subtly included within the true, inquiry and response come up together.
Communing with the source and communing with the process,
It includes integration and includes the road.
Merging is auspicious; do not violate it.
Naturally real yet inconceivable,
It is not within the province of delusion or enlightenment.
With causal conditions, time and season, quiescently it shines bright.
In its fineness it fits into spacelessness;
In its greatness it is utterly beyond location.
A hairsbreadth's deviation will fail to accord with the proper attunement.
Now there are sudden and gradual,
In connection with which are set up basic approaches.
Once basic approaches are distinguished, then there are guiding rules.
But even though the basis is reached and the approach comprehended,
True eternity still flows.

Outwardly still while inwardly moving,
Like a tethered colt, a trapped rat—
The ancient saints pitied them, and bestowed upon them the teaching;
According to their delusions, they called black as white—
When erroneous imaginations cease, the acquiescent mind realizes itself.
If you want to conform to the ancient way,
Please observe the ancients of former times;
When about to fulfill the way of buddhahood, one gazed at a tree for ten eons,
Like a tiger leaving part of its prey, a horse with a white left hind leg.
Because there is the base, there are jewel pedestals, fine clothing;
Because there is the startlingly different, there are house cat and cow.
Yi, with his archer's skill, could hit a target at a hundred paces;
But when arrow points meet head on,
What has this to do with the power of skill?
When the wooden man begins to sing, the stone woman gets up to dance;
It's not within reach of feeling or discrimination—
How could it admit of consideration in thought?
A minister serves the lord, a son obeys the father.
Not obeying is not filial, and not serving is no help.
Practice secretly, working within, as though a fool, like an idiot—
If you can actualize continuity, this is called the host within the host.

Chapter 6

Host and Guest: The "Song of the Jewel Mirror Samadhi" by Tozan Ryokai

INTRODUCTION

The teaching of thusness has been intimately communicated
by buddhas and ancestors.
Now you have it, so keep it well.

The Heart Sutra tells us everything is empty. For someone who is suffering, confused, and unclear about what to do about their life, emptiness—even if it is seen as the lively fluidity of no-thingness rather than the hollowness of despair—may not seem a great comfort. Our clients, after all, come to us when their lives seem chaotic and there is nothing they can hold on to. They are usually in enough distress that they cannot see their way clearly; their thoughts and feelings are so loud that they cannot hear their inner voice. In such a state, it's hard to find the freedom the Heart Sutra offers. To offer them emptiness may seem like pouring water on a drowning man.

Therapists know that when clients come to us gripped by irrational fears, it does not help much to say, "Really, there is nothing to be afraid of." Clients often know intellectually that there is nothing to be scared of, but their experience insists the fear is quite real. The Heart Sutra awakens us to emptiness by telling us there is "no body, no mind, no stopping, no origination," but if someone is losing their vision, going deaf, or facing terminal cancer, it may not help much to just say to them, "You know really, when you look at things from the absolute point of view, there are no eyes or ears, no birth or death." We have to somehow reconcile the truth of absolute emptiness with the fact that we fully experience ourselves as having eyes and noses, thoughts and feelings. These are matters of life and death.

Tozan Ryokai, the author of the "Song of the Jewel Mirror Samadhi", had similar questions about this:[2]

> While still young, Tozan Ryokai read the Heart Sutra with a teacher. When he reached the place where it said, "There is no eye, ear, nose, tongue, body, or mind," he suddenly felt his face with his hand. He asked his teacher, "I have eyes, ears, nose, tongue, and the rest. Why does the scripture say that they do not exist?"
>
> His teacher was amazed and said with regret, "I am not the teacher for you," and sent him to Zen Master Ling-mo on Mt. Wu-hsieh.

Tozan was confused and felt his face with his hand. When we are lost in a fog we act similarly: We pinch ourselves, splash water on our face, or stamp our feet; we are trying to wake up, to find the firmness of real ground beneath our feet. Tozan's Song of the Jewel Mirror Samadhi is about the "thusness" that grounds our lives.

In Buddhist parlance, "thusness" is shorthand for saying: truth as it is, things as they are. This truth is the absolute ground, the basic principle on which everything depends and that everything expresses. Whether in our daily lives, our Zen, or our psychotherapeutic practice, we all seek something fundamental:

> Ruiyan asked Yantou, "What is the fundamental constant principle?"
> Yantou said, "Moving."
> Ruiyan said, "When moving, what then?"
> Yantou said, "You don't see the fundamental constant principle."
> Ruiyan stood there thinking.
> Yantou said, "If you agree, you are not yet free of sense and matter: if you don't agree, you'll be forever sunk in birth and death."[3]

Like Ruiyan in the above story, we all are looking for something constant that we can rely on. But our lives are in continual flux; in our very searching, we are moving and cannot see that the fundamental principle of our lives is to be moving. If we cannot see the fluidity to everything in our life, we may become rigid and get stuck; if we try to step out of our narrow boats to explore the flowing stream, we may be swept away by the current, tumbled over and over. When we experience that everything in our life is moving, including us, we may have troubles finding our bearings.

The need to commune with the fundamental principle of our lives is often most urgent when it is most difficult. There are times in our lives when all our strengths seem to fail us. There are times in all our lives when we find we cannot laugh the way we used to, when we become tired of hanging on, when we pray and are met by silence, when our faith dissolves, even against our will. Our loved ones get sick and die; our love itself sometimes turns into disappointment, frustration, and anger. We age, and our memory fails; our logic deserts us in the face of strong emotion. We try to fall back on what has worked in the past, and it fails; we search for firm ground and find quicksand. Here in California, the very ground on which we stand sometimes quakes beneath our feet. We can feel suffocated, dead inside, lost:

> Brian was a middle-aged man who was feeling ambivalent about whether to stay in his long-term marriage. Most of his life he had felt emotionally constricted and armored. He tended to be overintellectualized and had difficulties enjoying himself.
>
> He had recently fallen in love with another woman. He felt guilty and conflicted about this and did not act on his love; he loved her from afar. But for the first time he had begun to feel some excitement in his life. He wasn't sure what to do, but the prospect of love stirred up many painful emotions and old issues, so Brian sought out psychotherapy. At the outset of the therapy, however, the sessions had an arid feel; Brian discussed his ambivalent desires but did so in a controlled, distant fashion that displayed little emotion.
>
> Then a few sessions later he suddenly started shaking. He fought hard against any "unseemly" display, but sobs came in overwhelming waves as he began to describe a series of childhood traumas. It turned out that when he was a little boy he was often taken care of by his fundamentalist grandparents. If he got into any mischief or displayed any "unacceptable" emotions, his grandparents would repeatedly take him out to their barn, beat him to "drive the devil out," tie him up, and hang him from a rafter by his ankles. Then they would take a bucket of water and submerge his head in it until he inhaled water, choked, and lost consciousness. He was a little boy; he loved and feared his grandparents, but they were literally killing him, and he reacted to this by shutting down and assuming a rigid control of any spontaneous feelings or behaviors that could lead to punishment.
>
> "They drowned my heart," he cried.

For several years, every time I sat down to do zazen I would experience tremendous pain in my back. I went to physical therapists, chiropractors, body workers, neurologists, psychotherapists. They all helped a bit, but although I received treatment and did my exercises regularly, the pain continued. It was accompanied by a tightness that seemed to block the flow of breathing and drain my energy. I knew there was some physical basis to this (I have a mild case of scoliosis) but I also knew there was a psychological and spiritual component I was missing. I could tell I was holding on tightly to something, although I couldn't tell what I was so fearful about. I tried psychotherapy, without any change. I tried relaxing into my pain, I tried softening around the constriction, I tried refocusing with various meditative techniques. I tried not doing anything and just accepting that this was the way it was.

I became frustrated and angry with myself, with my doctors, with Zen practice. I was being a "good boy," I was doing everything I was "supposed to," why was I locked in so much suffering? I found myself tense, irritable, unsatisfied. Sitting on the cushion, I became obsessed with how my posture was never quite right. I found it difficult to find a balance between accepting my imperfections and pain and working on finding some balance or peace. No matter how hard I tried to work, no matter how much I tried to give up and accept the situation, each meditation session became a struggle, off-balance. Something was not letting go.

I had dim memories of what meditation could feel like when it was balanced and whole. I had some inchoate sense of a larger container, a wordless foundation to my practice, but it seemed far away: I could not touch it. I would read, "The teaching of thusness has been intimately communicated; now you have it, so keep it well," and know that such thusness existed: But it seemed to exist as a phantom, just out of reach. How could I keep it well, with a body that ached and went off balance no matter how much physical therapy, yoga, acupuncture, and chiropracty I went to? How could I keep it well with a mind that careened between obsession and anger, depression and pride?

I felt that my practice had become self-centered, so I tried to rededicate myself to serving others, to loving my family and enjoying my work. But something in me seemed to dry up. Although I would go to the clinic, bow to my clients, and attempt to face them with openness, something kept closing down. I became more irritable with my family. I found myself just going through my paces, just getting by. Vacations, exercise, psychotherapy, meditation retreats, long hikes in the mountains, trying this, trying that, trying just to stay aware—nothing helped.

I began to worry that this might be the way the rest of my life might be.

I didn't know what else to do, so I kept sitting zazen. The pain and suffering continued. At the end of the year, in mid-December, I attended a week-long meditation retreat, a sesshin. This is the traditional sesshin to mark Buddha's enlightenment, but I experienced no peace. Everything felt grim. I tried to tell myself, "Grimness is OK," but that didn't make it any less grim.

It was the depth of winter, and I didn't know what I could rely on. I felt I'd "lost it."

THE SOURCE OF PRACTICE

> *Outwardly still while inwardly moving,*
> *Like a tethered colt, a trapped rat—*
> *The ancient saints pitied them, and bestowed upon them the teaching;*
> *According to their delusions, they called black as white—*
> *When erroneous imaginations cease, the acquiescent mind realizes itself.*

Many of us live lives of quiet desperation, feeling like tethered colts or trapped rats. Outwardly we may seem still, but inwardly we often are trapped in confusion and emotional distress. Many times we hear a client say, "I put on a good face, but inside I don't know where I am." We have strength and potential, but we hobble ourselves by our fears and angers; we corner ourselves in our expectations and prejudices. We seek out a teacher, or a therapist, sometimes because we think we've "lost it" (although It cannot be lost) and sometimes dimly apprehending that we "have it" but are unsure how to "keep It well."

We have learned to not trust ourselves; we are caught in the fundamental delusion that truth and happiness lie far away, that they are the property of ancient saints rather than right at hand. When we feel in pain, bad about ourselves, or disappointed in those closest to us, it is hard to have faith that just letting go of our erroneous imaginations is sufficient. We sometimes are so full of self-disgust that we fear if we ease up on our conditioned styles of thinking and customary habits, we will discover not an acquiescent mind but a seething cauldron within us. We sometimes fear that even if we do discover some transient peace or calm, it will be vulnerable to outside interference.

In our first session Arlene, a twenty-eight-year-old woman, told me she had been in psychotherapy before without much benefit. She said that ever since she had been a teenager she had felt anxious. When she got tense, she would fight the feelings for a while and then eventually either go get drunk or eat compulsively to take the feelings away. Both of these would satisfy her temporarily, but then she would feel guilty and anxious about what she'd done. Then the cycle would start all over.

During the session she began to explore the possibility that she was not so much sick as sensitive. She felt America was a rather frenzied place, which tended to set off her anxiety. She'd been visiting Greece since she was eleven years old and had spent a few months there recently; she discovered that eating under the open sky, away from television and traffic jams, she had been able to calm down.

She was able to identify how her anxiety had "allies" in the culture around her, with magazine covers and televisions blaring instructions on what she "should" be as a woman, reinforcing any insecurities she might have about herself. We explored what allies she had for counteracting the messages society promoted and maintaining her sense of being able to trust herself and feel a sense of calm and equilibrium. She said that for most of her life she had had no allies for soothing herself besides eating and drinking, but recently something had changed.

Just a week or two before as she had begun to feel anxious, she found herself doodling, and her drawing helped give her some distance from her anxiety. She had said to herself, "Well, let me see what happens if I just let myself be anxious and kind of notice what it's like." To her surprise, she found the anxiety dissipated after a few hours.

We discussed how the "knack" involved was to not push away the experience but not get swept up in it either. I asked if she were aware that what she had just discovered, spontaneously, was a skill—a kind of mindfulness practice—that many people went to stress management classes, meditation centers, and so forth to learn. I asked her what she thought would happen if she continued to cultivate her "mindful doodling."

She felt optimistic, but also fearful. She didn't feel that she could rely on herself. She was sure "doodling" wouldn't be enough, that she'd get swept up in her anxiety and old habits and not be able to step back enough to listen to herself, let herself have her feelings, and find her own true vision. So she was planning to leave the country in about two months to move to Greece.

We seek outside ourselves. Like Arlene, we all know the feeling of wanting to get away from it all; we seek to find a peaceful sanctuary in some place other than where we are. A client goes off to a clinic to see a therapist; a Zen student goes off to a meditation retreat to see an enlightened teacher; a therapist goes to a program or a workshop to see a famous clinician. We think that they have what we don't: Perhaps they have the Answer; perhaps they can provide that fundamental something on which we are looking to rely.

We are seeking that which, when we enter the midnight of our lives, will shine bright and act as a guide, removing pain, showing the way. We seek contact with our foundation, the Absolute Reality of our lives that moves us and to which we return again and again, whether we are aware of it or not. We're looking for It.

The "Song of the Jewel Mirror Samadhi" refers to It as "the teaching of thusness." We all have It, rely on It, and express It; It has been communicated to us intimately as our birthright. In Zen we say that It has been communicated to us even before we are born; It is the basis on which birth and death rest, this Ground of Being, this Fabric from which the material of our life is cut.

What is It?

For the Zen student, this is a basic koan.

When Tozan was leaving Ungan he asked, "After you die, if someone asks me, What was the truth you taught, what should I say?"

After a long pause Ungan responded, "Just this, just this."

Tozan sank deep into thought. Ungan said, "In order to understand the truth, investigate the matter thoroughly."

Tozan was still embroiled in his doubts.

What is "just this, just this" for therapists and clients? What is the truth on which psychotherapy rests? We may intuitively feel that it is important for us to be able to accept our clients as "just this," whatever problems they present with. We may sense that if we can avoid getting caught in self-conscious awkwardness, some healing can occur if client and therapist simply sit down with each other and let their meeting be "just this." But we worry. We feel we need to do something more. "Just sitting" sometimes doesn't feel like enough, whether it is the "just sitting" of zazen or the "just sitting" of listening and responding to each other in the therapy office: We denigrate it as mere "doodling." Even if we have positive experiences through letting life be "just this," we and our clients often remain embroiled in doubts.

At the first meeting of the "Help for Headaches" class, we usually mention that if you become frightened of a headache, you have two problems instead of one: Instead of dealing with just pain, you have to deal with the pain and the fear. We suggest that people try eliminating fear from their next headache by letting themselves experience the headache as if it were the first time, adopting an attitude of curiosity rather than trepidation.

The following week Hillary (one of the participants) said that she'd been interested in the idea that headaches invoke fear as an ally. A few days later she had begun to get a bad migraine. Worried that the headache would incapacitate her, she was getting ready to drive to the hospital for an injection to head off the pain when she became aware of how her fear was in the driver's seat. So she decided to experiment with just observing the headache instead. She said to herself: "OK, let's not anticipate and be scared. Let's just see what it's like."

She calmed herself down and just let the headache be what it was. To her surprise, it went away in a few hours without any medication.

"I'm pretty skeptical about all this mind-body stuff," Hillary said. "But that was interesting. Still, I can't accept the idea that just letting the headache be what it was could have been enough to make a difference. Maybe the medication I've been taking for a while did the trick."

Hillary let the headache be "just this." Arlene let her anxiety be "just this." When they did this, they let "erroneous imaginations cease." They began to let go of their thoughts about their experience and allowed the experience to be complete in and of itself. When we stop worrying about whether our anxiety will master us, when we stop anticipating how long the headache will go on, we stop separating ourselves from our experience. At that moment the headache or anxiety has no history: It neither goes nor comes, it's just there. We're just there too.

If we drop our expectations and "considerations in thought" we allow each experience to be fresh and new; we become like "a babe in the world, complete" in our immersion and wonder at our experience. The toddler who falls down doesn't initially cry; for the innocent toddler, a scraped knee is just a scraped knee, and the sensations are what they are. It is only later that, learning to anticipate pain, a scraped knee becomes occasion for distress. When we have a headache or anxiety we acquire thoughts and feelings about them, but the headache and anxiety are not our thoughts and feelings about them. The headache and the anxiety are just what they are. The empty thusness of headaches and anxieties are "naturally real but inconceivable." Our thoughts and feelings can reflect experience but cannot capture it.

If we stop discriminating and making up scenarios about the reality of our life, we're just left with the reality. A headache is not painful, it's just pain. An anxiety is not worrisome, it's just worry. It's not deluded or enlightened, bad or good—it's just what it is.

Hillary and Arlene both had a positive experience when they were able to let go and open up to the reality of their experience, letting it be as it was. Each of them came close to "just this." Yet neither of them could feel comfortable trusting what happened too much. Neither felt entirely secure relying on their life being as it is. Therapists have a similar difficulty. Sometimes clients improve in psychotherapy and we are bothered by the fact that we cannot clearly identify what the cause was for the change; we feel we did not do enough to explain the good outcome. Even if "just this" seems to be enough, we tend to rely on our sophisticated theories and powerful techniques, just as Hillary relies on medication and Arlene places her hopes on a move to Greece.

We don't like the answer, "just this." We tend to look for something else, something special. We are looking for something bigger to rely on, like the sincere student in the following interchange:

> At Berkeley Zen Center, someone once asked our teacher: "What can I rely on?"
> He thought a moment, then replied: "You can count on life being exactly the way it is."

We may like this answer in the abstract. But usually we have problems accepting our lives being exactly the way they are. We have some idea of what life "should" be, and some fantasy of being able to control things so that our life will conform to our vision. We tend to have an uneasy feeling that if we accept life being the way it is, this will turn into passive fatalism and leave us completely at the whims of fate.

So if things are not going the way we want, when life says: "This is it," our response is often a heartfelt "Noooooooo!" The managed care company rejects our paperwork, our son marries somebody we don't like, we get the flu just when we have a vacation planned, and we say "this can't be happening." We try to deny life. But everything that happens, whether we like it or not, is one more facet of our existence. Life shows itself to us through many faces:

> Master Ma was unwell.
> The monastery superintendent asked,
> "Master, how is your venerable state these days?"
> The Great Teacher said,
> "Sun face buddha, moon face buddha."[4]

In the morning we wake up, stretch, and rub our eyes. In the evening we lie down, yawn, and go to sleep. The morning's light and the evening's darkness are each complete. When we get divorced, we feel sad; when we meet someone new, we feel excited. We only get into problems if we feel sad about being sad—that's depression—and excited about being excited—that's anxiety.

If we stop to look at what's happening with us, we see our whole life as it is this moment, and life looks back at us and says: "Here we are." It's quite concrete. At this moment of writing, I have a cold. My throat hurts. My thoughts pause for a moment: It's dark and cold outside, the cup of tea is warm in my hands, the hard disk of the computer is whirring. At this moment of reading, there is a book, a chair, some light, some feeling. That's it, neither more nor less. There's nothing special about it. It's quite palpable.

> A monk asked Yunmen, "What is talk transcending the buddhas and ancestors?"
> Yunmen said, "Sesame cake."[5]
> Another time, a monk asked Yunmen, "What is Buddha?'
> Yunmen said, "Dried shit stick."[6]

Often we feel that our lives are shitty. Yet even if our lives are sweet and well-baked, we want to make more of them—surely my life is more than just this cake?

We met Sarah in a previous chapter, when she was feeling guilty about divorcing her depressed, alcoholic husband and questioning her ability to get involved in intimate, loving relationships. Her feelings of guilt eventually subsided, but then she went through a period in which she was feeling mostly sad and stale. For the past month or so she had felt that her life was boring.

Sarah said that nothing excited her. She would do various things to distract herself but couldn't really take an interest in anything. She was unable to work on her art (although she continued sketching). The men she met were either intriguingly mysterious but unreliable or stable but dull. She had a vision of life being either monotonous or, if she sought to escape that (as she sometimes did, in less-than-wise quests for adventurous liaisons) frenzied.

Sarah was annoyed at herself for feeling this way. She wondered out loud: Was this some flaw in her? Would she always become dissatisfied with any relationship she was in, find it tedious after a while, be unable to renew it and fly off to some adventure? Was she doomed to oscillate between frenzied, brittle excitement and flat ennui? Was she doomed to never feel satisfied, always be yearning for something else?

At the same time, she admitted that she had moments at which something felt different. The other day she had seen a hawk in the sky and felt very "present": content just to see the hawk circle and feel the breeze on her face.

I said, "And you can just hear that hawk thinking: 'Circling round and round, nothing new here, how boring to be just circling... is there more to life than catching the next air current?... Here I am looking for a mouse. Mouse for breakfast, mouse for lunch, mouse for dinner... I'm so tired of mice... there must be more to being a hawk than this!'"

Sarah laughed. She thought that the hawk wouldn't be able to fly very well, let alone be able to swoop down and catch its dinner, if it kept doubting its life that way.

I wondered if it might not be a good idea for her to try something boring on purpose, to discover how to renew her interest in the midst of mundane existence. I suggested that maybe she should decide to eat the same dinner day after day for a week or two and see what happened.

She blushed and said that she already did that. She was a bit embarrassed, because in California what you eat is often judged as being politically correct or incorrect. But Sarah confessed she really enjoyed Australian tea muffins. She would go for periods where she would eat them three times a day for many days (supplementing her diet, of course, with other foods for nutrition). She told me enthusiastically how she appreciated each detail of the muffins: their biscuit-like texture, the way they took butter, the way they toasted brown. And, Sarah said, whenever she ate the muffins as a mainstay that way, when she ate something different, it really stood out: It tasted so wonderful!

We discussed ways of extending this "muffin mind" into ways of relating to her self and to the people around her. Sarah described how sometimes she could just enjoy the moment; she could be driving her car and just enjoy driving, rather than driving to get somewhere. Instead of going from point A to point B she would just be where she was.

Still, for some time Sarah kept asking herself: "Is this all there is?" She worried that she was missing out on something; she still kept grasping at trying to understand, seeking excitement, looking for something grand. She had to practice for a while to find a way of being calm in the midst of thrilling novelty and joyful in the midst of her ordinary activity.

Sarah started to find the basis of her life in an Australian muffin. Proust found a world in a cup of tea and a madeleine; Blake found a world in a grain of sand. These bits and pieces are the stuff of our life, and of the universe itself. When we look for something beyond our immediate experience, we miss It. The "thusness" of existence is always available to us, but we often have troubles seeing it, hearing it, and accepting it.

Tozan Ryokai, the author of "Song of the Jewel Mirror Samadhi", had his own difficulties understanding "thusness" when he heard a teacher, Echu, instruct a monk in "the teaching of the nonsentient" by setting forth the stuff of our ordinary lives. Tozan told his teacher Isan what he had heard:

A monk had asked, "What is the Mind of the ancient Buddhas?"

Echu replied, "Fences and walls, tiles and pebbles."

The monk commented, "But are not fences, walls, tiles and pebbles non-sentient things?"

Echu answered that they were.

The monk asked, "Do they comprehend what teaching the Dharma is?"

Echu said, "They constantly teach, vigorously teach, ceaselessly and without rest."...

After some further dialogue, Echu said, "Surely you have seen in the Avatamsaka Scripture the passage, 'Worlds teach, sentient things teach, and all things of the past, present, and future teach."

When Tozan had finished the whole account, Isan said,

"I have IT here with me too, only it is rare to encounter a REAL PERSON."

Tozan respectfully asked, "Since I am not yet clear about the matter, would you please instruct me?"

Isan raised up his fountain scepter and asked, "Do you understand?"

Tozan replied, "No, I don't. Please explain."

Isan replied, "Speech born of father and mother will never explain IT for you— I can't explain it to you in words."

WORDS

> *Just to depict it in literary form is to relegate it to defilement....*
> *Ultimately it does not apprehend anything, because its speech*
> *is not yet correct.*
> *Although it is not fabricated, it is not without speech.*

Every encounter with ordinary life brings us the teaching of thusness, but we cannot depict this teaching in words without "relegating it to defilement." Words let us express ourselves to ourselves and to others, but they also let us deceive ourselves and confuse others. Words alone cannot convey experience, because the word is not the experience to which it points. Words are only pointers. As one Zen teacher said, "Words can describe things, but they are not truth itself."[7] In psychotherapy, we say that the map is not the territory; in Zen we distinguish between the finger pointing at the moon and the moon itself.

Part of a therapist's job is helping clients point out their experiences and talk about their lives; an equally important part of the job is helping clients learn how to become silent and still. Sometimes there are so many words in our heads we and our clients can't hear ourselves, let alone hear or express It. It's not just words that are noisy: We express ourselves through body gestures, facial expressions, songs and sculptures, dramas and drawings. All of these expressions are potentially wonderful, but sometimes we need to go beyond them by returning to silence.[8]

Finding a silent space of wonder beyond speech and thought is essential, because we get ensnared in thoughts and words and mistake them for our reality. Words set up a basic division: When you point at something, you separate yourself from the thing you're pointing at. However, when we go back to a place where speech is not "correct," we do not apprehend any thing; we stop trying to grasp our experience as an object and become one with the experience itself.

Silence makes listening possible, and listening is, of course, crucial to psychotherapy. If we are able to really listen to our clients, our clients start to hear themselves through our hearing them. When one stream meets another, both become deeper. Unless we are familiar with the quiet, still place where flowing streams spring from, however, it may be hard to know how to find water. Part of both Zen and psychotherapy is slowing things down enough so we can stop, listen, and make a fresh start.

> Hypnosis, progressive muscle relaxation, breathing, and imagery techniques all help clients learn how to go to a place beyond words and movement, to relax enough so they can listen to their lives. In addition, I sometimes like to suggest to clients that as they relax and focus within, they can notice a particular muscle they usually don't pay much attention to: the big, thick muscle within their head—the tongue. With the facial muscles relaxed, with no need to have any particular expression on their face, with no need to do anything in particular, no need to feel anything in particular, no need to think anything in particular, they can let their tongues find a place within the mouth to rest. They can notice that the tongue is usually moving, shaping sounds to form words, but there's no need to be busy with that now. As the tongue relaxes, thoughts can slow down as well; they can just have whatever experience they're having, without having to put it into words or thoughts.

Sometimes as a client goes deeper into his or her feelings and thoughts, not just in guided exercises but also in the course of an ongoing therapeutic conversation, the client's speech becomes slower, more awkward, and he or she falls into silence. Then he or she might say, "I can't put it into words." This is often a good sign; it can mean the client is dropping his or her usual ideas about experience and getting closer to the ineffable experience itself. Faced with ungraspable experience, we're often struck dumb and approach that place to which Zen master Amban refers: "Buddha, according to a sutra, once said: 'Stop, stop. Do not speak. The ultimate truth is not even to think.'"[9]

Still, Buddha *said* this. Amban, after quoting Buddha's advice to not speak or think, goes on to comment: "Where did that so-called teaching come from? How is it that one could not even think it? Suppose someone spoke about it, then what became of it? Buddha himself was a great chatterbox."

Having plunged into the speechless, absolute "thusness" of existence in which no thing is named or created but just is, we still have to find a way to express It. To do this we often must use language, whether it is a language of words or of gestures. "Although It is not fabricated, It is not without speech." As Fayan puts it, "Names arise from before naming."[10] Reaching silence, we must speak. And although all speech is a kind of defilement, this is the realm in which we live. We are continuously translating the silent "thusness" of our experience into articulated forms.

Thus our lives are poetry: finding expressions for the inexpressible. Poetry is not what gets lost in translation, but the act of translating itself. Translation is not merely a matter of looking up the meaning of individual words; if that were so, a dictionary and a grammar rule book would suffice. The translator's true work consists of finding different forms for meaning. The task of the therapist is to help clients translate their experiences to themselves in ways so that the translation opens up new possibilities rather than shutting them down.

A certain amount of accuracy is a precondition for, but not the measure of, a translation. There are translations that are a little less literal, or a little more complete at capturing multiple nuances; some capture the rhythms and music of the words, while others convey the images. The heart of emptiness teaches us there is no "core essence" to experience; we cannot capture "the" meaning in one "ultimately accurate" translation. We do best to look at several translations, each of which reflects some different facet of the source. In the process of translating back and forth, we learn not only new meanings, but also a good deal about the languages being used, the art of poetry, the poet, the process of translation, and even, possibly, the translator.

Looking at different facets of meaning in psychotherapy, we ask our clients to tell their stories over and over; we are not trying to get more accurate details, but to discover how each time the story is a little different. In Zen, we hear the same question asked again and again and receive different and sometimes even apparently contradictory answers. A monk asks, "Does a dog have Buddha nature?" and one time the response is "Yes," another time the response is "No."[11] We ask "What is Buddha?" and get an infinity of answers: "Sesame cake"; "Three pounds of flax "[12]; "Hui Chao."

The same is true of the way in which we put our lives into words: There are different stories we can tell and no ultimately "correct" speech except the babble of the moment. When we realize this, we paradoxically make it possible to come closer to the essential nature of an experience, because then we are traveling toward a horizoning rather than a thing. We come closer to our original Self through making multiple interpretations and translations, if we can only listen to what the interpreter is telling us.

> Tozan asked Ungan, "What should I do when I want to meet my original Self?"
> Ungan replied, "Ask the interpreter—ask the messenger."
> Tozan said, "I'm asking right now."
> Ungan asked, "What is he telling you?"

THE INQUIRING IMPULSE

> *"Baba wawa"—is there anything said or not?*
> *The meaning is not in the words, yet it responds to the inquiring impulse....*
> *Subtly included within the true, inquiry and response come up together.*

We are constantly translating our experience to ourselves and to others, but we often don't listen to the interpreter. Inquiry and response often don't flow smoothly. Virtually all of us have some difficulty deciphering the messages of our lives.

Psychotherapists sometimes intervene in this process by offering interpretations or reframings; often, however, clients seem unwilling to entertain alternative descriptions of their lives. After all, how can we expect clients to attend to therapists' messages if they cannot listen to what their own interpreters are telling them?

In psychotherapy, even if we ask questions carefully crafted to help deepen experience—such as the "unique redescription" or "experience of experience" questions drafted by White and Epston[13]—clients often can't respond. A client tells us how he or she stood up against his or her anger and managed to forgive someone and perform a kind deed; we ask, "What does this tell you about yourself?" and he or she says, "I don't know." If we ask clients why they did something, they often are not able to give a clear reason. At the very onset of treatment, we frequently ask, "What brings you here?" and the client often responds, "I don't know."

Some clients cannot find words; other clients get lost in a sea of words. Clients sometimes talk on and on but as we listen to them we realize that we have no idea what the issue is. Therapists also sometimes talk excessively: We find ourselves filling up the silence with a response although we still are unclear about our point. We don't do this only in the consulting room. Even with the people we most love we often find ourselves either falling silent or babbling. This can happen with painful topics, and also with topics at which we are so filled with wonder or happiness that we can't articulate well.

In our confusion, we all babble at each other in the language of "baba wawa." We may think we are being clear and direct, but our words snare us. This happens especially if we listen and talk from a self-centered perspective that is mostly concerned with what we stand to gain or lose from the interchange. If we wish to hear each other—whether it be as client and therapist, partner and spouse, or student and teacher—we must learn to attend instead to the inquiring impulse, to the source from which "baba wawa" springs.

Sometimes we have to babble in order to recover our sense of wonder or strengthen ourselves to face the truth; sometimes, immersed in truth or wonder, we babble. At such times it can be hard to understand our selves and the people talking to us. When we are in the midst of babbling "baba wawa," is there anything said or not?

> Rabbi Levi Yitzhak once came to an inn where many merchants were stopping on the way to market their wares. The place was far from the rabbi's home town and so no one knew the holy man. In the early morning the guests wanted to pray, but since there was only a single pair of phylacteries[14] in the whole house, one after another put them on and rattled off his prayer, and handed them on to the next.
>
> When they had all prayed, Rabbi Levi Yitzhak called the young men to him, saying that he wanted to ask them something. When they had come close, he looked gravely into their faces and said, slowly and intensely, prolonging each word:
>
> "Ma—ma—ma; va—va—va."
>
> "What do you mean?" cried the young men, but he only repeated the same meaningless syllables. Then they took him for a fool.
>
> But now the rabbi said: "How is it you do not understand this language which you yourselves have just used in speaking to God?"
>
> For a moment the young men were taken aback and stood silent. Then one of them said:
>
> "Have you never seen a child in the cradle, who does not yet know how to put sounds together into words? Have you not heard him make bawling sounds, such as 'Ma—ma—ma; va—va—va'? All the sages and scholars in the world cannot understand him but the moment his mother comes, she knows exactly what he means."
>
> When the rabbi heard this answer, he began to dance for joy.[15]

The fact is that even when we babble at each other, something inside us still understands and responds. Our babbling is part of a necessary process. We babble because we don't know quite what we're saying; we're fumbling for something we only dimly perceive. We know it's there but can't quite put our finger on it. Zen sometimes uses the metaphor of being half-awake, half-asleep and groping behind you for the pillow your head is resting on.

Sharing the same source, united in our humanity, we speak a common language beyond words that allows us to understand each others' inquiring impulse. Our ability to respond to the inquiry of "baba wawa" comes from something larger than ourselves. We are able to catch the intention behind the words, because our response takes its qualities from its parents: wisdom and compassion.

In Buddhism the incarnation of wisdom (the Prajnaparamita) is depicted as female, the incarnation of compassion (Avalokitesvara) is male; these are the parents of our response to the inquiring impulse. When parents respond to their babbling infant, they respond out of care and compassion. Parents do not respond to their baby's babbling in academic English; they babble back in baby-talk that is slightly more grammatical. In doing so, the infant learns ordered speech, the parents relearn spontaneity. Our parents understand our babbling questions that seek them out, because our parents know something about seeking: Our parents sought each other out. Our mother's and father's inquiring impulses were given room to wander and meet each other. Our parents gave birth to us; in giving birth to us, their inquiring impulse gave birth to our inquiring impulse.

The inquiring impulse responds to the inquiring impulse. Parent responds to child who responds to parent. Therapist responds to client who responds to therapist. It is our responsiveness to each other and all the myriad things of the world that constitutes us as living beings.

There is still the question of *how* to respond to each other. We are back to a problem to which we alluded earlier: When we meet each other, the absolute "thusness" of our interbeing exists just as it is, far beyond language's ability to capture it or silence's ability to obscure it. So we have to find a way to express It beyond words or silence. Wu-tsu posed this problem in a koan:

> Wu-tsu said,
> "When you meet a Zen master on the road, do not make your greeting with words or with silence.
> What are you going to do?"
> Wu-men makes a verse in reply:

> > Meeting a Zen master on the road,
> > don't make your greeting with words or with silence;
> > a punch in the jaw!
> > If you want to realize—just realize.[16]

Psychotherapy sometimes runs the risk of becoming an activity in which clients mostly talk about their experience instead of delving into experience itself. This can lead to new labels rather than to new life. Often we unwittingly abet this process by having clients fill out a questionnaire before the first therapy interview, in which we ask them to greet us with written words rather than their whole selves. Both Zen practice and psychotherapy can benefit from a sense of a certain urgency that emphasizes action rather than abstraction. For this reason, I often prefer to initiate psychotherapy with something like the following:

> In the clinic in which I work, clients are given a questionnaire to fill out before their first meeting with the therapist. Most of them hand me the questionnaire when they first meet me. I tell them, "Because you've taken the time to fill this out, I should take the time to read this." I read it while they watch, then lift it up in my hands and say,

"This is all I know about you—except for the fact that there's a lot more to you and your life than what's on this paper."

Then I drop the paper on the desk. I turn and face the person in front of me and take a moment to make eye contact and greet them nonverbally. Then I say something such as: "So what brings you here? Tell me what you wanted to get out of coming here today—then let's do it."

There's no substitute for doing. Thought is not enough. Therapists know that clients sometimes make the mistake of believing that thinking about something is the same as making it real. We have a wish we could be more assertive; we go to therapy and discuss being assertive, hoping that talking about it will make us less timid. Then our boss asks us to do something, and we don't say no. We have a wish to be enlightened; we go sit on our meditation cushions hoping it will lead to some special state, but when we have an opportunity to be kind to someone, we turn aside. We substitute the idea, the shadow, for the reality of the act.

If we want to get beyond our fantasies of "life-as-we-wish-it-to-be" and plunge into the reality of our lives, we cannot just cogitate and wait. "If we want to realize—just realize." In order to get beyond sound and silence we need to do something, feel something even if it's a blow to the jaw that temporarily stuns us. If we conceptualize, we retreat from the world into our images of it; ideas can float in a timeless, intangible vagueness. When we act, we are naturally real; our actions take us out of the realm of the hypothetical and help us find out who we are concretely right here, right now.

REALIZING BEYOND IDEAL AND ORDINARY

> Naturally real yet inconceivable,
> It is not within the province of delusion or enlightenment....
> It's not within reach of feeling or discrimination—
> How could it admit of consideration in thought?

When we respond to people and events, we usually employ some kind of representation. In order to express the ineffable "thusness" of our being we use words, images, and gestures to represent our experience to ourselves and each other. Yet as we swim in the sea of our life and death, conceptual thought (whether it be in words or images) always squeezes experience into less than what it is. Standing in a garden, we look around and see a picture in our minds; but the picture of a garden doesn't bear fruit.

Our feeling that the water is cold is just our feeling, not the water itself. Our thought that the ocean is rough is not the water itself. The water isn't warm or cold, rough or smooth; it's simply what it is. Our minds cannot grasp it. Our anticipation and memory, our desire and fear of what the next wave will bring, all are forms of imagination. If we get too caught up in our fantasies about the waves we like and our nightmares about the waves that can crush us, our thoughts may interfere with meeting each wave as it is. If we want to encounter the ocean directly, we need to let our erroneous imaginations cease and let our minds acquiesce to the ocean being Itself, rather than what we want it to be.

The Reality of the ocean transcends our thoughts and feelings about it: It transcends discriminating definitions of beautiful and ugly, holy and profane. It even transcends our ideas about being or nonbeing, existence or nonexistence. The ocean is "naturally real yet inconceivable; It is not within the province of delusion or enlightenment. It's not within reach of feeling or discrimination—How could it admit of consideration in thought?"

If we wish to truly know the ocean as It is and find our place in It, we need to stop trying to grasp it by classifying it according to our partial conceptions. Each instant of our lives is like a sudden shock, an explosion: When the thunder claps for a moment we are neither thinking nor not-thinking, moving or still. The glare of the lightning flash finds us neither tainted nor pure but completely illuminates us where we are. As Echu says:

> If, right now, within all your actions, the two classes of the mundane and the holy do not arise or cease in the least way, then this involves a True Consciousness that does not depend on being or non-being and is ablaze with keen awareness, with no delusionary emotional feelings or binding [personal preferences or] attachments.... there is not the least degree of emotional judgmentalism or intellectual discrimination.... Tozan said "You must comprehend IT in this way so that you can dedicate yourself at once to That Which Is.... That Which Is is steadfast and unmoving, a clear, bright, constant Knowing....
>
> Were you to try to seize this state, you would never realize It because It takes on no form, It is 'non-existent.'
>
> Were you to try to be rid of It, you could not separate yourself from It because It has accompanied you from the very beginning of time; It is not 'non-existent.'...

Tozan and Echu tell us to let go of our ideas, our self-centered judgments and personal preferences, so that we can dedicate ourselves to That Which Is by fully accepting each thing, each person who comes to us each moment. The irony is that if we start pursuing That Which Is somewhere other than where we are, we miss it. When we start identifying the details of our ordinary lives as somehow less than ideal, we think that there is some big picture we are missing out on.

We go to school and study "Psychotherapy." But "Psychotherapy" is only a name, an abstract idea. In our daily work we can only find the reality of psychotherapy in fragments of ordinary conversations between actual therapists and actual clients. These interactions rarely match our image of the Ideal Therapy. Similarly, we may study Zen to realize our True Self, but when we sit down on a particular cushion in a particular place we may find our self feeling uncomfortable, bored, or distracted; it doesn't match our image of Ideal Enlightenment.

If we are feeling that there must be some grandiose Ideal we are missing, we may start looking for Truth somewhere other than in the mundane details of our lives. Clients often come to psychotherapy and students often come to Zen seeking the ideal life. Both psychotherapy and Zen, however, are not about the Ideal we desire but about dealing with the life that is right in front of us; they are about finding the ideal in the ordinary and the ordinary in the ideal.

Our search for the ideal is founded on the Platonic notion that Real Essences lie "deeper than" or "behind" the concrete manifestation of things appearing in the here-and-now. We learn in psychology to dig beneath the surface; we learn in Zen to not be deceived by appearances. Unfortunately, the search for True Reality "behind" our immediate experience can leave the idealistic student searching for a saintly perfection; it can lead the obsessional to seek a life free from germs and contamination; it can lead a pain patient to pursue a mythical cure that will forever alleviate all discomfort. Psychotherapists sometimes feel dissatisfied with the fumbling efforts, full of mistakes, that respond to the actual person before them and search for the essence of psychotherapy in manualized therapeutic techniques designed for more prototypical patients. These kinds of idealistic searches are sometimes productive, but they can also lead to chronic dissatisfaction or even frustrated paralysis.

Zen insists that we find Reality right where we are and the ideal not separate from the real: We say, "The lotus blooms in the mud." The Heart Sutra teaches us the truth of emptiness, that there is no ideal "essence" to seek. Without essences, however, what are we left with? Ordinary life. Just this: thusness.

Long ago Diogenes said, "I have never seen Plato's Tea-ness and Cup-ness, but I have visited him and seen his tea and his cups." I have never heard a client recite a Narrative, but I have heard clients tell anecdotes about themselves. I have never touched Transference, but I have been touched by a client's strong feelings. I have never seen a Schema, but I have witnessed clients break free of their unhappy images by taking concrete small actions that embrace the concrete details of their lives:

I was seeing Len, a forty-six-year-old man with depression and panic attacks who would daydream about the creative things he wanted to do—in particular, quilting—but would never actually do anything about it. Len had a habit of overcommitting himself; he felt unable to say no to people to whom he was close and often wound up doing so much for others that he left no time to carry out his own projects. Then he would feel resentful in his relationships but would not want to make waves, so he would withdraw by smoking too much marijuana. He would think of things to say to his lover but not say them. He would "zone out," get irritable, and occasionally lose his temper; this would lead him to say more bad things about himself and he would feel unworthy and inadequate and fear rejection. He would "atone" for his angry outbursts by outwardly doing more for others but would withdraw further emotionally. Then he would mute his dysphoria by using more marijuana, meanwhile berating himself for not doing the creative things he wanted to do.

He would obsess but not act. He was quite aware of this, and this led him to be more down on himself. He felt he was doomed to being a compulsive perfectionistic martyr, unable to accept himself or others, and that he would never make the leap from dreams to action.

Although we addressed his depression, marijuana use, and lack of assertiveness with the usual therapeutic techniques, for a while not much changed. Then one day he came into the session very excited. He told me his life had altered substantially.

He had done quite a bit since our last meeting. He had completed some of his paperwork, made a baby quilt he enjoyed giving to friends, and gone to social gatherings he previously would have avoided. He had started an open and frank discussion with his lover about some of the problems in their relationship. He was feeling more accepting of himself and others, feeling more comfortable in general, and enjoying his life more. He had scheduled an appointment to get his cataract removed and in general felt he was dispelling the clouds and seeing things clearer.

On follow-up he reported that he had eliminated his marijuana use, cut back on his overtime work, become more assertive and "present" in his interpersonal relationships, and resumed his creative activities. His relationship with his partner improved, he had fewer migraines, he enjoyed himself more and became much less compulsive.

What had made the difference? He said he had found "the trick:" taking pleasure in the mundane details that made up the activities of his life and tackling tasks one bit at a time. He was quite eloquent about this and I took down what he said:

> I've stopped trying to push the universe. I've been able to step back from putting my nose on the grindstone and gotten a wider perspective on life. I've noticed there's a sort of space that occurs between starting and stopping....
>
> I'm not procrastinating any more. I've discovered how to focus on the apple, not the whole orchard. The trick is, instead of putting off things until they seem huge, I do a little bit of what I need to, even if it's just to organize stuff into separate piles. Instead of throwing the whole woodpile on at once I work at something for a bit and if I get tired, bored, or mentally fatigued, I take a break and do something else. That way, instead of pushing myself to continue and getting burned out, I keep a reserve of energy, and I'm able to come back to the job the next day. When I tackled things bit by bit this way, I felt like I'd taken a step and accomplished something. I was amazed, actually, at how much I got done.
>
> It's funny but, dealing with life one thing at a time this way, I've begun to feel that the little bits of work involved are the spice of life. I'm more aware of the textures, colors, and other little things around me....
>
> Instead of expecting I could flip a switch and have everything turn miraculously OK, I learned that going step-by-step gives me a sense that I'll continue to grow in new directions. Before, I would fantasize about the finished product, but wouldn't give any acknowledgment to the practical steps I had to take to see it through; then I'd get discouraged when things took longer than I had imagined. But once I was able to not get caught in being compulsive about the outcome, I was able to take pleasure in each step of the doing of the project.
>
> Going to the store to buy the thread, picking out the material and the color, allowing myself to ask for help from the salesperson—all of these are integral parts of making the quilt.

Like Len, we often find ourselves in a position in which it feels like there is a chasm between the thought and the deed, between the perfection (or frustrated perfectionism) of the Grand Scheme of Things and the "pettiness" of the little details that comprise our imperfect personal lives. Therapy and Zen practice are each in their own way about going to the store to buy the thread, and then sewing one stitch at a time. When we do this, we close the gap between the patchwork pieces and the whole quilt.

SEEKER OF UNITY: THE ABSOLUTE AND RELATIVE

Filling a silver bowl with snow, hiding a heron in the moonlight—
When you array them, they're not the same;
When you mix them, you know where they are.
Because there is the base, there are jewel pedestals, fine clothing;
Because there is the startlingly different, there are house cat and cow.

It is like the six lines of the double split hexagram;
The relative and absolute integrate - piled up, they make three;
The complete transformation makes five.
It is like the taste of the five-flavored herb, like the diamond thunderbolt.

As in any quilt, the independent pieces of our lives can only exist relative to each other; they are separate parts of a larger whole. The separate bits and pieces of our selves, the relative realities of our individual lives, are founded in and are part of some larger Absolute Reality.

As clients and therapists, lovers and Zen students, we are always seeking to touch the Absolute Reality of our lives. This Absolute Reality is, in turn, always seeking to know itself, but it can only realize itself through dividing into the infinite variety of its singular components. Truth emerges not as some grandiose abstraction but through asking a particular question and responding with a particular answer.

We, and our clients, can only know our undivided wholeness by experiencing our dividedness and separation. The source, the ground, the Absolute Reality on which our lives are founded is a seamless unity, boundless and nameless, silent and vast. We can only live in the world as recognizable entities, however, if we have boundaries and names. But as soon as we have boundaries and names, we seem to set up a division: We start to feel separate from the undivided unity that is our foundation.

This is the basic dilemma of our lives: how to feel connected, although apart. Therapy addresses our sense of disconnectedness if we feel personally alienated from ourselves and our world; religion addresses the basic issue of how the Godhead can be broken into many pieces and still remain whole.

Buddhism describes this through the interplay of emptiness and form, Absolute and Relative. Catholicism has its mystery of a Trinity that is also One. In Jewish mysticism we have a precreation story that describes how God, existing as the original primordial Unity, in order to know Itself separated Itself into vessels to hold Itself. The vessels, however, could not contain the glory: They burst into millions of pieces, the pieces of creation, each with a divine spark that longs to be liberated. In Jewish mysticism, the Shekhina is the seeker of unity who aims to rejoin the sparks into their fundamental wholeness, a wholeness that is apparently fragmented but that has never really been lost.

The "Song of the Jewel Mirror Samadhi" is fundamentally about the same question: How do we integrate the Absolute and the Relative, separateness and togetherness, part and whole? In technical Buddhist terms, these involve Tozan's Five Ranks, which describe how form and image behold each other in the larger jeweled mirror, how the relative and absolute integrate in piles of three and five:

> The five ranks have to do with emptiness and form, or the Real and the Apparent, or the Absolute and the Relative. So the first rank is called the Apparent within the Real. And the second one is called the Real within the Apparent. And the third one is the Apparent coming from the Real, and the Real coming from the Apparent. And these are the three fundamental basics, the fundamental base, the three legs.
>
> The first rank is like emptiness is emptiness. And the second one is like form is form. And the third one is form is emptiness and emptiness is form.
>
> In order to make this less intellectual, though, instead of talking about the Absolute and the Relative or Form and Emptiness or the Real and the Seeming, as the two aspects, let's talk about water and waves.
>
> The first rank is the water within the waves. And the second rank is the waves within the water. And the third rank is waves are water and water is waves... no difference.
>
> It's a kind of pattern of our life, or outline of our life. The first rank is about water being just water. [Water is empty of divisions; it just flows. If you try to hold on to it, it slips between your fingers. It isn't confined in any particular shape or essential form. In the sunlight it evaporates; in the cold it freezes.] When you understand that water is just water, and you understand the nature of water completely, then it's how you live in the various configurations of water and find your way.
>
> Enlightenment begins from finding ourself in the first rank where emptiness is emptiness. Finding ourself at the bottom of the ocean, just immersing ourselves in water. As a matter of fact, though, we can't stay in the first rank. The rule is: you can't stay in the first rank. We have to move out, and start swimming. And all the rest of the ranks are about how we swim, and what is the goal of swimming, actually. Where are we swimming to, and how do we do it?
>
> In Zen meditation we sink to the bottom of the ocean. When we go home, we find we are swimming in the waves, the turbulent sea of this ocean. But that's also water; that's what we have to understand. That's what Tozan is telling us. That's also water. The waves are water. Waves are not something apart from water.

[In the second rank form is form. It's the "thusness" of things. Waves are just waves. Some are huge and powerful, others are gently rolling. Everything appears in its own shape and nature. Things are as they are: just this, just this. We are each as we are.]

The third rank is where going back and forth between water and waves is no problem. Form is emptiness and emptiness is form... equal. And this is actually where we live our life of practice. It's called the coming from within the going to, the going to within the coming from. Total freedom. Perfect equilibrium of form and emptiness, water and waves. Not so easy to achieve.[17]

Because we have the Absolute, we have a basis that gives rise to all the myriad relative things in which the Absolute is realized: jewels, clothing, each nonsentient thing and each sentient being with its own unique, startling characteristics. We have house cats and cows, obsessionals and hysterics, therapists and clients, neurotics and psychotics, Zen teachers and Zen students. Each is a piece of the Puzzle; each patch of cloth recognizing the others as different parts of the same Quilt.

Ultimately all people come from the same fabric; we are all, as Sullivan said, more human than otherwise. We're all waves in the sea of humanity. We emerge from the same background: Place us in a crowd, stand back, and who can see the white heron against the moonlight? Yet we're all different, and it is our differences that give us enough perspective to stand back and, seeing each other, rediscover our connectedness.

We look at each other and discover our unique differences; but when we look at each other we can also discover how we are like each other and inextricably linked. There is a nice illustration of this in J.R.R. Tolkien's story *The Hobbit* when the naive but lovable hero, Bilbo, meets the sinister but somehow pitiable-lovable Gollum, a twisted creature who dwells in the dark. Bilbo and Gollum are two aspects of one whole. Bilbo wants Gollum to show him the way out; Gollum wants to eat Bilbo. So they have a riddle game to determine the outcome, and along the way the following riddle comes up:

> An eye in a blue face
> Saw an eye in a green face.
> "That eye, is like to this eye"
> Said the first eye,
> "But in low place,
> Not in high place."

An excellent koan! Tolkien gives the following answer:

Gollum had been underground a long long time, and was forgetting this sort of thing. But... Gollum brought up memories of ages and ages and ages before, when he lived with his grandmother in a hole in a bank by a river.

"Ss, sss, my preciouss" he said. "Sun on the daisies it means, it does."[18]

Whenever one being—sentient or nonsentient—encounters another, it is the sun and daisy meeting and discovering themselves through each other. Both do so against the background of a limitless sky. Each is in its own place. Mix them up together, and you discover who/what/where they are.

This is what we do in psychotherapy. We discover that just as all change depends on stability and all stability on change, all our individual uniqueness depends on our commonalties, and all our commonality depends on our uniqueness. When we form relationships with each other, one member of the couple can be the sun while the other member is the daisy.

> In couples' communication class the other night, we were talking about how to listen to each other by being open to what the other person thinks and feels.
>
> A man asked, "But really, don't we want to convince the other person to come around to our point of view? Isn't that the point of arguing in the first place?"
>
> His wife responded, "There, you see, that's the whole problem. Arguing isn't about convincing each other, it's about understanding each other. You have to be able to listen to the other person and appreciate what they're saying. That's the only way you'll come to a common understanding of what the problem is, and you have to have that in order to solve the problem."
>
> I replied, "You're both right. It's helpful to be clear about your own point of view and try to get it across. It's also helpful to realize your view isn't the only view, and to be curious about your partner's perspective. When you're talking with each other you need to hold both aspects of the discussion."
>
> Another man objected: "But this idea of coming to a common understanding about the problem won't work. You're two different people; you won't have a common understanding of the problem. At most you'll get some overlap. That's why we're always at each other's throats, because we always have a different take on the problem."
>
> I remembered sun on the daisies, eyes looking at each other in different places, and said: "We each have two eyes, don't we? And you know how we see: Each eye has a slightly different perspective on what's in front of it. If we look at the world through only one eye, what happens? It looks flat, two-dimensional. Because each of our eyes has a slightly different perspective, the brain can compare them and find their samenesses and differences. Then we see the world in greater depth; that's how we get three-D vision.
>
> "Imagine what would happen if your two eyes kept fighting about which one was 'right.' You'd get pretty confused and frustrated, wouldn't you? Each eye has its own perspective, it's not right or wrong. But when you combine them, something bigger emerges.
>
> "What would happen if in your relationship, you thought of each of you as one eye? When you put your two eyes together, how might you see the world differently?"

In psychotherapy, client and therapist each provide one eye. We go back and forth between perspectives, and something emerges that cannot be predicted from either perspective alone. This is true of all our relationships with people and with things. Each moment of our experience offers an "eye" on our whole life, so each experience we have widens our life further. Our lives are not just three-dimensional: Our lives are deep with many, many dimensions, each level larger than the last. In the larger scheme of things, each sentient being who has ever lived or will live and each nonsentient object that has ever existed or will exist is an "eye" of Absolute Reality, of an unimaginably huge Whole.

We know that the Whole is always larger than the part. The therapeutic relationship is larger than the individual client and the individual therapist. The whole therapy is larger than the series of individual sessions. The whole of our life is larger than the problem and larger than the solution; the whole of our life is larger than our suffering and larger than our happiness. The whole of our lives contains every thing and every person we encounter, every action we do, every thought and feeling we have. The whole of our lives contains every bit of our life, bar none.

Yet each fragment of therapy, each fragment of our lives, is complete in itself. It is its own whole. At that moment, there is nothing else. Each piece of our experience tends to feel separate as it claims our complete attention for itself. I feel separate from you. I am separate from you and from the things around me. I am the center of the universe.

The same holds true for you, however: You exist complete in and of yourself. You exist separate from other people and the things around you. You are also the center of the universe.

How can we each be the center of the universe? This may sound esoteric or idealistic, but it's a very practical question. This is the question we work with in Zen practice and also in psychotherapy. In Zen we try to discover how we can pay attention to each moment as the center of the universe. In psychotherapy we try to pay attention to each client as the center of the universe.

Clients may respond to our undivided attention with various degrees of appreciation, relief, defensiveness, and anxiety. Nevertheless, the experience of finding one's self at the center is basically healing. It feels good. At a certain point, however, doubt often creeps in. The client says: "You treat me as the center of the universe, but it's false because you treat all your clients this way. How can I be the center of the universe when you treat everyone that way? Anyway, I can't treat myself as the center of the universe. That's selfish and wrong."

The solution to this objection comes in realizing that the only way we can realize our self at the center of the universe is by treating *each and every* being we encounter as the center of the universe. The difficulty in doing this comes in finding the relationship between the many parts, the many centers of the universe, the many wholes, and the Whole. How do they connect? Each piece of our experience, to the extent that it appears to have its own separate identity, starts to feels disconnected from the other pieces. Making love seems separate from arguing. Our divorce feels separate from our marriage. Our vacation feels separate from our work. Our birth feels separate from our death. Our role as a therapist feels separate from our roles in our family life, and the activities of our daily life feel separate from sitting on a cushion staring at the wall.

The part loses sight of the whole; it feels like it is separate from the whole, even though the whole can only be constituted by its parts. We know that the whole contains its parts, but when we think about this we often envision something like pebbles in a jar. We get an image of a container with pieces sitting in it separate from the container. *But the container of therapy, of Zen practice, and of life itself is not separate from what It contains.* Absolute Reality is not separate from the relative bits and pieces in which it appears. The individual fragment—the individual person or thing; the physical form, the thought, the feeling, the sensation, the impulse, the awareness—is complete itself.

In Buddhism, the way each mundane thing coarises with the entire Absolute is sometimes called "the teaching of the nonsentient." The teaching of the nonsentient is the teaching of ordinary life: pebbles, rocks, tiles.

Every individual nonsentient thing—every rock, every tree and tile—is always naturally realizing Itself. Every individual sentient being is also always naturally realizing Itself. Everything is always teaching us how to go back and forth between the whole equation and the individual terms, between the big picture and the small detail, between our particular lives and our human interconnectedness, between our specific actions and our underlying intentions, between our fragments of experience and the overall meaning of our lives. Therapy is made of individuals meeting to rediscover a fundamental wholeness. Life is made of discrete experiences that provide the threads for a rich tapestry. Water comes from the ocean, but the ocean is made of water.

> So when we understand the nature of water, that's enlightenment. And when we find our way through, that's our practice—practice within enlightenment, as Dogen Zenji says: Even though we're swimming on the top of the water through the waves with our arms, our feet are firmly planted on the bottom of the ocean. We never leave the bottom of the ocean, no matter what kind of wave we're swimming in.
>
> We do this by finding ourselves on each moment. We easily get out of balance and we don't pay much attention to this fundamental way of life. We overlook it in our dash, in our running. So Buddhist life is to pay attention to this point, this fundamental point: how to find ourself on each moment.

FINDING OUR SELVES

> *It is like facing a jewel mirror; form and image behold each other—*
> *You are not it—it actually is you.*

Buddhist life is about finding our selves on each moment. But we often feel lost; we often feel we don't know who, what, or where we are. When we try to find ourselves in the waves of our life we get tossed about; sometimes we ride the crests, and other times we get pulled into the troughs.

Buddhism teaches us that, paradoxically, what gets in the way of finding our selves is our tendency to develop self-centered expectations. We begin to relate to the waves only insofar as how they affect us, rather than as themselves. In turbulence we may feel alarmed or excited; in calm waters we may feel relaxed or bored. We start distinguishing whether a particular wave is pleasant or unpleasant, difficult or easy to ride. Once our critical faculty starts to differentiate between good and bad waves, we start looking for something special. We may go around the world searching for the Ultimate Wave. We may become invested in being able to figure the waves out, to gain some special knowledge of the waves so we can be a Real Surfer. Each wave becomes a kind of extension of ourself, of our hopes and fears.

To realize ourselves as a Real Person, a Real Surfer, we need to learn to listen to the teaching of the nonsentient. Each wave teaches us; each wave rests on the whole Ocean. Each wave carries the truth of our lives, because regardless of whether the wave is large or small, rough or smooth, right now on this wave the wave is my life. Salt water surfs my skin, which ripples in tune to the motion of my muscles as I try to keep my balance: Sunlight plays on the neurons of my retina setting up a cascade of electrical impulses whose ripples reflect the motion of the water beneath my feet. This wave is this moment of me.

It takes most of us a while to understand this teaching of the nonsentient and enjoy our ride together. It took Tozan a while, too. After discussing matters with his teacher Isan, Tozan still didn't understand the teaching of the nonsentient and its relationship to being a Real Person. So Isan sent him to Ungan, and they had a conversation very similar to the one Tozan had overheard between Echu and the monk; at the end Ungan quoted the Amida sutra and said:

> Streams, birds, and trees all, without exception, praise the Buddha, praise the Dharma.

At this point, Tozan was enlightened. But he still had his questions. Enlightenment is not the Answer to Everything. So Tozan asked Ungan to summarize his teaching, and Ungan said, "Just this, just this." Tozan still didn't get it. He left Ungan and walked away embroiled in doubts.

> But later, as he was walking on a bridge crossing a river, Tozan caught a glimpse of his reflection in the water. At that point he became greatly awakened to all the previous teachings and said in a verse:

> > Truly I should not seek for the Truth from others
> > For then it will be far from me.
> > I now go on alone,
> > But I meet HIM everywhere.
> > He now is surely me,
> > But I am not Him.
> > When we understand this,
> > We are directly one with thusness—instantaneously with the Truth.

In his confusion, Tozan was in the position most of our clients—and most of us—are in, caught in doubts that prevent us from seeing that each of us is a Real

Person, and that we meet this Real Person everywhere. Sometimes we are so close to ourselves that we cannot see ourselves; sometimes we are so far from others that we cannot see them. Tozan needed a walk by himself, a bridge, a river.

When we are lost and confused, psychotherapy can help by giving us time out from the swirl of daily life and a chance to step back and get some new perspective. The therapist sometimes acts as a bridge, sometimes as a stream. Sometimes we offer the client a place to stand, so that she can look around and see herself reflected in the life that takes place through the lives of all those around her. At other times, a client's lifestream can be so roiled and muddy that the therapist needs to provide a calm, still pool in which the client can look and see himself reflected.

Even when we try to see clearly, however, our vision often gets muddied and we are unable to see ourselves and others because we make a double mistake. On the one hand, we "seek for the Truth from others." We look outside ourselves. We cannot believe that the solution to our sufferings lies right at hand; we keep searching for happiness and for our true self as something apart from what we are right now. On the other hand, we harbor a secret hope that there is a hidden, special Truth deep within us that makes us something special. We compound the mistake of being other-centered with the mistake of being self-centered.

We get confused: We seek It in others, we seek It in our selves; we seek to return to some peace we think we had before our present upset; we think that we can only find happiness after resolving our present problems. In our search, we overlook It shining forth every where, every who, every what, every when.

We look for It outside of us, erroneously believing that we will be able to grasp It, take It inside us, and then we will become something special. We have a fantasy that whatever It is that we lack, if we can only somehow grasp the secret knowledge—if we can only hear the nonsentient, find our Inner Child, become fully analyzed or enlightened—then we'll be something extraordinary. We have grandiose narcissistic desires; yes, we know we're flawed, but once that flaw is repaired, we secretly hope that the world will be our oyster and our flaws will turn into pearls. My hope is that I will actually be It: number one, the big cheese, the brilliant therapist, the Zen master.

When we pursue It from this misdirected other-centered/self-centered standpoint, we have grandiose visions. We're like Ahab pursuing Moby Dick; we feel maimed, vengeful, but also on a quest to exorcise our demons, to find a special jewel that will redeem our lives. Too easily this quest, because it is based on realizing self-centered desires through appropriating something valuable from a person or thing outside ourselves, becomes high tragedy: When we act like Ahab we are like

> The maniac here hunting like a jewel
> The rare ambiguous monster that had maimed his sex,
> Hatred for hatred ending in a scream,
> The unexplained survivor breaking off the nightmare—
> All that was intricate and false; the truth was simple.

> Evil is unspectacular and always human,
> And shares our bed and eats at our own table,
> And we are introduced to Goodness every day,
> Even in drawing-rooms among a crowd of faults;
> He has a name like Billy and is almost perfect,
> But wears a stammer like a decoration.[19]

It's romantic to think of ourselves as tragic heroes on a mythic quest for It. The truth, however, is considerably more humble and more wonderful. I cannot be It, but It actually is me. It does not discriminate between mundane and holy, monsters and jewels. Monsters and jewels are both introductions to our true selves, providing we can share our bed and table with them as members of our family. Too often, however, we prefer to push our monsters off into some hellish netherworld and imagine that our jewel is far away on a distant, heavenly pedestal.

When we fight some terrible monster, we are tempted to disavow any kinship with the monster: We say, "That's not me, I'm not it." This kind of pushing the bad outside me and disidentifying with it is a form of projection. But we do something similar if we admire some ideal role model or try to identify with some heroic quality we think we need to take into us; we perform the flip side of projection if we try to purchase, grab, or swallow the jewel to possess it and say, "That's mine." When we say, "That's mine," we are wanting to say, "That's me, I'm it." Introjection is projection's twin. Both are a form of erroneous imagination.

The problem with both projection and introjection lies in their dualistic view that inherently discriminates between "good" and "bad," "inside" and "outside," "me" and "not-me." Any time we do this we get caught in a world of separate things rather than a world of dancing relationships. Once we separate a part of ourself from ourself and place it "out there" rather than "in here," we get caught in a delusion that we are isolated and disconnected from the rest of the universe.

If we feel disconnected, we may try to put the good inside us to help ourselves think, "I'm It, Number 1, Great and Good." If we try to place the good inside us and distance ourselves from the bad, we are projecting/introjecting. We are also projecting/introjecting, however, whenever we think we're bad and others hold the key to goodness. The fact is that whenever we discriminate, whenever we pick and choose, whenever we say "that's good and that's bad," we set up a division that creates problems. We discriminate in an attempt to grasp at It: holding on and pushing away, we try to possess or dispossess ourselves of good and evil.

But we cannot seize It or be rid of It. It is beyond our ability to possess It or, for that matter, to reject It, because we do not own the world. The whale we name Moby Dick is not ours to kill, but a rejected part of ourself we have projected outward and are running away from even as we pursue it.

Our small personal egos cannot own or possess enlightenment but can be open to It. Streams, birds, and trees preach the dharma, but the bird singing is not *my* bird singing, the tree standing is not *my* tree standing, the stream flowing is not mine to appropriate for selfish profit. When the bird sings, it is not that I hear it and grasp it; rather, the bird offers a universe in which I can find myself. As Aitken-Roshi puts it:

> When birdsong is loud in the trees
> I vow with all beings
> to put down my work and to listen,
> recreated as song.[20]

I am not It; It actually is me. I am not here; rather, here is what I am. At the moment the bird sings and fills my hearing before "I" stop to hear it, the birdsong is my life. I owe my life to birdsong; I am its servant. Whenever a client visits me, she is not my client; I serve her as her therapist. My life and hers are inextricably intertwined, each realizing the other, each making what is real, real.

Our whole Self, our Life, is vast as the ocean. The ocean with its water and waves is beyond the province of good and bad, beyond the province of Ahabs and Moby Dicks, demons and angels, delusion and enlightenment, beyond the possibility of ownership or loss. If we stop projecting ourselves—our fears and desires, our hopes and hurts—onto It, Moby Dick is just a whale, my problem is just a problem, and enlightenment is just drinking the cup of tea in front of us. If instead of engaging in battles with our projections we simply accept our imperfections and let go of our virtues, they can meet each other and dissolve. Then we're left with just us who we are, just life, That Which Is. Each being, in being just Itself, is marvelous and reflects the wonder of the entire universe. Every thing in the universe is constantly and vigorously teaching.

> "Continually and vigorously teaching" means that, at no time, does It not manifest Itself. Because everything down to the croaking of bullfrogs and the mumbling of earthworms comes to be revealed, it is continual teaching, energetic teaching, without ceasing. Just look carefully.

The path of true awareness simply involves looking carefully, without projection or introjection, putting aside ideas of self and other. Realizing It involves letting go of personal preferences or discriminating things as being either mundane or holy. It is no thing special.

When our clients come to us, when as students we go in desperation to the Zendo, we may feel less like singing streams or soaring eagles and more like croaking bullfrogs and crawling earthworms. We may feel they, or we, are muddy, coarse, and slimy: not grand at all. When we speak to our clients or our Zen teacher, we stammer like Billy Budd. We'd prefer to be something grander, or at least to have some grand thing to worship that gives us a sense of special importance. If we seek for some grand thing to rely on, however, we will always be frustrated because then we set up a basic separation between "I" and "It."

PLUNGING IN

If you're excited it becomes a pitfall;
If you miss it, you fall into retrospective hesitation.
Turning away and touching are both wrong, for it is like a
mass of fire.

Once we feel separated from our source, we are caught in the dilemma of touching or turning away from It. If we lose our connection to our source we have troubles being conscious with It if we are only conscious of "I" and of "It" as separate things. We then become excessively self-conscious, and this makes it difficult to hum along with, let alone hear, the music of the nonsentient because we start magnifying overmuch the part we play and have difficulties trusting the larger forces at work.

Shishibodai asked Kakurokuna, "As I wish to pursue the Way to enlightenment, how should I exert my mind in order to do it?

Kakurokuna answered, "If you would pursue the Way, there is no situation where you need to exert your mind."

Shishibodai asked, "If I do not exert myself, who will perform the work of Buddha?"

Kakurokuna replied, "If you are involved in exerting, there will be no merit or virtue; if you do not make yourself perform, then that is 'the work of Buddha'. A scripture says: 'The merit and virtue in what I perform is due to there being no egocentric 'I'.'"[21]

If we emphasize our "I" we put too much stock in our own abilities, both by overinflating them and by fearing that they are inadequate to the tasks at hand. If we make the mistake of thinking "I" can be "It" rather than appreciating that "It" is me, we easily get caught in a dichotomous world of delusion versus enlightenment, saints versus sinners:

After Echu told the monk that fences, walls, tiles, pebbles, and other nonsentient things "constantly teach, vigorously teach," the monk was somewhat distressed.

The monk asked, "Then why can't I hear it?"

Echu said, "You don't hear it, but don't hinder that which does hear it."

The monk asked, "I wonder if anyone else can hear it?"

Echu said, "The holy ones can hear it."

The monk asked, "Can you hear it?"

Echu said, "No, I do not."

The monk asked, "If you can't hear it, how do you know that the nonsentient preach the Dharma?"

Echu said, "Fortunately, I can't hear it. If I did hear it, I would be the same as the holy ones and then you would not be able to hear me preach the Dharma."

The monk asked, "If that is so, then are they irrelevant for sentient beings?"

Echu said, "It is for the benefit of sentient beings that I teach the Dharma, I do not teach it for the benefit of the saintly."

The monk wants to know why he can't hear the teaching of the nonsentient. He is still somewhat self-conscious; perhaps he fears something is wrong with him or, alternatively, perhaps he still hopes "he" can be "It." Perhaps he has some fantasy of enlightenment as something special, that hearing the teaching of the nonsentient will provide a mystic experience in which he'll acquire magical powers, become a holy saint, and receive all the answers. If we get excited hoping to become proud eagles, however, we also may fear we're pitiful worms; then we may hesitate to do anything that might show us in that light. We can get stuck on either side of touching or turning away, once we separate the eagle from the earthworm.

Echu says, in effect, "Stop worrying about 'sentient' and 'nonsentient,' 'you' and 'it,' 'self' and 'other,' 'saintly' or 'ignorant.' Don't worry about some special, hidden meaning, just pay attention to everything around you and you'll discover all the details of your mundane life are always teaching." This is good guidance for therapists. Our work as therapists is not meant for clients who are "saints"—that is, for "good patients" who fit our theories and act in the ideal way the books say they should. Conversely, in order to do therapy, the therapist need not be a "saint" who has some special knowledge of Enlightened Psychological Wholeness.

Both therapists and clients tend to yearn for a Master Therapist. Therapists attend workshops hoping that a Master Therapist will give us a Special Teaching we can pass on to our clients. Clients look at the books on our walls and think that we know how to be a good parent, a compassionate spouse, a successful worker: They look to us for a Special Teaching.

Experienced therapists do have some good hints for clients and other therapists about techniques that often work. Basically, however, therapy is for ordinary sentient beings, working with ordinary therapists, and the Teachings we can hear and transmit are less absolute than we might think. The state of our knowledge is reflected in the joke about the developmental psychologist who, when he was still childless, wrote a book titled, *How to Raise Your Child.* At this point, he still had Ideal Knowledge. Eventually he got married and had a child; when the second edition of his book came out he needed to retitle it, *Some Suggestions About How to Raise Your Child.* By the time he had another child, the third edition became, *Some Possible Suggestions About Things Which Sometimes Work When Raising Your Child.*

Real life, as opposed to idealized formulas, teaches us that we do not have all the answers. Daily life teaches us that there is no cause to be an arrogant expert or a sanctimonious saint. The waves of our life are constantly teaching us that we can't ride them without getting wet. Real life teaches us how to be humble and human.

We go to psychotherapy to become "Whole"; we go to Zen to become a Real Person. This Real Person, however, is completely ordinary. Echu said to the monk questioning him: "If you and I were saints, we'd never be able to have this conversation. I teach for ordinary sentient beings, not for the saintly. I'm nothing special. I don't hear the nonsentient. I'm not holy."

It is our mundane ordinary existence that keeps us moving and helps us avoid getting caught in either turning away from or touching the burning fires of our lives. Our unholy imperfections provide the fuel for the flames: Our imperfect lives are always luminous.

We are constantly confronted by the smoldering embers of our worst habits and the dim sparks of our most cherished wishes, by the blue flame of the world's alluring beauty and the red tongue of the world's fearsome evils. If we turn away from the fire, we may not be able to outrun the inferno as it burns out of control; if we evade the conflagration, we may freeze. If we mindlessly touch the fire, we can easily get burnt. If in our pride we discard too much material as being unworthy of the fire, our critical judgments may starve the fire of necessary fuel; if in our anxiety we try to confine the fire to a small, easily controlled space, inhibiting our passions may smother the source of our energy.

In contrast, as we practice letting go of our expectations and fears, we find that the ground of acceptance is wide enough to support light and dark, fire and water. Instead of picking and choosing among our bits and pieces, we begin to discover that every scrap of our experience finds its place. By taking the path of working with our fragments, we rediscover our wholeness through an effortless effort that is neither turning away nor touching.

Facing the mass of fire this way, instead of being tortured by our burning desires, we are warmed by the flames even as we are the fuel that burns freely and merrily. Standing at the center of the pyre, acknowledging our self-centered urges and allowing them to be consumed, we have the opportunity to commune with the blaze and, moving along with it, enjoy momentary flickers of incandescent joy.

COMMUNING

> *Communing with the source and communing with the process,*
> *It includes integration and includes the road.*

When we stand at the center of the fire, we are communing with the source and communing with the process. Burning, we transform into light. We hesitate to do this, however, for fear we'll be consumed. We hesitate to plunge into the ocean of our life. Sometimes we put a toe in the water and find it freezing; we hug ourselves against its cold and draw back. Other times we look at the ocean and the waves seem too big; unsure we'll be able to ride the waves and fearful of drowning, we wait on shore for the sea to turn calm. We may wait our whole life. Stranded on shore by our fears, how can we learn to trust the water, trust ourselves, and plunge in?

When my daughter was seven years old, she had a terrible time learning to swim. She had learned the fundamentals in swim classes but was scared to take off on her own. She was rather thin and didn't have much natural buoyancy. She also sensed that her learning to swim was important to me and felt caught between conflicting desires:

She wanted to please me but wanted to do things her way. She hoped to swim like a champion but feared she would fail. She wanted to be brave but was frightened.

I was in a pool with her one day while she tried to swim a few feet to me. She would run into the pitfall of being overexcited: She would try so hard that her muscles would tighten up, which would make her start to sink, which would make her try harder. She would arch her back and lift her head out of the water, which would make her sink more and frighten her more. In her fear she would pull back, hesitate, and fall into anxiety and "retrospective hesitation." She would stop for a while, then overcome her irresolution by revving herself up to try again, and repeat the cycle.

After a few attempts, I urged her to stop swimming and just let herself play in the water. But she was determined to swim. Time and again she would take a breath, hold it, splash and flail about, sink down, and then grab at me gasping, spluttering, scared.

A stranger in the pool with his children offered me and my daughter a little inflatable, brightly colored plastic float to put under her. I nearly refused. I had been told to never teach swimming with the use of flotation aids; supposedly they give a false sense of security and allow you to go out too far, so if you slip off, not knowing how to swim, you can drown. But my two-year-old was also in the pool wanting attention, and my seven-year-old was trying too hard and wanted to play on the float.

So she put the float under her stomach and paddled off around the pool while I did other things. At first she was enthused; gradually, she got bored with the float. She slipped off and swam a few yards to me. I asked her to go back and get the float so we could return it. She splashed and swam back to the float. She got on for a while again, got bored again, slipped off and swam to me, leaving the float behind. Suddenly she realized she wasn't using the float and in surprise and delight called out:

"Daddy, Look! I'm swimming!"

Swimming is fairly simple: Lie on your back or stomach, kick your feet, windmill your arms, and turn your head to breathe. We get confused, however, by the expectations of others and ourselves. We lose confidence and search for aids, for a flotation device to keep us going. This can be a therapeutic technique, a meditation focus, or a rubber ducky. The advantage of such aids is real, but it is not what they purport to give us: They have no more power than the "magic feather" that Dumbo used to give him faith he could fly. The advantage of the aids and techniques is that they help us to forget ourselves so we can plunge in wholeheartedly. If we stop fighting ourselves and stop fighting the water, the sincerity of our full effort meets the buoyancy of our source and we discover that we're already in the water, we're already swimming.

Even as the waves crash over and turn us so that we don't know which way is up, something beyond our conscious ability buoys us up and supports our effort. At any one moment there are huge complementary forces at work on each of us: Gravity pulls us and winds seek to sweep us away; compassion pulls us to respond to each other and self-consciousness seeks to sink us in our isolated thoughts.

Given the basic interrelatedness of all things, when something comes up we will naturally have some response and will be responded to. But it's hard to have faith in this. So long as I feel "I" must be "It"—so long as I feel I must control the process of therapy or meditation—I will worry about doing things correctly and mistrust my reactions. In psychotherapy, if a moment comes up that calls for an intervention, if I obsess overmuch about whether my feelings constitute countertransference or if my intervention will be effective, I may get confused and lose the spontaneity so essential for a genuine meeting. If I feel pressured to bear the responsibility for the therapy myself, I may worry about how the client will respond to my response and hold back or rush in. If I feel compelled to remain in charge of "my" zazen, I will become frustrated and tight, progressively more awkward during the process of meditation, and more isolated from the universal source that supports my efforts.

When I realize "It" is actually "me," I can relax and let therapy and meditation find their course. When I join my client in the process of psychotherapy I discover that we share a common source: We're both swimming in the same sea.

> When I started graduate school my first client was a man in a high-security prison treatment center for sexually dangerous persons. He had been described to me as "six-foot-four and violent."
>
> "What do I do?" I asked my adviser. I was sure there was some book that told the correct things to say in treatment. Not having found any book with specific instructions, I worried that I might through my ineptitude hurt my client or (more reluctantly acknowledged, given the nature of this client) that the client could hurt me. I worried that if I said something it would be the wrong thing, but I also worried if I didn't say the right things it also would be wrong. I wanted to know what I should be doing, and this paralyzed me.
>
> My adviser simply reflected my concerns back to me—a bit of training I did not appreciate at the time. But even if he had told me what questions to ask or given me explicit instructions for how to listen—directions that would have alleviated my anxiety but limited my openness—such directions wouldn't have helped very much. I had to learn to trust my ability to relate to other people and respond flexibly to whatever situations came up.
>
> After I'd met with this client for several months, one day he became annoyed at something I'd said and started to tell me in considerable detail how he could beat me into a pulp. I was locked up behind bars with him in the midst of a deserted cell block, with the nearest guard some distance away. I felt quite unprotected. I felt threatened and wanted to yell for help, but I was terrified that if I called a guard it would provoke the client to attack me. I began to fall into the pitfall of excitement, in the form of intense fear. Worrying that whatever I said could provoke an attack, I fell into retrospective hesitation, but I also felt that not saying anything could provoke an attack.
>
> I realized that I was in a place where there was no way out. In the midst of my terror I began to realize that I had no alternative but to accept the situation, and at this point something curious happened: I began to calm down. I realized that if he did attack me it was unlikely that he could kill me in the few minutes that would intervene between my calling out and a guard coming. I realized I would do what I could: If he did kill me, then he would kill me, but in the meantime there wasn't much sense in worrying about it. If he attacked me but didn't kill me, all I had to fear was pain, and I could handle pain. It was just pain, not annihilation.

As I began to accept the situation, I started to realize that my feeling of being caught in a trap with no escape mirrored some of what my client was feeling. I started to recognize the sense of helplessness and suffocation that lay behind my client's anger. This was not the time or place to voice these in an interpretation, but as I began to empathize more I started to relax and listen to my client instead of to my fears. As I calmed down, my client calmed down too. It started to feel less like we were opposing one another, and more like we were communing with each other in a shared place. The threat passed.

The times when we are most fearful and "at sea" are the times we most need to settle down. This is easier if we can trust that there is a certain amount of "give" to the universe, a natural tendency for our feet to settle at the bottom of the ocean even if we are navigating choppy surface waves. In order to swim, we have to learn how to join the water. In order to do psychotherapy, we have to learn how to immerse ourselves in meeting and merge with the music of the dance.

TUNING

> *Merging is auspicious; do not violate it....*
> *A hairsbreadth's deviation will fail to accord with the proper*
> *attunement.*

Merging has something of a bad reputation in psychotherapy; it is often associated with psychotic symbiosis and a loss of autonomy. Yet merging also holds the allure of being "in the zone," that place every athlete knows in which bat and ball, body and mind are one fluid whole. At such times there is nothing to attain, just the pleasure of concerted connection. If we are playing in an orchestra, we find ourselves playing in tune with everyone else, serving the movement of the music. If we are surfing, we let go of self-conscious striving and just enjoy the sun on the sea, the wind on our face, the movement of the water beneath us; on each individual wave, we are in harmony with the whole ocean.

It's not always easy to find this auspicious place of merging. Even once we find that place, we easily violate it, because a very small deviation will throw us off. If we are surfing, we slip slightly and lose our balance; if we are playing music, our lip gets tired and our sound goes out of tune. If we are doing psychotherapy, our mind wanders and our client experiences some failure of empathy.

Often when this happens it's because we are bringing some element of self-centeredness to the process. When our mind wanders in psychotherapy, we usually are thinking of our own issues. When we are surfing or playing music, we run into problems if we are trying to perform well enough to impress others or if we are scared of embarrassing ourselves by falling off the board or flubbing our solo. We tie ourselves in knots with a string whose two ends are trying to succeed and fearing to fail.

A surfer who is showing off is in danger of falling on his face. In music we will lose the attunement if we start to think we're something special and the rest of the orchestra should be following our pitch rather than vice versa. As therapists, we make mistakes if we think we've achieved such a deep understanding of our client that the client should follow our lead, rather than the reverse. This interrupts and violates the client's music. An incident early in my career as a therapist taught me a valuable lesson:

> I was seeing Tim during my internship at an inpatient psychiatric ward. This was back in the days when people still could stay in the hospital for weeks or months for intensive psychotherapy, so I was seeing him almost daily for several months of psychodynamic psychotherapy.
>
> Tim was a Vietnam veteran who was in agonies of guilt, a carpenter who one day while working with his brother-law had gotten into an argument and suddenly snatched up a hammer and attacked him. Tim hadn't just swiped at his brother-in-law in a momentary lapse; he had hit him again and again, smashing his head repeatedly with the hammer in a kind of rageful trance. This was particularly shocking because Tim was a peaceable fellow with no history of previous violent acts. In fact he liked his brother-in-law, and had no grudge or animosity toward him.
>
> Tim had a documented seizure disorder and we wondered if this could have been a contributing factor. He professed to have no memory of actually doing the deed but still readily took responsibility for what he had done. He felt tremendously guilty and remorseful. He was full of self-recriminations and fears that he might do something violent again without wanting to. Tim was tense and couldn't sleep; he would pace the halls of the hospital asking himself how he could have possibly done this, literally wringing his hands in self-disgust and horror.
>
> I learned a bit about Tim's history. He had come from a large working-class family and was the eldest son. His father had been alcoholic and physically abusive. Tim had taken the first opportunity he could to leave home and enlist in the army, where he had seen combat duty in Vietnam. On returning home, he had married his girlfriend and begun to raise a family of his own.
>
> Tim was a responsible father and husband. But over the past year he had begun to have intrusive memories of his Vietnam experiences; he would push them away, only to have them come back as vivid visual images or nightmares that would provoke intense anxiety. In particular, Tim would remember how in Vietnam he worked the "body detail:" After a battle, he was responsible for going to the battlefield and picking up the dead bodies. Tim recounted in grisly detail picking up severed arms, legs, heads, and throwing them like so much offal onto an open flatbed truck, to be dumped into a pit later on. He had hidden his horror behind gallows humor at the expense of feeling increasingly emotionally numb.
>
> After two months of intensive psychotherapy, I thought we had a good therapeutic alliance but still felt I was missing something; neither Tim nor I could quite understand how his post–traumatic stress disorder and his Vietnam experiences, however horrific, had led to such a violent act. Tim remained fearful of himself and tormented by guilt.
>
> At the time I was studying Ralph Greenson's writings on empathy.[22] In addition to very helpful recommendations on how to construct an internal "working model" of clients, Greenson relates several incidents of remarkable intuitive understanding that

can emerge from the empathic process. He cites several examples in which a therapist divined a crucial bit of a client's personal history even though the client couldn't tell the therapist directly. A client might comment on a book being upside down on the therapist's bookshelf, and the therapist would say, "Why haven't you told me that you're pregnant?"

The prospect of this kind of knowing thrilled me. It was early enough in my training that I thought therapists should have special powers of understanding, and I wanted to experience something like this. I also sincerely wanted to understand my client better, to help us get past the impasse we'd apparently reached.

One day near Christmas time, Tim was talking about what Christmas was like when he was growing up, and how awful it was to live in fear of whether his alcoholic father would turn violent. He described a particular incident when he was a teenager: His father had become suddenly enraged and hit him with such force that he had literally knocked the patient through a wall.

I was putting this into my internal "working model" of the client and trying to feel my way into understanding Tim's experience. Suddenly the image of an angry adolescent, strong with youth yet powerless before his unjustly violent father, was superimposed over the severed human body parts and the blood and violence of the Vietnam war. Simultaneously this image coupled with what I had read about military "fraggings." The images coalesced, and I *knew* what had happened that Tim wasn't telling me or anyone else. I turned to him and said: "Why haven't you told me about killing your commanding officer?"

Tim looked at me, stunned. "How did you know that?" he yelled. Then he blurted out the story.

Tim's commanding officer had been ambitious. In order to earn more points for himself with his superiors he would repeatedly send his soldiers out into unnecessary combats in which many men died, meanwhile staying safely back at the rear himself. After a while Tim, sickened by tossing body parts of his fellows onto the garbage heap, couldn't tolerate it any longer. Together with some of the other enlisted men, they put a grenade under the commanding officer's bunk and blew him up. They'd never told anyone about it, and nobody had ever found out. Most of the men in the unit had been relieved. Tim felt this action had saved many people's lives but also felt intensely guilty about it.

I felt that at last we had the pieces of the puzzle that would help the therapy progress. But my client was deeply shaken. "How did you know that?" he kept saying. Despite my belated reassurances to the contrary, he felt I could read his mind, that he couldn't keep any secrets from me. He felt terribly invaded.

He couldn't tolerate it. The next evening, he evaded the staff and ran away from the hospital. I tried to contact him but couldn't locate him.

To this day, I have no idea what happened to him after that. But I do have a sense of what I did wrong. In my sincere desire to understand and help my client, we were able to become finely attuned and have some deep merging and understanding; but in my personal excitement at being able to do this, I invaded my client and committed a fundamental act of disrespect. I thought I had some special therapeutic ability to understand him, but my egocentrism blinded me to my client's needs. My empathy was enough to know his past experience but insufficient to appreciate his current experience of his past, which required keeping this particular door shut between us at this time.

I violated the balance of our merging in the therapy process; in so doing I fractured the relationship and lost the attunement of our work together.

To avoid violating the intimacy of merging, it's important to maintain deep respect for the separateness of each autonomous container. In the balance between parts and wholes, self and others, Absolute and relative, it is the fragile boundaries that give shape to experience and make merging possible.

As living beings we are united in an overarching wholeness, but life is composed of bits and pieces, so we need to respond to the specific circumstances of our lives. We live embedded in the world as surely as a fish swims in the ocean, carried by waves that reflect the pull of the moon on the earth: But although it helps to be aware that I am swimming in the ocean, it doesn't help to breathe in water and drown. There is no wave separate from water, but if we are surfing we need to pay attention to the specific form of this particular wave that is about to break right now, right here.

Because we are separate, bounded beings, we need to make constant small adjustments in order to accord with the proper attunement. Anyone who has ever played in a musical ensemble knows that we are always going out of tune. Even if we give up getting other people to tune to us and realize we have to keep in tune with them, it's not possible to tune up once and then stay in tune the rest of the concert. As the concert progresses, our instruments change pitch as the heat in the hall rises; our lips and fingers get looser as we play. So, in between movements, musicians stop and retune.

We have to accept the need for constant retuning. This is especially true in psychotherapy, in which there is no clear standard: It's not obvious what would constitute "A = 440" in an interpersonal relationship. So to the extent that clients and therapists are members of an orchestra, we need to find a way for us to constantly be listening to both the music and each other.

We are constantly going out of tune. We lose our balance in zazen; we make errors in psychotherapy. This isn't always addressed in our training. Both psychotherapy and zazen usually present teaching examples—case histories or koans—in which something dazzling happens because the people involved are really "in tune" with each other. These are very inspiring but problematical if they lead us to think that when we have mastered our practice we will always feel comfortable and "with it." Neither psychotherapy nor zazen guarantees we'll always be in the right place: They simply help us practice finding our right place again and again and again.

> After an experience of enlightenment, as he prepared to begin teaching, Ungan asked his teacher Isan whether he would be able to avoid messing up. He queried: "When I leave my teacher, will I be able to avoid violating my master's teaching?"
> Ungan answered, "No."[23]

We can't avoid messing up. Sometimes we get excited; sometimes we hesitate. We sit in a session with a client and think about whether to say something:

By the time we're finished thinking, it's too late. Our client feels abandoned, rejected, unheard. We feel touched or startled by something a client says and blurt something in response: It turns out to be just the wrong thing to say.

We and our clients always remain fully human, ordinary people. But ordinary people, however flawed, are ever so much more interesting than perfect ideal ones. Unlike ideal types, everyday people keep changing unexpectedly. Our actual clients are always teaching us by displaying the reality that lies beyond the purview of textbooks or abstract formulations. We cannot hope to acquire sufficient knowledge that will give us the skill to always respond to each client in the optimal way. But this doesn't mean we stop studying. If a client lets us know that we've made a mistake, it teaches us to eternally renew our studies each moment.

So when we err it helps to remember that we practice Zen not for saints, but for ordinary beings; we practice psychotherapy not for the approval of master therapists, but for the client in all of us. We practice to develop some skills that we know will always fall short and need constant revision. Despite the fact that we often feel awkward and at a loss, we keep looking to recover our balance and find our way. This is the core of our practice.

PRACTICE AND SKILL

If you want to conform to the ancient way,
Please observe the ancients of former times;
When about to fulfill the way of buddhahood, one gazed at a tree for ten eons,
Like a tiger leaving part of its prey, a horse with a white left hind leg.
Now there are sudden and gradual,
In connection with which are set up basic approaches.
Once basic approaches are distinguished, Then there are guiding rules.
But even though the basis is reached and the approach comprehended,
True eternity still flows....
Yi, with his archer's skill, could hit a target at a hundred paces;
But when arrow points meet head on,
What has this to do with the power of skill?

As we seek to find our way in Zen and in psychotherapy, we sometimes lose our sense of direction. When we ask: "How do I accord with the proper attunement?" we are in the position of the New Yorker who, in the old joke, asked the cabby: "How do I get to Carnegie Hall?" The cabby gives the only possible answer: "Practice, practice."

Disciplined practice develops the forms within which spontaneity can play. In Zen practice we adopt a rather rigid set of rules—how to sit, how to bow, how to wash our eating bowls—to help us clear our minds of our preconceptions and rediscover the world afresh. In psychotherapeutic practice we adopt a structure that governs how we work with clients, so that we are liberated from conventional social responses and can approach our clients from a new perspective. There are many different models for practice; there are distinct schools of Zen and various psychotherapeutic approaches. Whichever form we choose, our determination and sincerity are at least as important as the content of the particular model. We need to practice with the determination that devotes ten eons, if need be, to the task at hand; we need to practice with a willingness to give up all our preconceived notions and expectations, like a tiger willing to leave part of its prey. When we practice in this fashion, we're right in Carnegie Hall each moment.

As we practice, our learning basically proceeds in three steps: First we must study a model; then we must try to become the model by practicing its prescriptions; finally we must leave the model behind to allow new forms to emerge.

First we have to study the ancients' ways; all practice begins by careful observation. As Tozan says, "If you want to conform to the ancient way, please observe the ancients of former times." If we want to be a psychodynamic therapist, we observe what skilled psychoanalysts have done; if we want to be a narrative therapist, we observe what skilled storytellers have done. If we want to be a composer, we study Bach and Beethoven's works to learn the guiding rules.

After learning the guiding rules, we need to practice the basic approaches. We won't be able to absorb the teachings of Bach, Freud, or Dogen just by reading a book about them or browsing through their work. To know how to do something, we have to do it; we have to live in the shoes of the ancients. So to become a composer of music, we practice writing Bach chorales and Beethoven fugues before attempting our own symphonies; to become a hypnotherapist, we practice the standard hypnotic inductions before branching off to our own naturalistic methods for inducing trance. Zen students read Dogen's rules for meditation, observe how their teacher practices, and try to sit zazen in the same way.

We practice these forms by doing the same things over and over again until they become second nature. The musician plays her or his scales again and again and again. The Zen student sits down, breathes, notices the mind wandering, and comes back to the breath again and again and again. The psychotherapist learns a model of therapy and tries again and again and again to find the moving interpretation, the empathic reflection, the skillful assignment, the liberating story. As we immerse ourselves in the ancients' ways we begin to appreciate their perspective; when we observe our teachers and practice doing things the way they do we put something of ourselves aside; we expand beyond our familiar ways of thinking or working. We begin to understand Freud's theory of unconscious processes not from the standpoint of "let-it-all-hang-out" afternoon television talk shows, but in the context of Victorian repression; we start to hear Beethoven's dissonances sounding as harsh as they did in his classical epoch rather than listening to them in our current context of hot jazz and rock.

Usually at this point we begin to absorb some of the methods that we are studying and start to develop some specific skills. In Zen, we may be able to sit quietly for longer periods of time; in psychotherapy, we may acquire some powerful techniques. The danger here is that we may rely overmuch on our skills. Zen students may make a fetish of attending long meditation retreats and neglect their practice with their families and friends. In psychotherapy, the down side of knowing techniques is that sometimes we feel overeager to use them *on* a client rather than *with* a client. Particularly in these days of empirically validated treatments designed for particular conditions (matched not to people, but to diagnoses), we can get overly focused on skillful techniques. Sometimes, these constitute a mistake.

Back in the mid-1970s I took a course in behavioral medicine from Dave Mostofsky. He was studying the application of behavioral learning principles to the treatment of seizure disorders, but he also consulted to institutional settings, helping them set up operant conditioning programs. Dave related the following incident to us:

A local residential home for mentally retarded children called him in to consult. They had a mentally retarded six-year-old boy, Johnny, who had a seizure disorder. The problem was that Johnny would self-induce grand mal seizures by waving his right hand before his eyes. He would fall down and cause quite a commotion. The staff was worried that he would hurt himself, so they had tried to stop him.

First, they had tried tying his right hand behind him. The boy just used his left hand to induce seizures. Then, they tried tying both hands behind him. Johnny would blink his eyes to induce seizures. They didn't know what else to do, so they called Dave in to set up a system of behavioral rewards and punishments, which were particularly in vogue in those days.

Dave was somewhat daunted by the case but, given the seriousness of the boy's condition, agreed to give it a try. He started to prepare an operant conditioning schedule, but then he had an idea that he decided to try before going to the considerable lengths it would take to institute such a program.

He asked to speak to Johnny. The staff brought Johnny to him, and Dave knelt down to speak to him.

"Johnny," Dave said, "Have you noticed that when you wave your hands in front of your eyes or blink your eyes you fall down?"

Johnny nodded yes.

"Johnny," Dave said, "The staff is worried that you could hurt yourself when you fall down."

Johnny nodded.

"Johnny," Dave said, "The staff would like you to stop waving your hands in front of your eyes and blinking, so you won't fall down any more."

"Okay!" Johnny said.

Johnny was as good as his word. The seizures stopped. No complicated program was required.

Dave had good operant conditioning skills; he could hit his target behaviors. He recognized, however, that what was needed here was not an archery match but a meeting.

As therapists it is useful to master techniques to help us treat specific conditions. It also helps to remember that when we sit down with a client, our technique provides the vehicle but not the heart for the healing. "I" am not "It." The source of healing does not come from my ability in isolation but from some larger meeting. I can notch the arrow and pull the bow, but the arrow's flight depends on the physics of mass and gravity, of the forces of wind and air resistance; its accuracy depends on the stillness or motion of the target relative to the arrow's trajectory. Depending on whether the target is hard or soft, willing or unwilling, the arrow will bounce off or be taken in.

No matter how skilled or well-meaning I may be, I cannot make a meeting happen; I can only be open to the possibility of meeting with each other. If we study the ancients and practice their ways, we set up a meeting between them and us, but no matter how much we practice we cannot force ourselves to become copies of them. Because we admire our teachers and models, we try to become like them by absorbing and applying their methods. After a while, however, we start to realize that however much we try to be faithful to the original, we inevitably fail. Our solution to a Bach chorale doesn't sound quite right; responding to a koan with Dogen's answer provides an accurate quotation but does not open the gate to our own life; our mouthing of the words of an Eriksonian hypnotic induction leaves a client unmoved.

We start to learn something very valuable. We learn that we cannot be someone else: not Beethoven, not Dogen, not Freud. We find that even if we succeeded in copying our model exactly, we would be left not with a new work but only with an imitation. Imitations don't work in either Zen or psychotherapy:

> Whenever Gutei was asked a question about Zen, he simply raised one finger.
>
> A boy attendant began to imitate him in this way. One day a visitor asked the boy what his master preached, and the boy raised a finger.
>
> Hearing about this, Gutei seized the boy and cut off his finger with a knife. As the boy ran from the room, screaming with pain, Gutei called to him.
>
> When the boy stopped and turned his head, Gutei raised a finger. In that instant the boy was suddenly enlightened.[24]

> One day in [Carl Whitaker's] office, a mother left her infant's bottle. When the next patient commented on it, Whitaker offered him the bottle.
>
> From then on, bottle feeding became an important technique in the weaponry of his team of therapists, who encouraged their patients to regress, using the bottle as a prop. The therapists were full of excitement, and so were the sessions. Patients brought meaningful associations, and therapy achieved new dimensions. For a while, it seemed that The Technique had been found.
>
> But with the passage of time, the excitement wore off. Patients and therapists became less enthusiastic, and ultimately bored. Finally milk became not a pathway, but plain milk.... The Technique was useful as long as it produced excitement and curiosity in the therapist. Like the Wizard of Oz's medal, which gave courage only to the courageous, technique is only a vehicle for the therapist's [and client's] creative exploration.[25]

As we practice over and over again we gradually learn that practice does not deepen so long as we are attempting to replicate a past experience: Sometimes gradually, sometimes suddenly, we learn how to practice over and over in a way so that each time becomes fresh. We practice over and over so that each time we re-create experience: conceiving it, giving it birth, bringing it into new being in every repetition. Children know how to do this: They can do the same thing over and over again and discover something new each time and take pleasure in it. We need to relearn this skill; then our re-creation becomes recreation, and what we thought was the drudgery of practice becomes the joy of spontaneous play. When we practice like this, every once in a while we hit the right note. For that moment, we become the Ancients in a new form. Realizing the Ancients in a fresh, new way revitalizes them even as it gives us a form, a pathway to express our selves: The chain of succession is renewed and eternity flows.

Each therapist, client, and Zen student must find his or her own way to practice the Ancients' way. The apprentice imitates the master but must create her own masterpieces. This is not a moral dictum but a practical fact. The reason that imitation doesn't work is that if we imitate we are usually copying an image rather than a reality. We think we can imitate Bach by writing a chorale using his rules of harmony. Bach, however, never wrote according to a set of rules; the rules we associate with Bach are merely summaries that later musicologists abstracted by studying his works and codifying his practice. His compositions are full of "exceptions" to the rules, because the "rules" were not the living reality of his work. When Bach sat down at the harpsichord, he did not follow a manual of composition: He simply made music.

Therapists and Zen students struggling to reconcile their studies with their practice can take some guidance from this. We need to learn the basic approaches and guiding rules, but we need to do so with full knowledge that they will not cover all eventualities; the manual won't tell us how to respond to the unpredictable variety of the myriad circumstances we encounter in our clinical work and in our lives. If having learned the rules we try to constrict our experience to accord to what we have learned, we may not leave room for the necessary reality in front of us that confounds our expectations.

I saw Elizabeth in a twelve-session time-limited psychotherapy following the model of James Mann.[26] Elizabeth's presenting problem involved a pattern of being unassertive. She would please others excessively because she felt afraid that if she did not, people would abandon her; she also became anxious and guilty if she did something for herself, such as take a vacation or even go to a movie. All this was explored in some depth during the treatment, and Elizabeth made considerable gains. She became more assertive both in the transference relationship and in her life at large; she became more able to recognize her own wishes and act on them in appropriate ways.

Predictably, termination activated fears that by having asserted herself within therapy she was "causing" herself to be abandoned by ending treatment. In the penultimate session she was able to grapple with her newfound ability to "go it alone without supports" if need be and treat herself well. In the very last session, however, the perspective shifted. Rather than focusing on how others might abandon her, she was able to talk about how, fearing loss, she would protect herself from becoming close to people. She talked movingly about how she felt close to me and did not want to leave. She found it very hard to think we would never see each other again. As she told me about this, we could each feel the relationship between us palpably deepen. Elizabeth hesitated; she appeared to be in considerable conflict and distress. Then she seemed to summon up her courage and, taking a deep breath, told me that she felt she would not be true to her self or what she had learned in the therapy if she did not assert herself and tell me she wanted to see me for at least one more session.

I was in something of a quandary. Following the rules of Mann's model, I had been very clear we would meet for twelve, and only twelve, sessions. The twelve-session limit is crucial to the effectiveness of this psychotherapy; during the initial phases of the treatment it is supposed to activate a client's unconscious fantasies for a magical cure through a timeless symbiosis with a powerful and empathic helper. The termination then becomes crucial for working through the painful disappointments of empathic failures and feelings of loss inherent in all relationships bounded by finite time. In order to bring home the intensity of loss and activate the ambivalence involved, the therapist not only avoids extending the treatment contract but indicates that when the 12 sessions are up they will not plan to ever meet each other again. This usually results in a very painful, but very intense and powerful, brief therapy. I had experimented in the past with "fudging" the twelve-session limit and discovered it usually resulted in watering down the effectiveness of the treatment and deprived it of needed emotional force.

I had, in fact, during the course of our meetings turned down other requests by Elizabeth and enforced the frustrations inherent in this kind of treatment; doing this had helped Elizabeth explore many issues. I learned that when she was growing up, Elizabeth almost never asked for anything for herself from her parents, but on the rare occasions when she had, they had been withholding, critical, and shaming. She had dealt with this by closing herself off and denying her needs.

I hesitated before responding to Elizabeth's request to extend the therapy. Both the "rule" and my past experience suggested that I should deny Elizabeth's request. Somehow, however, the rule didn't feel right. Responding to Elizabeth's courageous willingness to open herself up and run the risk of being turned away by flatly refusing her was too much like repeating what she had experienced in her family of origin. Elizabeth and I discussed the issue for a while; together we decided it was important to leave the termination date up to her, so that she could stop when she felt ready and not when an authority figure told her she should feel ready.

Two sessions later—on the 14th session—she said she was ready to stop. Elizabeth said now that she felt it was her choice. She could say goodbye to me without having to pretend that it wasn't painful or that she wasn't scared, but also without having to pretend that she wasn't strong enough to be able to do it or that we hadn't accomplished something positive and meaningful together. We were able to discuss how even after saying goodbye we would go on remembering each other and we both acknowledged, with mutual expressions of appreciation, the value of our work together.

We shook hands, and Elizabeth left the room with both of us experiencing a strong sense of mutual fondness, satisfaction, and sadness. I remained in the room a few more minutes, savoring what I thought was the end of the therapy. However, there was a coda to come.

There was a knock on the door. Elizabeth came back in, stating that she had left her keys behind. She picked up the keys, and said, "I guess I really don't want to leave, do I? But now I've got my keys. I can go now."

We looked at each other silently; as our eyes met, Elizabeth and I smiled. Our smile acknowledged the truth of both her literal statement and the metaphor for the end of our work together. We did not see each other again, but I had a colleague do a follow-up a year later and found that Elizabeth continued to do well.

We had not followed the rules, but perhaps this was a place where the manual of twelve-session time-limited therapy needed to be put aside. In the process we each had to learn to trust our own and each others' intuition, and the process that linked us together.

In the face of the uncertainties of psychotherapy and Zen practice, it is helpful to know that there is something going on that is beyond basic approaches and guiding rules. Skill may help us better aim our arrow in the direction of our client, but however skilled we may be, we cannot control the trajectory of our of client's arrow's flight. When we touch each other in relationship, something transpires in the joining that is beyond the powers of skill.

Sitting on our cushion, whether or not we are successful in assuming the posture of a particular form of Zen practice, so long as we are practicing not just for ourselves but for the benefit of all beings, true eternity is flowing. Sitting in the psychotherapy office, whether or not we are acting according to the rules of a particular form of therapy, we re-create psychotherapy anew with each client so long as we approach the relationship from the standpoint of service.

SERVING

A minister serves the lord, a son obeys the father.
Not obeying is not filial, and not serving is no help.

When two arrows strike each other in midair both turn incandescent in the sparks that fly. Still, each travels in the direction in which it was aimed; each of us is a separate dart with its own agenda. We must pursue our individual courses as minister or lord, parent or child, teacher or student, therapist or client. When the different courses of our lives collide, must one arrow subordinate its interests to the others? Or is it possible that, by following its trajectory faithfully, each arrow can serve the other by helping it find its target in itself?

Neither psychotherapy nor Zen practice can be just for ourselves, or our arrows will be on solo flights and miss each other. At the same time, if our practice is not for ourselves, we stand in danger of feeling subordinated or dominated by others: Then we may stop serving and fall into resentful servility.

If we mostly serve ourselves, we may cloak ourselves in a "professional" detachment that can become insensitive to the needs of others. If on the other hand we do not watch out for our own interests, we may feel drained by the importunities of clients who feel needy, or we can feel overwhelmed by the demands of employers seeking to increase our productivity. Facing a mass of fire in our daily work, we stand at risk of burning out rather than being warmed and illuminated by the flames.

On spiritual paths, if we mostly serve ourselves we may become secure but arrogant in a narrow faith. If on the other hand we do not pay sufficient attention to ourselves and think spirituality is identical with self-abnegation, we may fall into a different trap: If we adopt the role of faithful devotee without any self-interest, we may avoid making our own personal choices. If we don't do the necessary hard work to make our individual selves a lamp, this can leave us forever dependent on reflecting others' light.

In its images of minister and lord, child and parent, the "Song of the Jewel Mirror Samadhi" raises the question of who we obey and how we serve. We want to know what are the ultimate aims of our endeavor, so that we can tailor our efforts relative to those ends. Therapists in these days of managed care are finding the issue particularly confusing because there is considerable conflict about who is our master. Often we feel caught between a client's needs and an insurance company's limits; more and more, the marketplace intrudes into the therapeutic setting. These economic issues make the problem of conflicts of interest in the therapeutic setting very concrete. However, there has always been some friction about whose interests should rule when client meets clinician.

As therapists, we often prefer to avoid acknowledging that clients' needs also serve to advance professional interests. Our clients' money provides us a source of income; our clients' admiration and gratitude provide us a source of narcissistic gratification; our clients' problems provide us topics for research studies and journal articles to advance our professional prestige. Where clients are seen as patients and research subjects, therapists are usually viewed as experts with privileged knowledge of what constitutes problems and what qualifies as treatment. Then, as lords of the clinic, we set the times our clients can come and the fees they must pay and determine the questionnaires they are supposed to fill out.

Of course there has always been a counterweight to this trend, which places clients' needs foremost. In client-centered therapy, the client is the source of wisdom, growth, and health; the therapist exists only to support and follow the client. The problem here is that it is possible to become overly concerned with clients' individual hurts and needs so that their personal desires become the rulers of the process. This can ignore the legitimate interests of people outside the immediate therapy who have a relationship with the client (e.g., family members, employers) or with the therapist (e.g., other clients who may need the time slot the client is occupying; third-party payers and clinic employers trying to remain economically viable). If we work with a client as if he or she exists in a vacuum, sometimes therapy can lead a client to be overly self-absorbed or isolated; we probably all know people who have been in therapy who can talk, and think, only of themselves. When the client is lord of the clinic, it is possible to mistake selfishness for self-actualization.[27]

Faced with conflicting potential masters with a claim on the therapy process, we may want to identify a superordinate ideal, a sovereign ruler who provides us with some absolute reference point. We have various potential gods in our lives: We may wish to be minister to the lord of Personal Growth; we may wish to devote ourselves to Scientific Truth; we may bow to Economic Necessity; we may try to act faithful to the God of our spiritual path. We may not be so clear in our minds about this but just have some vague feeling, when caught between different demands, that we would like some ultimate ruler, some cause larger than the trivialities of our daily tasks, whom we can serve in good conscience.

Faced with many masters, who ultimately do we serve? There is a Zen koan that pertains to this issue. In Buddhism, there are many Buddhas: Shakyamuni is the historical Buddha who appeared in India 2000 years ago; Maitreya is the Buddha who will appear in the future. No particular Buddha is "superior" to another, and there is nothing "above" Buddha: Buddhism does not identify a Supreme Being. Yet Buddhism emphasizes our practice is a kind of service. Who, then, do we serve?

> Wu-tsu said, "Shakyamuni and Maitreya are servants of another. Tell me, who is that other?"[28] I asked my teacher, Sojun Mel Weitsman, this question. "What master do the Buddhas serve?"
> He answered: "They serve each other."

As therapists and clients, as Zen students and teachers, together with all sentient and nonsentient beings, we are always serving each other. We make a mistake if we try to pin service down to one side or another. The minister serves the lord, but the lord also serves the minister. Emptiness is not "more fundamental" than form; the Heart Sutra reminds us that form is emptiness, emptiness is form. The Absolute is not "more important" than the Relative; the Sandokai reminds us the Absolute and the Relative are like two arrows meeting in midair. In the "Song of the Jewel Mirror Samadhi," Tozan's Five Ranks invokes the interplay of relative and Absolute, self and other, minister and lord, child and parent. The fourth rank deals with

> The relation of us to the Absolute. Our filial piety is how we give power to the Absolute, and the Absolute empowers us. Rather than taking power, rather than trying to take power from the Absolute, [we] allow the Absolute to do the empowerment.
> The fourth rank is the perfecting of that kind of activity. Real freedom, but still with an awareness of self and other, or an awareness of Absolute and relative working

together. The fourth rank is [about]... how we swim in the waves, no matter what kind of waves they are. And how we help others to do that, and how we... really devote ourselves to doing that.

In the fourth rank the relative and Absolute integrate by bowing to each other and offering each other mutual devotion. This kind of service is mutually empowering. But in our culture we often get confused about the issue of service.

Service implies a server and a served, and we tend to feel uncomfortable with the idea of hierarchy. On the one hand, we tend to think that if we are a servant, we're somehow one-down, humiliated, or dishonored. Serving becomes confused with submission, selfless giving becomes confused with martyrdom or being taken advantage of. So we try to protect ourselves by demanding something in return for our service. If we're a parent, we expect our children to appreciate us; if we're a therapist, we expect to receive a good salary or perhaps some prestige from our position; if we're a Zen student, perhaps we think we deserve peace of mind. If we're a waiter or waitress, we expect a tip. Then we get angry if our service is not "appropriately" rewarded. Other cultures have a different tradition: The server feels honored by the opportunity to serve, so that serving well is its own reward. In those countries offering a waiter a tip is regarded as a demeaning insult; it implies the waiter takes no intrinsic value from the work of helping others feel comfortable and happy, that the waiter is a "flunky" with no internal integrity.

On the other hand, serving sometimes gets confused with superiority. If we have some talent we can employ in service, we sometimes feel we know more or can do something better than someone else; the simple fact of having knowledge or skill gets contaminated by the idea that somehow it makes us exceptional or special. Therapists sometimes feel superior about how well they serve their "impaired" clients; religious practitioners sometimes feel superior about devoting their lives to serving "deluded" humanity. We often have conflicts about this feeling and may defend ourselves against it by going to the other extreme: We deny our intellect, strength, or special abilities. If we efface ourselves in this way, we do not take responsibility for making full use of our gifts.

We get confused if we think a talent is *our* talent. The Fourth Rank is about realizing that our gifts do not lie in us but in an interchange; we give our talents to the Source that provides our talents. We give power to the Absolute, and the Absolute empowers us. We serve Service, and let the Service do the serving. We just need to get out of the way by doing our part and not worrying about who's on the top or bottom.

The fact is that we all are lords and all servants. There is always someone who knows more than we do, and someone who knows less. There is always someone stronger and someone weaker. We are all weak and strong, knowledgeable and ignorant. If we start to discriminate about who needs to be served and who owes service, we will get confused. If we serve for the sake of serving well, service honors both the server and the served. We serve and are served not to get some thing, but as a natural expression of our enjoyment of each other.

Some years ago, my wife, two daughters, and I volunteered to help prepare a dinner at a shelter for homeless men. As we drove there, my wife and I felt anxious about whether the men would act appropriately with our children. We felt awkward and didn't know how we'd be able to relate to the men: Would we be in a noble, "one-up" position that would be embarrassing? Conversely, would we feel threatened? Would the men, humiliated from their treatment by society, be aggressively hostile and act inappropriately with our young children?

We were not prepared for what happened: We enjoyed cooking the meal with our coworkers, and we enjoyed serving the meal and eating dinner with the men. The men we served were appreciative without being servile; they joked with our children and helped keep things running smoothly as the food was distributed. Their ability to maintain good humor in the face of difficult circumstances helped inspire us. When we sat down to eat together, we had some interesting conversations.

We now go serve at the homeless shelter on a regular basis. When we tell friends about it, they sometimes think we're doing something charitable. It's hard to explain that we do this not to do anything special, but simply because it's enjoyable. If before we go to the homeless shelter we've had a family argument or are feeling depressed about something or stressed about work, usually by the time we leave the shelter we're feeling tired but content. It's a good way to spend time with each other and the people in our community.

As we serve each other we discover that we give of ourselves not from obligation or a desire to feel appreciated or to be nobly charitable: We give simply because we enjoy giving. If we give this way, it also enables us to enjoy receiving others' gifts to us. If we are in need and someone gives us what we need, we can accept the gift without shame or humiliation. If we have done something for someone else and they serve us in return, we need not feel they are returning what is our due as a quid pro quo. Rather, serving and being served are expressions of our basic nature; giving and receiving are not creditor/debtor transactions but relations of love.

As we all know, however, the exchange of love is not always easy. Having been hurt or abandoned before, it is sometimes difficult to open ourselves up to receive the gift of love; we may worry about the strings that are attached. Conversely, having been rejected or taken advantage of before, it is sometimes difficult to offer the gift of love; we worry about being disappointed or drained. If we relate to others by keeping accounts of how much we put out or receive, we may feel guilty with undeserved wealth or angry at being poor, deprived of what we see as our fair share. Either way can lead to discouragement and despair, to feeling flooded or drained. What serves to keep us afloat in the play of these tidal forces of the heart?

A few months ago one of our dearest friends entered the final stages of terminal cancer; at the time his family was in considerable financial trouble. My wife flew up to be with our friend and his family and to help them sort out their finances, while I stayed home with our younger daughter.

When my wife returned from the trip, she was exhausted. As soon as she got back from the airport and entered the house she collapsed on the couch and started telling me how chaotic and emotionally charged the visit had been. There had been lots of people at our friends' house, all of them feeling grief at his impending death and panic at the family's impending bankruptcy. Everyone felt helpless; because my wife is a good organizer, a compassionate listener, and very competent at financial matters, during the visit everyone had turned to her for advice and support even while they remained in denial about the severity of both the illness and the money situation.

My wife felt drained. She told me she felt badly that at a certain point, after feeling pulled in many directions by the people there, all of whom she loved, she began to feel as if her compassion had run out. She started to feel resentful. She wanted to have some room for her own grief and some time to say goodbye to our dying friend but felt forced to take care of business details. She wanted to be giving but found herself wanting our friends to take more responsibility for the situation. She wanted to be there for them emotionally but found herself closing off, and she felt distressed at closing off.

While she was saying this to me, I found myself closing off to her. My mind was wandering and my feelings were shutting down. I said to myself that I had also had a difficult weekend: I had been taking care of the household, I had my own work and family pressures, I didn't have the energy to listen to my wife. I started to feel resentful; couldn't she understand that I had my limits, too? I started to feel judgmental: She had gone up there to help out, why couldn't she just push herself a bit more, put herself aside, and serve the friends she had gone up there to help out?

Then I became aware of the judgmentalism in my thoughts, the anger in my feelings, the tension in my body. I started to realize that I was closing off because my wife was voicing the exact same issues that I was having problems with. In my wife's fatigue I could feel my tiredness at shouldering what I felt were constant demands. In my wife's irritation that our friends weren't taking more responsibility for their economic difficulties I could see my own irritation at some colleagues and clients who I felt were not taking full responsibility for their situation and were relying on me more than I felt was appropriate. My wife's issues about feeling obligated to attend to other peoples' feelings rather than her own emotions were the same issues that I experienced in dealing with my adolescent daughters, with my clients, and, at this moment, with my wife.

I saw I was having the same troubles giving to my wife that my wife had experienced giving to our friends. I realized I was feeling something similar to the difficulties my clients and colleagues were expressing: a sense that too much was expected, that it was impossible to meet all the demands, and a desire to have someone else to lean on.

As I became more in touch with how my feelings echoed those of the very people I was irritated with, I became more aware of my connection with everyone else. Then something started to open up, and the irritability of obligations dissolved in a sense of appreciation and gratitude at shared effort.

I was able to sense that my wife was not demanding something from me but sharing something of herself. Instead of having to do something to serve her needs, we could serve each other just by sitting there, acknowledging the impossible situation we're all in, and leaving room for compassion for us all. We could enjoy sharing our difficulties and in doing so appreciate the love we had for each other.

We're all asked for too much. Life makes seemingly impossible demands on us. But that's what's so wonderful: Life forces us to constantly stretch beyond ourselves. We have a choice, however: We can stretch feeling isolated, depleted, and resentful, or we can stretch feeling connected to each other stretching. As coworkers and clients, siblings and strangers, parents and children, we are cohosts for the irritations and pleasures, the inadequacies and triumphs of our lives. As cohosts, we serve and are served by each other; we move back and forth sometimes being the guest, sometimes being the host, facilitating both sides of service.

Service is enjoyable because it is not an obligatory exchange, but a cooperative sharing. Serving is an expression of intimacy, not a strain on the muscles of the heart but a strain in a song. When we serve and are served, we are singing with each other. Family and friends, clients and therapists, givers and receivers are each unique voices in a vast chorus.

We are always finding our place in the chorus. When our service is intimate song we are always taking the shape of the melody being sung, yet we are always singing in our own voice. There will be people who can sing higher or lower, louder or softer. Sometimes we sing through a sore throat or sing off-key. It's still singing. So long as I don't insist that you can only join in my preconceived compositions, there is room for us to harmonize together. Even if we don't feel like serving or singing, it doesn't help to try to wriggle out of it because we are always all intimately interconnected; our doom is to have each of our acts be a note in a larger melody that forms a theme in an ongoing composition.

Sometimes we have troubles hearing the music and we don't feel like singing. This is at least in part what practice is about: how to sing even when we don't feel like singing, how to sing even if singing seems impossible. When we sing to each other and listen to each others' songs, we serve and are served by each other and connect to our source; we connect self and other, minister and lord, Absolute and relative, because *we serve the source of song by singing*. Because of this, when we cannot sing, our singing calls forth song in others and the music continuously streams forth.

SINGING

> With causal conditions, time and season, quiescently it shines bright....
> It is bright just at midnight; it doesn't appear at dawn.
> It acts as a guide for beings—its use removes all pains....
> It is like the taste of the five-flavored herb, like the diamond thunderbolt....
> In its fineness it fits into spacelessness;

In its greatness it is utterly beyond location....
When the wooden man begins to sing, the stone woman gets
up to dance.

Singing helps us find the music in our lives even in the midst of a psychological or spiritual midnight. At such times we may feel either parched or flooded, like we are burning in a hot cauldron or freezing to death in the dark. Clients often come to psychotherapists at such times, seeking a way out of their discomfort like the monk in the following koan who seeks to avoid the pain of heat and cold:

> A monk asked Tung Shan, "When cold and heat come, how can we avoid them?"
>   Shan said, "Why don't you go to the place where there is no cold or heat?"
>   The monk said, "What is the place where there is no cold or heat?"
>   Tung Shan said, "When it's cold, the cold finishes the monk; when it's hot, the heat finishes the monk."
>   Yuan Wu says: It's not this season. [Cold and heat] are right in your face, right on your head. Where are you?...[29]

Tung Shan bids us not to flee from our experience but to plunge into it. In this spirit Yuan Wu asks, when we are immersed in our experience, where is our original self? We have learned from Tozan that "I am not It; It actually is me," so we begin to understand: In the midst of the cold, the bite in the air is us. In the midst of the fire, the flames constitute our lives.

We tend to feel threatened by alterations in the climate of our lives. If in the midst of a crisis staring us in the face someone asks us Yuan Wu's question, "Where are you?" we may be tempted to answer, "Anywhere but here." But we cannot say who we are if we avoid the circumstances of our lives. Some of us tend to be afraid of pain and depression, so we flee them by seeking frenziedly to hold on to being happy, healthy, and excited. Some of us tend to be afraid of happiness and intimacy, so we flee them by hanging on to our misery and loneliness. Neither selective strategy works well, because our life experience is multifarious and ungraspable: It has a greatness that goes beyond location and a fineness that needs no space at all. So in order to answer "where are you?" we must find the fullness of our lives wherever we are each moment, even in the midst of our discomfort.

In the face of the changing conditions of our life we often become rigid. Even if we know that something needs to change, our fears tell us to grab hold of our sense of ourselves. So we often try to hang on to just the familiar pieces of our experience and shut out the rest. If we grasp tightly in this way we are wooden men and stone women, whether we sit on a meditation cushion or in a client's or a therapist's chair.

Zen practice and psychotherapy can help us deal with the fact that our lives are not bland: Our lives have the complex tang of the five-flavored herb. Life is always tasty. Even if it is sour or bitter, there is a fullness to life that fills our palate as surely as there is beauty and peace in the midst of ugliness and terror. The tastes of life arise in our interminglings. Where self and other meet each other, where

Absolute and relative play guest and host to each other, this is the jewel mirror samadhi: the mirror and subject fulfilling each other and shining bright.

This jeweled mirror has many facets and reflects them all. Sometimes as therapists we provide a mirror to client experiences that are traumatic and horrifying; sometimes in Zen meditation we encounter stone walls or visions of frightening demons. The mirror reflects them all but is like a glistening stream of water that reflects whatever faces it; the stream remains unsullied by the images. Even if it is in danger of being choked by debris, the strong currents of the river can help it break free.

At the beginning of this chapter we met Brian, the middle-aged man whose grandparents had "drowned his heart." To protect himself, he had constricted his emotional palette and lived most of his life without much color, music, or joy.

But strong feelings of love had unlocked something in him, even though he didn't know what to do about them. During the therapy, he had some catharsis in talking about his childhood torture and sharing it with somebody: His crying seemed to resuscitate his heart. Outside of the therapy, he was entertaining new possibilities for his relationships. He tentatively began to share some of his doubts with his wife, and to explore the feelings he had for the other woman he had fallen in love with. He formed a close friendship with another man and with him tried various spiritual exercises. He started being more creative and spontaneous in his work and changed the way he related to his colleagues. As he did all this, he not only began to be aware of his own feelings but became more sensitive to the feelings of the people around him. He discovered he was sensitive and empathic, and what became most important to him spiritually was finding ways of touching other peoples' lives. To do this, he began working with his friend on a book project.

By the end of therapy he had finished his book. He titled the book, *What If?* Each page had a question and a response, such as the following:

> What if...
>> you are more aware now than you have ever been?
>>> Were you aware of that?
> What if...
>> your every act is an act of love?
>>> Who has your heart touched today?

After being traumatized at some fundamental level and fearing other people would drown him, this man had been deeply afraid; he had adopted a rigid armor that closed himself off to life. But he found compassion for himself and for others; he broke free of his previous conditioning and discovered in his connectedness to others a new sense of awareness and joy. When he least expected it, something in him unexpectedly opened up to creativity and love.

Therapy and Zen practice are about discovering openings that allow us to find ways to dance and sing even in the midst of fear and despair. To do this we need to realize that there is some experience deeper than trauma, something that brings us back to the most fundamental tendency we have to grow and live out our lives.

Grass will spring up even through concrete and cover the fields of old battles with verdant green. In the words of a Zen saying, "The real does not conceal the false, the crooked does not hide the straight."

People who struggle with illness really appreciate good health; people who struggle with tyranny know how to enjoy the freedoms they create despite the watchful eyes of oppression. Oppression comes in many forms: We may be dominated by political powers; we may be tyrannized by our thoughts and feelings; we may feel dominated by illness or imprisoned by aggression or fear. The ultimate triumph of tyranny only comes, however, if we react to our difficulties by cringing back and avoid meeting the full experience of our lives: Then we feel isolated from others and trapped within ourselves.

For this reason, psychotherapy must be about sharing the flavors of life. What shines out in the diamond thunderbolt is the fact that our being is inter-being. The wooden man in therapy—be he therapist or client—can only find his singing voice in the midst of a duet; the stone woman in Zen meditation can only find the dance by waltzing with the pain in her knees and the cushion on which she sits. If our lives are solitary essences they are tasteless, restricted to a single flavor, constricted to a single theme. When our lives are connected, we can take pleasure in the fact that songs come in many forms.

There are songs of joy and sorrow, love songs and the blues; we have revolutionary ballads and hymns to creation. Songs match their conditions just as our lives have their seasons. Each melody has its own key; each season is "just this" and expresses its own being on a field far beyond form and emptiness:

> Spring has hundreds of flowers;
> Autumn, the clear moon.
> Summer has cool winds;
> Winter has snow.
> When busyness doesn't take your mind—
> that's your chance.[30]

When in psychotherapy or Zen practice we clear a space so that we are not caught in the busy machinations of our minds, in the fears and hopes we have about the seasons, we can encounter each season as Itself. In the cycles of growth and decay, birth and death, even the earth needs a rest: Winter has its own lessons to teach.

I was going through the winter I described at the beginning of this chapter. Meditation wasn't "working." I had pain in my back, constriction of my breath, depression. I felt I didn't have room to breathe. I went to a week-long sesshin (meditation retreat) and had a difficult time.

No matter how much I tried to relax and settle in, the breath was constricted. I hung on through sheer stubbornness—perhaps obsessiveness? Although in each moment of meditation I would try to settle in to my experience of the immediate moment without judging it as good or bad, another part of me would say, with each breath:

"This is awful. Stop this. Quit." It wasn't so clear that quitting wasn't a good idea: Maybe continuing wasn't practice but just an obsessional neurosis. Maybe quitting wouldn't be laziness or defeat but simply acknowledging the part of me that said, "You're not giving yourself room to breathe."

I talked to a friend, a very experienced Zen student, about this. I told him how I was trying hard but felt trapped by my own trying. He suggested I just stay with each experience as it came up without attempting to alter it or do anything about it. I told him that's what I was trying to do. When I felt discomfort, I tried to open myself to, smile at, and accept the discomfort. But I still felt caught in a struggle with myself.

My friend said to me, "No, Bob, you don't understand. When you do all that, you're still trying, you're still *doing* something. You're still holding on. *Just let go and be with whatever's happening.*"

I felt a jolt; I could feel the force of his suggestion. I tried to implement his advice during the remainder of that day's meditation but I kept getting in my own way: I still felt frustrated and conflicted.

When I went out to my car at the end of the day's meditations to drive home and get some sleep before coming back for the next day of the retreat, I discovered that during my meditations someone had thrown a rock through the window of my car and stolen my compact-disc player. I couldn't see the full extent of the damage in the dark, but it looked pretty extensive. There was broken glass all over.

I was annoyed. It seemed that one more obstacle had been put in my path. It had been difficult to arrange my work and family life to attend the meditation retreat; it seemed that whenever I tried to attend a retreat, something came up to interfere. I asked myself, "Won't I ever be able to attend a sesshin without interruptions?" I thought, "Here I was meditating all day, fighting the battle about sticking with the program, and someone does this. Now I'll have to deal with this the next day rather than going to the retreat." Part of me was relieved to get away from the anguish of my zazen; I also felt guilty at feeling relieved. I felt frustrated at how I tied myself in knots.

I woke up feeling depressed. I took the car in to be repaired and had to wait for an hour. During that time I went to a restaurant to get a bite to eat. The meal was awful. While eating, I read an article by John Tarrant, a contemporary Zen teacher, in which he wrote: "The ordeal here is in the descent, the dark pain... the grief of the personal, the surrender of the fantasies of being pure.... When we make this sacrifice we are welcomed into a more specific community of the human, the family, the life of the passions, companionship... in terms of spirit it's fine if we die, yes, today would be OK. [But] soul wants to see its daughter graduate from college."[31]

I cried reading this. Then, walking back to the repair shop, I noticed a person sitting in his car at a stoplight, frowning. I could see that he had his own difficulties, and I felt some compassion for him. Suddenly, my self-preoccupations and obsessions dropped away and the breeze and sunshine were very wonderful. The glass window of personal partiality shattered: I was able to reexperience my connectedness with all beings in suffering and happiness.

A compact-disc player stolen? No more playing of the old, worn tracks. A rock through the window? Wonderful! Wonderful! With the window open, the air flows through. I could breathe again.

Returning to the Zendo, walking slowly with everyone else, I saw a candle burning. Underneath the flame, the yellow wax was melting into a hot liquid. Its light taught clearly: No flame without wax. Sometimes the wax might congeal and seem all too solid and unyielding; sometimes the wax might not like heating up and melting; but wax and flame together give off light.

Some days after the meditation retreat, I was driving to work in the morning and noticed how brown the hills were. Here in California, throughout the summer there is little rain. The hills turn brown. When a friend of mine visited, I took her up into the hills to a viewpoint with a vast panorama. She was disappointed at the dry, dusty hills. "There's no green," she said.

The hills turn brown gradually. It's easy to accustom oneself to drought, to not see it, to just tolerate it. Driving this morning in November, however, still with no rain and the hills dusty brown, a single green-leafed tree appeared around a curve, sharply defined against the drab background.

When the hills are brown, the blossoming tree shows itself clearly.

Somehow, even at the lowest ebbs of life, in our darkest hours, something is still flowing. Bright just at midnight, some light shines forth. Just when all our efforts seem exhausted, just when our Zen practice seems impossible, just when therapy seems to have failed, some spark ignites and in the deep darkness, the light of a single candle flame can be seen for miles.

HOSTING

> Practice secretly, working within, as though a fool, like an idiot—
> If you can actualize continuity, this is called the host within the host.

The brown hill acts as a host for the blossoming tree. The blossoming tree gives its leaves back to the soil and hosts the hillside. The branches of the tree also host myriad birds, each of which acts as host for the birdsongs that teach us to sing through sunshine and rain, even if everything in our life tells us we cannot sing.

But the hill doesn't make a big deal about itself: It simply offers itself to the tree, providing soil into which the tree can put down roots. The tree doesn't advertise itself but provides a place for the birds' nests. The host who wants to make her guest feel comfortable doesn't call attention to the effort that went into preparing the meal. Hosts "practice secretly, working within." The host appreciates that the guest gives him an opportunity to play the host; in doing so, the guest acts as host to the host.

When a client gets better, the therapist doesn't say, "I cured you. I'm great." If as therapists we are invested in being the vehicle for a client's cure, even though we may mean well, our pride can overshadow the deep roots and inherent phototropism of our client's growth. On the other hand, if at the end of a therapy the client thanks us for our efforts, we'd be ungracious to disparage their thanks; if we insist "I did nothing, you did everything" we can leave a client feeling they're alone, with no one to admire their blossoms, enjoy their fruit, or lend some water during a dry spell. Either way denies the mutuality of our meeting and serving each other.

Guests and hosts are always linked. As therapists, we provide a space in which our clients can realize their selves; our clients give us an opportunity to work as therapists and in this way realize our selves. In therapy we are constantly guiding by following, and following by guiding. We are opening our house to our client at the same time as the client is opening his or her house to us: We are hosts within hosts, and somehow in this process we bring each other forth and realize that we are continuously our true selves.

In the midst of our activity, we host each other. In the midst of our mutual hosting we tend to forget our selves; we may not be clear about what we are doing or who is contributing what. When we or our client find some freedom, often we are not quite sure how it happened. But there is a sense that as we stumble around, although we are not doing anything brilliant or special, even at the times when we are having difficulties and feel like we're floundering, there is still some sense, some foolish faith that something larger than our individual efforts is moving and opening us up. This is the fifth rank.

> The fifth stage is where everything's forgotten. There's no sense of relative or Absolute... no need to think about in terms of relative or Absolute because it's so well integrated that there's no duality whatsoever. The fifth rank is, no matter what you do, you can't sink. Whether you're down at the bottom or the top, it doesn't matter, there's no way you can sink. Or, sinking is OK, and floating is OK.
>
> And this is the stage of the fool. The idiot. No particular sense of accomplishment or flag of distinction between self or other. No sense of hierarchy or position. Whatever happens is life itself. No more striving. When you can completely let go, this effort is not yours or someone else's. You don't know whose effort it is... it's one organism that's working together in harmony.
>
> It's sometimes expressed as "foolish old man." Bumbles around, can't find his glasses, but in his bumbling, in his stumbling, without trying, without thinking about it, without doing anything special, he inadvertently brings sentient beings to enlightenment....
>
> Hakuin uses a koan to express it: "And up on his mountain top he hires foolish wise man and he and they together fill up the well with snow."

Sometimes Zen practice is called "selling water by the river." We do the same thing in psychotherapy, in which we are constantly filling up the well with snow, healing a client who is already whole. Psychotherapy is about realizing wellness, discovering the depths of the well by adding to its pool. The well absorbs the frozen water we give to it and gives us back refreshing fluid water to quench our thirst.

The play of filling up the well with snow goes on and on. There is no moment in which it is not happening, no stopping or starting. Life and death, health and sickness, distress and joy are in constant, continuous flow.

Often our lives feel like they stutter, jerk around, start and stop. We feel divided into different pieces of ourselves, that the world is broken into separate fragments. All the bits and pieces of our lives are related to each other; they fit together in a fundamental unity, but this unity is not always easy to see. We can only realize this unity and fit the pieces together by working with each piece separately: each client, each breath, each step. Zen practice and psychotherapy are about putting the pieces together, one by one.

So even though we don't quite know what we're doing, we continue to do our work as therapists and Zen students. We simply do what needs to be done without having to worry about It or separate ourselves from It. We fumble around, performing the useless activity of talking and listening, exchanging words that in their fragmentary nature cannot possibly convey all there is to our experience. Sometimes we catch glimpses of the picture formed by the whole jigsaw puzzle: This makes it a little easier to have some sense of what we're doing. Our basic job, however, involves the practice of picking up one piece, placing it next to another, turning it around and around to see if it fits, dropping it if need be and reaching for another piece. We search for the pieces that snap together, and once we've found one union, we go on to the next piece. We do this again and again: If we do it continuously, we discover that each piece is a facet of the Jewel Mirror.

Tozan reminds us that the Jewel Mirror Samadhi is a *song*. We form this song with our whole body and our whole mind. When it is quiet enough, we realize that every movement we make creates sound: In an anechoic chamber, you can hear the beating of your heart and the high-pitched whine of your nervous system. Leaning forward in our chair, our clothes rustle and our bones creak. Lying asleep, the bellows of our breath recreates the music of surf and waves. Thoughts and feelings play a tune that gets expressed in a word, a facial expression, a hand pulling back or reaching out. We are always singing the story of our lives, creating tones absorbed, reflected, and actualized in the concert hall of the universe.

When we think we have problems singing, or even when we think we are singing superbly, we don't need to go around broadcasting it: We only need to find our place in the symphony that is continuously playing. We are one voice in a polyphonic composition. As we sing, our notes are always part of a larger chorus, so we don't want any one voice to stand out: We want them to blend so that together they create a rich harmony. We're all just one instrument in a vast orchestra, but the orchestra will sound different with the loss of a single clarinet. We serve the music, and the music serves us. In this unimaginable and ungraspable Sound that is always there yet always changing, we are host and guest, hosting within the host.

The Jeweled Mirror is reflecting and reflected in millions of facets, throughout universes of experiences, infinities of a moment. The "Song of the Jewel Mirror Samadhi" is a song about serving and being served, about appearing sometimes as client, sometimes as therapist: of reconciling teacher and student, Absolute and relative, host and guest, body and mind, lover and beloved. Together and apart are a song and dance routine that can animate us even when we feel like wooden men and stone women. In our psychotherapeutic and Zen practice, all we need do is enjoy linking the discrete steps into a spirited dance, enjoy lifting our voices in the delight of concerted effort.

For Fran Tribe

Death is not a stranger.
She needs no visa to enter,
Is her own passport to return home.
She does not even need a name for us to recognize her.

Like a mother we must rail against
(insisting we must break from her to be our precious selves apart,
still indebted for our birth,
for her dark ontogenetic soil)
she smiles on our discomfort at her embrace,
settles for a chaste kiss on the cheek.

Knowing more than we
She needs no ornament,
Her face holds no particular expression
Not because she's cold or disapproving,
but because she's simply a mirror that strips us of our masks
she pierces our heart
teaches us another way to greet all life with equal love.

Her sharp tongue may goad us to journey in strange lands
But like a mother she comforts our hurts
Even when we are outraged at the pain
constantly offers us her strong hands and soft lap.

Beyond all our efforts to comprehend her
Beyond all our efforts to bargain and come to terms
She does not bide her time nor plan nor remember
she does not come for us at the end
but is always there for us,
sufficiently herself.

A frightening refuge an effortless challenge
reminding us our home is always here

the yeasty smell of baking bread
the mysterious solidity of black, slick ice
playing with her husband the sun to jointly engender a permanent wind
blowing over the whole world
making the sea restless
smoothing the land's uneven hills.

Like a mother death takes our fear of disappearance
Plays peek-a-boo with our fright
Greets our startled laughter with welcome, sparkling eyes.

Chapter 7

Actualizing the Fundamental Point

1

As all things are buddha-dharma, there is delusion and real-
ization, practice, and birth and death, and there are buddhas and
sentient beings.

Each of us belongs. We are always, every moment, completely and uniquely ourselves: Laughing or crying, sleeping or alert, we have ten fingers and ten toes, each with its unique bones and muscles, each pointing in a slightly different direction. Clients and therapists sit in different chairs and face myriad things from varied angles. Everything, everyone is a teacher, an apprentice, a song. Each instant we present ourselves to the world and the world presents itself to us in infinite variety.

As the myriad things are without an abiding self, there is no
delusion, no realization, no buddha, no sentient beings, no birth
and death.

Insert a ring into some soapy water, blow on it, and a bubble appears: Sunlight forms a glistening rainbow on the bubble's thin surface. Our lives are like this.

Rainbows cannot be grasped; they move along with us. In rainbows there is no color separate from sunlight and mist, no sunlight and mist separate from color. We are rainbows dependent on special conditions in order to be ourselves:

We have no existence separate from those defining conditions, which are constantly changing. We divide the rainbow by naming its colors, but red, yellow, orange, green, blue, indigo, violet don't exist: These are colorful labels, not colors themselves.

We search for our self in our component colors. We think our thoughts are important. We feel our feelings are ourselves. We sense the solidity of our sensations. We experience the urgency of our urges and cling to the awareness of being conscious. Each of these fragments wants to assert the primacy of its being; each lays claim to being the core of our existence.

But none of these abides as a constant fundament. Thoughts are just thoughts. Feelings are just feelings. Sensations are just sensations. Impulses are just impulses. Consciousness is just consciousness. Each arises in response to something that is arising in response to something else. Each appears in concert with all the others, dancing with each other and the world, depending on its surroundings to give it shape.

We and the world arise together, linked by mutual need and love: We cannot exist alone. Client and therapist give up their names as they dance with each other and manifest themselves sometimes as a blossoming plant in the deep earth, sometimes as a shooting star in the vast heavens.

> *The buddha way is, basically, leaping clear of the many and*
> *the one; thus there are birth and death, delusion and realization,*
> *sentient beings and buddhas.*

We have an open invitation to embrace it all, to swim in this world in all its particular varieties and all its vast, embracing infinity. Each of our clients is unique and universal; every session of sitting zazen is the same complete surprise; our lover's embrace is each time completely different, and intimately familiar.

Psychotherapeutic and Zen practice are about not getting caught in separateness or merging, about cooking our whole life when we chop this particular carrot. Psychotherapy and Zen help us find the wisdom in what we thought was our foolishness and the foolishness in what we thought was our wisdom. Psychotherapy and Zen are about letting ourselves die so that we can emerge from our cocoons to live in some new, unanticipated but not wholly unfamiliar form.

Practice is dancing, tracing out the steps that bridge delusion and realization, no delusion and no realization. Practice is the interplay of treating our client for a problem and appreciating our client for what she or he is. In the dance of practice we find our balance between seeing ourselves as separate from our clients and seeing that we and our clients are one: We discover our individual selves through our common roots.

> *Yet in attachment blossoms fall, and in aversion weeds spread.*

Sometimes when we are dancing we say to ourselves: "This is great! I wish it could go on forever!" Fearing the music will stop, we clutch at our partner and they tighten up; the movement of the flowing dance becomes a desperate attempt to force time to stand still. Instead of losing ourselves in the rhythm, we lose the rhythm.

Sometimes when we are dancing we decide we don't like our partner, or we don't like ourselves; we judge the music to be too slow or too fast, too sharp or too flat. Then the dance becomes an ordeal, something we must either bear with, escape from, or destroy.

As soon as we try to hold on tight and attach to ourselves the objects of our love or desire, they slip away from us; as soon as we try to avoid what we most fear, we shackle ourselves with the ball and chain of aversion. Phobic clients are prisoners not to their fears, but to the avoidance of their fears; depressed clients mourning a disappointment are prisoners not to their dashed hopes, but to their attachment to their forlorn yearning. As insomniacs we suffer not from sleep deprivation but from our hope Morpheus will render us unconscious and help us avoid the terror of being wakeful in the deep darkness of our night.

I write this in the early hours of the morning, having woken up with a reaction to some medication I took.

I wanted to reject my agitation and go back to bed; I didn't want to have tachycardia and racing thoughts. I wanted to run after sleep and grasp the peacefulness of slumber. Of course, the more I chased sleep and ran from insomnia, the more I became tied up in knots.

Finally I got up, sat down, and did zazen for an hour. The misery of agitation and the sad yearning for peace came together: Sitting settled down in the midst of both. As a space cleared, agitation became energy; wakefulness became opportunity; yearning for peace became calm acceptance of things being the way It is. Aitken Roshi expresses it:

> When wakeful at two in the morning
> I vow with all beings
> to light incense and sit on my cushion—
> it's time that I really wake up.[1]

2

To carry yourself forward and experience myriad things is delusion. That myriad things come forth and experience themselves is awakening.

We want to wake up, but we're all full of ourselves. Psychotherapy runs the danger of having us focus overmuch on carrying ourselves forward. When we're preoccupied with how *I* feel, with what *I* want, with what *I* hope for and fear, we restrict our field of vision. We do this not necessarily in grand acts of selfishness, but by thoughtlessly sleepwalking through the details of our lives.

When we throw a tea bag into some hot water to grab its caffeine, if we are using the tea just to satisfy our need for alertness and do not allow the tea to come forth itself, we won't truly wake up to appreciate the experience. When we brew a cup of tea mindfully, heating the cup first, listening to the sound of the water bubbling, pouring piping hot water over the tea leaves to help them release their flavor to the brew, we recognize that we, tea, cup, and water all realize our own existence through each other. Then when we sip the tea, we can taste it and awaken with each other.

What's true of tea is true of husbands, wives, clients and therapists, children, dogs, Zen students, the clothes we wear and the air we breathe. If we use them rather than cherish them, we will miss out on our lives. If psychotherapy is overly preoccupied with being too useful, it can transmit the idea that not just therapists but also clients and employers, lovers and enemies, trees and flowers must be useful things.

If we are full with use, we can easily feel used up. If there is no-thing useful about Zen or psychotherapy we have space to realize how our self and the self of every person, leaf, and teacup is always coming forth. Then when we open our eyes, we see the world springing forth to greet us as we greet it.

Hello. Hello. Hello.

> *Those who have great realization of delusion are buddhas; those who are greatly deluded about realization are sentient beings. Further, there are those who continue realizing beyond realization, who are in delusion throughout delusion.*

When we are sure we know what are we seeing, we blind ourselves. When I think I've "got it together," that I know myself and know the people around me, I can delude myself greatly.

As a therapist I may think my studies have given me knowledge about people: that I can understand a client because his or her symptoms seem similar to something I read in a book; that helping a client involves doling out advice and providing expertise. As a husband, I may feel certain that because I've seen my wife's reactions to life over the course of twenty years, I can know what she'll feel in certain situations. I may mistake the false security of the lie that we can always respond to each other in predictable ways for the riskier mysteries of true intimacy with its unpredictable, constant changes.

If I feel I know things I stand in danger of exploring no further, of excluding what doesn't fit, of insulating myself against surprise. Thinking I am open and enlightened, knowledgeable and wise, is rank ignorance and delusion. If I feel I don't need to pay attention to the obstacles I place between myself and my clients, lovers, and the world, I reinforce the ruts of my preconceptions and expectations.

When I realize that I don't know anything, that I *can't* know any thing completely, when I realize that I am always inevitably swimming through a sea of my expectations and filters, I can wake up. I can be aware of my unawareness; I can befriend my illiteracy and tutor it kindly. I can smile at the illusions in which I wrap myself, accept them and let them go. Then I am constantly rediscovering myself, my clients, and the whole world anew each moment. This is practice.

> *When buddhas are truly buddhas they do not necessarily notice that they are buddhas. However, they are actualized buddhas, who go on actualizing buddhas.*

A couple came to me one day for their first session of psychotherapy. It subsequently turned out that they had a rather typical pattern: When the husband didn't help out around the house, his wife felt she was left holding the bag and became angry. She would then demand that he do his chores in a way he felt was demeaning, to which he then responded by digging in his heels.

When I asked what brought them to the clinic, however, they were quite apologetic to me and annoyed with themselves because, although they knew they needed couples' counseling, they said that for the past two weeks things had been going better. Although they had gotten to the point of wanting a divorce because of their constant arguing, for the past two weeks they hadn't had any major blow-ups.

I asked them what had happened. Alhough neither of them had previously articulated it to each other, or even to themselves, this is what they told me:

The husband had begun to recognize how much effort it cost his wife to work at a job, come home, and deal with the house and their child. He saw the pain she was in, struggling with depression, avoiding taking an antidepressant so she could continue to nurse their young child. So recently, instead of backing off, he began to do some things for her without waiting for her to ask. He decided even if she criticized and scolded him, he would help her out as best he could.

Meanwhile, the wife realized she had been talking down to her husband and had been carping at him for small things. She understood that he worked long hours at his job, and that he was tired when he came home. She recognized that because of his attention-deficit disorder (undiagnosed until he was an adult) he had always felt somewhat insecure and was sensitive to criticism.

She determined that rather than get angry when she saw some task undone, when she needed something from him she would calm herself down and ask nicely. Instead of focusing on what he didn't do and criticize, she started to express her appreciation for whatever efforts he did make. She decided that even if he pulled back or failed to do some of the things she wanted, she would help him out by expressing her affection for him as much as she could.

Here in the therapist's office: Buddha actualizing Buddha.

3

> *When you see forms or hear sounds fully engaging body-and-mind, you grasp things directly. Unlike things and their reflections in the mirror, and unlike the moon and its reflection in the water, when one side is illuminated the other side is dark.*

If I engage with my clients through the reflections of cogitative musing, I meet them indirectly, through a glass darkly; the conceptual structures we erect to filter our immediate experience throw up veils between our selves and each other. Then we run the risk that what appears in the mirror will be the mists and shadows of imagination. But when we can only imagine our clients, we can only imagine ourselves.

Responding to someone by fully engaging body and mind means dropping body and mind: Grasping something directly involves letting go of ourselves and becoming the thing we thought to grasp at. Listening and talking with a client, if we bring full sincerity to the task and put our selves aside we listen with our eyes, our thighs, our toes, our spine; clients' lamentations and crows are apprehended through open pores until my breath moves with your sighs and my eyes twinkle at your chuckles. Touching each other, we resonate to each others' music, responding with our ears, our hands, our teeth, our breath, our heart.

When we engage fully, without reflection or conception, everything is just as it is, complete. When the client who slashed her wrists holds out her hands, her scars speak to us of the music of despair: When the same client turns in her chair, the light catches her long pianist's fingers. When she is slashing her wrists, she is not playing the piano; when she is playing the piano, she is not slashing her wrists. She is completely herself in each activity but need not be caught defining herself by only one of them. She need only face the ancient mirror of her true self, which reflects everything completely.

When *everything* is continuously reflected and nothing remains, there is no reflection or deception: no thing added, no thing gained. Just complete, ongoing activity. The bright mirror reflects only the face that appears to it: the clear mirror reflects clarity. When the two mirrors face each other, no thing appears and no thing is left out.[2]

When client and therapist come forth in this way, they appear fully. Appearing fully means that whatever is expressed at the time is completely itself. Tears are salty, laughter is infectious. What's there is there. When the client cries, it is just crying; there is no thing other than crying in the entire universe. Even the memory of laughter is obliterated. When sorrow is completely illuminated, happiness is dark.

This being so, the client's crying cannot be a signal for anything else. A kiss is just a kiss, a sigh is just a sigh: Time does not go by but is *realized* as the client's and therapist's entire lives rise up complete each moment. If the client's tears fill the whole universe client, therapist, and tears disappear in the pristine clarity of pure experience; there is no suffering and no release from suffering. In another moment, client and therapist smile, and another universe appears.

Within each session of psychotherapy we are born, live, and die countless times. Fully engaging body and mind, client and therapist are constantly realizing universes beyond universes in each word, each sigh, each smile.

To study the buddha way is to study the self. To study the self
is to forget the self. To forget the self is to be actualized by myriad
things. When actualized by myriad things, your body and mind as
well as the bodies and minds of others drop away. No trace of
realization remains, and this no-trace continues endlessly.

In psychotherapy we often talk about finding our selves; in Zen we often talk about forgetting our selves. The two are flip sides of a coin but are not always what they seem. A client may get lost in a self-effacement that suppresses and hides her self, rather than forgetting and finding her self. A Zen student may isolate himself in an arrogant humility whose purported emptiness does not take account of the needs of other people in his life.

"If we do not see ourselves we are not capable of seeing others.... If we cannot see others we cannot see ourselves."[3] As I study myself studying myself studying others, however, sometimes I get confused. In the midst of the process of merging and separating sometimes I feel like I'm losing track, so I stop to ask (even though I'm not sure who I'm asking): What's going on here? Who is who?

In our activity, we *are*. But our activity cannot take place in isolation. In our activity together we discover who we are; we discover I am that I am. Thus, *we* are *who*. We are *who* we are.

But we are constantly running from who we are. We have troubles accepting I am that I am, so we fall into confusion and doubt; we shrink from our lives and fear our deaths.

Shirley came to me feeling chronically anxious and depressed. She had some mild obsessional symptoms, low-grade dysthymia, and difficulties letting go of some old hurts in her marriage. She talked about these issues for a while, then gradually revealed her hidden secret, the one that really shamed her: She confessed she was tormented by the idea of death. She experienced panic attacks whenever she thought of dying. She remembered lying awake in bed at night in her room even as a little girl, thinking of death, feeling paralyzed with terror. She was sure that this meant she was crazy.

My mother, when she was a little girl, heard someone say that "the good die young," so she lay awake in bed each night saying every curse word she could think of, hoping to avoid being good, hoping not to die. I thought of her fright, and the fears that arose during my own and my loved ones' brushes with death, and tried to engage Shirley in the common humanity of our fears, hoping she would feel less isolated. But Shirley continued to insist that her fear of death was a mark of some twisted inadequacy, an indicator that something was wrong with her.

She decided she wanted to take an antidepressant medicine and attend a group for dealing with panic attacks. She benefited from both treatments and was more able to keep her anxiety within manageable limits. But her fear of death remained a constant undercurrent running through her life. She said she couldn't enjoy anything fully, because in the midst of her enjoyment, she would say to herself: "But this won't last. I'm going to die. What good is it?"

I thought of the Buddhist saying, "Knowing the glass will break, I handle it carefully and enjoy it fully." Shirley made clear that for her the fragile, transitory nature of the glass was a source of constant grief. I considered offering various Buddhist meditation techniques devoted to confronting impermanence and death, and various psychotherapeutic desensitization methods. But Shirley had no interest in pursuing these; she was only concerned about how her preoccupation with the issue of death—this universal question that confronts us all—was another sign of her pathology.

So we pursued her concerns. We poked around for some unconscious or psychodynamic meaning to her fears but got nowhere. As we continued our conversation each of us often was surprised and flummoxed by the other's reactions, to the point at which we each felt unclear about where our discussion was going; yet there was a sense of intimacy as we both became absorbed in the dialogue.

Finally I didn't know what to do, except to consider the possibility that her fear of death was a form of studying the self. I asked her: "Is it possible your fear of death is a signal? Could some part of you be asking you to pay attention to something?"

She was a bit nonplused. This was a strange idea. What could her fear of death possibly be saying to her?

"Well," I said, "maybe it's a way of asking yourself if your life is meaningful and satisfying? Maybe it's a way of asking you to look at your life and live it in a way so that when you do die, you'll be able to look back and say, 'That was a good life.' What do you think would happen if every time you started to think about fearing death you asked yourself, 'What's the meaning of my life?'"

She didn't resonate to this at all. She said it didn't make sense for her to explore the meaning of her life. In a matter of fact, almost cheerful way, she stated it was obvious that *her* life couldn't be meaningful, because she was just an insignificant librarian with crazy ideas.

She didn't seem upset about this. She had clearly been brought up to be sweet but self-effacing, modest to the point of invisibility. It seemed that talking about the issue of the meaning of her life was not threatening, but simply so peculiar that it was as if I were speaking to her in a foreign language. I started to wonder whether I was inappropriately posing to Shirley a philosophical or moral dilemma that interested me but was irrelevant to her. I tried taking a slightly different tack:

"Maybe your fear of death isn't a question about meaning, but about who you really are. What do you think would happen if each time you felt fear of death you said to yourself: 'Who am I?'"

Shirley replied, "But I know who I am. I'm a thirty-nine-year-old mousy, anxious, white lady."

I asked, "Are you sure that's who you are? There's millions of thirty-nine-year-old anxious white women. What makes you you? How do you know who you are?"

She replied, "This is very confusing. I'm a librarian. I like to know where everything is, I can put a number to everything and assign it to its place."

I asked, "Is that the essence of what being a librarian is about?"

She paused. "Well, no... that's part of it. But it's really about sharing knowledge with others."

I was very interested in her statement. I wondered what it would mean to Shirley if who she was had something to do with sharing knowledge with others. By the end of the session, Shirley told me she felt somewhat confused but intrigued.

As we interacted with each other, Shirley and I became absorbed in studying each other; immersed in the dialogue, at times we started to forget about ourselves, find each other, and find ourselves. In our discussion, we shared our knowing and our not-knowing. If we are attached to either knowledge or not-knowing, this is ignorance. If we are open but unattached to both knowledge and not-knowing, this stimulates a sense of wonder and discovery.

Death is the ultimate expression of our not-knowing. I think Shirley's fear of death arose in part because, in thinking about the cessation of her existence, her self-consciousness reasserted itself but in a morbid form: She felt that she had no special place in the chain of being. I think it was quite encouraging that something in Shirley rebelled against extending her self-effacement this far, even if it had to express itself in the form of fear. In denying and hiding her self, Shirley could not see how she was actualized by the myriad things. In this position death becomes a frightening annihilation, a disappearance rather than a transformation. The fact is, every being has its own place from which it interacts with all being.

If we feel isolated from the chain of being, life and death seem chasms apart. In reality, however, life is just a way of realizing ourselves by remembering ourselves; death is just a way of realizing ourselves by forgetting ourselves. Each forms a mirror for the other to study itself. We find our place each moment by dying to one moment and waking up to another.

If we neither shrink from our lives nor fear our deaths, we immerse our selves completely in our activity and forget our selves. If we forget ourselves, we leave room to be actualized by myriad things. "Those who get the message of the lute forget its strings."[4] The lute player becomes the lute and is actualized in notes forming melodies. Working at her job in the library, when Shirley is absorbed reading a novel, she becomes a book; when she helps someone research a topic, she becomes a host for knowledge and knowledge seekers. Like all of us, Shirley is a book, but not just a book: She is also a whole library.

Libraries are not inert stone walls filled with collections of volumes: Because people and books pass in and out, libraries are fields for the continual re-circulation of wonder. If a library is so self-effacing it does not acknowledge its self as a library, it will stop retiring outdated books from its stacks and fail to bring in new works. It will cease to exist as a library and instead become, at best, a museum. On the other hand, if a library is self-aggrandizing and thinks of itself as something special, it will become inaccessible: As a repository for valuable things, it will place metal detectors at the entrances and lock the doors at night.

If the library is neither self-effacing nor self-promoting, if it studies itself by forgetting itself, it finds itself in the activity of sharing. Then its doors are always open; it becomes an open book. Readers come and go freely, texts and records circulate. Then even if the library's shelves and walls are demolished to make way for a K-Mart, even if its books are taken away and its students forced to wander in other realms, having shared itself the library goes on being shared. Even if it dies, the library finds itself disseminated over and over, forever in all directions.

5

When you first seek dharma, you imagine you are far away
from its environs. But dharma is already correctly transmitted; you
are immediately your original self.

When we seek the dharma, we are investigating

"the Buddhist teaching of a thousand sutras and the Bodhisattva teaching of ten thousand scriptures: 'Who are you and where are you from?'"[5]

When we study this question, searching for our true selves, we may feel we need a library in which to study. We sometimes forget we *are* the library of our self, and that our research is a re-searching.

Clients go to psychotherapy and Zen students go to Zendos hoping to find a special place where they can meet their selves. We tend to think our quest requires a journey to some other place than where we are, that we need to meet some other person than who we are. We have troubles seeing that every moment, every place we are immediately our original self.

When we are upset we say, "I'm not myself." At such times we lose sight of who we are because, unable to embrace our wholeness, we get caught in a partial view: Lost in the woods, we see only trees. Feeling depressed, the whole world seems to be sadness far from any prospect of joy. Sick with cancer, our body seems immersed in dying far removed from any prospect of life; abandoned by our lover, we feel we are unlovable far from any prospect of intimacy.

Life gets under our skin. If we have a splinter in our finger and put our hand up in front of our eyes to take it out, our eyes see only the splinter and the hand. As therapists we invite our clients to tell us of their splintered hurts, to share the pain of fragmentation. Yet at the same time, we have to be careful not to mistake the injured hand for the whole world. Clients coming to psychotherapy usually can see only the splinters of their selves; in the intensity of clients' pain and frustration, both clients and therapists may feel tempted to cut off the offending hand. We wish to eliminate our pain, eradicate our imperfections, cure our symptoms.

This will not work: The world includes our hurting hand as surely as it includes splinters. All our human frailties are also who we are. We are not just our symptoms, but neither can we exist apart from them. Our true nature includes our foolishness and our ignorance along with our wisdom and our realization. In fact, it is their interplay that constitutes our existence so that we are always immediately ourselves.

The truth of our lives is not destroyed by our false starts; in fact, the right ways of living can only be discovered through recognizing our wrong turns and retracing our steps. The desire for wholeness that motivates clients to seek therapy springs up along with their pain. Therapy is a transmission of self to self that takes place not in a distant discourse but as an intimate intercourse. Zen practice is not an uncovering of our original nature but a rediscovery of our natural origins, a realization that all our being is interbeing.

The connectedness of interbeing means that our identity is not an essence obscured by an illusion; a mountain is not a rock obscured by trees or a ridge hidden under snow. All the pieces of our lives arise together.

> All my life false and real, right and wrong tangled.
> Playing with the moon, ridiculing wind, listening to birds...
> Many years wasted seeing the mountain covered with snow.
> This winter I suddenly realize snow makes a mountain.[6]

6

When you ride in a boat and watch the shore, you might assume that the shore is moving. But when you keep your eyes closely on the boat, you can see that the boat moves. Similarly, if you examine the myriad things with a confused body and mind you might suppose that your mind and nature are permanent. When you practice intimately and return to where you are, it will be clear that nothing at all has unchanging self.

By virtue of its height, the mountain's cool air attracts clouds and catches the snow from the ocean. The snows pile up: Glaciers carve the cliffs and valleys of the mountain's flanks. The heavy ice of our suffering sculpts the Yosemite of our souls. This interdependence is the truth of all existence, but we often have difficulties seeing It and grasp instead at the bits and pieces of things.

We think snow melts but the mountain stays solid, but the snow's freezing cracks boulders and the spring runoff erodes the granite bed. Although in the absolute sense everything is always moving, from the relative standpoint when one thing moves, something else stays still. So in order to study ourselves we stop what we're doing: We meditate, or go to a therapy session, in an effort to step out of the stream of our lives so that we can see what's going on. We want to take a break, to get some perspective so that we're not just carried along by the currents.

As a useful first step in both psychotherapy and Zen practice we need to step back: We need to pay attention, study ourselves, observe ourselves. As we do this we sometimes get the impression that we can "have" a dispassionate observer within us who stands still, untouched by the thoughts/feelings/sensations/modes of consciousness that are constantly moving. Thinking "I" can stand apart and get a handle on at least the movement of "my" inner life, I try to pin down the schemas and conditioned habits that seem to rule me in an effort to be free of them. Perhaps I label my thoughts in mindfulness meditation or answer back my irrational thinking in cognitive therapy.

But as I go deeper—perhaps as I begin to observe myself observing—I start to realize that "I" cannot take control of "me," because no matter how much I try to step aside, I am always immersed in the stream of my life.

Fayan asked Elder Jiao,"Did you come by boat or by land?"
Jiao said, "By boat."
Fayan said, "Where is the boat?"
Jiao said, "The boat is on the river."[7]

Our minds and bodies provide a boat for us on the moving river of our living and dying. Not only is the river always flowing: The boat is too. Any action we take in our life is like tossing a ball on swift-flowing water:

A monk asked T'ou Tzu, "What is the meaning of 'Tossing a ball on swift-flowing water?'"
T'ou Tzu said,
"Moment to moment, nonstop flow."[8]

Our lives are nonstop flow, so we also must be constantly flowing. Sailing our boat, we are always making small adjustments. We must frequently trim our sails and turn our rudder, while all the time we are rocking up and down, back and forth on the waves. The sails and rudder, the hand that adjusts them, the water that they cleave, all move. If we just point ourselves in one direction, say, "This is who I am," and see everything in our life from the standpoint of an illusory, unchanging self-identity—one independent of other people and separate from the activities of our life—then we are riding in the boat and watching the shore move.

As therapists we like to think of ourselves, or at least the therapeutic container, as a well-ballasted yacht that is solidly anchored, providing a refuge for our client's fragile skiff. If we think we remain still while the shore of our client moves, however, we'll fail to notice how when we ask a client a question, or even when we shift position in our chair, the therapy-craft shifts under us. Therapist and client are in the same boat, and neither can remain unmoved when the deck rolls in the waves.

Constant flow: The boat is always moving, the water is moving, and the shore is always moving. Each has its own flow and responds to and influences the others'. The earth spins on its axis as it hurtles through space, cycling through light and darkness; the crust of the planet expands in sunlight and contracts in the cool of the night. From the standpoint of a sailor, the shore is a goal to be reached, a harbor of stability. The moon, however, casts its light down to a coastline eaten by waves as it rotates with its world. Earth, moon, wind, and light are all moving. The stars circle overhead, and their dance provides an opportunity for navigation.

As therapists we strive to be a pure lake in which our client, bending down, may see the purity of his own reflection. Nonetheless, there are constant currents in the depths of the lake, companions to gentle ripples on the surface. If the lake is still and frozen, it assumes a milky-white opaqueness; the client may be able to skate across it but looking down sees nothing. Under a firmament of stars on a warm summer night, caressed by a gentle breeze, a client may venture into the lake or perhaps throw in a stone and be wet through by the splash. Water and watcher both change, each imbued by the other.

The stone the client throws into the lake sinks to the bottom and joins the lakebed. Is the lakebed separate from the lake, the stone, the thrower, the breeze, the stars?

7

> *Firewood becomes ash, and it does not become firewood again. Yet, do not suppose that the ash is future and the firewood past. You should understand that firewood abides in the phenomenal expression of firewood, which fully includes past and future and is independent of past and future. Ash abides in the phenomenal expression of ash, which fully includes future and past. Just as firewood does not become firewood again after it is ash, you do not return to birth after death.*

Under the heat of the sun, a lake dries up and becomes a meadow. A meadow fills up with trees and becomes a forest. A forest goes up in flames and seeds are flung forth to sprout anew. Our whole life takes place through particular phenomenal expressions, each a phase of being that at all times is intimately connected with all other beings.

At the same time, each phenomenal expression is each moment purely itself. When the lake is a lake, we don't lie down on its grassy bed, even though the grassy bed is there. Once the lake turns into a meadow, we don't need a bathing suit to traverse it, even though there is water in every blade of grass.

Each moment we express our whole life, but only as we are that moment. Alhough we are constantly growing and changing, sometimes the images we hold of ourselves lag behind; then sometimes it takes a moment of realization to come back to where we are now.

Once upon a time Joan had been a tortured teenager, an anorexic dancer. Now she enjoyed being a mother, a wife, and a dance teacher. Recently she had felt she was getting a little bit lost in her family roles, doing things mostly for others. So she decided to do something special for herself and enrolled in a dance class.

At her first class, Joan looked around and saw that most of the other class members were girls in their late teens, most of whom had the thin bodies of adolescents driven by their inner demons into starving themselves. Joan looked at her own body and saw a slim dancer's body, but it was clearly the body of a mature thirty-two-year-old mother, not the body of a teenager. For a moment Joan felt insecure about how she looked; as she caught herself comparing her body to these young girls', she worried briefly whether she'd be drawn back into anorexia. Then she relaxed. She said, "I realized I feel happy with myself as I am."

I just repeated back her statement—"I'm happy as I am"—and we took joy in sharing her ability to openly accept herself, even though her body was no longer that of an ideal dancer or dream-like model.

Out of curiosity, I asked her: "What's it like to enjoy being a real woman in a woman's real body?"

She at first dismissed this as a rather ordinary truism of no consequence, saying matter-of-factly that her body had changed because, "I'm a woman now, not a girl." Then she stopped, somewhat startled. She had heard what she herself said and repeated it back to herself, with increasing awareness: "I *am* a woman, not a girl... "

We discussed how this would make a difference when she dealt with some family-of-origin issues about which she was concerned. She realized that she would be speaking to her parents not as a teenager, but as an adult. She would be talking to her mother not just as a daughter, but also as a mother. We had a nice discussion about mothers, mother-in-laws, the community of women, and the social messages that she and all women grapple with.

Joan had changed; even when she revisited an old way of being, she did so from a new perspective. We can't step into the same stream twice. However much our society's advertising promises that skin creams will bring back the complexion of youth, the fact is that women don't turn into girls. What may be less obvious is that girls also don't turn into women.

Like the forest, a child contains the seeds of future growth: But when she is playing kickball, a little girl is just a little girl playing kickball. Her mother may revisit her childhood playground, but even if she plays kickball, she'll do so with a woman's legs. An elderly woman may watch her daughter and granddaughter playing on the same field and perceive their relationship clearly through her experienced eyes, however dim her vision.

A little girl is not a half-grown adult, but a little girl. An adult woman is not half-child, half-crone. An old woman is not a decayed version of a little girl, but a mature matriarch. Girls, women, and wise crones are all temporary states, each complete in and of itself. We can't go back, but we also can't go forward. At every age, we are who we are, where we are, when we are.

Each instant we are identifiably ourselves, displaying the unpolished finish of our unfinished business. If we were finally finished, we would be something other than the reality we are: constant change that neither comes nor goes but blooms expressively each moment.

> *This being so, it is an established way in buddha-dharma to deny that birth turns into death. Accordingly, birth is understood as no-birth. It is an unshakable teaching in Buddha's discourse that death does not turn into birth. Accordingly, death is understood as no-death.*
>
> *Birth is an expression complete this moment. Death is an expression complete this moment. They are like winter and spring. You do not call winter the beginning of spring, nor summer the end of spring.*

Time does not flow from past to future. If we are caught in that perception, it is like being on a train and thinking that the telephone poles are moving. We do not move through time, but in our moment-by-moment existence, in our constant changing, we express time. As we respond to each moment, our facial expression changes: Expressing ourselves, we give time a human face.

When our expressions of our self change, we don't turn into something else, we simply are a new person each moment. We can never *change* who we are, but we can *be* ourselves differently each moment, a whole new person in a whole new universe.

We can never go forward or back: There's no place other than here. There is no progress or regression, only constant realization in this moment. If I drive from San Francisco to Yosemite, San Francisco does not turn into Yosemite. Yet the waters of the High Sierra feed the waves of San Francisco Bay in a continuous flow; there is no San Francisco Bay separate from the snow, the rain, the ocean. Still, if I think I am driving *to* and *from* my home in San Francisco and my vacation in Yosemite, remembering one place and anticipating the other I may miss the California poppies blazing orange along the roadway.

Our life's journey is not a linear progression *from* birth *to* death. Each moment of our life is entirely itself. Each moment of our experience has no beginning and no end; it covers the entire universe of our existence. Our lives are always burning fiercely: As fuel and flame meet each other, each flicker of the blaze is all-consuming, no matter what its particular expression. In psychotherapy, when therapist and client meet each other it is like the mountain meeting the river: sometimes an earthquake in spring, sometimes an avalanche in winter; sometimes the ice cracking open a boulder, sometimes the melting of the snow to feed the sparkling stream. Each is complete that moment, needing no purpose or goal to justify its undivided activity. The avalanche isn't trying to move the boulders in the scree: The melting snow isn't trying to turn the pebbles in the stream. Yet the landscape is constantly being transformed.

So in therapy, we do not go from one partial place to another. The first session of a therapy blooms completely as the first session: At that time, if a client is depressed or anxious, that is where they are. We needn't call depression the beginning of happiness, or anxiety the beginning of fearlessness. Nonetheless, if we have clients track their moods hour-by-hour, they will see they fluctuate through all the colors of experience that spring up in response to the wild variety of our life. In the sixth session of a twelve-session therapy, a client is not half-cured and the therapy is not half-baked: We do not call a client's smile the end of sadness, or a client's courage the end of fear. We continue to respond to the moving circumstances of our lives. At the end of a therapy, the last session blooms completely as the last session: Rather than clinging to a cure for life, we practice saying hello when it's time to say hello, saying goodbye when it's time to say goodbye. Letting each moment of each session be itself, we practice letting ourselves be ourselves. Then in a moment therapists and clients meet themselves meeting each other.

We are all just a moment here and a moment there. If we open up and give ourselves fully to our experience, we are constantly dying and being born. At the moment we die, we die completely. At the moment we live, we live completely.

At this moment as you read you are on this page. You can only read the page in front of you. The previous page did not become this page, and even if you turn back a page, on rereading you and it will be different. The second time is the second time, the first is the first.

Therapy takes place one page at a time. We practice our psychotherapy by finding what page we are on, and turning the page. As we do this we appear fully reflected in our activity on each spot, each moment. This is enlightened practice.

8

> *Enlightenment is like the moon reflected on the water. The moon does not get wet, nor is the water broken. Although its light is wide and great, the moon is reflected even in a puddle an inch wide. The whole moon and the entire sky are reflected in dewdrops on the grass, or even in one drop of water.*
>
> *Enlightenment does not divide you, just as the moon does not break the water. You cannot hinder enlightenment, just as a drop of water does not hinder the moon in the sky.*
>
> *The depth of the drop is the height of the moon. Each reflection, however long or short its duration, manifests the vastness of the dewdrop, and realizes the limitlessness of the moonlight in the sky.*

Looking into each other's eyes, we see not just ourselves: We see our retina looking back at us, holding the image of ourself seeing ourself in the other, ad infinitum. The tiny circle of the other person's retina is enough to show us a cascade of entire universes.

In reflecting each other, we find ourselves and lose ourselves. In order to get our bearings, sometimes we draw the lines that define you and me, client and therapist, healthy and sick, delusion and enlightenment. At this point, however, the lines we draw sometimes seem to divide us and highlight our apparent hindrances.

We look back at our pasts and feel that we were hurt so badly, we cannot possibly love fully. We look at the schedules that seem to outline our future and feel we cannot possibly find enough time to have a meaningful psychotherapy. We look at the diagnoses that are supposed to chart the possibilities of interpersonal relatedness and feel we cannot reach a client across the boundaries of a personality disorder.

In all this we mistake the map for the territory; we confuse the moon in the water with the moon itself. The fact is that regardless of our thoughts about the matter, if we put our hand in the water, we get completely wet; if we stand on the bank of the lake, our reflection in the water and our shadow on the shore are both full expressions of moonlight. Each reflection is complete enlightenment.

Enlightenment is nothing special but a simple reality: As we respond to and reflect all around us, we show our nature. In realizing the client, the nature of the therapy manifests itself: soothing or stimulating, plumbing the depths of feeling or exploring the surfaces of life's unexplored territories. In reflecting the moon, the nature of the water manifests itself: shallow or deep, choppy or smooth. Just as the moon is reflected in a drop of water or a mile-long lake, so both therapist and client appear fully as they meet, whether it be in a single session or a five-year analysis. Each form of the lake is a phase of the moon; each moment of the therapy is a season of our life.

Our life takes place under a sky that does not get in the way of either limitless light or boundless dark. In the dark, stars appear; in light, we can see landscapes of necessary action.

9

When dharma does not fill your whole body and mind, you think it is already sufficient. When dharma fills your body and mind, you understand that something is missing.

When I passed the psychology licensing exams, I thought my training was sufficient.

I thought at least I knew what I did not know, that within the areas in which I specialized my expertise sufficed. But my clients wouldn't say the lines assigned to them by the textbooks and treatment manuals I had studied. A man I treated with systematic desensitization for a phobia insisted on talking about his childhood. A woman I treated for a post–traumatic stress disorder did not review the story of her trauma but brought a phonograph player to her sessions and danced. Transference interpretations often brought neither insight nor resistance, but only polite disbelief; strategic paradoxes were defused by common sense.

Secretly, I began to doubt myself and feel I was an incompetent therapist.

When I first started going to Berkeley Zen Center, I thought my prior ten years of mostly solitary Zen practice were sufficient.

I thought I'd solved a few koans and knew how to sit unmoving and calm. Practicing with other people, however, I was disconcerted when I entered a period in which meditation led not to serenity but to intrusive memories of childhood injuries and waves of depression and anxiety. Searching for sudden, instant enlightenment, I was dismayed to hear Uchiyama-roshi say, "I tell everyone who comes to study with me, 'Sit zazen for ten years,' because nobody would study with me if I told them, 'Sit zazen for 20 years.'"

Secretly, I began to doubt myself and feel that if ten years was not sufficient, twenty years would not be enough for me to realize enlightenment.

When I became a father, I was insecure. But I hoped that the combination of a good relationship with my wife, a library of books on child-rearing, and well-intentioned love for my daughters would suffice me as a parent and allow me to act as guide for my children.

> I found instead I rarely knew what to do myself, let alone how to guide my children. I didn't know how to respond when, coming home to greet my two-year-old daughter, she would run down the street smiling and calling my name, holding out her hands to me as I knelt down to give her a hug, but then stop two feet away from me and refuse to come any closer. After work I felt emotionally drained and irritable; I had troubles summoning the smiles and laughter I wished to give in response to the love my daughters offered and the attention they demanded. In the face of their tears and tantrums I would grin uncomfortably from anxiety, rather than react calmly with the discipline or comfort I thought the situation called for.
> Secretly, I began to doubt myself and feel inadequate as a father.

My doubts came from feeling that I was missing something. All along the way, however, my clients, family, and Zen practice kept giving me clues. My clients did not need a technically perfect therapist, but one who could respond to them from an acceptance of his own imperfections. My daughters did not need a guide so much as someone who could support their beginners' minds by cultivating his own curiosity, learning to parent just by being interested in their discoveries rather than passing on his own. My Zen teachers would remind me that when I didn't know where my pilgrimage was heading, not-knowing was nearest. What I was missing was being able to feel comfortable with my incompleteness.

Something is always missing. So long as that frightens me, I will be seeking to fill the gap with some answer, some doctrine. Then my uncertainty and yearning leaves me prey to people who claim they have the Answer: political tyrants, dogmatic religious fundamentalists, and therapists who market themselves with false hopes of fashionable cures. All of them ask me to believe in them, but clinging to beliefs is a good way to lose faith. Faith arises when we don't know what to do, when we don't know what to expect, when we don't know what to believe.

Faith is founded in our realization that our completeness lies in our incompleteness, that our insufficiency creates the field on which we actualize our selves. If I feel self-sufficient as a therapist, Zen student, parent, or lover, I may have the illusion that I can realize my identity without the relationships that actualize that identity. I may forget that I cannot be a therapist without a client, I cannot be a Zen student without a sangha, I cannot be a parent without children, and I cannot be a lover without a beloved.

We are all incomplete. There is a gap between me and my self, between me and your self, between me and the world's self. Faced by the gap, we call to each other and listen not for the Answer, but for the pure sound beyond ourself that our selves respond to. If we feel full of ourselves and self-sufficient, there's no room for the sound to reverberate: We become circumscribed in the bland circles of our certainty.

> *For example, when you sail out in a boat to the middle of an ocean where no land is in sight, and view the four directions, the ocean looks circular, and does not look any other way. But the ocean is neither round nor square; its features are infinite in variety. It is like a palace. It is like a jewel. It only looks circular as far as you can see at that time. All things are like this.*

From a distance, the coastline looks to be a smooth arc. When we actually walk on it, we find there are many nooks and crannies, inlets and promontories.[9] The closer we get, the more detail we see. The closer I get to being a parent the more attention I pay to the variety of ways in which a diaper can be changed and the variety of meanings in my baby's cries. The closer I get to being a Zen student, the more intimate I become with the cushion beneath me, with the varieties of the beings who sit and walk next to me, with the infinite varieties of thoughts, feelings, sensations, consciousnesses that breathe in and out with me.

The closer I get to being a therapist, the more I realize that treatment does not take place in some ideal space but only arises in a particular meeting place on a particular chair, a particular form of chart in which to record the notes of the meeting, a particular person presenting a unique form of the variety of problems that come up in life. Clients' presenting problems often fit a classic diagnosis until we start asking more questions. The more questions we ask, the more individual variations we discover. The client stops being a type and starts to become a human being. This is true of all people and all the objects of the world.

We cannot discover each other, or even ourselves, in prisons whose round walls are constructed of expectant knowledge and whose square cells are erected from the materials of desire. We can only meet in a crenallated palace: Here the irregular shapes of you and me are bricked together into walls; these walls support windows and doors, the openings you and I offer to each other. This palace rests on a deep foundation; the palace's high towers offers lofty overlooks of landscapes whose horizons stretch infinitely far. Approaching the landscape at eye level we discover its specific features, seeing just as much as our eye can see.

> *Though there are many features in the dusty world and the world beyond conditions, you see and understand only what your eye of practice can reach. In order to learn the nature of the myriad things, you must know that although they may look round or square, the other features of oceans and mountains are infinite in variety; whole worlds are there. It is so not only around you, but also directly beneath your feet, or in a drop of water.*

If I only see what I am prepared to see, I may not be able to see either where or who I am. Columbus never saw the New World, but only the Indies he expected; he never realized he was a poor navigator but an excellent explorer. The carpenter looks at a piece of wood and sees a house; the instrument maker looks at a piece of wood and sees a violin. So long as I am attached to a particular view of my self or the world, that view limits my vision.

As therapists we can only see as much of a client at any time as our position allows. So long as we anchor in diagnosis, we will see the client as a personality disorder or a phobia; so long as we anchor in psychodynamics, we will see the client as hopes, wishes, and fears; so long as we anchor in cognitive processes, we will see the client as thoughts, assumptions, and expectations; so long as we anchor in narratives, we will see the client as a series of stories. These are all necessarily incomplete.

So long as we see the client from the standpoint of a therapist looking at a client, he or she will look like a client as far as we, as therapists, can see. When we realize the person right in front of us is a whole world, we discover that the person we thought of as a client is a sculptor and a gardener as well as a parent and a child: She laughs and cries, learns and yearns, drives a car, and teaches the art of birth and death. We discover that the person we thought of as a therapist is a jazz singer and a spy; he smiles and frowns, hikes in the mountains and in awed ignorance gazes at the darkness of an eclipse and the bright tail of a comet.

Cultivating our eye of practice helps us expand our appreciation for the infinite variety of life manifesting itself each moment. Both therapeutic and Zen practice require that we do not stay put in the safe harbors and comfortable berths of our ideas but rather pull anchor and find ourselves on a continual journeying. Sometimes we dream of where our journey will take us, but we can only *see* where we are this moment. Sometimes that means seeing we are in a fog. Sometimes that means seeing the clear cliffs of home. The water slaps the boat: The sound wakes us up, and the spray wets us through completely. The client's litany of rhythmic grief gives way to a sudden laugh: Our conceptions drop away and the world's heart opens up in a moment. Then wherever we are, in fog or sunshine we are home together.

10

A fish swims in the ocean, and no matter how far it swims there is no end to the water. A bird flies in the sky, and no matter how far it flies there is no end to the air. However, the fish and the bird have never left their elements. When their activity is large their field is large. When their need is small their field is small. Thus, each of them totally covers its full range, and each of them totally experiences its realm.

If the bird leaves the air it will die at once. If the fish leaves the water it will die at once.

Know that water is life and air is life. The bird is life and the fish is life. Life must be the bird and life must be the fish.

It is possible to illustrate this with more analogies. Practice,
enlightenment, and people are like this.

Standing in the midst of where we are, our experience covers the total realm of our existence. Sitting in the therapy office, arguing with a lover, strolling by the sea or on a mountain peak our whole body is engaged: Consciousness illuminates whatever it lights upon hearing sounds, seeing sights, smelling smells, tasting tastes, touching sensations, feeling feelings, and thinking thoughts. However out of place we may feel—frightened crossing an emotional bridge, alienated dealing with a difficult workplace, awkward in the formal atmosphere of a Zendo—still we are always in our element. Each place is the field, the ocean, the sky at which our whole life takes place that moment. A pebble in our shoe can become the whole earth on a long hike. A child's smile can become the whole ocean of joy at the gravesite of our father.

All our experience is our life. This field is immense, a whole firmament to explore, but if we are ego-centered, we confine our activity to a narrow range. If I am fired by a client and see only my own frustration, I will not learn anything from my countertransference. If I am meditating and only concerned about my own enlightenment, I will become annoyed at the fidgeting of the enlightened being next to me rather than appreciate how her efforts and sufferings are constantly teaching. If I am going through a divorce and think only of my current loneliness without grappling with my spouse's unhappiness, I won't learn how I held back from the relationship or how I might connect better in the future.

Although our preoccupations with our small personal concerns restrict our activities to a small area, our yearning to be other than we are kills us in countless small deaths. If we find ourselves in the salty sea of our tears, we may not like being a small fish in an ocean of hurt. We wish we could leave our element for another. Faced with sharks and undertows, we imagine we'd prefer the air in which we could fly free as a bird, conveniently forgetting that the sky also houses hawks and downdrafts.

This yearning for something else is like being in a restaurant with a meal in front of me, unhappy about what's on my plate. So I sneak a look at the food the other diners are eating. In the midst of my marriage I envy the sexual freedom of my single friend; in the midst of my parenting I envy the neat house of the childless couple I'm visiting. Sitting in the Zendo on my cushion, I'm sure the person sitting in a chair has less pain. Juggling the demands of brief therapy and managed care, I long to live the life of a clinician who can do "real" long-term psychotherapy in private practice.

This life immediately in front of me, however, is always my private practice. We cannot live somebody else's life or digest another person's food. As soon as I sneak a look at the food on someone else's plate, as soon as I anticipate my next course or compare what I am eating to meals I've had before, I will not enjoy the sunshine in the despised Brussels sprouts sitting on my plate. I'm leaving my element, missing what's right in front of me and dying a little in the process, because I'm missing my life.

> For many years I've had a long commute. I get restless, frustrated, bored. I turn on the car radio and daydream. Then I don't see the ice plants blooming in the center strip or hear the deep thrum of the road singing the tale of each vehicle whose weight it bears. I fail to appreciate the miracles around me.
>
> Early this morning I leave off writing this book and go to wake up my daughter. It's time to prepare for school. Drowsily she wants to tell me her dream of snickerdoodles and strangers. I half-listen, but I want to get back to writing my book. If I don't stop and listen to my daughter, I won't enjoy her smile and her languorous stretch as she wakes up. I'll miss an opportunity to wake up along with her.

We cannot live another place, another time. We cannot live any life other than the one we are experiencing this moment, this place. Sometimes when life presents to us something we don't like we say, "That's not my cup of tea." But this experience right now, bitter or sweet, smooth or rough, is the beverage at hand; if we don't want to miss our lives we need to be able to drink deeply of whatever's in our cup. If we're sad or mad going through a divorce, we are sad or mad going through a divorce. If we feel we're floundering working with a difficult client, that's the kind of fish we are in the choppy sea we're navigating. If we're meditating and our back spasms leave us unbalanced and in pain, we're unbalanced and in pain, feeling like a bird with crippled wings struggling with strong gusts of wind.

Psychotherapy and Zen practice are about recognizing and responding to life however we find it. Then we don't miss our lives.

Practice is about opening up to a universe that includes the fish and the bird, appreciating the deeps of the sea that allow a fish to fend off the seagull's attack and the expanse of the atmosphere that gives a bird room to fly. Practice is about accepting myself as a fish, studying my self by studying the ocean. Practice is about accepting myself as a bird, studying myself by studying the air.

Practice is about finding my place as a bird or a fish, regardless of what species I would like to be or think I ought to be:

> When I was young, I really wanted to be a composer. I did my undergraduate major in music. It was hard to accept that I don't have a composer's ear and discover my own way of listening, my own way of singing.
>
> I really wanted to be a Zen practitioner with fierce strength and deep gravity. It was hard to accept that I'm a short high-strung guy with a somewhat crooked spine and discover the pleasures in my tendencies to joke and laugh.
>
> I wanted to be a wise psychoanalyst who saw a few patients and practiced piano in the quiet between sessions. It was hard to accept that I'm in a frenzied clinic, where any open space in my day is immediately filled by another new client. It was difficult to see many people for just a few sessions until I discovered that this provides endless opportunities for finding my place with each person, each session.

Each of us can only talk in his or her own particular voice. We can only walk on our own two feet. We can only swim with our own two arms and navigate by the guide of our own sincerity. However well-intentioned, we cannot be other than who we are, where we are.

Before his death, Rabbi Zusya said "In the coming world, they will not ask me, 'Why were you not Moses?' They will ask me: 'Why were you not Zusya?'"[10]

My task as both therapist and Zen student is not to become some ideal person, some messianic savior in a mythic past or ideal feature, but rather to become myself right here, right now. Zen and psychotherapy are about waking up to the fact that *here* IT is as I am, that *this* is my song, *this* is my posture, *this* is my temple and sanctuary, *this* is my life; that this Nature leaves room for all the varieties of nature, that Self leaves room for me to realize my self swimming and flying as my particular self:

> Clear water all the way to the bottom;
> a fish swims like a fish.
> Vast sky transparent throughout;
> a bird flies like a bird.[11]

11

Now if a bird or a fish tries to reach the end of its element before moving in it, this bird or this fish will not find its way or its place. When you find your place where you are, practice occurs, actualizing the fundamental point. When you find your way at this moment, practice occurs, actualizing the fundamental point; for the place, the way, is neither large nor small, neither yours nor others.' The place, the way, has not carried over from the past and it is not merely arising now.

Accordingly, in the practice-enlightenment of the buddha way, meeting one thing is mastering it—doing one practice is practicing completely.

A fish can't get to the bottom of the ocean without swimming; a bird can't get to the upper reaches of the atmosphere without flying. We daydream a lot, imagining who we'd like to be. But thinking isn't doing: Fantasizing movement isn't the same as moving.

Actualization must be real rather than imagined. This is more difficult than it sounds, because there is often some discrepancy between our idealized vision and our actual conditions.

These days therapists' work situations rarely match our ideal image of what therapy "should" be like. In my own rushed life, working in the hectic clinic in which I'm employed I often think to myself: "If only I could have a little more time, and see this client for more sessions." But I work in a place where we have only a few sessions with clients. Sometimes this is frustrating.

When life is particularly hectic at my clinic and I yearn to work more leisurely or at least more thoroughly, I sometimes remember seeing an episode of M*A*S*H, the old television show about doctors practicing field medicine on the battlefields of the Korean War. In one particular episode Charles Winchester, a very upper-crust, very superior surgeon from Boston, gets transferred into the M*A*S*H field unit. He takes one look at the grubby surgeons who have been out near the battle lines for a year, sneers at their rough ways, and disparages the crudeness of their surgical setup.

During a battle a load of wounded are airlifted in. Winchester goes to the makeshift operating room and smugly says: "Now let me show you how it's done. Observe. I do one thing at a time, I do it perfectly, and then I move on."

When I saw this I had very mixed feelings. For all his smug snobbishness, I admired Winchester's careful thoroughness and single-minded focus. It seemed very much in keeping with Zen ideals.

But while Winchester was working slowly and perfectly in the operating room, patients were dying. A flood of casualties kept coming. The other doctors had to say to him, "Charles, while you're making beautiful stitches closing up that wound, the patients on the other tables are bleeding to death. This isn't Mass General Hospital. This is meatball surgery." Winchester had a hard time adapting. He was exhausted and shaken by the end of his shift.

Excising a brain tumor is fine work, but so is meatball surgery. Each has its own flavor, requiring its own actions. One can make a wonderful dish out of meatballs and spaghetti, so long as we don't pretend we're preparing veal sautéed in truffles and wine.

I try to remember this when I'm working in the short-term rush of my clinic. I try to remember that this is the water in which I need to learn to swim.

Like Winchester, we all have our vision of the best way to do things. Like Winchester, we experience some rude shocks when we are on the front lines of our life and are forced to deal with some messy realities. Our lives are rarely sterile operating rooms; life often does not give us the opportunity to finish one thing before presenting us with another demand. Our reveries usually don't include the mundane acts necessary to realize our romantic notions of ourselves, but each mundane act is its own complete practice.

We may have a vision of therapy as an existential encounter, but the work often consists of dealing with missed appointments, answering voice mails, filling out the paperwork for disability requests and wrestling with client recalcitrance. We may have a vision of Zen as calm serenity in a community of selfless companions, but the practice involves dealing with our greed, desire, and anger as they arise on our meditation cushion and in our dealings with the people in our lives. We may have a vision of home as a place for loving intimacy, but much of family life consists of dealing with how our spouse disappoints us on our birthday and our children rebel when it comes time to clean the house or walk the dog. Just as we have some ideal vision of how things should be, we also hold some image of how we should be: wise therapists, unruffled Zen students, kind parents, loving spouses. In the face of our difficult life circumstances, we often don't act the way we feel we should.

Although our situation may be far from how we imagined it would be, we can only find our way in the actual place where we are. Answering the phone, filling out our paperwork, reacting to our child's temper tantrum when we're already late for an appointment, meditating while our neighbor cranks up the volume on his stereo, we express ourselves as we actually are rather than how we like to think of ourselves. In this spot, there is usually some gap between our image and our reality. Then we may feel that there is some problem with the world or some problem with ourselves. We may spend our lives trying to find some place where the external circumstances match our image of how they should be or seeking a cure to help us correspond to our ideal image of ourself. Yet no matter how hard we try, we cannot live our life in some ideal fashion, free from external and internal problems.

Our practice lies not in ridding ourselves of our problems but in finding our problems again and again, each time in more subtle forms, until we are on intimate terms with them. Then we start to experience freedom. This is not a freedom from fear and sadness, for these are still frequent companions in a world filled with suffering and hurt. Rather, this is a freedom from isolation and disconnectedness, a freedom that celebrates the realities of our lives.

The reality of our life takes place at the gap. This is our element. The only way we can close the gap and realize our vision is to move within the concrete realities of this particular moment. Then we can find fulfillment by meeting one thing each moment and taking the necessary action. Sometimes this involves singing a lullaby to our cooing baby; sometimes this involves cleaning up our own vomit. In therapy, Zen practice, and life, there are no insignificant moments, nor does anything special happen. We are how we sit straight on a cushion, how we look a client in the eyes, how we take a deep breath in an argument with our spouse. Finding our place in our current element, we realize ourselves and each other every where, every when.

Our lives arise in particular actions at particular places, moment by moment: not in the past, not in the future. It is not even possible to grasp the "now." Our lives arise in the moment, but this moment does not consist of some discrete, very small instant of time: It is not measurable. The point on which life arises is *continually* arising, and the place of the moment is *completely* saturated with life. This means that our entire life appears each moment. Our entire existence, as therapist and client, is continually right where we are standing. Finding where we are standing is practice.

In therapy one person meets another at a certain time and a particular place. This meeting is neither the therapist's nor the client's, neither mine nor yours. The continuous activity of this meeting is infinitely wide and infinitesimally particular. Sometimes our meeting focuses on a single issue, sometimes it ranges over wide fields of meaning. Sometimes we have only a session in which to work with a client. Sometimes we have years. Each is a lifetime. Each handshake is a complete therapy. Each moment of therapy totally expresses the entire being of client and therapist, for each moment is life itself. There's no need to wait for something else. There's no need to hope for some other time, some other place. Here is where we actualize the fundamental point.

12

Here is the place; here the way unfolds. The boundary of realization is not distinct, for the realization comes forth simultaneously with the mastery of buddha-dharma.

Do not suppose that what you realize becomes your knowledge and is grasped by your consciousness. Although actualized immediately, the inconceivable may not be apparent. Its appearance is beyond your knowledge.

Here we are, this moment. I am sitting in a room, different from the room you are in, now. Yet at the same time we are both in the same place: right here, reading and being read, your eyes seeing my thoughts shaped by inky letters spread out on the sinews of trees. I forget myself writing, and you forget yourself reading. I discover my self writing to you; as you react to this, you hear yourself listening to me. Our lives are unfolding right here, right now: In the practice of this single small act we are realizing each other by waking up to the enlightenment we share with all beings.

Practicing with each other, we do not *attain* realization: Practice simply puts our realization into play. Our realization is our enjoyment of each others' play, our play expresses our delight in each others' practice. In this practice-realization, mastery involves responsiveness; it requires a deepening of the relationships in which we engage and are engaged, a willingness to be being called to our calling. Mastery is not a matter of achieving domination and control of our subject, but a matter of coming forth together with our subject.

When some realization comes forth in our practice of either Zen or psychotherapy, it is not *my* or *your* accomplishment. Realization is larger than us: As we touch it and are touched by it, it fills us completely and enlarges us beyond our small ideas of ourselves. If we try to take individual credit for it or copyright it, we diminish it and, losing contact with It, feel once again diminished ourselves, bereft of any mastery. True mastery leads not to pride, but to unfathomable wonder.

When we begin to practice Zen, we think we will gain enlightenment. Eventually we come to understand that "I" trying to grasp "It" is like a dog chasing its tail. "I" cannot know "It" without standing back and losing It. Practicing the buddha-dharma, we cultivate kindness, compassion, joy, and acceptance and realize the kindness, compassion, joy, and acceptance that surrounds us and supports our effort.

When we begin to practice psychotherapy, we think we will cure patients. Eventually we come to understand that clients and therapists are both bigger than their ideas about themselves: Each embodies knowledge that they do not know they know. Practicing the skills of therapy, we rehearse our therapeutic techniques again and again not so we can make clients do what we think they ought to, but so that we can respond to the inquiring impulse that is born and dies at the boundary it crosses.

What *I* know in psychotherapy is not so important as what *we* discover. Healing is a two-way relationship; knowledge only arises from acknowledging our ignorance so that we can participate in the intimacy of learning from each other. The immediacy of this activity takes place on a field far beyond any ideas of each other we can hold on to. We cannot find our way by standing still nor by retracing well-worn roads. Instead, our mastery rests on an inconceivable mystery: how we are constantly realizing ourselves by laying down a path in walking.

We master a piece of music by letting it master us. Listening to the music, it plays upon us and we realize what it's saying by becoming its song without words. When our breath passes over our lips or a bow strokes a string, at the boundary of the meeting point both vibrate to each other's tone. Sounding the notes with our fingers or our lips, stumbling through one phrase as we practice it again and again, we enter the melody as it enters us. The phrase tells us how it wants to be performed and begins to make sense to us through our senses; our heart beats to its rhythm and our breathing synchronizes with the flow of the song. The music realizes itself through our singing; we realize our singing in the music.

The same is true for the music of any activity. Gardening, we learn to think like a plant. By practicing our golf swing again and again, our mastery of the stroke comes forth as our arm becomes an extension of the club. By driving a car, our mastery of the road comes forth simultaneously with our movements that respond to the road's directions: It bends us to its curves. Practicing the skills of parenting, we come to realize that as children we grew up simultaneously with our parents, each learning from the other, touching and touched by the indistinct but necessary boundaries of love.

13

> Zen master Baoche of Mt. Mayu was fanning himself. A monk approached and said, "Master, the nature of wind is permanent and there is no place it does not reach. Why, then, do you fan yourself?"
>
> "Although you understand that the nature of the wind is permanent," Baoche replied, "you do not understand the meaning of its reaching everywhere."
>
> "What is the meaning of its reaching everywhere?" asked the monk again. The master just kept fanning himself. The monk bowed deeply.
>
> The actualization of the buddha-dharma, the vital path of its correct transmission, is like this. If you say that you do not need

> to fan yourself because the nature of wind is permanent and you
> can have wind without fanning, you will understand neither per-
> manence nor the nature of wind. The nature of wind is permanent;
> because of that, the wind of the buddha's house brings forth the
> gold of the earth and makes fragrant the cream of the long river.

Love is neither tainted nor pure. We all have our personal selfish agendas; we all want to get something out of what we're doing. We also all have our generous intentions that sincerely aim beyond ourselves to a larger wholeness; we all have ways of putting forth effort without desire for personal reward, of putting forth effort for the thing itself, for no particular reason or sense of gain. We all are continuously self-centered, and at the same time continuously Self-centered.

The question for our practice is how we go about uniting the two.

Because there is a difference between self and Self, winds rise up. Whenever there is a difference in temperature or pressure between two places, this generates a wind that seeks to connect the differing areas and reach a greater sense of equilibrium. Everything in nature, including ourselves, is always looking to find its balance. Because conditions are always changing, however, any equilibrium is brief, local, and relative; there is no permanent, fixed atmosphere, but rather a constant flow that connects every place, every being on earth. Each being, each physical object absorbs heat and radiates heat: We are constantly exchanging energy with each other. The nature of wind is permanent. Although the nature of wind is permanent, we need to fan ourselves if we want to be able to cool off in the heat of the moment.

Having some theoretical knowledge of psychopathology and psychotherapeutic technique is not the same as practicing psychotherapy. Having some abstract understanding of spirituality is the not same as putting that spirituality into practice.[12] If we want to understand what's real, we have to make it real: We have to real-ize every bit of It ourselves.

> Once when an ancient Buddhist saint was walking over mud, a novice asked him, "How can you do it yourself, Venerable One?"
> The saint said, "If I don't do it, who will do it for me?"[13]

It's up to each one of us. Secondhand experience or watered-down versions won't do; there are no Cliff Notes for our lives, no Reader's Digest abridgments of Zen or psychotherapeutic practice.

When we put our realization into practice, we actualize the nature of wind: We actualize our own enlightened being. We do this not in some abstruse place where ideal personal lives unfold in transcendent relationships. We realize our lives in the real place where we are. Our relationships with our loved ones are marked with hurt as well as healing, disappointment as well as satisfaction, anger as well as love. Life presents us with the myriad things; we may sometimes not have much choice about what life brings us, but we can choose how we practice with whatever comes.

In the course of our lives, time and again we find ourselves tossed on difficult winds and waves. We can fight the waves and practice hate. We can feel wronged by something someone did ten years ago and let our entire world become an ocean of resentment. But we also have the opportunity to relax in the ebb and flow of the waters by practicing loving kindness. We can forgive ignorance and wrongs, let go of greed and envy, and act to promote the happiness of all beings. Then our entire world can become a sea of acceptance and kindness, a sky of compassion and joy.

We actualize the fundamental point swimming at the meeting of wave and water, breathing at the intersection of wind and air, living in the service of the larger firmament of love. We do this by studying ourselves, asking, "Who am I?" We all want to discover, "Who am I?" We want to discover our true nature. But we run into problems because we think our true nature is like some elemental ore, buried deep and out of sight.

Prospecting for who I am, I hope to make some discovery that will enrich me personally and allow me to stake a valuable claim. Although I may fear that my inner core consists of some base substance as dull and heavy as lead, still I hope to find gold deep within the mine of my self. But as I continue my search, I begin to discover that this "who I am" is like the wind: It reaches everywhere I see, everything I touch. In some kind of simple alchemy, it turns out that wherever I go, there I am.[14]

As this becomes clearer my search for my true self stops digging for a fabulous one-time find and becomes instead the pleasures of continual finding. I become less anxious about defining once and for all *who* I am and more curious about *how* I am: because the wind reaches everywhere, the question "Who or what am I?" transmutes into, "How shall I live my life at this place and moment, swimming on this wave, in this ocean?" When I make my answer and plunge into this particular moment with full sincerity, I forget myself and find realization in myriad things. This is actualizing the fundamental point.

The fundamental point comes down to how we can actualize the inquiring impulse as best we can: Given our limited vision, how can we harmonize the warring elements of our nature into a harmonious counterpoint that, by embracing all of life and death, sings songs of loving-kindness? The fundamental point does not come down to whether our self is ultimately characterized as Good or Bad, Talented or Worthless, Enlightened or Deluded. The fundamental point comes down to the myriad specific details of how we carry out our daily activities with everyone and everything around us. Our practice involves finding our true selves each moment in the place we are: buttering bread, folding laundry, helping our child with homework, listening to our parent's unwanted advice, smiling, or arguing with our lover. Sitting on a cushion or in a therapist's or client's chair, we begin to learn not how to turn ourselves into some desired ideal image but rather how to realize ourselves as living, breathing beings.

Actualizing the fundamental point does not lead to some grand Answer, some state of extraordinary understanding in which we attain something special and then rest on what we have accomplished. Actualizing the fundamental point leads nowhere but finds Itself in our ordinary life of constant, ongoing practice-realization. Practice without realization would be a mindless golem; realization without practice would be a disembodied ghost. Practice and realization always arise together and help each other out. Practice and realization intersect at the horizon of our lives: the cloud meeting the mountain, dry granite glistening moistly in a shaft of sunlight, ocean touching the sky.

Practicing our realization we begin to understand: This mind, right here, this moment, is Buddha: Treat it with respect. Realizing our practice we begin to understand: This body, right here, this moment, is enlightened delusion: Treat it with kindness and compassion. Practice-realization is a natural unfolding of loving-kindness. It is simple and matter-of-fact. It does not call attention to itself; practice-realization simply is our way of expressing our understanding in action as best we know how at this point.

> Recently, during a lecture at Berkeley Zen Center, someone asked a question about Zen practice:
> "You mentioned something about making sure you act with compassion and love. I haven't heard much talk about that in Zen. Could you say something more about that?"
> Sojun was somewhat surprised by the question.
> "We don't talk that much about it," he replied. "We try to just live it."

Zen and psychotherapy offer us forms for practicing and realizing how to just live our lives. They don't provide recipes, but they do nourish us and inspire us to keep cooking with all the mundane ingredients we have at our disposal.

Any kind of practice, however, can become dull and lifeless. Whether it be playing piano, learning gymnastics, sitting zazen, or doing psychotherapy, practice can involve either drudgery or play; practice can become a monotonous obligation or an anxious obsession. Practice can also be something we come back to as a source of energy and strength. If practice is to enliven and revitalize us rather than drain us, the practice needs a strong foundation that can be renewed again and again.

The Buddhist precepts provide the foundation for Zen practice. The precepts offer a guide for how to treat ourselves and others; they point us in the direction of right action. When we commit ourselves to following the Buddha-way, we have a ceremony to take the precepts, but this is not a one-time event; each month at the new moon we renew our vows to follow the precepts. Renewing our vows, we renew the precepts; in doing this we actualize the precepts and actualize our lives.

The precepts are a good container for the conduct of our lives, for the practice of Zen and the process of psychotherapy. But the precepts are rather general: They don't tell us what to do. We each have to make the precepts our own. This is the process of fanning, of refining our lives even as we are tossed around by life. As this happens, the turbulence of the water smoothes and polishes the pebbles it deposits on the shores.

In our daily lives we thrash about as the streams of our life plunge down-hill searching for the ocean; this cascade gives off a dazzling froth as we refine the gold of our lives from the gravel of the riverbed. But froth can be confusing, and gold can give way to greed, hate, and delusion. So we return to the precepts to remind us how to refine our lives: how to fan ourselves moment by moment. Although we lose our way again and again, we come back to the precepts again and again as a way of locating our center of gravity; this helps us enjoy our prac-tice of finding our balance in the ever-shifting winds that blow us toward new equilibriums.

Practicing the precepts is not an onerous task, full of moralistic "shoulds" and "shouldn'ts." The precepts teach us about actualizing ourselves with others, others with ourselves, others with others, and ourselves with ourselves; this actualization brings forth treasure everywhere.

Practicing the precepts is a joyful journey of discovering how to treasure ourselves and treasure others, renewing our wonder again and again.

Practicing the precepts is about appreciating the life we have, the people and the things around us, enjoying the light of ourselves and others refracted in the jewel of life.

Practicing the precepts is about finding ourselves on the page we are on now, and rediscovering ourselves fresh each moment in the act of turning the page.

Thank you for reading this book, allowing me to practice with you. In grat-itude, may I say: Please treasure yourself and all around you. In companionship, may I suggest: Please continue fanning yourself. Please turn the page.

PRECEPTS

I vow to refrain from all evil.
It is the abode of the law of all Buddhas; it is the source of the law of all Buddhas.

I vow to make every effort to live in enlightenment.
It is the teaching of anuttara samyaksambodhi and the path of the one who practices and that which is practiced.

I vow to live and be lived for the benefit of all beings.
It is transcending profane and holy and taking self and others across.

I vow not to kill.
By not killing life the buddha tree seed grows. Transmit the life of Buddha and do not kill.

I vow not to take what is not given.
The self and objects are such as they are. Two yet one. The gate of liberation stands open.

I vow not to misuse sexuality.
Let the three wheels of self, objects and action be pure. With nothing to desire one goes along together with the Buddhas.

I vow to refrain from false speech.
The Dharma Wheel turns from the beginning. There is neither surplus nor lack. The sweet dew saturates all and harvests the truth.

I vow to refrain from intoxicants.
Originally pure, don't defile. This is the great awareness.

I vow not to slander.
In the Buddha Dharma, go together, appreciate together, realize together and actualize together. Don't permit fault-finding. Don't permit haphazard talk, do not corrupt the way.

I vow not to praise self at the expense of others.
Buddhas and Ancestors realize the vast sky and the great earth. When they manifest the noble body, there is neither inside nor outside in emptiness. When they manifest the Dharma body there is not even a bit of earth on the ground.

I vow not to be avaricious.
One phrase, one verse—that is the ten thousand things and one hundred grasses; one dharma, one realization—is all Buddhas and Ancestors. Therefore, from the beginning, there has been no stinginess at all.

I vow not to harbor ill will.
Not negative, not positive, neither real nor unreal, there is an ocean of illuminated clouds and an ocean of bright clouds.

I vow not to abuse the three treasures.
To expound the Dharma with this body is foremost. The virtue returns to the ocean of reality. It is unfathomable; we just accept it with respect and gratitude.

Notes

PREFACE AND MEAL CHANT

[1] A word about the case vignettes that appear in this book. I occasionally have an opportunity to audiotape or videotape sessions, but most of the case accounts in the book are taken from my process notes. Thus quotations from clients or my own words are generally not verbatim but represent my best recollection. In general I have done my best to not revise the material to make it sound better, but I have occasionally made minor changes in an attempt to improve readability or to convey the flavor of a session. I have also sometimes combined several sessions or several interchanges within a session into a single vignette.

Some of the cases involve narrative therapies in which there has been an exchange of letters between the client and myself. At such times, I record the material verbatim and note that explicitly. At other times, for purposes of illustration I have combined several clients into a prototypical vignette. When I do this, I also note it explicitly.

In general, then, except when I explicitly note a case as either verbatim or a compilation, the case examples are paraphrasings from process notes taken immediately after a session.

[2] This chant is used at Berkeley Zen Center before formal meals eaten in the Zendo. The compilation and translation is by Mel Weitsman.

The issue of greeting whatever comes our way in life with equal appreciation is a central issue in Zen practice. It often is expressed in the context of practical daily concerns, such as food. In "Instructions for the Zen Cook," Zen Master Dogen offers some helpful instructions:

"When making a soup with ordinary greens, do not be carried away by feelings of dislike towards them nor regard them lightly; neither jump for joy simply because you have been given ingredients of superior quality to make a special dish... a dish is not necessarily superior because you have prepared it with choice ingredients, nor is a soup inferior because you have made it with ordinary greens. When handling and selecting greens, do so wholeheartedly, with a pure mind, and without trying to evaluate their quality, in the same way in which you would prepare a splendid feast. The many rivers which flow into the ocean become the one taste of the ocean; when they flow into the pure ocean of the dharma there are no such distinctions as delicacies or plain food, there is just one taste, and it is the buddhadharma, the world itself as it is.... Never feel aversion toward plain ingredients.... make the best use of whatever greens you have." In *From the Zen Kitchen to Enlightenment: Refining Your Life*. T. Wright, trans. New York: Weatherhill, 1983, pp. 7–13.

CHAPTER 1

[1] This is a translation of Zen Master Eihei Dogen's Zazen-Gi by Dan Welch and Kazuaki Tanahashi. It appears in K. Tanahashi, ed., *Moon in a Dewdrop: Writings of Zen Master Dogen*. San Francisco: North Point Press, 1985, pp. 29–30.

[2] Sawaki Kodo Roshi, quoted in K. Uchiyama Roshi, *The Zen Teaching of "Homeless" Kodo*. Kyoto, Japan: Kyoto Soto Zen Center, c/o Sosenji, 1990.

[3] This is a koan, the seventh case in a famous collection of Zen koans called *The Blue Cliff Record* (T. Cleary and J.C. Cleary, trans. Boston: Shambhala Publications, 1992, p. 46).

[4] D. Brazier, *Zen Therapy*. New York: John Wiley, 1995. This book offers a good primer of Buddhist psychology and its application to humanistic psychotherapy.

[5] Family systems therapy has long been interested in the nature of paradoxical interventions. I have argued previously ("Paradox as Epistemological Jump." *Family Process 21*(1), 1982, pp. 85–90.) that paradox is not a technique to be applied by a therapist "onto" a client. Rather, paradox is the living, shimmering relationship whose multiple strands and contrasting colors constitute our lives.

[6] Here I am paraphrasing the Diamond Sutra, which more specifically states: "It is impossible to retain past mind, impossible to hold on to present mind, and impossible to grasp future mind." (*The Diamond Sutra and The Sutra of Hui-Neng*, A. F. Price, W. Mou-lam, trans. Boston: Shambhala, 1990, p. 39.)

[7] Case 45 in *Book of Serenity: One Hundred Zen Dialogues*. T. Cleary, trans. Hudson, NY: Lindisfarne Press, 1990, p. 191. The book is also available from Wheelwright Press, San Francisco Zen Center, 300 Page Street, San Francisco, CA 94102.

[8] R. Aitken, *The Dragon Who Never Sleeps*. Berkeley, CA: Parallax Press, 1992. This is a wonderful collection of *gathas*, which traditionally are little four-line poems designed to strengthen one's Buddhist practice. Robert Aitken has written a series of modern *gathas* for us and gathered them together in this book.

CHAPTER 2

[1] These are excerpts from each of the ten sections of Zen Master Eihei Dogen's Gakudo Yojin-shu. I have combined two translations: one, "Guidelines for Studying the Way," was translated by Ed Brown and Kazuaki Tanahashi and appears in K. Tanahashi, ed., *Moon in a Dewdrop: Writings of Zen Master Dogen*. San Francisco: North Point Press, 1985, pp. 31–43. The other, titled "Points to Watch in Practicing the Way," was translated by Okumura Shohaku. It appears in *Dogen Zen*, Kyoto, Japan: Soto Zen Center (Shoinji Temple), 1988, pp. 1–42.

[2] There are many accounts of the life of Buddha. Thich Nhat Hanh tells the story in beautiful, simple prose in *Old Path White Clouds*. Berkeley, CA: Parallax Press, 1991.

[3] Mark Epstein has a nice discussion of the psychological consequences of impermanence in his excellent book, *Thoughts Without a Thinker* (New York: Basic Books, 1995). He focuses on the narcissistic injury involved in the realization of impermanence and vulnerability, calling the First Noble Truth one of *humiliation*.

[4] My colleague Haim Omer and I have written of this in our paper, "Diseases of Hope and the Work of Despair." *Psychotherapy, 34*(3), 1997, pp. 225–232.

[5] See, for example, J. Dyckman, "A Communications Model of Panic Disorder." *Anxiety Disorders Practice Journal, 1*, 1994, pp. 77–82.

[6] There are many versions of this story. One appears in Nyogen Senzaki's *101 Zen Stories*, itself a translation into English of a book called the *Shaseki-shu*, written late in the 13th century by the Japanese Zen teacher Muju. The story can be found in Paul Reps's compilation *Zen Flesh, Zen Bones*. Garden City, NY: Anchor/Doubleday, no date, pp. 22–23.

[7] In this regard, it's interesting to reconsider Freud's notion of fixation. This was originally an "economic" notion of how mental "energy" got "trapped." It later came to take on the notion of "excessive preoccupation" with an issue due to a failure to successfully find a resolution to some developmental conflict. But a different way of approaching the matter lies in the fact that, although

fixations do tend to arise at developmental crises, they are not so much "failures" to resolve them but a "successful" attempt to freeze the developmental moment in time, to "fix" the "site." The "fix" is not in the sense of repair, but in the sense of capturing it in an unchanging psychological stasis that can be repeated over and over again. Fixations are denials of impermanence.

[8] There are various versions of this vignette in different Buddhist traditions. The vignette is quoted in both Stephen Levine's *Who Dies?* (New York: Doubleday, 1982, pp. 98–99) and Mark Epstein, *Thoughts Without a Thinker* (see n. 3), pp. 80–81.

[9] Good books on solution-oriented therapy include the works of Steve de Shazer (starting with *Keys to Solution in Brief Therapy.* New York: Norton, 1985) and Bill O'Hanlon (e.g., W. H. O'Hanlon & M. Weiner-Davis, *In Search of Solutions: A New Direction in Psychotherapy.* New York: Norton, 1989). Another good introduction can be found in J. Walter & J. Peller, *Becoming Solution-Focused in Brief Therapy.* New York: Brunner/Mazel, 1992. For introductions to solution-oriented or strategic brief therapies that incorporate (sometimes tacitly) a Buddhist perspective, readers might find my book chapter, "Strategic Psychotherapy," (in R. Wells & V. Gianetti, eds., *Handbook of the Brief Psychotherapies.* New York: Plenum, pp. 351–404) and my recent journal article, "Form, Formlessness and Formulation," (*Journal of Psychotherapy Integration, 6*(2), 1997, pp. 107–117) helpful.

[10] Case 43 in the Mumonkan. Here I am using Robert Aitken's translation in his book *The Gateless Barrier: The Wu-Men Kuan.* San Francisco: North Point Press, 1990, pp. 261–264. The book by Aitken-Roshi continues a long Zen tradition of offering commentaries on this classic collection of koans. Throughout the text, when using cases from the Mumonkan, I usually have collated the Aitken translation with the translation by Paul Reps, available in Reps' *Zen Flesh, Zen Bones* (see n. 6). For convenience's sake, I provide the reference and page numbers for just the Aitken version.

[11] Moshe relates this in his book, *Single Session Therapy.* San Francisco: Jossey-Bass, 1990. Another good reference for the topic of single-session therapy is M. Hoyt, R. Rosenbaum, & M. Talmon, "Planned Single-Session Therapy," in S. Budman, M. Hoyt, & S. Friedman, eds., *The First Session in Brief Therapy: A Book of Cases.* New York: Guilford, 1992, pp. 59–86.

[12] We often think changes in the natural world occur only via small increments through gradual evolution. Recent geological evidence suggests, however, that the world can also change abruptly through "punctuated evolution." Sudden discrete events such as meteorite strikes can cause profound, long-term "structural" changes in both the physical and biological realms (S. J. Gould, *The Panda's Thumb.* New York: W.W. Norton, 1980).

I have previously related this incident in several of my writings on single-session psychotherapy, including my 1994 journal article, "Single-Session Therapies: Intrinsic Integration?" (*Journal of Psychotherapy Integration 4*(3), 1994, 229–252), and a coauthored book chapter, R. Rosenbaum, M. Hoyt, & M. Talmon, "The Challenge of Single-Session Psychotherapies: Creating Pivotal Moments," in R. Wells & V. Gianetti, eds., *Handbook of the Brief Psychotherapies.* New York: Plenum, 1990, pp.165–192.

[13] This case is a compilation of several clients.

[14] The anecdote and commentary appear in Robert Aitken's discussion of Case 5 of the Mumonkan in *The Gateless Barrier: The Wu-Men Kuan* (see n. 11).

[15] Case 7 in the Mumonkan in Aitken's translation (see n. 11).

[16] There are many excellent sources of material on mindfulness practice. Helpful texts include, from the Vipassana/Zen tradition, Thich Nhat Hanh's *The Miracle of Mindfulness* (Boston: Beacon, 1992) and Joseph Goldstein's and Jack Kornfield's *Seeking the Heart of Wisdom: The Path of Insight Meditation* (Boston: Shambhala, 1987); from a more Zen perspective, the books of Charlotte Joko Beck (*Everyday Zen.* New York: Harper & Row, 1989; *Nothing Special.* New York: Harper & Row, 1993). Jon Kabat-Zinn's *Full Catastrophe Living* (New York: Delacorte Press, 1990) was a milestone in the application of mindfulness in medical settings. For those wishing a discussion of mindfulness and its role in psychotherapy, both the Mark Epstein and David Brazier books cited in chapter 1 are excellent.

[17] I am indebted to Taitetsu Unno, from whom I had the good fortune to take an undergraduate course in religion at Smith College, for first pointing this out to me.

[18] Shunryu Suzuki Daiosho, founder of San Francisco and Tassajara Zen Centers, said this. The quote is from a collection of his talks, *Zen Mind, Beginner's Mind* (New York: Weatherhill, 1970, p. 21). This wonderful little book is a perennial best-seller within the world of Zen literature, and an excellent gate to Soto Zen practice.

[19] Case 96 in *Book of Serenity: One Hundred Zen Dialogues,* T. Cleary, trans. Hudson, NY: Lindisfarne Press, 1990, p. 412.

[20] Case 20 in *Book of Serenity: One Hundred Zen Dialogues* (see n. 19).

[21] Henry Littlefield. I'd like to express my appreciation to him for his help during my college years.

[22] Case 9 in the Mumonkan in Aitken's translation (see n. 11). For the sake of readability, I have substituted the word "eons" for the original's "kalpas," which technically is the period of time between a world's creation and its destruction in Buddhist cosmology.

[23] This appears in Aitken-Roshi's commentary on the koan of the nonattained Buddha, case 9 in the Mumonkan cited in this chapter, pp. 67–68.

[24] This appears in Dogen's "Bodhisattva's Four Methods of Guidance," a translation of the Bodaisatta Shisho-ho, translated by Lew Richmond and Kazuaki Tanahashi, in K. Tanahashi, ed., *Moon in a Dewdrop: Writings of Zen Master Dogen.* San Francisco: North Point Press, 1985, p. 45.

[25] In the same fascicle and same page quoted previously (see n. 24).

[26] I am paraphrasing this anecdote of Hui-neng's dharma transmission rather freely. Hui-neng's own account appears in "Sutra Spoken by the Sixth Patriarch on the High Seat of the Treasure of the True Law," in *The Diamond Sutra and The Sutra of Hui-neng*, A.F. Price & Wong Mou-lam, trans. Boston: Shambhala, 1990, pp. 69–74.

[27] There are many accounts of the Buddha's enlightenment. This quote is taken from Keizan Jokin, *The Denkoroku: The Record of the Transmission of the Light,* H. Nearman, trans. Mount Shasta, CA: Shasta Abbey, 1993.

[28] The "Mountains and Waters Sutra" is a translation of Dogen's Sansui-kyo, translated by Arnold Kotler and Kazuaki Tanahashi, in K. Tanahashi, ed., *Moon in a Dewdrop: Writings of Zen Master Dogen* (see n. 24).

[29] A brief version of this case first appeared in Haim Omer's and my article, "Diseases of Hope and the Work of Despair." *Psychotherapy*, *34*(3), 1997, pp. 225–232.

[30] From a translation of Dogen's Uji, "The Time-Being," D. Welch and K. Tanahashi, trans., in K. Tanahashi, ed., *Moon in a Dewdrop: Writings of Zen Master Dogen* (see n. 25).

[31] Case 4 in *Book of Serenity: One Hundred Zen Dialogues* (see n. 19), p. 17.

CHAPTER 3

[1] This is an adaptation by Sojun Mel Weitsman of a translation by G. Constant Lounsbery that appears in *Buddhist Meditation.* Tucson, AZ: Omen Press, 1973.

[2] Case 87 in *The Blue Cliff Record,* T. Cleary & J.C. Cleary, trans. Boston: Shambhala Publications, 1992, p. 477.

[3] Readers of J.R.R. Tolkien's *The Lord of the Rings* (Boston: Houghton-Mifflin, ed. 2, p. 41) will recognize the phrase as Bilbo's description of himself at his 111th birthday, prior to resuming his travels after possessing the Ring for a long time.

[4] I have heard this story from several people orally, but have not been able to track down its source.

[5] Many different versions of this story are available. One version appears in I. Shah, *Tales of the Dervis.* New York: E.P. Dutton, 1969, p. 191.

[6] Quoted in R. Aitken, *The Mind of Clover: Essays in Zen Buddhist Ethics.* San Francisco: North Point Press, pp. 37–38. The original is in Kajitani Sonin, ed., *Shumon Kattoshu (The Traditional Tangled Wisteria Collection).* Tokyo: Hozokan, 1982, pp. 342–344.

[7] This anecdote appears several places. The version here appears in Dogen's fascicle "Kokyo," translated as "The Ancient Mirror." Dogen Zenji, *Shobogenzo: The Eye and Treasury of the True Law*, vol. II. K. Nishiyama & J. Stevens, trans. Tokyo, Japan: Kawata Press. 1977, p. 58.

[8] See, for example, Thomas Cleary's translation of Dogen's *Eihei Koroku* in *Rational Zen: The Mind of Dogen Zenji*. Boston: Shambala, 1995, p.48.

[9] Case 19, Mumonkan. Here I am using the Reps translation, *Zen Flesh, Zen Bones* (Garden City, NY: Anchor/Doubleday, no date), p. 105.

[10] From *Porgy and Bess,* by George Gershwin, Du Bose Heyward, and Ira Gershwin. Miami, FL: Warner Brothers, 1935.

[11] Bankei, *The Unborn: The Life and Teaching of Zen Master Bankei, 1622–1693,* N. Waddell, trans. San Francisco: North Point Press, pp. 61–62.

[12] Thich Nhat Hanh told this anecdote during a lecture in Berkeley, California, around 1988.

[13] J. Parappully, *Finding the Plentifulness in the Darkness; Transforming Trauma into Gift*. Unpublished doctoral dissertation, California Institute of Integral Studies, San Francisco, CA, 1997.

[14] T. N. Hanh, *Old Path White Clouds*. Berkeley, CA: Parallax Press, 1991, p. 275.

[15] Case 94 in *Book of Serenity: One Hundred Zen Dialogues,* T. Cleary, trans. Hudson, NY: Lindisfarne Press, 1990, p. 402.

[16] I have not been able to find the reference for this poem and am writing it from memory, so I may not be quoting it accurately. The poem appeared on a well-known poster commonly seen on the walls of college dorms in the United States in the late 1960s.

CHAPTER 4

[1] This unpublished translation of the Sandokai is by Sojun Mel Weitsman, abbott of Berkeley Zen Center. He is the Sojun-sensei of the dialogue presented elsewhere in this chapter. Another translation and interesting discussion appears in Sheng-Yen, *The Infinite Mirror*. Elmhurst, NY: Dharma Drum Publications, 1990, pp. 5–64. There the Sandokai is translated as "Inquiry Into Matching Halves."

[2] When they do this, somehow the examples always resort to *physical* reality: "He really hit her, didn't he? You can't deny that!" Therapists need to remember Freud's great discovery: Psychological reality is no less (and no more) "real" than physical reality. Ideas cannot be touched but are just as real as tangible things.

[3] The two-way nature of interpersonal interaction is exemplified by the relational model within psychoanalytic approaches (e.g., L. Aron, *A Meeting of Minds*. Hillsdale, NJ: The Analytic Press, 1996; S.A. Mitchel, "Recent Developments in Psychoanalytic Theorizing." *Journal of Psychotherapy Integration,* 4(2),1994, pp. 93–103). Within the cognitive-therapy approach, M. Mahoney (*Human Change Processes*. New York: Basic Books, 1991) and Safran and Segal (*Interpersonal Process in Cognitive Therapy*. New York: Basic Books, 1991) stress the interpersonal components of what is sometimes seen as a "technique-oriented" model. Systemic psychotherapies, of course, have always stressed the mutual nature of interpersonal influence.

[4] This can be subtle. I had a colleague who practiced narrative therapy, which espouses a constructivist perspective that maintains it is oppressive to impose our own views on anyone else. However, my colleague was afraid to present cases to his group supervision, because it felt like the "narrative police" would criticize him if his involvement with his patients deviated from the "politically correct" line.

CHAPTER 5

[1] This (unpublished) translation of the Heart Sutra was compiled from various sources by Peter Schneider.

[2] This chapter is based in large part on a chapter coauthored with John Dyckman, "No Self? No Problem?" which appeared in M. Hoyt, ed., *Constructive Therapies*, vol. II, NY: Guilford, 1997, pp. 238–274. John's help and friendship have been invaluable to me.

[3] T. N. Hanh, *The Heart of Understanding*. Berkeley, CA: Parallax Press, 1992.

[4] Case 2 in *Book of Serenity: One Hundred Zen Dialogues,* T. Cleary, trans. Hudson, NY: Lindisfarne Press, 1990, p. 6.

[5] Robert Ayllmer used this phrase to sum up the key assumption of Bowenian systems therapy when he was teaching a seminar on that subject at the Boston VA in 1978.

[6] This is embodied by the theatrical work of Peter Brooks, who titled his book *The Empty Space* (New York: Simon and Schuster, 1978).

[7] Reps, *Zen Flesh, Zen Bones*. Garden City, NY: Anchor/Doubleday, no date, p. 5.

[8] M.H. Erickson, *Life Reframing in Hypnosis*. New York: Irvington, 1985, p. 3.

[9] B. Keeney, *Aesthetics of Change*. New York: Guilford Press, 1983.

[10] A favorite saying of Gregory Bateson, but one drawn originally by A. Korzybski (*Science and Sanity*, ed. 4. Clinton, MA: Colonial Press, 1973).

[11] I provided a nearly complete transcript of this case in my chapter "Heavy Ideals: A Strategic Single-Session Therapy," in R. Wells & V. Ginaetti, eds., *Casebook of the Brief Psychotherapies*. New York: Plenum, 1993, pp. 109–128. I also cited this case in "Single-Session Therapy: Intrinsic Integration." (*Journal of Psychotherapy Integration, 4*(3), 1994, pp. 229–252). I have felt some concern about the role deceit played in this case, yet it still somehow feels that the intervention was true to the client's needs. This is discussed more fully in both references.

[12] E. Dickinson, *The Complete Poems of Emily Dickinson*, T. Johnson, ed. Boston: Little, Brown, 1960, p. 133. Original work c. 1861. The other Dickinson citation later on in this chapter is from the same poem.

[13] S. de Shazer, *Keys to Solution in Brief Therapy*. New York: W.W. Norton, 1985.

[14] M. White & D. Epston, *Narrative Means to Therapeutic Ends*. New York: W.W. Norton, 1990.

[15] Mark Epstein, in his book of the same title, offers an insightful exploration of the psychodynamics of "Thoughts Without a Thinker." New York: Basic Books, 1995.

[16] S. Freud, *The Ego and the Id*, J. Strachey, trans., vol. XIX of *Standard Edition of the Complete Works of Sigmund Freud*. London: Hogarth Press, 1961, pp. 3–66. (Original work published 1923).

[17] Case 88 in *Book of Serenity: One Hundred Zen Dialogues*, T. Cleary, trans. Hudson, NY: Lindisfarne Press, 1990, p. 377.

[18] Bateson, G. *Mind and Nature: A Necessary Unity*. New York: Bantam, 1979. Bateson's book focuses on mind and nature, but leaves out bodies. In his urgency to convey the importance of relationships rather than reifications, Bateson was fond of asserting that minds can exist without bodies. This is true, if what we mean by mind is not limited to brains and flesh. However, minds (and relationships) always are embodied in some tangible form, whether it be planets and suns or dendrites and axons.

[19] M. Merleau-Ponty, *Signs*, R. McCleary, trans. Evanston, IL: Northwestern University Press, 1964.

[20] Consciousness takes different forms. When I look at a rock I can be conscious *of* the object I perceive as separate from me, the observer; this is what we think of when we usually think of consciousness. When I bang my shin and pain shoots through my whole body until I see stars, I am conscious *by* the experience; my consciousness can be subsumed by an intense sensation, thought, or feeling that seems to "take over" and to be "running the show" of awareness.

Another form of consciousness exists, however, that straddles the previous two: Consciousness-*with* coexists with a changing stimulus in such a way that it simultaneously is determining and being determined by the shifting quality of awareness. When I am riding a bicycle without particularly thinking about it, consciousness resides in my sense of balancing this way and that, of the wind on my face and the pedals under my feet. The movement of the bicycle under me lends a certain quality to my awareness of the experience, but simultaneously the awareness I give to the experience changes the feel of the ride. Take another example: When I listen to music I am conscious *with* the music. The music invokes my awareness and gives it some quality (brisk music alerts me, slow music relaxes the currents of my consciousness, etc.), but at the same time the music starts to take on the quality of awareness I bring to it; if I "relax into" a slow tempo the music may sound rhythmically "right," but if I "push" the tempo and mentally hurry it along, the music may sound slack or lugubrious.

Consciousness *with* is particularly relevant to therapists because it is the kind of consciousness involved in participant-observation; it is the consciousness that arises interpersonally when therapists work with clients and when couples touch each other; it is the consciousness that arises intrapersonally when we touch ourselves physically (e.g., one hand massaging the other) or when we touch ourselves mentally (e.g., when we mindfully become aware of our awareness).

[21] A. Bohart, "Experiencing: The Basis of Psychotherapy." *Journal of Psychotherapy Integration, 3*(1), pp. 51–68, 1993.

[22] F. Varela, E. Thompson, & E. Rosch, *The Embodied Mind*. Cambridge, MA: MIT Press, 1991. They point out that the essential problem is the idea that experience needs to be *represented* by a self separate from that experience. The issue is not one of how the body is represented "in" the mind. This view perpetuates a mind-body dualism that is particularly pernicious and leads to fruitless debates regarding whether the locus of "the self" resides in body, mind, or somewhere "in between." Views of self-identity that treat it as internalized representations or schemes tend to ignore the action component. When self and experience are united in embodied action, there is no need to "re-present" experience "out there" to a self "in here." Varela et. al. offer the image of "laying down a path in walking" as a metaphor for how self and experience are inextricably tied.

[23] W. Yeats, "Among School Children," in R. Finneran, ed., *The Collected Poems of W.B. Yeats*. New York: Collier Books, 1989, p. 217. (Original work published 1928).

[24] W. R. Bion, "Notes on Memory and Desire." *Psychoanalytic Forum, 2*, 1967, pp. 271–280.

[25] Case 2 in the Mumonkan in Aitken's translation, *The Gateless Barrier: The Wu-Men Kuan*. San Francisco: North Point Press, 1990, pp. 19–21.

[26] S. Suzuki, *Zen Mind, Beginner's Mind*, T. Dixon, ed. New York: Weatherhill., 1970, p. 36.

[27] Reps (see n. 7), p. 18.

[28] M.J. Horowitz, "Short-term Dynamic Therapy of Stress Response Syndromes," in P. Crits-Christoph & J. Barber, eds., *Handbook of Short-Term Dynamic Psychotherapy*. New York: Basic Books, 1991, pp. 166–198.

[29] Modern theories of recall tell us that our memories do not consist of encoded engrams that we save in a mental attic and later recover from a storeroom in the brain (W. Friedman, "Memory for the Time of Past Events." *Psychological Bulletin, 113*(1), 1993, pp. 44–66). Memory does not necessarily involve a process of going to a warehouse, retrieving a videotape of a past event, inserting it in a VCR and replaying it. Rather, memory is more like being an actor in a live production of a play; even though the same scene from the same script may be repeated night after night, each time it will be reenacted with a slightly different rhythm between the players, a slightly different interpretation, a varied expression (D. Edelman, quoted by S. Levy in "Dr. Edelman's Brain" *The New Yorker,* May 2, 1994, pp. 70–71). If we see memory not as bits and pieces but as a process of active reconstructing, our individual history does not consist of accruals of experience but the shifting constraints we place on our potential selves.

[30] This perspective is strongly influenced by H.S. Sullivan, e.g. *The Interpersonal Theory of Psychiatry*. New York: Norton, 1953.

[31] This crucial point is made by postmodernist and feminist writers who stress the inherent relational and contextual nature of self, e.g. J. Jordan, J. Miller, I. Stiver, & J. Surrey, eds., *Women's Growth in Connection: Writings from the Stone Center*. New York: Guilford, 1991.

[32] Thomas Merton, "The Joy of Fishes," in *The Way of Chuang Tzu*. New York: New Directions, 1965, pp. 97–98.

[33] Self arises at an intersection of multiple planes that defines a meeting point. In geometry, by definition, all points are dimensionless—i.e., empty.

[34] Martin Heidegger (*Discourse on Thinking*, J. Anderson & E. H. Freund, trans. New York: Harper & Row, 1966) has described the process of thinking as a cultivation of wonder, an existential exploration he terms *horizoning*.

[35] Thomas Cleary's translation of Dogen's *Eihei Koroku*, in *Rational Zen: The Mind of Dogen Zenji*. Boston: Shambala, 1995, p. 51.

CHAPTER 6

[1] This is the version of the *Hokyo Zamai* that we chant at Berkeley Zen Center. The translation is by T. Cleary and appears in *Timeless Spring* (New York: Weatherhill, 1980, pp. 39–41. Another translation and interesting discussion appears in Sheng-Yen, *The Infinite Mirror*. Elmhurst, NY: Dharma Drum Publications, 1990, pp. 65–123. Here the title is translated as "Song of the Precious Mirror Samadhi."

[2] Throughout this chapter I quote from the section of Keizan Zenji's *Denkoroku* that describes the life and teaching of Tozan Ryokai. I am using a compilation of two translations, one by Francis Cook (*The Record of Transmitting the Light*. Center Publications, 1991, pp. 174–179) and one by Hubert Nearman (*The Denkoroku, or, The Record of the Transmission of the Light*. Mount Shasta, CA: Shasta Abbey Press, 1993), together with some additional translations by Sojun Mel Weitsman during a course he taught on the subject at Berkeley Zen Center. I rely mostly on the Nearman translation.

[3] Case 75 in *Book of Serenity: One Hundred Zen Dialogues,* T. Cleary, trans. Hudson, NY: Lindisfarne Press, 1990, p. 316.

[4] Case 36 in *Book of Serenity: One Hundred Zen Dialogues* (see n. 3), p. 160.

[5] Case 78 *Book of Serenity: One Hundred Zen Dialogues* (see n. 3), p. 332.

[6] Case 21 in the Mumonkan in Aitken's translation, *The Gateless Barrier: The Wu-Men Kuan*. San Francisco: North Point Press, 1990, p. 137.

[7] Nangaku, quoted by Dogen in Bukkyo, "Buddhist Sutras," in Dogen Zenji, *Shobogenzo: The Eye and Treasury of the True Law*, #70, vol. III, K. Nishiyama & J. Stevens, trans. Tokyo, Japan: Kawata Press, 1977, p. 81.

[8] This is the subject, and title, of a nice book by Dainin Katagiri Roshi, *Returning to Silence: Zen Practice in Daily Life*. Boston: Shambala Productions, 1988.

[9] From "Amban's Addition" to the Mumonkan. The text can be found in Paul Reps, ed., *Zen Flesh, Zen Bones*. Garden City, NY: Anchor/Doubleday, no date, p. 128.

[10] Case 74 in *Book of Serenity: One Hundred Zen Dialogues* (see n. 3), p. 311.

[11] Case 18 in *Book of Serenity: One Hundred Zen Dialogues* (see n. 3), p. 76.

[12] Case 18 in the Mumonkan in Aitken's translation (see n. 6), p. 120.

[13] These are put forward in Michael White's "The Process of Questioning: A Therapy of Literary Merit?" (*Dulwich Centre Newletter*, Winter 1988, pp. 37–46) and also in "Deconstruction and Therapy" (*Dulwich Centre Newletter*, no. 3, 1991). David Epston describes the philosophy clearly in "Extending the Conversation" (*The Networker*, November/December 1994, pp. 31–39, 62–63).

[14] Religious Jews don phylacteries daily to pray. Phylacteries consist of two small boxes, with straps attached so they can be wrapped around the arm and forehead; within the box is a small piece of paper with the Biblical inscription: "And thou shalt bind them for a sign upon thine hand, and they shall be for frontlets between thine eyes."

[15] From Martin Buber, *Tales of the Hasidim: Early Masters*, O. Marx, trans. New York: Schocken Books, 1947, p. 214.

[16] Case 36 in the Mumonkan. I have compiled Aitken's translation (see n. 6), p. 221, with Rep's version (see n. 9).

[17] This, and the subsequent quotations explaining Tozan's Five Ranks, come from a series of lectures Sojun Mel Weitsman gave on the subject.

[18] J.R.R. Tolkien, *The Hobbit*. Boston: Houghton Mifflin, 1966, pp. 85–86.

[19] W.H. Auden, "Herman Melville," in *Collected Shorter Poems, 1927–1957*. New York: Random House (Vintage Books), 1975, pp. 145–146.

[20] This gatha is in Aitken's *The Dragon Who Never Sleeps*. Berkeley, CA: Parallax Press, 1992.

[21] From the portion of the *Denkoroku* that describes the life and teaching of Shishibodai. In the translation by Hubert Nearman (Mount Shasta, CA: Shasta Abbey Press, 1993) this appears on p. 131.

[22] There are a number of excellent papers, as well as his excellent textbook on psychoanalytic technique. Perhaps the classic paper is R. Greenson, "Empathy and its Vicissitudes," *International Journal of Psychoanalysis, 41,* 1960, pp. 418–424. Greenson describes a technique wherein the therapist, listening to the client, constructs a kind of internal "working model" of the client that is not

just an intellectual construction but a kind of partial identification with the client. The therapist puts together all his knowledge of the client's experiences, behaviors, fantasies, memories, defenses, and so forth and then diminishes his internal resistance, adds his theoretical knowledge, his conception of the client's potentials, and his own (the therapist's) personal experiences with similar situations, real and fantasized. The therapist then goes back and forth between entering this internal model, stepping back from it to observe, listening further to the client, and gradually deepening his understanding.

[23] I am paraphrasing this section of the *Denkoroku* rather freely.

[24] This is case 3 in the Mumonkan; I am using a compilation of the Aitken (see n. 6) and Reps (see n. 9) translations.

[25] S. Minuchin & H.C. Fishman, *Family Therapy Techniques.* Cambridge, MA: Harvard University Press, 1981, pp. 286–287.

[26] J. Mann, *Time-Limited Psychotherapy.* Cambridge, MA: Harvard University Press, 1973. Also, J. Mann & R. Goldman, *A Casebook in Time-Limited Psychotherapy.* New York: McGraw-Hill, 1982.

[27] David Brazier has called attention to this in *Zen Therapy: Transcending the Sorrows of the Human Mind* (New York: John Wiley, 1995).

[28] Case 45 in the Mumonkan, Aitken's translation (see n. 6), p. 269.

[29] Case 43 in *The Blue Cliff Record.* I am using a variation of a translation we used at Berkeley Zen Center, based on the translation by T. Cleary and J.C. Cleary (Boston: Shambhala Publications, 1992, p. 258).

[30] This is the poem that my teacher, Sojun Mel Weitsman, wrote on the back of my rakusu when I received lay ordination from him. It is by Wu-men and appears in Case 19 ("Ordinary Mind Is the Tao") of the Mumonkan. The last two lines are sometimes translated as, "If your mind isn't clouded by unnecessary things, this is the best season of your life."

[31] J. Tarrant, "Soul in Zen." *Blind Donkey.* Santa Rosa, CA: California Diamond Sangha.

CHAPTER 7

[1] The gatha is from R. Aitken, *The Dragon Who Never Sleeps.* Berkeley, CA: Parallax Press, 1992.

[2] There is a wonderful fascicle by Dogen called *Kokyo (The Ancient Mirror)*, which treats this issue extensively (in *Shobogenzo: The Eye and Treasury of the True Law,* K. Nishiyama & J. Stevens, trans. Tokyo, Japan: Kawata Press, 1977, pp. 45–59.

[3] Dogen's fascicle *Henzan,* "Direct Study under a Master," in *Shobogenzo: The Eye and Treasury of the True Law,* vol. II (see n. 2), p. 96.

[4] This appears in the commentary of Case 51 in *Book of Serenity: One Hundred Zen Dialogues,* T. Cleary, trans. Hudson, NY: Lindisfarne Press, 1990, p. 216.

[5] Dogen's fascile *Bukkyo,* "Buddist Sutras," in *Shobogenzo: The Eye and Treasury of the True Law,* vol. III (see n. 2), p. 81.

[6] Eihei Dogen's "Snow," translated by D. Schneider and Kazuaki Tanahashi. It appears in K. Tanahashi, ed., *Moon in a Dewdrop: Writings of Zen Master Dogen.* San Francisco: North Point Press, 1985, p. 217.

[7] Case 51 in *Book of Serenity: One Hundred Zen Dialogues* (see n. 5), p. 215.

[8] Case 80 in *The Blue Cliff Record,* T. Cleary & J.C. Cleary, trans. Boston: Shambhala Publications, 1992, p. 437.

[9] In fact, Mandelbrot demonstrated mathematically, in his paper "How Long is the Coastline of Great Britain," that even though they enclose a finite area, all shorelines are infinite in length. This is described in J. Gleick, *Chaos: Making a New Science.* New York: Penguin Books, 1987.

[10] From Martin Buber's *Tales of the Hasidim: Early Masters,* O. Marx, trans. New York: Schocken Books, 1947, pp. 251.

[11] From Eihei Dogen's "The Point of Zazen, after Zen Master Hongzhi," translated by P. Whalen and Kazuaki Tanahashi. It appears in K. Tanahashi (see n. 6), pp. 218–219.

[12] Uchiyama-roshi, in *From the Zen Kitchen to Enlightenment: Refining Your Life*. T. Wright, trans. New York: Weatherhill, 1983, reminds us that it is not enough to know that the wind's nature is permanent. That is, to have some experience of enlightenment, we must also practice that enlightenment.

[13] Thomas Cleary's translation of Dogen's *Eihei Koroku* in *Rational Zen: The Mind of Dogen Zenji*. Boston: Shambala, 1995, p. 52.

[14] J. Kabat-Zinn, *Wherever You Go, There You Are: Mindfulness Meditation in Everyday Life*. New York: Hyperion, 1994.